C0-GLH-328

OXFORD WORLD'S CLASSICS

FROGS AND OTHER PLAYS

ARISTOPHANES (*c*.450–385) was the most important poet of Old Comedy, the exuberant, satirical, and often obscene form of festival drama which flourished during the heyday of classical Athenian culture in the fifth century BC. Much of his career fell within the years of the prolonged Peloponnesian War between Athens and Sparta (431–404); three of his plays, *Acharnians* (425), *Peace* (421), and *Lysistrata* (411), draw on the war, though in highly fantastic fashion, for inspiration. The earlier part of his career was dominated by issues from the city's democratic politics and by scurrilous treatment of the demagogue Kleon, especially in *Knights* (424) and, more obliquely, in his comedy on the law courts, *Wasps* (422). But Aristophanes also showed a leaning towards cultural themes: hence his caricature of the philosopher Sokrates in *Clouds* (423), and later his burlesque of materials from the tragic stage in both *Women at the Thesmophoria* (411) and *Frogs* (405). A vein of sheer absurdity and dreamlike wish-fulfilment runs through his work, reaching a kind of *ne plus ultra* in the cosmic triumph of Peisetairos, the man-bird-god, in *Birds* (414). His last two surviving plays, *Assembly-Women* (*c*.393) and *Wealth* (388), partly represent a change of direction for the genre, moving away from a biting, uninhibited ethos towards the gentler humour of character and situation which was eventually to generate the New Comedy of Menander.

STEPHEN HALLIWELL is Professor of Greek at the University of St Andrews and a Fellow of both the British Academy and the Royal Society of Edinburgh. He taught previously in the Universities of Oxford, London, Cambridge and Birmingham, and has held several visiting professorships in Belgium, Canada, Italy and the USA. His extensive publications on Greek literature and philosophy include *The Aesthetics of Mimesis* (2002), *Greek Laughter: A Study of Cultural Psychology from Homer to Early Christianity* (2008), and *Between Ecstasy and Truth: Interpretations of Greek Poetics from Homer to Longinus* (OUP, 2011).

OXFORD WORLD'S CLASSICS

For over 100 years Oxford World's Classics have brought readers closer to the world's great literature. Now with over 700 titles—from the 4,000-year-old myths of Mesopotamia to the twentieth century's greatest novels—the series makes available lesser-known as well as celebrated writing.

The pocket-sized hardbacks of the early years contained introductions by Virginia Woolf, T. S. Eliot, Graham Greene, and other literary figures which enriched the experience of reading. Today the series is recognized for its fine scholarship and reliability in texts that span world literature, drama and poetry, religion, philosophy and politics. Each edition includes perceptive commentary and essential background information to meet the changing needs of readers.

OXFORD WORLD'S CLASSICS

ARISTOPHANES

Frogs and Other Plays

Translated with an Introduction and Notes by

STEPHEN HALLIWELL

OXFORD

UNIVERSITY PRESS

OXFORD
UNIVERSITY PRESS

Great Clarendon Street, Oxford OX2 6DP
United Kingdom

Oxford University Press is a department of the University of Oxford.
It furthers the University's objective of excellence in research, scholarship, and education by publishing worldwide. Oxford is a registered trade mark of Oxford University Press in the UK and in certain other countries

© Stephen Halliwell 2015

The moral rights of the author have been asserted

First Published in 2015, as *Aristophanes: Clouds, Women at the Thesmophoria, Frogs*
First published as an Oxford World's Classics paperback 2016
Impression: 12

All rights reserved. No part of this publication may be reproduced, stored in a retrieval system, or transmitted, in any form or by any means, without the prior permission in writing of Oxford University Press, or as expressly permitted by law, by licence or under terms agreed with the appropriate reprographics rights organization. Enquiries concerning reproduction outside the scope of the above should be sent to the Rights Department, Oxford University Press, at the address above

You must not circulate this work in any other form
and you must impose this same condition on any acquirer

British Library Cataloguing in Publication Data
Data available

Library of Congress Control Number: 2016934368

ISBN 978-0-19-282409-7

Printed and bound in Great Britain by Clays Ltd, Elcograf S.p.A.

PREFACE

THIS is the second volume of a new verse translation of the eleven surviving plays of Aristophanes. The first, containing *Birds*, *Lysistrata*, *Assembly-Women*, and *Wealth*, was published in 1997 and appeared in the World's Classics series in 1998. The approach I have adopted as translator attempts to combine historical accuracy with a sufficiently fluent style to engage the imagination of modern readers: the principles on which my translations are based are explained in more detail in the Introduction ('Translating Aristophanes'). The Introduction as a whole remains substantially the same as in the previous volume, though I have made numerous small revisions of wording and added a few further points.

In the vexed matter of the spelling of ancient Greek names, I have aimed for reasonable but inevitably less than perfect consistency. While I have largely preferred more authentically Greek to Latinized spellings, I have sometimes kept familiar English forms where their pronunciation assists the rhythms of the translation. Most dates are BC; the exceptions, especially in the part of the Introduction entitled 'Aristophanes and Posterity', will be obvious. The Index of Names contains only people, places, and institutions mentioned in the translation itself; technical terms relating to theatrical performance are explained in the sections of the general Introduction entitled 'Formality and Performance' and 'Stage Directions'. Marginal numerals in the translation refer to the standard lineation of the Greek text (following the editions specified in the Select Bibliography).

I have benefited from discussing some of the intractable problems of translating Aristophanes with my partner, Margaret-Anne Hutton.

S.H.

St Andrews
Summer 2014

CONTENTS

INTRODUCTION

Aristophanes' Career in Context

DESPITE the numerous difficulties, psychological as well as cultural, which make the workings of comedy and humour notoriously resistant to analysis, it is possible to identify within the Western traditions of comic drama two major types which broadly define the opposite ends of a spectrum. These types first emerged in successive phases of ancient Athenian culture and came to be known in antiquity itself by the basic chronological labels of 'Old' and 'New' Comedy.[1]

Old Comedy, whose roots lay partly in the folk practices of popular festivity, had its heyday in the second half of the fifth century. Its ethos, as we see from the surviving plays of Aristophanes, is quintessentially zany, fantastic, scurrilous, and larger-than-life. Its treatment of both character and action shows slight concern for consistency, plausibility, or coherence. And it tends to rely on a mentality which is physically reductive and crudely cynical. New Comedy, by contrast, which flourished in the time of Menander and other playwrights during the later fourth and third centuries, is marked by semi-realistic if somewhat stylized characterization, integrated and neatly resolved plots, benign sentimentality, and an underlying tolerance. Its central interest is in recurrent tensions in human relationships, both within the family and on a larger social scale. And it is the ancestor, via the Roman reworking of Greek plays by Plautus, Terence, and others (and the vernacular adaptation of Roman comedy itself in fifteenth-century Italy and subsequently in other countries too), of later European 'comedy of manners'.

The history of ancient Greek comedy was, in its larger trajectory, a process of evolution from the first to the second of these styles of theatre and humour. On a micro-level, however, the process was hardly a linear, let alone a teleologically driven, progression. Between around 480 and 300 BC probably more than one thousand

[1] For the intermediate category of so-called 'Middle Comedy', a term which broadly describes plays of the first half of the fourth century, see the Introductions to *Assembly-Women* and *Wealth* in the first volume of this translation.

comic plays were staged at the official Athenian dramatic festivals (see below). Since the overwhelming majority of those plays are lost (leaving us, though, with thousands of fragments to stimulate and tantalize our imaginations), we naturally cannot chart the whole history of the genre in detail. But we can be sure that it was a matter of perpetual theatrical experimentation and (re-)invention, teeming with dramatic forms and features which even in principle could hardly be fitted into a single schema of historical reconstruction. This must have been especially true of the period of Old Comedy in the later fifth and early fourth centuries—the period for which our primary evidence is the remarkable collection of extant plays by Aristophanes.

In a career which stretched from 427 to the mid-380s, Aristophanes wrote more than forty plays for the Athenian theatre. The eleven which remain demonstrate that the dominant traits of his comic style were unrestrained exuberance, irreverence, and indecency, embodied in a repertoire of dramatic techniques which revels in the topsy-turvy mixing and jumbling of categories (mythical and actual, human and animal, male and female, abstract and concrete, real and pretended, public and private), as well as in the creative manipulation of many disparate registers of language and poetry. To appreciate Aristophanes' comic world at a distance of two-and-a-half millennia, we need to open our minds to a multifaceted genre of theatre in which vulgarity and sophistication, far-fetched extravagance and down-to-earth grossness, constantly rub shoulders. But we also need a historical framework of understanding, without which the cultural specificity of Old Comedy will elude us.

At the time of Aristophanes' birth (probably around 450–445), comedy had been part of the official programme at the City (or Great) Dionysia festival, celebrated in late March or early April each year, for close to two generations (since 487/6, to be precise). It was added to the schedule of the Lenaia (late January), another festival of Dionysos, not long before 440, when Aristophanes was a boy or adolescent. By the second half of the fifth century, inclusion in these festivals meant performance—for comedy as for tragedy—by professional actors (though chorus-members were ordinary citizens) at technically high standards of production worthy of major state-organized celebrations. But prior to that, Attic comedy had had a long prehistory in a range of improvised and popular entertainments performed by 'volunteers'. That last term, evidently denoting enthusiastic amateurs, is

Aristotle's (*Poetics* 4.1449a2), in a passage where he also picks out as the most prominent forerunner of the dramatic genre of comedy the semi-ritualized celebrations which he calls *phallika*, 'phallic processions/songs' (4.1449a10–13). As it happens, Aristophanes himself incorporates a phallic procession into one of his surviving plays, at *Acharnians* 241–79, where we can catch something of the heady atmosphere of festive ceremonial, bawdy revels, and personal scurrility which might have marked such occasions.[2] Here the setting is the carefree and egotistical hedonism of the Rural Dionysia (a local not a centralized festival), as celebrated by the protagonist Dikaiopolis. The scene is in one sense a symbol of Old Comedy's own Dionysiac spirit, but the fact that Aristophanes can dramatize a phallic procession of this type in (perhaps) parodic fashion is itself a sign, albeit a nicely ambiguous one, of how far Athenian comedy had acquired a status above its earthy origins. Beginning from the sub-literary level of folk 'mummery' and festival sideshows, comedy had by the mid-fifth century developed into a poetic and theatrical genre that was able to sustain a coexistence alongside tragedy at two major civic festivals. In the Rural Dionysia scene of *Acharnians*, we see Aristophanes taking a wry glance at Old Comedy's local roots from the elevation of a state-sponsored dramatic competition. This—as quite commonly in Aristophanes—is comedy looking at itself in its own (distorting) mirror.

Aristophanes reveals an awareness of the history and traditions of his genre above all in the parabasis of *Knights* (514–44),[3] where he surveys a trio of important predecessors: Magnes, whose career went back close to the official beginnings of comedy at the Dionysia (his first victory occurred *c.*480); Kratinos,[4] whose early plays were staged in the mid-450s, but who was still active at this time and actually competing against *Knights* in 424; and Krates, whose career fell largely in the 440s, and perhaps the early 430s, at a time when Aristophanes is likely to have attended the theatre as a boy. Although the references

[2] A comparable example is the Eleusinian procession in the parodos of *Frogs* (316–459), which refers to a mixture of earnestness and mirth at 389–90 and culminates in a representation of communal, festive abuse at 416–30: choral satire is particularly well adapted for evoking the spirit of collective, ritualized exhilaration of this kind. Cf. S. Halliwell, *Greek Laughter* (Cambridge, 2008), 206–14.

[3] On the nature of the parabasis, see the later section on 'Formality and Performance'.

[4] For Kratinos, see my note on *Frogs* 357.

to these three figures are coloured and embroidered with fictional freedom, they do give us some valuable hints about those aspects of the development of fifth-century comedy which might have seemed salient to a playwright of Aristophanes' generation. The passage highlights, for one thing, the visual and musico-choreographic elements which had become so fundamental to comedy's theatrical style, and in which it is reasonable to accept that Magnes had been a pioneer.[5] It mentions also the highly 'urbane' type of wit supposedly characteristic of Krates, whose plays may well have been notable for a less scurrilous seam of humour than was practised by most of his contemporaries.[6] Yet above all it foregrounds, and mock-heroically burlesques, the satirical power of Kratinos, who had dominated the comic theatre of the 440s and 430s (winning a total of nine first prizes) and had specialized in vehement topical ridicule whose targets included Athens' greatest politician, none other than Perikles. For all its rhetorical contrivance, then, this part of *Knights* conveys an underlying artistic self-consciousness which recognizes the wide range of comic resources made available by the theatrical history of the genre in Athens.

The ostensible purpose of Aristophanes' comments on some of his predecessors in *Knights* is to explain why he had not taken personal charge of the staging of his plays until that date (424). The explanation takes the form of emphasizing, with the colourful elaboration already mentioned, what a complicated and hazardous business it is to produce a comedy in front of a mass festival audience of Athenians. It is plausible that this was the chief reason why Aristophanes, who may have been as young as eighteen when his first play (*Banqueters*) was staged in 427, turned in the early years of his career to a specialist producer/director, Kallistratos (who may have had qualifications as an actor too). Since Old Comedy employed a chorus of twenty-four dancers (compared to fifteen in tragedy), who needed months of vocal and choreographic training for their substantial and intricate routines,[7] the duties of the producer (*didaskalos*, lit. '(chorus-)trainer')

5 It is not insignificant for Aristophanes himself that Magnes' titles include *Birds* and *Frogs*.

6 At *Poetics*, 5.1449b7–9 Aristotle claims that Krates was the first comic poet at Athens to abandon the 'iambic mode'—i.e. scurrilous personal satire—and to concentrate on coherent plot-construction.

7 See below, 'Formality and Performance', for details of the chorus's main contributions to Old Comedy.

must have been onerous. Inexperience alone makes Aristophanes' early use of Kallistratos understandable; but the fact that several of his later plays as well were produced by others (see the Chronology), including Philonides (an actor-playwright himself), suggests that the technical sophistication of theatrical production was by this date becoming increasingly demanding and entailed professionalized skills in the rehearsal/staging of plays which not all poets felt comfortable assuming. The old convention of the combined poet-producer, which appears to have been the norm for both tragedy and comedy in the first half of the fifth century, was by now on the wane.

It would be fascinating if we could reconstruct in more precise terms how the career of a young playwright was launched in classical Athens. Unfortunately our evidence hardly allows us to do this in much detail; but in Aristophanes' case we do have tantalizing glimpses of some relevant conditions. *Clouds* 528 refers, in connection with the production of the earlier play *Banqueters*, to a group of people whom the author finds it 'a pleasure to mention': we are probably entitled to infer that these were backers or patrons, people of influence who helped to promote his entry into the official world of festival drama.[8] In this same passage Aristophanes talks of himself as an 'unmarried girl' whose baby had to be 'exposed' (i.e. abandoned) and was taken up by 'another girl'. The reality behind this ironically coy imagery is best interpreted, I think, as a situation in which a gifted but inexperienced new playwright needed extensive help in turning his works into successful, large-scale performances before an audience of many thousands. Aristophanes is nonetheless likely to have been involved himself in theatrical preparations even for his early plays, and *Knights* 541–4 (with its analogy to a hierarchy of functions on board a ship) suggests that he was steadily acquiring familiarity with the arts of production during the period 427–424.

As for the ability to write complex *texts* suitable for production, Aristophanes must have benefited both from a particularly thorough version of the education in poetry and music which was available to well-to-do Athenian sons,[9] and from many experiences, starting as a boy (cf. *Clouds* 539, *Peace* 50, 766, for the presence of boys),

[8] On the official procedures involved in having a play selected for performance, see 'Old Comedy and Dionysiac Festivity' below.

[9] See esp. Plato, *Protagoras* 325d–6c, for a description of this, with Aristophanes' own *Clouds* 961–72 for a partly travestied reflection of traditional musico-poetic schooling.

as a spectator himself in the theatre. But it is also possible that the preparations for, and even the early stages of, his career involved some element of poetic collaboration (of the kind known from other theatrical traditions, including Elizabethan–Jacobean England). The phenomenon of collaboration is, at any rate, apparently assumed at *Wasps* 1018–20, where there is a reference to secret assistance supposedly given by Aristophanes himself to other poets. This is yet another parabatic claim that is no doubt skewed by the rhetorical bragging expected of comic poets, but it does receive some support from other pieces of available evidence.[10] No one can now be confident about the practical circumstances of Aristophanes' 'apprenticeship' in the early to mid-420s, but given the nature of Athenian theatrical culture it is a reasonable supposition that they were many-stranded.

If a sense of comedy's rich theatrical history, as we saw in the parabasis of *Knights*, was one factor which helped shape Aristophanes' early development as a dramatist, another, though in a more diffuse way, must have been his awareness of working in the largest and most self-confident polis in Greece. Aristophanes grew up at a time when Athens was close to the zenith of its power and authority in the Greek world, during an era of political and cultural life dominated by the leadership of Perikles. The 440s and 430s saw, among much else, the building of the Parthenon as a monument to the imperial leadership and wealth of Athens, and the establishment of the city as a cosmopolitan centre which attracted artists, intellectuals, traders, tourists, and others from all round the Mediterranean and even beyond. It was in large part, however, Athens' very success as the head of an alliance[11] of Greek cities gradually transformed into a de facto empire which caused a steady deterioration in relations with her main rival, and leader of an alternative power-bloc, Sparta. Conflict came to a head in 431 with the outbreak of hostilities which were to run, with only short interruptions, till Athens' final defeat in 404, and which we now know (following Thucydides' conception of it) as the Peloponnesian War. Most of Aristophanes' career, including probably some three-quarters of his output, fell within the years of the war, as

[10] See my article, 'Authorial Collaboration in the Athenian Comic Theatre', *Greek, Roman, and Byzantine Studies*, 30 (1989), 515–28.

[11] The so-called Delian League, founded in 478–7 in the aftermath of the second Persian invasion: see Thucydides 1.96–7.

can readily be seen from the details of his surviving plays given in the Chronology.[12]

Aristophanes lived, then, through the period in which Athenian imperial hegemony was challenged and eventually defeated by Sparta and her allies; the last part of his career, in the early years of the fourth century, saw the rebuilding of Athens' position and the emergence of new power relations between the leading Greek city-states. Old Comedy of the kind practised by Aristophanes had been formed in most essential respects in the generation before him, not least under the influence of Kratinos' politically topical mode of satire (see above). It is no coincidence that the comic spirit found in Aristophanes' work presupposes—in its exuberance, freedom, and outrageousness—the democratic and cultural self-confidence which had been established in Athens, on the basis of imperial power and the economic prosperity flowing from it, between around 470 and 430. Equally, however, many of Aristophanes' plays were produced at a time when this self-confidence was being tested and threatened in a war which came to assume unprecedented proportions. Although we cannot precisely correlate the themes and emphases of Aristophanic comedy with the upheavals of the war years, we can at any rate see that without this context much that we find in his plays would not have taken the form that it does. The war itself became a recurrent starting-point for his plots: three of the extant works (*Acharnians*, *Peace*, *Lysistrata*) are in that basic sense 'war-plays', though it is important in each case to recognize how very selective, and even unreal, his comic treatment of the war actually is. Other features of Athens' particular historical situation find their echoes in Aristophanes' choice of subjects, among them the supposed workings of the democratic Assembly (*Acharnians*, *Assembly-Women*), the law-courts (*Wasps*), and the city's demagogic leadership in the years after Perikles' death (*Knights*), as well as the officialdom of Athenian imperialism (*Birds*). But it would be difficult to chart a consistent relationship between Aristophanes' themes and the changing currents of Athenian politics and society, especially once sufficient allowance is made for the uneven representation of the different phases of his career in the plays available to us.

The concentration of surviving works from the 420s probably

[12] For the chronology of the lost plays, see the Appendix to this volume.

leaves us with a rather unbalanced impression of the playwright's output, but it is nonetheless far from accidental. This was an intense stretch of Aristophanes' career: between 427 and the end of the decade he wrote a comedy for each of the major festivals, the City Dionysia and the Lenaia, in most years, and won several first prizes. As a result he became established, alongside his close contemporary Eupolis,[13] as outstanding among a new generation of comic dramatists. During these years he acquired an especially pungent satirical style which owed something to his most successful predecessor, Kratinos. While several playwrights in the 420s fell under the influence of Kratinos, it was Aristophanes who made particularly distinctive use of this influence by vigorously satirizing Kleon, the most prominent and potent politician in the city after the death of Perikles. Although Kleon himself may not have been an explicit target in *Babylonians* of 426, it was that play which provoked him into taking the unusual step of making an official complaint about the comic poet's treatment of Athens' relations with her allies. The gravamen of his complaint was probably that a subject of sensitive importance for the war had been mocked in a performance staged at the City Dionysia when ambassadors from the allied cities themselves were present.[14] This led in turn to the elaborately and scabrously allegorical attack on Kleon in *Knights*, and may have helped, in a way which Aristophanes himself could never have designed, to lend a frisson of controversy to the early years of the playwright's career.

Despite the nature of his clash with Kleon, the extent to which Aristophanes' choice of topics and satirical targets can be interpreted as politically motivated in a thoroughgoing sense remains a keenly disputed issue to which I shall return later in this Introduction (see 'Satire and Seriousness'). But it is worth pointing out here that the 420s witnessed a configuration of factors in Aristophanes' career—not only in terms of his recurrent concern with war and democratic politics, but also in his special attention to a single political leader—which was never subsequently repeated. After the Peace of

[13] On Eupolis, cf. my note on *Clouds* 553–7.

[14] For interpretation of this episode and its implications, see Halliwell, *Greek Laughter*, 248–9; for a different view, A. H. Sommerstein, 'Harassing the Satirist: The Alleged Attempts to Prosecute Aristophanes', in I. Sluiter and R. M. Rosen (eds.), *Free Speech in Classical Antiquity* (Leiden, 2004), 145–74. For what we do and do not know about *Babylonians*, see the Appendix.

Nikias in 421, which ended the first phase of the Peloponnesian War, Aristophanes appears to have deliberately moved in a rather different direction. Although we cannot take entirely at face-value the account he gives of this change at *Clouds* 545–62 (a passage revised a number of years after the first performance of 423), it is not meaningless that he there mocks his rivals for continuing to write plays about individual politicians, and boasts, with flamboyant aplomb, about his own perpetual search for comic originality. That passage is entertainingly tendentious, in the usual manner of the poet's parabatic pronouncements, but beneath its rhetoric there is a claim which does seem to be borne out by our other evidence for his career. In particular, after 420 Aristophanes appears never again to have devoted a play to a single political figure,[15] in the way in which, for example, the dramatist known as Plato comicus did on several occasions (with his *Peisandros*, *Hyperbolos*, and *Kleophon*), or Eupolis seems to have done once more around 415, when his *Baptai* ('*Bathers*') made Alkibiades its major butt. On the other hand, Aristophanes turned repeatedly after this date to mythological burlesque (some ten titles at least apparently belong in this category), but also to themes that were literary or broadly social in comic character. Of course, substantial political elements of a kind do appear in some of his post-420 plays, though in the two most obvious cases, *Lysistrata* and *Assembly-Women*, politics is transmuted into the extreme fantasy of 'women on top' plots, and there is relatively limited direct satire of contemporary individuals or political issues. So we do have some grounds for supposing that in the rather intense early years of his career Aristophanes had, so to speak, sated his appetite for bitingly political work, and thereafter sought to exploit different possibilities in the repertory of Old Comedy.

Old Comedy and Dionysiac Festivity

Comedy, like tragedy, was not available all year round at Athens in regular performances, but was staged only at a small number of festivals, of which the two main ones, the Lenaia and the City or Great Dionysia, have already been mentioned. The Lenaia took place in midwinter, the Dionysia in late winter or early spring; but plays

[15] This includes *Triphales*, which was once thought to have been about Alkibiades; see the Appendix.

for both were selected by major magistrates (Archons) months in advance. In submitting what was presumably an outline and/or provisional extracts, the poet was officially 'requesting a chorus' (cf. *Knights* 513), and in choosing a play the Archon 'granted a chorus', even though the costs of the twenty-four-man chorus, unlike the fees of the individual actors, were defrayed not by the state but by a *choregos* (a kind of sponsor or impresario) appointed for the purpose on criteria of personal wealth. The long period between selection and performance involved not only rehearsals and the making of costumes (including masks), but also completion and revision of the text. Traces of ongoing revision can be seen, for example, in the case of *Knights*, where gibes about Kleon's 'stolen' victory at Pylos (54–7, etc.) cannot have been inserted before around late August 425, or in that of *Frogs*, where references to the death of Sophokles (76–9, 787), who died some months later than Euripides, probably represent a fairly late addition to the text.[16]

The festive context is crucially important for the nature of Old Comedy. The Greek word *kômôdia* means 'revel-song'. A *kômos*, which might easily form part of a larger festival framework, typically consisted of an exuberantly celebratory, alcohol-fuelled procession accompanied by song and dance. The ethos of the *kômos* can be sensed at many points in Aristophanes' plays, but perhaps especially in the rumbustious endings of works like *Acharnians*, *Wasps*, *Peace*, and *Birds*: it is no accident that in such cases the opportunity for a *kômos* arises from, or becomes in some way associated with, a symposium (*Wasps*), a drinking-contest (*Acharnians*), or a wedding (*Peace*, *Birds*). The generic vitality and freedom of comedy stemmed, as we earlier saw that Aristotle suggested, from the improvisatory spirit of such practices as phallic processional-songs. The *kômos* was a kindred phenomenon—a mobile, high-spirited revel that lent itself to play-acting and uninhibited self-expression. The greater cultural 'respectability' which comedy had achieved by 487–6, when it was first given official status alongside tragedy in the Dionysia, must have reflected a perception of increasingly ambitious standards—poetic, dramatic, and theatrical—on the part of the genre's practitioners. But this elevation to the rank of state-organized festival performance did not erase the underlying comic impulse towards carnivalesque

[16] Cf. note 3 to my Introduction to *Frogs*.

absurdity, indecency, and vulgarity, all of which preserved a link with the genre's 'folk' origins.

That tragedies and comedies were performed during the same Dionysiac festivals, perhaps even sometimes on the same day,[17] itself epitomizes the double-headed nature of Athenian festivity. These festivals were both deeply serious, as events affirming the collective identity and communal activity of the democratic polis, and yet at the same time opportunities for a kind of liberated and liberating licence. We can observe these opposed yet complementary forces particularly clearly in the case of the City Dionysia. The festival, which usually lasted for five or six days, was an occasion in part for an exceptionally ostentatious display of Athenian pride and self-confidence. Visitors from all over the Greek world were present, including, as earlier mentioned, ambassadors from Athens' allied cities, who brought with them the tribute that embodied their subservience to Athenian hegemony.[18] Its framework, like that of many festivals, was provided by ceremonial processions, prayers, sacrifices, and rituals, and among its oldest elements was the performance of dithyrambs, choral hymns to Dionysos. In addition, the Dionysia contained important public proclamations, such as the bestowal of honorific crowns on public benefactors. Yet amidst all this solemnity there was also an air of abandon and 'play', with a heady release from quotidian routine. Much civic business, including that of the courts, was suspended for the festival's duration, and prisoners were bailed from the city's prisons. Feasting and revelling of various kinds took place, and it was this side of the festivities which accounted for the celebratory, *kômos*-conducive traditions from which comedy itself came into existence. If the serious dimension of the Dionysia was typified by ceremonies involving the city's war-orphans in the theatre itself,[19] comedy's *inversion* of civic seriousness is equally typified by a scene such as *Peace* 1270 ff., where the idea of preparing the young for the acceptance of patriotic-military values is exposed to the scorn of a protagonist bent on festive self-gratification.

[17] The point is disputed: see my note on *Birds* 789.

[18] Aristophanes mentions these aspects of the Dionysia when making a contrast with the Lenaia at *Acharnians* 502–8.

[19] The orphans were presented with suits of armour in the theatre, and some were given front seats for the dramatic performances: see Isokrates, *On the Peace* 82, Aischines, *Against Ktesiphon* 154.

The two features of Aristophanes' plays, and of Old Comedy more generally, which most conspicuously express this hedonistic aspect of the Dionysia (and, to a considerable extent, of the Lenaia too) are obscenity and satirical freedom. Both features could be loosely covered by the Greek term *aischrologia*, which means 'speaking what is shameful' (or, more pithily, 'filthy talk'). Comedy, that is to say, acted out an extreme but temporary escape from the norms of shame and inhibition which were an essential element in Athenian and Greek society. Sexual explicitness, mirroring the traditional practice of phallic songs, was built into the very fabric of comic performances in the shape of the phallus standardly worn by the actors and affording, together with their padded buttocks and belly, great scope for physical grotesqueness (cf. 'Stage Directions', below). It was further developed in frequent verbal and physical bawdy (including scatological crudity), such as the scenes between Philokleon and the prostitute in *Wasps* (1341 ff.), Kinesias and Myrrhine in *Lysistrata* (845 ff.), or the Archer and Elaphion in *Women at the Thesmophoria* (1181 ff.). The extent of this facet of Old Comedy should be read as a direct symptom of Dionysiac festivity and even of a kind of collective psychological regression—a sign of the genre's charter to throw off the inhibitions on sexual language and action which prevailed in the public sphere.

The same is broadly true of comedy's satirical freedom, which gave it a special privilege to lampoon and denigrate even the most prominent of citizens, including not only leading politicians such as Perikles and Kleon, but also the city's major military officers, the generals, during their tenure of office. (See further in 'Satire and Seriousness', below.) While the making of certain serious allegations in public life—such as that of being a 'shield-discarder' or military deserter—was prohibited by law, and would in any case have brought with it the direct risk of political or legal reprisals, comedy appears to have enjoyed a largely unlimited licence to ridicule and abuse, traditionally exempted as it was from the conditions applying to other types of public speech. This generalization is not substantially undermined by the fact that on rare occasions comedy's special freedoms generated political tensions, as when Kleon reacted adversely to Aristophanes' *Babylonians* in 426 (as mentioned above), and even produced attempts, always short-lived, to impose formal limits on what comic poets were permitted to say. The extreme autonomy which comedy had acquired by the mid-fifth century both reflected and required a buoyant Athenian culture to sustain it. When the city's affairs were under acute pressure, especially during war, even the liberty of comedy could be questioned. And in a longer historical overview we can see that the indulgence allowed to comic poets by Athenian democracy in the fifth century was an extraordinary experiment which gradually gave way, in the fourth, to a narrower spectrum of entertainment, eventually yielding the urbane inoffensiveness of New Comedy.

In the earlier part of this section I emphasized that Old Comedy was performed in the same cultural context as tragedy. The two genres shared many basic theatrical and dramatic conventions, such as the combination of actors and chorus, the use of masks, multiple role-playing by actors, and many of the same metres and verse-forms. It is plausible to suppose that comic poets were influenced by the desire to produce plays that could match tragedy for poetic and dramatic quality, while at the same time creating a variety of theatre that was in ethos the polar opposite of tragedy. We cannot now confidently reconstruct the lines of comedy's relationship to tragedy before the time of Aristophanes, though the fragments of earlier plays suggest that none of Aristophanes' predecessors manifested quite his degree of interest in the detailed parody and burlesquing of tragic materials. This would help to explain why Kratinos, who seems himself to have turned more readily to epic and lyric poetry for parodic possibilities, made one of his characters refer to someone as a 'Euripid-aristophanizer' (fr. 342), thereby jibing at Aristophanes' particular penchant—well illustrated for us now by *Acharnians* 393–488, the whole of *Women at the Thesmophoria*, the second half of *Frogs*, and an abundance of shorter 'paratragic' passages[20]—for converting Euripidean plays and motifs into a source of comic effects.

Aristophanes was certainly not alone in exploiting the capacity of comedy to be a kind of 'parasite' on tragedy, drawing nourishment for itself from the other genre's life-blood. But he does appear to have made a distinctive trait out of a type of humour which relies on

[20] The category of 'paratragedy' embraces a whole range of ways in which tragic language is playfully quoted, echoed, adapted, distorted, and manipulated by Aristophanes; it is not reducible to a single comic function of derision. See my Introduction to *Women at the Thesmophoria*.

a feeling for destabilizing shifts between the disparate voices of the two genres. The modern reader of his plays needs to bear this constantly in mind, since it is so often basic to both his conception of situations and to the fine texture of his writing. The first of these two aspects is easier to appreciate, since it involves overtly marked borrowing from one or more tragic models—as, for instance, in the *Telephos* parody at *Acharnians* 496 ff., where Dikaiopolis moves intricately in and out of the persona of a Euripidean hero, or in the elaborate series of parodic uses to which Euripides puts his own plays (especially *Helen* and *Andromeda*) in attempting to rescue his Kinsman in *Women at the Thesmophoria*. Evidently Aristophanes could count on his audience's extensive familiarity with tragedy (though not necessarily their recollection of individual passages) and their ability to follow the stylistic twists and turns of parody. In a sense, this is demonstrated even more tellingly by his habit of allowing the language and tone of tragedy to infect virtually any context with a momentary switch of register. A characteristically unannounced instance occurs near the start of *Clouds*, when Strepsiades, gloomily checking his list of debts in the middle of the night, drops into a short tragic phrase (linguistically unmistakable in the Greek as a departure from ordinary Attic) for just half a line:

> 'What burden next was mine'—after Pasias' loan?
> Three minas, chariot base and wheels: Ameinias.
>
> (*Clouds* 30–1)

The effect is so brief that the audience has to catch the effect instantaneously—or miss it altogether. A slightly longer example of a similar kind shows that even on this miniature scale Aristophanes can incorporate subtlety. In *Assembly-Women*, Blepyros inserts two (doctored) lines from Aischylos when lamenting the loss of his Assembly pay:

> BLEPYROS [*like a tragic actor*]. O alack alas!
> 'Antilochos, lament your fill for me
> And not for my—three obols. The loss is mine.'
> [*Normally*] But what was going on, to make this throng
> Turn up in such good time?
>
> (*Assembly-Women* 391–5)

Without warning, we have to adjust to the old Athenian's partial and fleeting assumption of the voice of Achilles, from Aischylos'

Myrmidons, lamenting the death of his companion Patroklos; and then to switch back to his ordinary citizen voice and his curiosity about the abnormally large numbers that had turned up for a meeting of the Assembly. Literary historians continue to argue about just how close a knowledge of specific tragic sources Aristophanes assumed in his audience. What is beyond doubt is that he looks for, and comically titillates, a finely tuned ear for the detailed incongruities of blended tragic and comic timbres. That he was able to do so tells us something about the hybrid cultural atmosphere of Athenian festive theatre, where the two genres were placed side by side yet embodied starkly opposed ranges of imaginative experience.

The Dynamics of Fantasy

Although it is hazardous to generalize about Old Comedy on the basis of just eleven plays out of many hundreds staged at Athens in the course of the fifth century, our appreciation of Aristophanes' comic artistry can benefit from a critical perspective which sets the specifics of individual works against the backcloth of generic characteristics. In this and the following section I shall explore in turn both aspects of a central paradox of the genre: its combination of imaginative fluidity with theatrical formality.

The fluidity of Old Comedy derives most obviously from the freedom with which it selects and develops its materials, and from the consequently wide range of humorous modes (satire, parody, caricature, burlesque, bawdy, farce, irony, wit) which it encompasses. Unlike tragedy, which with rare exceptions, such as Aischylos' *Persians* (based on the battle of Salamis), was confined to myths of what might be called 'heroic sufferings' (Aischines 3.153), comedy could and did take its subjects from virtually any and every source. The stuff of actual Athenian life, both high and low; figures and events from earlier Greek history; the stories of myth, fable, and folktale; life on Olympos and in Hades; the subject-matter and styles of other genres of poetry, including epic, tragedy, and lyric—all these (and more) were used, in assorted and unpredictable ways, to create the scenarios of comedy, though more often than not (in fact always, in our eleven plays) within the notional time-frame of 'the present' from the point of view of author and audience. Athenians attending the theatre to watch tragedies could have clearly anticipated the kinds of story they would be likely to see. The same people turning up for *comic* performances in the fifth century would probably have had no way of knowing what sort of characters or action they were about to watch:[21] hence, indeed, the typical element of 'mystery' at the start of an Aristophanic play, sometimes turned into active 'teasing' of the audience (esp. *Wasps* 54–87, *Peace* 43–8) or more generally embodied in the oddities and uncertainties of openings such as those of *Women at the Thesmophoria* and *Frogs*. A comic audience's expectations would have been limited to, on the one hand, certain formal theatrical conventions (see 'Formality and Performance'), and, on the other, the typical spirit of scurrility and festive indecency whose context I sketched in the previous section.

At the heart of Aristophanes' and Old Comedy's unpredictability lies the exercise of fantasy: the unfettered manipulation of ideas furnished by the full gamut of contemporary experience, cultural tradition, and sheer imagination. In *Women at the Thesmophoria*, for instance, Aristophanes fuses together two wildly improbable, not to say downright nonsensical, hypotheses: one, that the women of Athens might collectively (and in the secrecy of their annual Thesmophoria festival) plot 'revenge'—even to the point of a vote of condemnation to death!—against the tragic poet Euripides for the (supposedly negative) way he depicts female characters in his plays; the other, that Euripides himself might try to undermine the women's plans by disguising an ageing, boorishly misogynistic Kinsman as a woman and getting him to infiltrate the women's gathering on the Akropolis. The resulting scenario, carried to a further, ultra-absurdist level when Euripides tries to rescue the unmasked Kinsman by acting out scenes from his own plays, is a kind of comically doubled (if not tripled) case of 'life imitating art'.[22] *Frogs* stretches the parameters of fantasy even further by collapsing the space between the domains of gods and humans, as well as that between life on earth and the afterlife in the underworld, into a compound comic universe. Going on a long-distance journey with

[21] Spectators of tragedy could attend the 'preview' or proagon at which tragedians gave some sort of advance announcement of their forthcoming plays: see Plato, *Symposium* 194a, with E. Csapo and W. J. Slater, *The Context of Ancient Drama* (Ann Arbor, Mich., 1995), 105, 109–10. But we have no evidence for a comic proagon. Cf. the Appendix on Aristophanes' lost play *Proagon*.

[22] See my Introduction to *Women at the Thesmophoria* for the specific mechanisms of metatheatre, the confusion between life and theatre.

a donkey and slave, and expecting to stay in cheap roadside inns, is something any Greek could understand in realistic terms. But when the journey is that of a buffoonish Dionysos trying to emulate his brother Herakles by going down to bring someone back from Hades, we are in the sphere of a kind of comic myth-making.[23] And when we add Dionysos's aim of bringing back the recently deceased *Euripides*, the whole scenario, as with *Women at the Thesmophoria*, enters an archetypally Aristophanic territory in which 'art' and 'life' interact and interpenetrate in deliciously strange ways.

To gain a more detailed sense of some of the operations of Aristophanic fantasy, let us consider the almost Beckettesque opening of one of his plays, *Birds*.[24] The work starts in an unspecified rural setting (probably indicated, but only sketchily, in the original staging), where two elderly Athenians, their age and apparently rather ordinary social status indicated by their masks and costumes, are staggering around with birds on their wrists and with a variety of baggage and paraphernalia. They appear bewildered and lost, and so too, though with more amusement, might an audience be. For what are these old men doing? Their baggage probably suggests a long journey, perhaps even 'emigration', as well as the possibility of a sacrifice. But why are they using chained birds for orientation? As soon as Euelpides tells us that these are birds bought from a named Athenian market-trader, Philokrates (14), yet purchased with a view to finding *Tereus*, mythological Thracian king (15–16), we are faced with a binary frame of reference that is quintessentially Aristophanic. We are required not only to accept simultaneously, but also to allow to merge into one another, the real-life logic of the contemporary polis, where birds are for sale every day on market stalls, and the world of Greek myth, in which metamorphosis from man to bird is possible. We are invited, in other words, into a special comic universe, which both is and is not continuous with the Athens of the audience.

The inner workings of this comic universe are revealed more fully when Euelpides eventually turns to the audience at 27 ff. (an

[23] The start of *Frogs* may involve further subtextual mythological allusions as well: some spectators will have thought of the image of Hephaistos being brought back on a donkey to Olympos by Dionysos; see e.g. T. H. Carpenter, *Art and Myth in Ancient Greece* (London, 1991), ills. 2–15 (various). Aristophanes' opening vignette (with Xanthias for Hephaistos, Hades for Olympos) ironically inverts the myth in question.

[24] For Aristophanes and Samuel Beckett, cf. n. 105 below.

extra-dramatic gesture itself characteristic of Old Comedy) to explain the situation. Euelpides and Peisetairos are ageing Athenians looking for an escape from the oppressive reality of the city, especially its culture of litigation. That they are so old and yet prepared to turn to such a far-fetched means of release from their frustrations is itself significantly improbable. Aristophanes repeatedly associates the transformations effected by comic fantasy with elderly protagonists who become symbols of prodigious daring and/or rejuvenation (cf. *Acharnians*, *Knights*, *Wasps*, *Peace*, *Wealth*, as well as the gender-transformation of the Kinsman in *Women at the Thesmophoria*, *Clouds* offers a special variant of this motif). Moreover, the two old men in *Birds* do not speak as consistent individuals with whom reasonably predictable dealings would be possible, but as figures whose voices continually shift tone and level—now reflecting elements of social reality (concern over debts, etc.: compare *Clouds*), now engaging in the artificial joke exchanges of a comic double-act (e.g. 54–60), and generally displaying a capacity to tolerate incongruity in themselves as well as around them.

This quality of comically free-floating personality, familiar from the routines of stand-up comedians and clowns (and compare the very start of *Frogs* for precisely that kind of joke routine), is a hallmark of Aristophanic characterization and can best be described as quasi-improvisatory. It leaves the impression that, to invert a principle of Aristotle's, the figures often say what the playwright wants and not what (in realistic terms) the situation plausibly calls for.[25] It is the unrestrictedness of Aristophanic fantasy which gives rise to this malleability of persona (as likewise of plot), so that many of the leading characters in the plays are constructed more by aggregation than by integration: they are, so to speak, constantly reinvented—and/or appear constantly to reinvent themselves—as the work unfolds. We cannot coherently connect the world-weary Peisetairos who opens *Birds* with the world-ruling 'hero' who ends it, at any rate beyond the level at which all his behaviour issues from an underlying pursuit of the pleasure principle (see below).

[25] Cf. Aristotle, *Poetics* 16.1454b34–5: the principle applies, of course, to the serious genres of epic and tragedy. It would be instructive to see how far Aristophanic characterization could be effectively read as an inversion of Aristotle's own principles of characterization in *Poetics*, ch. 15.

Already, then, within the first fifty lines of *Birds*, Aristophanes has teased his audience with hints of quirky peculiarity, and then opened up for them a scenario which fuses the possible with the impossible, the real with the mythological, in a manner which can be carried further (with a whole sequence of unforeseen twists) by the rest of the plot. Comparable observations could be made about the openings of virtually all the extant plays. What is salient about the germinal conception of the fantasy fluctuates from case to case. In *Birds* it includes, for example, the cardinal use—as a link between the human and the ornithological—of a figure whose story was one of the most gruesome in Greek myth, involving as it did a combination of incest, rape, murder, and cannibalism. This provides, therefore, a particularly telling example of comedy's ability to convert and travesty tragic material for its own purposes; something analogous occurs with Trygaios' Bellerophon-like journey to Olympos in *Peace*. In other instances the hinge of the plot's fantasy is a complete transmutation of social and political conditions, as in *Acharnians*, where Dikaiopolis opposes the Assembly and its democratic officialdom single-handed; or *Lysistrata* and *Assembly-Women*, where the wives of Athens conspire to invert the normal relations of power and subservience between male and female. In *Knights* (where politicians are 'slaves' in the household of Demos, personification of the democratic citizenry) or *Wasps* (where a juror is persuaded to hear imaginary trials in his own house), the core of the action involves a semi-allegorical superimposition of the public (the *polis*) onto the domestic (the *oikos*)—or vice versa. In yet other cases, especially *Women at the Thesmophoria* and *Frogs*, it is an interplay, as already noted, between life and theatre which provides the impetus of the plot.

These rudimentary and partial observations ideally need much fuller refinement, and some of them will be picked up in the introductions to individual plays. But they usefully draw attention to the diversity of ways in which Aristophanes freely manipulates ideas and situations, creating in the process an imaginative space for the confusion of those very categories and distinctions whose maintenance is a general prerequisite of the social world outside the theatre. Various threads of connection can always be traced between the dramatic plane of fantasy and the contemporary viewpoint of the audience, but they are threads which every play, in its own way, takes it upon itself to tangle or even tie in knots.

In terms of what might be called narrative logic, the type of fantasy characteristic of Old Comedy has broad affinities with both *mythology*, from which we have seen that it often borrows (and distorts) materials, and *dreaming*.[26] In all three realms, the impossible becomes not only thinkable but capable of attainment. The mundane impediments which have to be faced in the real social world can be imaginatively ignored in the interests of some grand (and/or crazy) goal, whether this involves—to oversimplify—an engagement with deep-rooted cultural anxieties (myth), the enactment of basic fears and desires (dreaming), or the pleasure derived from allowing the imagination to blur and dissolve the normally accepted categories of experience (comic fantasy). Equally, and for much the same reason, Aristophanic comedy, dreams, and (perhaps to a lesser extent) myth all share a tendency towards dislocation, discontinuity, and the temporal telescoping of events, so that selective attention to key moments overrides the need for sequentially detailed cohesion. Finally, these three modes of thought commonly generate concrete, sensuous, or personified representation of abstract and general ideas. In Aristophanes' case, we find, for instance, the eponymous chorus of *Clouds*, emblematic (at first sight, anyway) of the nebulous notions 'worshipped' by otherworldly intellectuals like Sokrates; the chef-like figure of War with his pestle and mortar, at *Peace* 236 ff., as well as Peace herself, the statuesquely symbolic female, in the same play; the caricature of the Athenian people as a semi-senile householder, Demos, in *Knights*; the girl Princess, in *Birds*, incarnation of the cosmic power which passes from Zeus to Peisetairos; the seedy, castanet-playing, prostitute-like 'Muse' of Euripides in *Frogs* (1305 ff.), supposed embodiment of the tragedian's low-grade lyrics; and the blind god Wealth, in the play of the same name, whose entry into a house is tantamount to its acquisition of material prosperity.[27] Realization of the impossible, narrative discontinuity, and concrete embodiment of the abstract are recurrent, defining features of Aristophanic fantasy

[26] On the particular relevance of dreaming to the plot of *Birds*, see my Introduction to that play. Note also the start of *Wasps* (13 ff.), where the two slaves narrate dreams which exhibit, in miniature, characteristic elements of Aristophanic comedy itself: narrative discontinuity, the blurring of identities, and confusion of categories (especially human and animal).

[27] The idea of a domestic visit from Wealth, as a metaphor for prosperity, occurs in a fragment of the sixth-century iambic poet Hipponax (fr. 36 *IEG*).

which lend its creations an air of comic mythologization and dream-like transcendence of the ordinary.

I have already stressed how the figures who inhabit this fantasy world tend, though with many gradations, towards a semi-improvised, aggregative form of behaviour. But there is another component of Aristophanic characterization which deserves to be highlighted: the adventurous energy and egotistic proclivities of his protagonists.[28] This is a phenomenon which critics have often analysed in terms of wish-fulfilment. On this reading, individual characters give embodiment to strong psychological cravings, whether for material goods, power, sexual gratification, or a more generalized relief from the problems and pressures of reality. It is easy to find a prima facie justification in the surviving plays for this type of analysis. Aristophanic protagonists display a larger-than-life vitality which leads to the breaching of boundaries and the transgression of norms, whether those of class (e.g. with the peasant-farmers of *Acharnians* and *Peace*, or the Sausage-Seller in *Knights*, all of whom discover an improbable political prowess), of age (as with the elderly males of *Acharnians*, *Wasps*, *Peace*, and *Birds*, who experience a rejuvenation in their vigour, sexuality, capacities of persuasion, etc.), of law (as with Strepsiades' attempt in *Clouds* to refuse to pay his debts), of gender (as with the active heroines of *Lysistrata* and *Assembly-Women*, or, very differently, with Euripides' Kinsman in *Women at the Thesmophoria*), of 'biology' (as with the god-defying Trygaios in *Peace* or the semi-metamorphosed Peisetairos in *Birds*), and of death itself (as with Dionysos's bringing back of a poet from Hades in *Frogs*, though there we have the comic complication that the agent is a god).

Yet wish-fulfilment in its most self-centred forms is a far from invariable trait of these figures. In most plays the action of the central character(s) involves the exercise of a radical, problem-solving ingenuity, whether individual or collective; and in every case but one (the exception being *Clouds*[29]) the end result is the satisfaction of fundamental desires or the harmonization of previously conflicting

[28] It is no coincidence, in view of the previous paragraph, that these are features, respectively, of many myths and dreams.

[29] Strepsiades is ultimately left with the pleasure of revenge, but that does nothing to mitigate the outright failure of his original impulse to escape his creditors: see my Introduction to the play.

forces. In the broadest terms, a redistribution of power is a salient goal and/or achievement in *Knights*, *Birds*, *Lysistrata*, and *Assembly-Women*, though in all of these except *Knights*[30] it is coupled with some variety of sexual reward, which is also an achievement of the protagonists of *Acharnians*, *Wasps* (briefly, at least: 1341 ff.), and *Peace*. The attainment of wealth, or escape from the conditions which threaten or diminish it, is the primary aim that drives the protagonists of *Clouds* (where, however, it becomes diverted via an instrumental need for rhetorical prowess) and *Wealth*, as well as a benefit that accrues to Dikaiopolis in *Acharnians* and to almost everyone (via utopian 'communism') in *Assembly-Women*. The desire for peace, with the wider potential for prosperity (including wealth and sexual fertility) which it represents and presumptively creates, is the central goal of *Acharnians*, *Peace*, and *Lysistrata*; it also plays a subordinate part in *Knights* (1388 ff.) and *Birds*. *Women at the Thesmophoria* and *Frogs* are less easy to categorize in such basic terms, but both certainly fantasize a solution to difficulties and conflicts: the former resolves (or perhaps dissolves) the male/female and poetry/life tensions between Euripides and the city's women, while *Frogs* celebrates a triumphant finale that ostensibly equates Athenian 'salvation' with the recovery, via Aischylos, of ancestral wisdom, strength, and peace.

As even that schematic survey of the plays indicates, the model of comic fantasy as wish-fulfilment needs to be qualified by a recognition of the complexities and peculiarities of individual figures and their situations. Although egotism *qua* bold self-assertion is a recurrent characteristic, Aristophanic protagonists are certainly not uniform manifestations of a Freudian id or of purely selfish instincts. Peisetairos in *Birds* comes closest to this status: his original desire, shared with Euelpides, for a decadently sybaritic life (128–42) is eventually fulfilled in a blaze of cosmic glory in which, as already mentioned, Zeus-like power and sexual potency coalesce. Philokleon in *Wasps* is Peisetairos' nearest neighbour in terms of a craving for pleasure without responsibility, and this is equally true of him both in his role as juryman and in the rechannelled energies of the later scenes: what he loses by way of power over others in the courts he more than makes up for in the rampant, irrepressible sensuality of his new

[30] Even there we have the sexual symbolism/incarnation of the peace libations at 1388 ff.

social life. But other protagonists, with the exception of Strepsiades in *Clouds* (whose immoral ambitions remain finally unfulfilled), are impelled by mixed impulses.

This is true even of Euripides in *Women at the Thesmophoria*. While he acts at first purely to save himself from the vengeful wrath of the city's women (whom he takes, ludicrously, to be threatening his very life, 76–84), he finds himself having to play the role of rescuer to his Kinsman, now a 'hostage' of the women, during the second half of the play. In *Acharnians*, Dikaiopolis initially wants the city as a whole to make peace; the fantasy of his alternative one-man peace treaty stems from a thwarted political desire, not from sheer selfishness (though he has plenty of that for enjoyment of his exclusive privileges). What Dikaiopolis originally craved is what Trygaios actually brings about in *Peace*, with the help of the farmers whose class he belongs to: both the internal dynamics of the plot and the contemporary context of an imminent peace treaty between Athens and Sparta make the protagonist's achievement, like his marriage to Harvest, an emblem of something more-than-individual.

In the case of *Lysistrata*, *Assembly-Women*, and *Wealth*, the concerns of the main character for some kind of communal good are unequivocal. Chremylos, in *Wealth*, is troubled by a decline in moral behaviour and social justice; what he goes on to accomplish is restored prosperity, not just for himself but for all 'decent' people. Lysistrata and Praxagora are patently motivated by the interests not only of all women but of all Athenians (even, in Lysistrata's case, all Greece). Lysistrata cunningly controls the libido of both women and men—restricting the former in order to arouse the latter—for the sake of the higher goals of peace and marital concord; Praxagora goes further still, planning a female seizure of power in pursuit of permanent utopia for the entire polis. Different again is the Sausage-Seller of *Knights*, whose initial role as the *ne plus ultra* in political depravity (a role foisted on him by others: an unusual pattern[31]) is subsequently overtaken by the function of 'saviour' of the democracy. Finally, even the 'effeminately' sensualist Dionysos of *Frogs*, for whom the idea of bringing back Euripides from the dead

[31] The nearest parallel is *Women at the Thesmophoria*, where Euripides tries to enlist Agathon's services and then falls back on those of his Kinsman: here the pattern neatly fits Euripides' status as the playwright who tries to script the drama of his own life.

has a quasi-physical intensity (52–66) and is presented as an obsessive need of his own personality, turns out, in a typically late twist to the plot, to have a public-spirited interest in resurrecting from Hades a poet who can help (once again) to 'save' the city (1419). Whether the ending of *Frogs* (or of any other Aristophanic comedy) is given any real plausibility in that respect remains a matter for debate: see my Introduction to the play. But there is no doubt that the final stretch of the work at any rate broadens the god of drama's horizons beyond a desire for something that is his alone to enjoy.

Aristophanic protagonists, then, typically possess a determination, inventiveness, and confidence which make them suitable agents for the achievement of fantastic ends. But their specific motivations vary considerably, and can mutate in the course of a play without much regard for plausible consistency of character. Furthermore, the success and hedonistic gratification which usually come their way are not necessarily accompanied by outright self-centredness: to judge by the eleven plays we have, these characters are, or aspire to be, 'saviours' (of one kind or another) as often as they are egotists.

One important implication of these claims is that there are no straightforward conclusions to be drawn about the relationship between the protagonists of Old Comedy and the allegiances of the mass audiences which gathered for the Dionysiac festivals at Athens. In the past, critics have too often attempted to detect or construct correlations between Aristophanes' choice of characters and particular sections of Athenian society, especially the smallholder farmers who made up a substantial portion of the demos. Sociological hypotheses have led to critical judgements about the intrinsically 'sympathetic' nature of certain protagonists. But there are too many variables in the configurations of plot and protagonist to yield useful generalizations of this kind; each case needs considering on its merits. Needless to say, no hermeneutic paradigm based on alignment between audience and characters can readily encompass *Lysistrata* and *Assembly-Women*: even if we allow for the presence of *some* women in the audience, the great majority of spectators were certainly men.[32] Nor,

[32] My own view on this vexed issue is that no more than a few women attended the theatre in the fifth century; the position may gradually have changed in the fourth. For our (slight) evidence, see J. Rusten (ed.), *The Birth of Comedy* (Baltimore, 2011), 408–10, Csapo and Slater, *The Context of Ancient Drama*, 286–7, 290–2. Cf. my note on *Women at the Thesmophoria* 395–7.

for different but comparable reasons, can such a model do justice to *Women at the Thesmophoria* and *Frogs*: most Athenians were neither tragic poets like Euripides nor gods. Obviously, questions of audience sympathy go beyond the single factor of the protagonist's identity: in *Women at the Thesmophoria* there is the pairing of Euripides and his Kinsman to reckon with (though, while on the same side, they are evidently 'chalk and cheese', which blocks any easy 'sympathy' reading); in *Frogs*, the second half of the play sets up the polarization between Aischylos and Euripides, setting the split loyalties of Dionysos oscillating in the middle. But at the level of protagonists alone, even before further complications are taken into account, it is impossible to apply any sort of consistent formula for how spectators might have responded to the characters on stage.

That point holds up even in the case of certain recurrent 'types'. For example, Dikaiopolis in *Acharnians* and Trygaios in *Peace* both belong to the same broad class of peasant-farmers, yet the question of how 'sympathetic' either of them might have been to an Athenian audience at large cannot be treated independently of their specific contexts: above all, it makes a big difference that Dikaiopolis' opponents, the chorus of Acharnians, are farmers themselves. Strepsiades in *Clouds* is also from a rural background, but both his utter immorality and the distinctive nature of his marriage to an aristocratic woman give his case a peculiar slant. In *Knights*, on the other hand, the 'hero' or saviour of the democracy is a Sausage-Seller who can only represent a class of low urban workers, if he represents anything at all; yet the momentum of the allegorical satire, particularly in the later stages of the play, makes him apparently a figure with whom the audience is invited to side. It is arguable that in another case again, that of *Birds*, the protagonist is sociologically somewhat indeterminate, though conceivably thought of at one point (33, where there is reference to the characters' clear 'ancestry') as from a well-to-do family which has fallen on hard times.[33] But his salient features are old age and disillusionment with Athenian litigiousness; it is hard to see that this makes him identifiable in class terms for an audience. These examples bear out the difficulty of assimilating Aristophanic protagonists to a uniform model. They also indicate the danger of assuming

[33] It is possible that costume was used to mark him as a rustic, but if so the text gives no clue to this. His companion Euelpides is apparently given a rural deme at 496 (but a different one at 645!).

that the heterogeneous fantasies in which those protagonists become involved are designed to yield any one simple kind of satisfaction for the large, mixed audiences of Athenian citizens who watched the plays.[34]

Formality and Performance

Old Comedy is remarkable, as we have seen, for its festive freedom and the plasticity of its plots and protagonists. But it was also, and just as significantly, a genre which exhibited a high degree of formality and structural patterning—more so, perhaps surprisingly, even than tragedy. The origins of this formality have been often but inconclusively investigated. For our purposes it is enough to register that the fragments of Old Comedy establish that the main types of structure found in Aristophanes' surviving plays (and detailed below) were well established before his time and were the common property of comic poets in the second half of the fifth century. That is not, however, to suggest that the formality of the genre was static; Aristophanes' own works clearly show otherwise. Continual experiment with dramatic form was an important aspect of the evolution of Attic comedy, including the phase of so-called Middle Comedy represented by the last two extant Aristophanic plays, *Assembly-Women* and *Wealth*.

The formal conventions and structures to be discussed in this section have to be identified by modern readers on the printed page.[35] But it is essential to remember that for Aristophanes and his audience they were integral to *performance*, that is, to presentation through verbal/rhythmical shape, musical character, and visual reinforcement (especially dance). To understand something of the vividly animated theatricality of these elements, we need to know that comedy, like tragedy, used three principal 'modes' of poetry (and theatrical delivery):[36] first, the spoken verses of the iambic trimeter, a metre whose flexible rhythms can admit a large range of registers (from

[34] On the size of fifth-century theatre audiences, see my text with nn. 84–5 below.

[35] My translation marks the major formal sections of each play, in order to keep the reader alert to this aspect of comic theatricality.

[36] Cf. my further comments on these modes in 'Translating Aristophanes' below. Comedy also very occasionally admits short portions of prose, such as the chorus-leader's proclamation at *Women at the Thesmophoria* 295 ff., the Herald's announcements at *Acharnians* 43, 61, 123, or the Decree-Seller's utterances at *Birds* 1036 ff.

the colloquial to the high-flown); secondly, longer verses (tetrameters, in both iambic and other rhythms[37]), which were chanted or declaimed, often by the chorus-leader, to the accompaniment of the double pipes (*aulos*, pl. *auloi*)[38] and are now customarily bracketed together, with a term borrowed from music, as the 'recitative' mode; and, finally, full-blown song (in Greek, *melos*), again accompanied by the *aulos*, in lyric sections (whether sung by the chorus or sometimes by individual characters) which make use of a wide selection of rhythms but are frequently constructed in matching strophic pairs (strophe + antistrophe). Of these modes, the first and second depend on stichic metres—that is, those involving the repetition of regular 'lines'—whereas the lyrics comprise units of varying length. Choral song was supported and enhanced by choreography; the same was true with some cases of recitative as well.

In our surviving fifth-century tragedies the recitative mode is put to more limited use than in comedy, being predominantly limited to (part of) the entrance, or parodos, of the chorus in certain plays.[39] For the most part, tragedy is constructed from scenes of iambic speech/dialogue, alternating with the lyric songs or odes of the chorus (and sometimes the solo singing, monody, of characters).[40] Old Comedy too employs iambic speech and free-standing choral songs, but it also makes much more extensive use than tragedy of recitative, which it incorporates into large-scale structures of a strikingly formal, often symmetrical, type. This is all part-and-parcel of comedy's interest in a theatrically flamboyant and showy style of entertainment which maximizes the resources of both actors and singers/dancers. In this connection it is helpful to keep in mind two attributes of the comic chorus which differentiate it from the tragic variety: first its size, namely, twenty-four dancers as opposed to tragedy's fifteen (originally twelve); secondly its characteristically colourful and elaborate costuming, often involving animal-forms (wasps, birds, frogs, etc.) or the distinctive accoutrements of special groups such as the

[37] See further in n. 75.

[38] On the *aulos*, cf. also the later section 'Stage Directions'.

[39] It is ironic, therefore, that the development of musical recitative in early Italian opera was influenced by the belief that much of ancient tragedy was musically declaimed in a style halfway between speech and song; cf. C. V. Palisca, *Humanism in Italian Renaissance Thought* (New Haven, 1985), 408–33.

[40] Cf. *Frogs* 1330–63, with my notes, for parody of Euripidean monody.

cloud-deities of *Clouds* (though we can only guess how they were costumed), the charcoal-burners of *Acharnians*, the cavalry of *Knights*, or the old men (with logs, etc.) and women (carrying buckets of water) in *Lysistrata*. These features contribute to, and can be illuminated by, the three major formal units or sequences of Old Comedy—the parodos, agon, and parabasis—which I shall now consider in turn and which do so much to give a dramatic 'architecture' to most of Aristophanes' surviving works.

The parodos is the section of a play built around the entrance of the chorus into the *orchêstra* (see 'Stage Directions', below).[41] Aristophanes always treats it as a theatrical event in its own right: he organizes the parodos, which was clearly a formal convention long before his time, in such a way as to create a specific and usually extravagant effect on the situation in hand. The chorus's movements are choreographed to represent a particular kind of action, condition, or mood, ranging from the eager animosity of the charcoal-burners in *Acharnians* to the pathetic sluggishness of the old jurors in *Wasps*,[42] from the earthy robustness of the farmers in *Peace* (complete with spades, crowbars, and ropes) to the ethereally 'floating' remoteness of the cloud-deities in *Clouds*. In *Lysistrata*, the use of a divided chorus of Old Men and Women allows the parodos to foreground a confrontational clash between the gendered points of view of the two groups. Especially intriguing, but also problematic, is the case of *Frogs*, which has two quite separate choruses—the eponymous frog-chorus itself and the chorus of initiates in the underworld—and therefore arguably two parodoi (at 209 ff. and 316 ff.). Some scholars have believed that the frog-chorus is never actually visible (there is nothing in the text which proves that it is) but sings off-stage: if so, 209 ff. will be a kind of 'false' parodos. But those who, like myself, believe that the frog-chorus hopped around the *orchêstra* (presumably with amphibian costume to match its dance steps), in a way fully in keeping with the genre's traditions of animal choruses, will infer that Aristophanes has indeed here exploited the theatrical impact of a choral parodos twice over.

[41] A peculiar exception, which reflects developments associated with Middle Comedy, is *Assembly-Women*: here the chorus takes up its first formation precisely in order to *exit* at 285 ff. (it will return at 478 ff.). See my Introduction to the play.

[42] After the warning of waspishness at 223 ff., the parodos brings a humorous defeat of expectations; 404 ff. subsequently functions as a kind of deferred or postponed parodos of the chorus *qua* wasps.

No two parodoi are identical in form (the two in *Frogs*, just mentioned, are radically different in scale and structure). In fact, there is legitimate disagreement about how strictly to define and delimit the parodos of a comedy. Some scholars, using a narrower specification, would say that *Women at the Thesmophoria* does not even have a parodos, on the grounds that the text suggests that the women of the chorus enter silently as a crowd (by or at 295) and then sing as a foregathered group; by that criterion, *Assembly-Women* is more anomalous still (see n. 41). But that is a somewhat technical point which does not affect my general observations on the theatrical incisiveness of the parodos as the first choral contribution to a play.[43] Each parodos, understood flexibly in this way, manifests a variable amalgam of the three poetic modes explained above, especially recitative and song, moulded so as to express the dramatic interaction between chorus and characters. In *Knights*, for example, the choral entry comes in response to the request from one of the slaves for assistance in the fight against the Paphlagonian (242–6). It is entirely in recitative mode, whose rhythms here convey the mimicry of a galloping cavalry attack (247 ff.). Whether on pantomime-horses or in piggy-back fashion, the dancers manoeuvre themselves in quasi-equestrian formation, circling round, cornering, and eventually assaulting the Paphlagonian with (among other conspicuous gestures) kicks to the belly (273). The sight of cavalry drill would have been familiar to most Athenians from training-grounds in the city, but this parodos is a burlesque version of the practice and comically suffuses the model of equestrian exercises with the ethos of crude brawling, wrestling imagery, and political polemics.[44] Taken as a whole, from 247 to 302, the parodos of *Knights* constitutes a gradual crescendo of verbal and physical hostility: the effect of the Knights' onslaught is to embolden the Sausage-Seller, who gradually takes over the momentum of the campaign against the Paphlagonian.

In *Birds* the parodos is different in a number of respects. For one thing, it is unusually preceded, or initiated, by the appearance of four extra dancers in specially ostentatious bird-costumes on the roof of the stage building, the *skênê* (267–93). Aristophanes teases the

[43] Aristotle, *Poetics* 12.1452b22–3 (applicable to both tragedy and comedy), defines the parodos of a play simply as 'the first complete utterance' of the chorus.

[44] See my Introduction to *Knights* on the different levels of significance in the play's allegory.

audience at this point, raising the possibility that the whole chorus may enter individually on the roof, that is, 'in the air'. (I believe that the roof was also used as part of a long tease about the choral entry in *Clouds*, at 275 ff.; there the joke is on the bemused Strepsiades, not on the audience.) But at *Birds* 294, as the human characters look into the sky for further birds, the real chorus suddenly enters on ground-level in a flurry of running, wing-flapping, and screaming cries. All this multiform ornithological commotion is going on for sixteen lines (294–309) before the chorus-leader starts to chant, in recitative, on behalf of the group. Uniquely as far as the surviving plays go (but there were precedents and parallels in lost works), the twenty-four dancers are individually costumed to represent different species. Unlike the announced cavalry attack in *Knights*, this parodos initially projects a confusion of colour, movement, and sound, and it is a crucial part of the comic effect that only gradually, at least to the humans themselves, does it become apparent that the birds are collecting with menacing intentions. Also, whereas in *Knights* the chorus's hostility is a burlesque version of an obvious model—real-life cavalry manoeuvres—the birds' aggression incongruously endows the animal-chorus with a type of behaviour not naturally characteristic of it. At any rate, it seems likely, in view of the military language later in the encounter at 352 ff., that the parodos of *Birds* made use of choreography which included not only feathery agitation but also movements and gestures reminiscent of warfare. Here, as elsewhere in the play, the comedy engenders a deliberate confusion of the avian and the human.

After the preliminary information provided by the prologue of a comedy, the parodos usually carries with it a grand expansion of the play's scenario through a rich array of poetry, dance, and music. It sets up an interplay, whether of alliance or hostility, between characters and chorus (or even within the chorus itself, as we have noted in the case of *Lysistrata*). The parodos typically initiates or prepares for a drama of confrontation, which brings us to the second of the three major forms with which we are concerned. This is the agon, the 'contest' or 'debate'. Formal competition was a near-pervasive feature of Greek culture: the term *agôn* was applied to the adversarial contexts of law-court trials, debates in political assemblies, athletic events, military conflicts, as well as dramatic competitions themselves. Although military associations regularly attach themselves to the larger setting of a comic agon, it is the first of these areas—the sphere of verbal and argumentative contests—which lends the convention its predominant tone of acrimonious dialectic. Moreover, the agon not only provides the framework for a specific dramatic clash. It also allows for the opening up of general issues—political, educational, artistic, and so on—which go beyond the immediate situation in the play.

In its full form, the agon is a substantially symmetrical structure,[45] each half of which comprises (i) a lyric section, in which the chorus elaborates on its expectations of the speaker; (ii) a long stretch of recitative, introduced by an exhortation to the participants by the chorus, and containing the speaker's arguments themselves; (iii) a climactic conclusion and tail-piece to the recitative, consisting of shorter lines and more rapid rhythm—a kind of accelerando flourish. This is the form which occurs, for example, at *Clouds* 949–1104, *Wasps* 526–724, *Lysistrata* 476–607, *Frogs* 895–1098. The symmetry of the full agon thus constitutes a combination of songs and declamations, technically known as a syzygy, which we shall shortly meet again in the parabasis and whose main components can be set out in diagrammatic form as in Table 1.[46]

The importance of this symmetry is that it represents the harnessing of poetry, music, and (for the lyrics) dance, to create a theatrical design which in performance would be simultaneously aural and visual. Although the parodos and the agon both use a combination of

TABLE 1. *Symmetrical structure of the Aristophanic agon*

	First Half	Second Half
SONG/DANCE	(1) strophe: choral expectations	(1) antistrophe
RECITATIVE	(2) arguments (introduced by second exhortation)	(2) counter-arguments (with choral exhortation)
	(3) accelerando conclusion	(3) accelerando conclusion

[45] The agon proper is sometimes preceded by a preparatory recitative or pre-contest (e.g. *Clouds* 889–948, *Lysistrata* 467–75): I ignore this for present purposes.

[46] The technical terms normally used for the components are: ode/antode (songs); epirrhema/antepirrhema (arguments); katakeleusmos/antikatakeleusmos (exhortations); pnigos/antipnigos (conclusions).

song and recitative, it is easy to see why the agon but not the parodos should be usually symmetrical. Where the parodos forms a dynamic juncture, connecting the prologue to what follows (often the agon itself) and moving the action forward into a new phase, the agon supplies a framework in which the issues of a conflict can be squarely faced up to and, more often than not, resolved. Theatrical patterns mirror dramatic functions.

Just as in the case of the parodos, however, the precise deployment and function of the agon vary from play to play. It is sometimes argued that the norm is a single complete agon occurring in the first half of the drama, that is, before the main parabasis, and producing an outcome whose consequences are then explored (typically through a sequence of 'intruder-scenes', as in e.g. *Acharnians* or *Birds*) after the parabasis. But, as with so many aspects of Old Comedy, talk of norms can be misplaced: the scheme just indicated is strictly found in only two of the surviving works, *Wasps* and *Birds*, though in a third, *Lysistrata*, there is something close to it.[47] *Frogs*, by contrast, has an agon in the second half of the play, for it is only there that a contest between Aischylos and Euripides (an element not anticipated in the earlier scenes) can be staged. In *Knights* and *Clouds* there are actually two full agons.[48] In *Knights* this reflects the fact that most of the drama is an ongoing, serial conflict between the Sausage-Seller and the Paphlagonian, and is not settled until the latter's final defeat at 1263. In *Clouds*, on the other hand, the second agon—between father and son (1345–1451)—serves a comically ironic function by marking the reversal which Strepsiades suffers when Pheidippides turns against him the very sophistic education which he had originally so much wanted his son to acquire.

Several plays (*Peace*, *Assembly-Women*, and *Wealth*), on the other hand, possess only a half-agon, where formality of structure is retained but without the symmetry. In *Peace* (582–656), at least, this scaling down probably arises from the agon's adapted function as a means of explanation (of Peace's absence from Greece) rather than debate. In *Assembly-Women* and *Wealth* it is more likely a symptom of

[47] The victory won by the women at *Lysistrata* 607 is only over the Commissioner; resolution of the larger male/female conflict has to wait till much later in the play.

[48] Passages such as *Wasps* 334–402 and *Birds* 327–99 are also sometimes counted as preliminary agons: what is certainly germane is that these passages do display, on a smaller scale, the theatrical symmetry which gives the agon its distinctive shape.

the overall decline in large-scale theatrical formality, together with a general diminution of the chorus's role, which characterizes the period of Middle Comedy. In *Women at the Thesmophoria*, the function of an agon is fulfilled by an exchange of speeches—*contra* and *pro* Euripides—between the women and the disguised Kinsman at 372–573; but the last section of that scene, at 520–73, formally approximates to another half-agon. Finally, Aristophanes' earliest surviving play, *Acharnians*, has no formal agon at all, even though it does involve a scene of quasi-forensic confrontation in which Dikaiopolis has to defend himself against the chorus's aggressive allegation of treason. Here the omission of a structured agon seems to be motivated by the desire to give the protagonist a parody of the great speech of self-defence made by Telephos in Euripides' play of that name. There are other variables too in Aristophanes' manipulation of the agon, such as the difference between genuinely two-sided debates (e.g. *Clouds*, *Wasps*) and those dominated by a single party (e.g. *Birds* and *Lysistrata*). But enough has been said already to indicate that the agon is at the same time a structure of elaborate theatrical formality, and yet a dramatic unit which can be tailored in diverse ways to suit the particular details of any plot in which it finds a place.

Whereas the agon, like the parodos which I considered earlier, is always causally integrated into the plot, the last of the major formal sequences of Old Comedy, the parabasis, functions above all as a major interlude. The parabasis (English stress parábasis, plural parábases, Greek plural *parabaseis*) has often been thought to be a very old ingredient of the genre; there are various theories about whether it might originally have been placed at the beginning or end of a play. In the surviving comedies it is typically positioned somewhere towards the middle of the plot, the limiting cases being *Clouds* (510 ff.), where only a third of the play precedes it, and *Wasps* (1009 ff.), where it occurs two-thirds of the way through the work. The term parabasis means 'stepping forward': it is a performance routine in which the chorus, normally alone on-stage,[49] addresses itself directly to the audience and therefore stands outside the ongoing action of the plot. The full form of the routine is introduced by a short linking comment (song or recitative) on the preceding scene,

[49] *Women at the Thesmophoria* 785–845 is an exception: the Kinsman is on stage too, trapped at the altar of the Thesmophorion.

continues with the parabasis proper (a substantial recitative section of audience-address, sometimes called the 'anapaests', though that is not always the metre of the section), and is completed by a symmetrical pattern or syzygy—song and recitative; matching song and recitative—which is parallel to that of an agon. The structure is thus as indicated in Table 2.

This full form is found, with only small variations, in *Acharnians*, *Knights*, *Clouds*, *Wasps*, and *Birds*. *Peace*, *Lysistrata*, *Women at the Thesmophoria* (the only parabasis without songs), and *Frogs*[50] all have reduced or reorganized parabases, while by the time of *Assembly-Women* and *Wealth* the convention has disappeared altogether. This distribution tends to suggest that the parabasis exercised a declining appeal for poets and audiences in the later years of the fifth century and beyond. That inference is reinforced by the parallel disappearance of 'second parabases'. The works which have this latter component—usually a reduced version of the main parabatic form—are *Knights*, *Clouds*, *Wasps*, *Peace*, all from the 420s, and *Birds* of 414. But in the last five surviving plays of Aristophanes the only remaining trace of this phenomenon is the section of audience-address at *Assembly-Women* 1154–62.

Unlike the parodos and agon, where the choral element was interwoven with the world of the dramatic characters, the parabasis was an exclusively choral presentation which exploited to the full the vocal, choreographic, and visual aspects of the dancers. But that general observation fails to do justice to what is the most remarkable

TABLE 2. *Formal structure of the Aristophanic parabasis*

SONG/RECITATIVE	Linking comment, usually addressed by the chorus to departing character(s)
RECITATIVE	Parabasis proper ('anapaests'), addressed by the chorus to the audience
SONG	Strophe (typically a prayer/hymn)
RECITATIVE	Declamation ('epirrhema'), usually delivered in the chorus's dramatic identity
SONG	Antistrophe
RECITATIVE	Matching declamation ('antepirrhema')

[50] For an additional peculiarity of *Frogs*, see my notes on lines 354–71 and 674.

feature of the parabasis, namely its fluctuations and flexibility of 'voice'. There are three fundamental voices which can be adopted, in part or whole, by the chorus of a parabasis. The first is (ostensibly) that of the poet himself: this can be expressed in either the first person singular, as though the playwright were actually speaking (*Clouds* 518–62, all the more interesting for being a partly revised version which reacts to the first production of *Clouds* itself), or in the third person singular, with the chorus(-leader) 'reporting' a message from the poet (*Acharnians*, *Knights*, *Wasps*, and *Peace*): at *Acharnians* 659–64 and *Peace* 754 ff. there is a switch from third to first person within the same passage. The second voice is that of the chorus's dramatic identity, and this is the usual point of view from which they deliver the symmetrical series or syzygy of songs and recitatives (parts 3–6 in Table 2), as we see from all the surviving parabases (including those in reduced form) except *Peace* and *Frogs*. But here too there are variations of emphasis: in *Acharnians*, for example, one song reminds us of the chorus's primary status as charcoal-burners (665–75), but what follows represents the standpoint of old men in general. The third voice or persona sometimes assumed in the parabasis—as *Peace* (773 ff.) and *Frogs* (throughout)[51] demonstrate—is that of a comic, dramatic, or festival chorus pure and simple, without more specific signs of identity.

The availability of these different voices and frames of reference, often juxtaposed within a single parabasis, yields a particularly rich vehicle of poetry, humour, and thematic imagery. Indeed, the length of the parabasis, together with the fact that it never concretely affects the action of the play, makes it—unlike either the parodos or the agon—a strikingly free-standing form in its own right, which is the main reason why it has been the subject of so much speculation regarding its origins. Aristophanes' plays from the 420s suggest that the independence and the internal complexity of the parabasis gave it, at that stage of comedy's history, attractions for both playwrights and audiences. One of the most interesting of these attractions can be described as a kind of theatrical self-consciousness, to which I drew

[51] *Frogs* is actually a little more complex, for two reasons: first, the section of 'advice' (686 ff.) might be thought implicitly reminiscent of the convention of the poet's own parabatic voice; secondly, the references to 'sacred' choruses (674, 686) might be treated as reminders of the Initiates' identity, though, taken as a whole, the parabasis hardly makes this necessary.

attention in a previous section when discussing the parabasis of *Knights* (see 'Aristophanes' Career in Context'). It is a related point that the parabases of the early plays are used to build up an extravagantly rhetorical portrait of the poet's own character, standing, and ambitions, as well as the supposed shortcomings of his rivals.[52]

Perhaps Aristophanes' most virtuoso effort in this respect is the section of *Wasps* (1030 ff.) where he depicts himself as a new Herakles fighting against the terrifying monstrosity of the politician Kleon. The theatrical appeal of this passage seems to be vouched for by the fact that Aristophanes repeated these lines, almost verbatim, the following year in *Peace* (752 ff.). I shall have more to say in the next section about the nature of such Aristophanic bravado and boasting, but there is no doubt at all that in the earlier part of his career he was able to exploit very effectively the potential of the parabasis for ostensibly extra-dramatic entertainment. On the other hand, it is this particular feature of the parabasis which appears to have faded rather rapidly after the 420s, so that in *Birds*, *Lysistrata*, and *Women at the Thesmophoria* the chorus remains in its dramatic identity throughout the parabasis.[53] Given the more general evidence, already noted, for a decline in the parabasis during the later fifth century, it is a reasonable hypothesis that the intricacies of the form, which had once provided such elaborate scope for musico-poetic, comic, and choreographic flourishes, had come to seem too cumbersome and old-fashioned for the evolving tastes of dramatists and their public.[54]

I stressed at the outset of this section that we should not allow the technical analysis of compositional forms in Old Comedy to conceal their primarily theatrical character as structures in which meaning, rhythm, music, and dance all came together in a performative

[52] The fragments of other poets' works from roughly this period show that comic boasting and the denigration of rivals were found in their works too, though with some differences from Aristophanes: see A. H. Sommerstein, *Talking About Laughter* (Oxford, 2009), 116–35.

[53] *Frogs* (cf. n. 51) revives the tradition of parabatic 'advice', but not with overt reference to the supposed views or standing of the poet himself.

[54] It is often suggested that the diminution in choral elements (including the parabasis) visible by the time of *Assembly-Women* and *Wealth* was a result of Athens' impoverishment in the Peloponnesian War. Although economic factors may have played a part, I would prefer to look in the first instance for an explanation in terms of theatrical and dramatic evolution.

synthesis. The parodos, agon, and parabasis helped Aristophanes, as they did other poets, to give shape to his plays in ways which drew on yet constantly modified (and sometimes defeated) the expectations of his audience. Understanding something about these structural components allows us to form an idea of an important interface between convention and creativity, continuity and change, in Old Comedy.

Satire and Seriousness

The overwhelming impression created by Aristophanic humour is of an imaginative world that is unlimitedly fluid, grotesque, and absurd in its possibilities of both action and character. Despite this, scholars and critics have long been interested in seeking, and have often claimed to discover, a layer of 'serious' intent in the playwright's work. While fantasy is the dominant mode of Old Comedy, the materials on which fantasy operates its inventiveness and distortions are frequently drawn from the contemporary social and political world of Athens. It is, at root, the interplay (and tension) between fantasy and reality which has given rise to sharply contrasting judgements of Aristophanes' dramatic aims and values.

For a long time after the Renaissance the extremes of this disagreement were posed chiefly in moral terms, with Aristophanes regarded either as a shameless, indiscriminate jester or as a moral, didactic chastiser of reprobates. The play most often treated as a test-case in this debate was *Clouds*, where the question at issue was whether Aristophanes had wantonly attacked the blameless Sokrates, or had perhaps used the figure of Sokrates as a means of exposing the subversive fraudulence of very different types of intellectuals, especially the so-called Sophists. In eighteenth-century England, when an ideal of benevolent humour prevailed, the case of *Clouds* was cited so regularly in this connection that one literary historian has suggested that the period made the issue 'its peculiar property, by infinite repetition'.[55] Unsurprisingly, given the ethical aesthetics of the time, the standard reaction can be exemplified by Joseph Addison, who saw *Clouds* as a prominent illustration of satire's 'poisoned darts, which not only inflict a wound but make it incurable'.[56]

[55] S. M. Tave, *The Amiable Humorist* (Chicago, 1960), 23.
[56] *Spectator*, 23 (27 Mar. 1711).

From the early nineteenth century, however, the focus of debate over Aristophanic satire shifted markedly towards the arena of politics. The central questions, which have tended to dominate scholarship on the playwright ever since, became: was Aristophanes a committed, purposeful satirist, in his treatment of individual leaders and the workings of democracy? And, if so, where did he stand in terms of the major political affiliations of late fifth-century Athens? It was first in Germany, and subsequently elsewhere, that the basic interpretative positions were staked out, with the philosopher Hegel, among others, advancing a view of Aristophanes as a patriotically motivated teacher, and the translator Droysen delineating the opposing idea of the pure entertainer. For most of the last 150 years the majority view has been that Aristophanes *was* in some degree committed to expressing political judgements in his comedies, especially through the use of satire. But there has been much less agreement about exactly what those judgements were, or from what kind of general stance they were delivered.

Commonest is the inference that Aristophanes was some sort of 'conservative', which is defined in this context principally in terms of opposition to the radical democracy of the time and a hankering after an earlier, supposedly more moderate, era of Athenian politics.[57] But there have been many variations on and modifications to this inference, with arguments being advanced for Aristophanes the 'oligarch' (opposed to democracy *per se*), Aristophanes the true democrat (opposed above all to the abuse of power by demagogues and others), Aristophanes the champion of the rural classes—and other positions besides. There is not space to examine each of these possibilities here, nor the ascription of more particular commitments to the poet (such as an acute antipathy to the politician Kleon, for example, or passionate opposition to the war with Sparta). One objection to categorical formulations of Aristophanes' putative values or beliefs is that they are inevitably based on, and tend to simplify, a mass of comically and dramatically variegated material which by its very nature might be thought to destabilize the possibility of

[57] Aristophanes has also frequently been regarded as a 'cultural' conservative in matters of education, poetry, and music, despite the fact that his boasts about his own dramatic artistry stress originality and innovation (*Clouds* 545–8, *Wasps* 1053–9). See my Introductions to *Clouds* and *Frogs* for objections to simplified inferences about the poet's own views on topics such as these.

a consistent reading. It is therefore right that some of the more specific issues raised by the kinds of views I have mentioned should be addressed in my introductions to individual plays. What I shall attempt in the rest of this section is to offer some general reasons for caution about deducing Aristophanes' personal allegiances from his comedies.

The plays of Aristophanes contain such frank and often extreme satirical elements precisely because they belong to a special genre of festival entertainment. As I indicated earlier (see 'Old Comedy and Dionysiac Festivity'), Old Comedy enjoyed a peculiar freedom to break the taboos and contravene the norms which obtained in the social world at large, a freedom which expresses itself in obscenity as well as (and often at the same time as) satire. This freedom stemmed partly from 'folk' practices of scurrilous jesting and inebriated celebration of the kind which Aristophanes himself twice incorporates in his surviving plays.[58] What is so telling about this side of comedy is the 'irresponsibility' of its licence to ridicule, to lampoon, and to vilify. Despite some prima facie suggestions to the contrary (see 'Aristophanes Career in Context' on the special case of *Babylonians*), the playwrights of the genre were essentially exempted from any need to explain or answer for their choice of satirical targets. Unlike the personal abusiveness which undoubtedly played a part in the rivalries of political life, comedy was not usually constrained by the possibility of legal reprisals, nor by the pressures involved in persuading an audience to take a practical decision (other than the judges' voting of a prize to the best comedy) on a particular occasion. These differences are culturally and psychologically fundamental; without them it would be impossible to explain why classical Athens permitted comedy a type and degree of liberty (of speech and thought) which was not available in other contexts of public life. The result of the conditions in which Old Comedy thrived is that Aristophanic satire often takes on a sense of gratuitous irreverence of a kind it is hard to translate into the terms of serious authorial commitments.

In the case of many 'victims' of satire, comic prominence should be taken as a reflection less of scandalous notoriety than of the achievement of status and power within the city. This is most obviously

[58] See 'Aristophanes' Career in Context', with n. 2 above, for the phallic song at *Acharnians* 263 ff. and the Eleusinian mockery at *Frogs* 416 ff.

true of leading politicians, generals, and office-holders (Perikles, Kleon, Hyperbolos, Lamachos, etc.), and while our evidence is often inadequate for certainty, we can be confident that this was true of many of the lesser targets as well. Kleonymos, for example, is set up as a glutton and coward in several of Aristophanes' plays, but we know that he was politically prominent on more than one important occasion and we have some reason to connect him with Kleon in the 420s.[59] Similarly, the Kinesias who appears as both a vacuous poetaster and a physical freak, at *Birds* 1372 ff. and elsewhere, was very probably a much more significant figure, both culturally (as composer and chorus-trainer) and even politically, than we would ever guess from a literal-minded reading of his profile in Aristophanes. Naturally not all butts of satire were eminent or influential, but like many later satirists, Aristophanes did not waste much of his humour on utter social misfits or outcasts. Aristophanic derision has an intrinsically debasing and degrading thrust, and therefore an inbuilt tendency to direct itself against targets whose public standing permits a satisfying disparity between accepted realities outside the theatre and the grotesque reductiveness of comedy itself. In this respect Old Comedy's mockery of human beings is parallel to its burlesque presentation of the gods. Just as most readers would not now infer Aristophanes' own religious attitudes, nor prevailing currents of religious feeling in Athens, from the treatment of Hermes in *Peace*, *Birds*, or *Wealth*, of Iris and Poseidon in *Birds*, or of Dionysos in *Frogs*, so we should be highly circumspect about translating his satire of individual Athenians into a personal set of political or social convictions.

At this point we need to address a seemingly obvious objection. This amounts to the commonly stated orthodoxy that comic playwrights *did* possess, in their parabases (and occasionally elsewhere too), the means to communicate to their audiences the specific perspective from which they observed and judged the life of the polis. It is on the basis of parabatic passages where the chorus can speak either in the voice of the poet or on his behalf (see 'Formality and Performance', above) that Aristophanes has commonly been regarded as a professedly *engagé* dramatist. In *Acharnians* (633 ff.), for example, the chorus explains that Aristophanes believes himself to have been responsible for many benefits to the democracy, especially

[59] See the Index of Names in each volume of the translation.

by bringing to its attention in his recent play *Babylonians* (see the Appendix) the deceitful flattery used by foreign ambassadors who come to address the Assembly in Athens. The poet, they suggest, is not afraid to speak out in the interests of justice, and thereby to serve his people as adviser and teacher (645–58). In a similar vein, the chorus of *Wasps* reports Aristophanes' boast that he has not indulged in petty ridicule of ordinary people but has deployed his satire against the biggest of targets, namely the politician Kleon, here allegorically described as a monster whom it requires Heraklean powers to overcome (1029–35, cf. *Peace* 751–8). Aristophanes, the chorus claims, has fought and continues to fight on behalf of the Athenian people (*Wasps* 1037).

But it is naive to suppose that any such passage offers us the direct or authentic voice of the poet himself. The parabasis, though always standing outside the progress of the dramatic action, is none the less a full part of the comic performance. Its elaborate formality (rhythmical, musical, and choreographic), discussed in the previous section, provides a highly stylized routine which is a theatrical event in its own right. Moreover, the 'voice' of the poet in which the parabasis is sometimes delivered is a conventional fiction, an opportunity for comedy to ape and burlesque the postures of public discourse which were familiar to Athenian audiences from the political Assembly, the adversarial contests of the law-courts, and other democratic institutions.[60] When Aristophanes 'speaks' to the city in his parabases, whether in the first or third person, he can always be seen to be making use of a more-or-less parodic rhetoric by feigning the role of adviser and teacher to his fellow-citizens.

Of the two examples mentioned above, *Acharnians* provides a ripe instance of mock-rhetoric in two modes, both that of self-defence (Aristophanes is replying to the complaint made by Kleon about *Babylonians*: see above) and that of political advice. What gives the game away, above all, are the ludicrous claims at 643 ff.: first, that representatives of allied cities will now hurry to Athens with their annual tribute in order to have a chance to see Aristophanes himself; then, more preposterously still, that even the king of Persia is said to have remarked on the value of the poet to the Athenian war-effort (and

[60] Public oratory is burlesqued in a different way by being made the mode of discourse in which even *women* speak at their own festival meetings, *Women at the Thesmophoria* 372–519.

this is *Acharnians*, whose protagonist makes a private peace treaty!). In *Wasps*, similarly, Aristophanes' depiction of himself as a quasi-Heraklean enemy of Kleon is an exercise in extravagantly hyperbolical bluster, the spirit of which matches the comically outrageous terms (briefly anticipated at 35–6) in which Kleon is transformed into a physically repulsive mongrel. Finally, and very tellingly, the boast of fighting for the people (1037) is a transparently rhetorical cliché, and as such was twice satirized earlier in the play—ironically through the mouth of Philokleon himself (593), and directly by his son (667)—as a hallmark of slick, exploitative orators (593).

In short, there is nothing authoritative about anything said in the poet's name in a parabasis, since the poet's voice is part of, not a detached commentary on, the theatrically artificial and inflated world of the play.[61] Indeed, the kind of argument I have been criticizing could profitably be stood on its head: it is precisely the air of *mock*-seriousness, the posturing rhetoric, and the pretence of didactic influence found in some parabases which reinforce the grounds for supposing that Old Comedy is a perpetual creator of illusions and fabrications about itself as about everything else.

Even in the case of the one surviving parabasis, that of *Frogs*, where there is an apparent linkage to a political decision subsequently taken by the Athenians, caution is in order about relationships of cause and effect. The proposal that Athens should restore citizen rights to some of its disenfranchised citizens if they fight in the fleet (686–702)—a proposal, it is worth noting, advanced by the chorus of initiates, not in the name of the poet as such—is one that must have been already under consideration in certain quarters in the period 406–5.[62] Athens had a manpower shortage in the later years of the Peloponnesian War: hence the enfranchisement of slaves who fought at the battle of Arginousai, as this same passage of *Frogs* mentions. When the Athenians did in fact restore rights to some disenfranchised citizens in the final months of 405, as a result of the decree of Patrokleides (and after their disastrous naval defeat at the battle of

[61] The same is true of *Acharnians* 497–500, where Dikaiopolis prefaces his 'defence speech' with some remarks about comedy itself: to treat this as programmatic of the author's own stance, as has often been done, is to tear it out of the context of parody and metatheatre in which it is teasingly embedded.

[62] On the political/military context at the date of *Frogs*, see further in my Introduction to the play.

Aigospotamoi), this must have been because it had by then attracted the support of a sufficiently widespread body of opinion in the city, not directly because of Aristophanes' comedy. At most, the parabasis of *Frogs* was echoing and, as it were, cheering on a political sentiment that had already been conceived by some Athenians, not independently advocating a new political idea. That Aristophanes chose to include this material in his play probably tells us something about a growing mood in the city. But its place in the intricate web of threads which make up the total fabric of *Frogs* should not be exaggerated.

To return to the broader issue of satirical purpose in Aristophanes, it is practically inevitable that a form of comedy predicated on the licence to abuse, denigrate, and lampoon should sometimes give the *impression* of a politically committed position. In most social contexts forthright mockery is a weapon of aggression, superiority, or contempt. But Athenian democracy had allowed comic drama to develop, however riskily, as a festively 'protected' opportunity for scurrility without responsibility. (The point applies to the treatment of religion as well: nowhere outside comedy could a god like Dionysos be treated as a buffoon, as happens in *Frogs*.) From at least the time of Kratinos, in the generation before Aristophanes, poets had exploited this opportunity to expose leading politicians, generals, and other office-holders, as well as a range of lesser individuals, to the force of collective laughter. If we ask why this should have been so, it is impossible to avoid a culturally speculative model of explanation. Two factors of fundamental importance were stressed in my earlier section on 'Old Comedy and Dionysiac Festivity': one, the subliterary 'folk' roots of this variety of comic satire in old traditions of popular revelry; the other, the flourishing of Old Comedy during the period when Athenian democracy was actually most buoyant and prosperous (as well as confidently 'imperialist'), and therefore most comfortable about allowing elements of its world to be occasionally exposed to ridicule. We are probably dealing, in other words, with a type of collective celebration which was pre-democratic in origin, 'sub-democratic' in its psychological appeal to anti-authoritarian irreverence, and yet functionally democratic in the way it was embedded in the city's calendar of festivities.[63]

[63] For a fuller statement of this view of the genre's cultural psychology, see Halliwell, *Greek Laughter*, 243–63.

We need to remind ourselves here of a cultural paradox and puzzle. Dionysiac festivals at Athens were thought equally suitable settings for the performance of both tragedy and comedy. They were occasions when, on the one hand, the city distributed marks and awards of honour to pre-eminent citizens, but also when carnivalesque pleasures of ritual mockery and licensed obscenity were prominent in the form of masked revellers on wagons or floats who processed through the city hurling ribald abuse at one another and at the watching crowds.[64] It is as if the heady atmosphere of Dionysiac festivals was thought simultaneously appropriate for the opposing extremes of solemn, civic earnestness *and* disruptive, topsy-turvy play. More interestingly still, the recipients of honorific and satirical attention were in some cases the very same people, as, for example, with the city's generals, who were granted rights of front seating (*prohedria*) in the theatre,[65] but who might then find themselves, as Kleon and others did, the object of vilification in the very plays they were watching. Satirical mockery may, in a psychologically subtle way, have temporarily counterbalanced and inverted the possession of public power or esteem, but it is hard to believe that it could have been allowed to negate or cancel out these things.[66]

Nor does our other evidence, if assessed sensitively, encourage belief in comedy's potency as a direct influence on currents of public opinion in classical Athens. The case of Aristophanes' seemingly stormy relationship with the leading politician Kleon has been touched on more than once already. Whatever its other implications, it provides no cogent evidence that comedy could make a significant difference to the practicalities of democratic politics. On the contrary, it might be thought to throw into relief the asymmetry between 'real' and 'comic' politics. When, in the parabasis of *Clouds* (549–50), Aristophanes boasts that he had struck Kleon 'hard in the belly' and 'knocked him flat' (as if in an all-in wrestling contest) but had then moved on to other subject-matter for his plays (itself a claim that

[64] See Halliwell, *Greek Laughter*, 177–81. [65] See *Knights* 575, 702–4.

[66] Our only fifth-century observation on the satirical practices of Old Comedy is the claim in pseudo-Xenophon (so-called 'Old Oligarch'), *Constitution of the Athenians* 2.18, that the targets of comedy are largely 'the rich, noble, or powerful', not members of the common people: although this passage is hardly a precise formulation, it surely leaves the impression that comedy did not *change* anything in Athenian society.

is hard to square with serious political commitment), this is a self-evident piece of pseudo-political arrogance. If anything, Kleon's power and prestige in Athens had actually *risen*—as testified by his repeat election to generalships in 424–3 and 423–2—during the very period when Aristophanes' lampooning of him was at its most comically scabrous. Aristophanes himself betrays the paradox: he had supposedly knocked Kleon down when he was, in fact, 'at his height' or most powerful (*Clouds* 549).

Nor does another famous case, that of the references in Plato's *Apology* (18 c–19 c) to the treatment of Sokrates in *Clouds*, point in a different direction. Contrary to what is usually claimed, it is far from clear that Plato means to suggest that *Clouds* itself had been seriously responsible for having disseminated a negative perception of the philosopher. Rather, he makes Sokrates use the play as a pointed illustration of just how ludicrous the distortions of his life and character could become: Sokrates contrasts comic 'nonsense' with the 'animus and malice' shown by his real-life enemies and accusers.[67] The fact that *Clouds* had actually been something of a flop at its first performance in 423 (when Plato himself, moreover, was still a young child), as we learn from the play's revised parabasis (524–5), weakens even further any argument that might be constructed about its supposed influence on general Athenian attitudes to Sokrates in the late fifth century.

Because comic performances were limited to two main festivals in the year (though with some opportunity for smaller productions in local deme theatres),[68] they were not sufficiently integrated into the all-year-round processes of social and political life to impinge on the latter in any substantial way. This is not, however, to say that comedy was simply 'innocent fun'. Its unfettered freedom of speech permitted it to voice feelings of disgruntlement, exasperation, and cynicism which no doubt partially reflected the underside of political consciousness in the city. But we will be prone to considerable self-deception if we think that we now have much chance of picking our way through its distortions, absurdities, contradictions,

[67] For further detail on the references to Sokrates in Plato's *Apology*, see my Introduction to *Clouds*.

[68] See Rusten, *The Birth of Comedy*, 126–31, for inscriptional evidence on performances in deme theatres. Plato, *Republic* 5.475d, refers to theatre addicts who tried to go to as many local dramatic performances as they could.

and outrageous transformations of life, and coming out at the end with a coherent or steady sense of the playwright's own point of view. All humour tends to some extent towards the dissolution of sense, and the characteristic modes of Old Comedy do so to an exceptional degree. Aristophanes' theatrical strength lies in his multifarious talent for manipulating images and ideas into surprising yet satisfying scenarios. But anyone who looks to him for clear or deep insights into Athenian society is likely to be ultimately disappointed.

Translating Aristophanes

The translator of Aristophanes is confronted by challenges more varied and formidable than those posed by any other ancient author. There are three main sources of difficulty. First, Aristophanic verse encompasses many different linguistic registers; it frequently achieves its distinctive effects by piquant or incongruous combinations of these. As well as echoing and parodying other genres of Greek poetry—epic, lyric, and above all tragedy[69]—the stylistic range of Old Comedy constantly moves backwards and forwards between the colloquial and the elevated, the informal and the technical, the delicate and the gross. Secondly, large areas of Aristophanic humour are inextricably tied up with verbal details of imagery, puns, coinages, and other kinds of word-play, many of which are hard, if not impossible, to preserve in modern translation. Finally, Old Comedy is saturated with historically specific references to people, places, institutions, and assorted paraphernalia. These sometimes created problems even for post-classical Greek readers in antiquity,[70] and they continue to form a barrier to appreciation for those who are not extensively familiar with fifth-century Athenian culture. The conjunction of these various factors means that issues of fidelity of the sort which affect all fields of translation arise in an acute form with Aristophanes' work: the expectation of comic fluency and the desirability of historical accuracy make competing and often irreconcilable demands.

Translations are intrinsically ambivalent constructions. On the

[69] Cf. the earlier section, 'Old Comedy and Dionysiac Festivity'.

[70] For one example, see my discussion of Plutarch in 'Aristophanes and Posterity' below.

one hand, they implicitly invite us—and the more so the greater the cultural distance between their originals and ourselves—to extend our experience beyond the bounds of what is immediately available within our own language and its associated thought-world. On the other, they inevitably engage in some degree of assimilation by the very act of transference into the translator's/reader's language. Translators strive, according to their inclinations and purposes, either to strike a balance between these contrasting implications, or else to accentuate one at the expense of the other. In the case of comic texts, the temptation to prefer assimilation and modernization over the acknowledgement and savouring of historical distance is very considerable, for the simple reason that readers of comedy readily expect to be amused, and amusement is by nature a relatively spontaneous response which does not normally require a special effort of imagination or understanding. But the present translation tries, in the main, to resist this temptation, on the assumption that readers of Aristophanes should be looking for something other than a ready-made entertainment of a kind straightforwardly equivalent to, and interchangeable with, the products of their own culture.

My translation has accordingly been guided by the conviction that, while it is desirable to make Aristophanes as accessible as possible, accessibility must involve access *to* something that is not our own, rather than a modern substitute for it. The comic pleasure which can still be obtained from these plays depends on the willingness of readers to participate in a well-informed experience of a historically peculiar, even alien, mode of drama. What I have tried to provide are versions which approximate as closely to the original texture of Aristophanic poetry, and to the proclivities of Aristophanic humour, as is compatible with reasonable fluency in modern English. This means, for one thing, that I have generally retained as much as possible of the historical fabric of names, references, and allusions, so that readers will not at any rate be badly misled about the kinds of things Aristophanes wrote and imagined. It also, and equally importantly, means that I have chosen not to translate the plays into prose, since that would involve, in my judgement, too great (and comfortable) an assimilation to the dominant medium of comic drama in our own world, with a corresponding loss of the poetic forms which are so integral to the nature of Old Comedy. Here as elsewhere, however, some compromise is appropriate, as will become clear from further explanation of the verse-forms I have adopted.[71]

In the earlier section of this Introduction on 'Formality and Performance' I described Aristophanes' use of the three basic modes of dramatic poetry: speech (in iambic trimeters); chanted, and musically accompanied, 'recitative' (in longer lines of various rhythms); and lyrics (in often complex metrical units), also with musical accompaniment. These three modes pose distinct challenges to a translator. The spoken iambic trimeters call for a treatment which maintains a sense of tight verse structure while allowing for easy variation in phrasing (including division between speakers, a particular source of verbal give-and-take in Aristophanes[72]) and for a wide spectrum of registers and effects, including the colloquial,[73] though the latter is not quite as dominant a voice as many modern translators of Aristophanes have made it. Here I have adopted a five-beat line (with a little stretch for some Greek proper names) which represents a maximally supple version of blank verse, the so-called 'iambic pentameter'. This has three advantages to recommend it: first, it is not too far in metrical shape from the Greek iambic trimeter (making allowance for the difference between the quantitative rhythms of Greek verse and the dynamic stress-patterns of English);[74] secondly, it has a combination of regularity with flexibility which can cope with the gamut of styles employed, echoed, and parodied by Aristophanes in the spoken parts of his plays; thirdly, it has a historical embeddedness in English verse (particularly in the practice of dramatic

[71] In the case of oracles, which use dactylic hexameters (the metre of epic) in Greek, I have used accentual hexameters, despite the problems of this form in English: see e.g. *Knights* 1015 ff., *Birds* 967 ff., *Lysistrata* 770 ff.

[72] See e.g. *Clouds* 219, *Frogs* 51–7, 305–6. The maximum splitting of a line between speakers (six separate utterances) is found at *Wealth* 393. For similar effects in a different metre, see the sustained play with 'echoes' at *Women at the Thesmophoria* 1078–96.

[73] See Aristotle's well-known remark that 'the iambic trimeter, more than any other metre, has the rhythm of speech: an indication of this is that we speak many trimeters in conversation with one another' (*Poetics* 4.1449a24–7; cf. 22.1459a12, *Rhetoric* 3.8, 1408b33–5).

[74] If Greek iambics were assimilated to a stress-patterned metre, the result would be six main 'beats' in the line, as opposed to the five of blank verse. It is thus important to notice the difference between standard terminology for Greek and English metres. An English iambic 'trimeter' would have *three* beats, a 'tetrameter' four, etc.; for Greek units, '-meter' denotes a metron, which roughly corresponds to a pair of feet, hence two beats, in English rhythms. Cf. n. 75.

and satiric poets) which stretches back to the sixteenth century and which ought to make it conveniently familiar to modern readers. Unlike some other modern versions, my translations keep line-by-line step with the Greek text.

The recitative sections of Aristophanes' comedies use longer lines (tetrameters)[75] of iambic, trochaic, and anapaestic type, and occasionally other rhythms too. It is hardly feasible to match all of these rhythms with their nearest English equivalents. Trochaic rhythms in Greek typically had a springy quality, but it is hard to capture this consistently by English trochees, which cut too much against the grain of the language and tend to sound laboriously mannered. Even so, I have sometimes rendered shorter passages of Aristophanes' trochaic tetrameters as English trochaics (in lines of *eight* stresses): examples are *Clouds* 1115–30, the cloud-chorus's address to the judges in the 'second parabasis'; *Women at the Thesmophoria* 659–62, 687–8, where the chorus-leader's words accompany the chorus's stealthy search for an intruder, 830–45, part of the parabasis; *Frogs* 686–705, 718–37, also from the parabasis, where the chorus purport to instruct the city how to run its affairs. In some other cases, however, I have converted trochaic tetrameters into eight-stress *iambic* lines: examples include the second half of the parabasis of *Clouds* (575–94, 607–26), where the cloud-chorus delivers its political and religious 'advice' to the city.

Anapaests are even harder to sustain without either awkwardness or a rolling Gilbertian manner that palls when kept up for the length of passages in which this metre occurs in Aristophanes. The attempt by Swinburne to translate part of the parabasis of *Birds* (anapaestic tetrameters) into an English equivalent (anapaestic heptameters) shows that even a practised versifier is stretched to carry off the exercise without making a reader stumble;[76] and I give my reasons, in 'Aristophanes and Posterity' (below), for thinking it advisable to avoid endowing Aristophanes with the genial spirit of Gilbert and Sullivan. In the present volume, therefore, I have dispensed with

[75] In the Greek context, 'tetrameter' denotes four metra, which roughly correspond to either seven or eight English feet/beats; thus a Greek iambic tetrameter is approximately twice as long as the English line so-called (as e.g. in Marvell's 'To his Coy Mistress').

[76] Swinburne's version was first published in the *Athenaeum*, 30 Oct. 1880, then in his *Studies in Song* (London, 1880), 67–74; see *The Poems of Algernon Charles Swinburne*, v (London, 1904), 41–5. Smoother anapaests such as those of B. B. Rogers have the drawback of tending to become more monotonous.

regular anapaestic rhythms altogether.[77] Some anapaestic colouring can be kept, however, by the type of longer line which I use to translate most of Aristophanes' tetrameters (iambic, trochaic, and anapaestic): namely, a flexible version (allowing variable numbers of unstressed syllables) of the iambic heptameter (or, in its strictest form, the 'fourteener'), that is, an iambic line with seven main stresses.[78] The heptameter has enough fluency to accommodate the numerous kinds of material found in Aristophanes' Greek tetrameters, and enough declamatory formality to convey something of the slightly raised, stylized tone of the passages in question.[79] Examples in the present volume include extensive parts of the parodos of *Clouds* (starting from 263 onwards), where we are introduced to both Sokrates' and the chorus's supposed loftiness of mind; *Women at the Thesmophoria* 531–73, where Mika reacts with increasing indignation to the Kinsman's misogynistic speech; and the main sections of the agon between the poets at *Frogs* 907–70, 1006–76, where poetic principles are debated in set-piece exchanges. This leaves just one passage of recitative in the present three plays, namely the poetic 'autobiography' in the first part of the parabasis of *Clouds* (518–62). This is in a metre known as eupolidean, named after Aristophanes' contemporary and rival Eupolis (cf. *Clouds* 553)—the only example of it in the extant plays, though it certainly occurred elsewhere in comedy. I have rendered it in free verse.

Finally, the lyrics. Here it would be pointless to follow B. B. Rogers and several of his Victorian predecessors in aiming for anything like a consistent correlation with Greek rhythms, since too many of the latter, even when turned into stress metres, would make no recognizable pattern to a modern ear. In some passages, however, part of the rhythmical ethos can be captured in at least an approximate manner, either by the 'shape' and length of metrical phrases or, occasionally, by some of their dominant rhythms. My general strategy in this area has been to employ a fluid free-verse technique. Aristophanic

[77] For a short example in the previous volume of this series, see *Birds* 209–22, where anapaests well suit the Hoopoe's excited summons to his nightingale wife.

[78] The English metre is sometimes divided into alternating lines of four and three stresses, as in Coleridge's *Rhyme of the Ancient Mariner*. My treatment of the end of heptameters allows both 'masculine' (final syllable stressed) and 'feminine' (final syllable unstressed) cadences. The same is true of my occasional longer trochaic lines.

[79] For related reasons, I render anapaestic dimeters into iambic tetrameters in the snappily stylized tit-for-tat abuse in the pre-agon at *Clouds* 889–948.

lyrics, which can involve characters as well as chorus, vary greatly in style and tone both within and between plays. Some are quite prosaic in diction and sentiment but given a perky song-and-dance tautness by their rhythms: *Clouds* 1303–20 (where the chorus anticipates the undoing of Strepsiades) and *Women at the Thesmophoria* 520–30 (the chorus's initial shock at the Kinsman's misogyny) are cases in point. Others are integrated into stage action in various ways: see, for example, Strepsiades' torment by bedbugs at *Clouds* 700–22, the women's hunt for an intruder at *Women at the Thesmophoria* 659–88, or the famous contest between the rowing Dionysos and the croaking frogs at *Frogs* 209–67. The spectrum of Aristophanic lyrics reaches all the way, in fact, from ditties of shameless vulgarity and outright obscenity (*Frogs* 416–30, 542–8) to exercises in pseudo-religious elevation (e.g. *Clouds* 275–90, *Women at the Thesmophoria* 312–30)—not forgetting the various kinds of lyric parody which Aristophanes so relishes and of which *Women at the Thesmophoria* 101–29, 1015–55, and *Frogs* 1261–1363 provide virtuoso specimens. While it is impossible to mirror all this in modern English, translation of the lyrics calls for maximum pliancy in both formal and linguistic terms.[80] In reading the lyrics, readers in turn need to stretch their imaginations and seek some sense of what must have been contributed by the lost music and choreography.

I referred at the start of this section to three main categories of difficulty facing any translator of Aristophanes. The problem of mixed and unexpectedly shifting stylistic registers—above all, the typical Aristophanic juxtapositioning of 'high' and 'low'—is ubiquitous. In coming to terms with it I have made use, where appropriate, of 'stage directions' (see the next section), as well as quotation-marks, designed to prompt and guide the aural imagination. In the case of puns and word-play, one is at the mercy of luck and of the latent verbal potential of English: *Clouds* 28–9, with its pun on 'driving' chariots and 'driving crazy', is one of the rare cases where one can stick close to the Greek yet hit a similar note in English. Usually the most one can hope to achieve in translation is something which indicates the spirit though hardly the precise 'ring' of the original joke. At *Clouds* 23–4, for instance, Strepsiades sarcastically plays on the (accidental and

[80] One resource I have abstained from, however, is the structural use of rhyme, despite its appeal to some other Aristophanic translators. I have never been quite able to convince myself that it serves a useful purpose in this context.

partial) sound-resemblance between the term for a branded pedigree horse and a verb which refers to having one of his eyes knocked out: I resort to 'dashing racer' and 'dashed out' to signal the interplay between the aural and the semantic. At *Clouds* 32–3 something of the same sort is happily available to match Strepsiades' pun on cleaning a horse and being taken, as we say, 'to the cleaners'. More complex is *Women at the Thesmophoria* 842–5, where the chorus's disparaging remarks about the mother of the politician Hyperbolos and her supposed moneylending activities play with two senses of the noun *tokos*, 'offspring' and 'financial interest'. I have tried to capture the point with the following English paronomasia: '*You* deserve no fruit from your loans: how could you, given the fruit of your loins!' (845). But very often nothing even as approximate as that can be contrived. How, for example, can one get anywhere linguistically near the pun at *Frogs* 418, where the politician Archedemos is said not even to have (literally) 'grown phratry-members' by the age of seven? To be introduced as a young child to a phratry or kinship group was a normal part of becoming a legitimate citizen; but the word for 'phratry members' is quite similar to the word for 'permanent teeth'. A translator is entitled to despair at such moments. We can, in any case, hardly ever expect to *savour* puns in an ancient language; there is something about punning which taps into an instinctive feel for the language.[81] Given that fact, one option is to be independently inventive. But that is for less historically focused translations than this one. In keeping with the general aims of the present version, I have tried never to stray too far from the verbal details of the text, since it is these which cumulatively create the flavour of Aristophanic humour. As already explained, the same principle has been largely applied to the various topical references which embed the plays in their time and place.

Yet there remain difficult linguistic choices to face. These can be illustrated by the contrasting problems of oaths and dialects. The use of oaths is commonplace in Aristophanes' plays. The main reason for this is undoubtedly that they were a general feature of real Attic speech at all levels. Many of them, such as the commonest of all ('by Zeus'), functioned as little more than expletives or exclamations.

[81] We are badly placed to judge which puns in Aristophanes would have struck his audience as successful: when Dover, in his commentary on *Clouds* (see the Bibliography), calls the pun at lines 23–4 cited in my text above as 'one of [Aristophanes'] feeblest', I cannot see how he can tell that.

Others lend varying degrees of intensification or emotional colour to their utterances. And some have further significance, for example as markers of female speech[82] or as the basis of local comic effect. In the latter category belong, for instance, Strepsiades' oath by Zeus in the very act of doubting the god's existence at *Clouds* 1234, Poseidon's oath by himself at *Birds* 1614, the Commissioner's oath by Poseidon at *Lysistrata* 403 when responding to the old men's complaint about their watery suffering, or Dionysos's partly stifled cries to Apollo and Poseidon (which he tries to pretend are quotations from poetry) at *Frogs* 659 and 664. To translate each and every oath literally would probably lead to an excessively arch effect in English. To omit most of them, on the other hand, would be to lose both a distinctive feature of Athenian speech patterns and a source of much verbal pointing of comic dialogue. I have tried, therefore, to keep a fair proportion of oaths, especially those which are salient in one way or another.

In the case of dialects, however, I have diverged from the practice of most earlier translators by declining to employ a systematic differentiation of speech patterns in the case of characters who are depicted in the Greek as speaking dialects other than Attic (principally, the Megarian and Boiotian in *Acharnians*, Lampito in *Lysistrata*). This is for the simple but fundamental reason that no appropriate equivalent, making sense in both linguistic and cultural terms, is readily available. Athenians must have heard other Greek dialects spoken on many occasions, in the streets of their own city as well as elsewhere; the dialects as such were not intrinsically amusing, though their Aristophanic versions may contain some comic details.[83] In particular, giving the three characters in question a 'funny accent' is not the point. Many translators in the past have made Lampito speak Scots, but this is, and always was, unsuitable in a version which can be read as well in Scotland (where I happen to teach!) as anywhere else. Other translators have opted for a dialectal element which can be perceived, from the point of view of the implicit readership or audience, as markedly rustic or backward; in America, this usually means

[82] See the notes on *Women at the Thesmophoria* 254, 383, 594.

[83] See, for instance, Lampito's perhaps excessive and mannered use of a Spartan form of oath (esp. *Lysistrata* 81–90). The visitors in *Acharnians* too have speech features which are markedly comic, but these can be conveyed in translation independently of an overall dialectal colouring. Plato, *Laws* 1.642c shows that Greeks could in principle enjoy the sound of dialects other than their own.

a hillbilly variety of speech. But such a strategy is certainly inapt for Lampito, and probably for the two characters in *Acharnians* too, since we have no reason to suppose that Athenians perceived the relevant dialects in this light. I have therefore eschewed the use of a consistent dialectal presentation of these characters, while allowing individually comic speech peculiarities to come through in the translation.

The Skythian Archer in *Women at the Thesmophoria* (like, more briefly, Pseudartabas in *Acharnians* and the Triballian god in *Birds*) is, however, a different matter. He is a 'barbarian'; his speech—unlike that, it is worth noting, of every other slave in Aristophanes—is correspondingly defective. There is no real alternative to giving him a strongly yet indeterminately pidginized form of English. But even here Aristophanes is playing subtle language-games: the Skythian's egregious errors still fit the verse rhythms flawlessly, and part of their effect depends less on their morphological or grammatical faults *per se* than on the extreme clash of speech registers which they set up with the poetry of Euripidean tragedy.

Stage Directions

The Theatre of Dionysos in Athens, on the south-east slope of the Akropolis, was the location for the dramatic performances at both the City Dionysia and, almost certainly, the Lenaia too (cf. 'Aristophanes' Career', above). The details of its fifth-century form are contentious, since the archaeological remains are mostly of much later date and literary evidence is scanty. But in recent years there has been an emergent consensus that the area for the audience's wooden benches on the hillside, and therefore the size of the audience, was smaller in the late-fifth century than previously supposed. Many scholars now believe that Aristophanes' comedies would have been watched by around 5,000–7,000 spectators (including some non-Athenians at the Dionysia, fewer at the Lenaia).[84] That is still, however, a substantial proportion of the citizen body, representing

[84] See e.g. M. Revermann, *Comic Business* (Oxford, 2006), 168–9, D. K. Roselli, *Theater of the People: Spectators and Society in Ancient Athens* (Austin, Tex., 2011), 64–75 (arguing for additional spectators outside the official seating area). For the wooden benches on which most spectators sat, cf. *Women at the Thesmophoria* 395, though there may have been stone seating for dignitaries at the front. Cf. n. 32 on the vexed question of whether women attended the theatre in this period.

approximately the same scale of attendance as at political Assembly meetings.[85]

As for the performance space itself in the Theatre of Dionysos, the main components were a substantial, probably wooden stage building (*skênê*), and, in front of it, a large area, possibly rectilinear and elongated (trapezoidal) rather than circular in shape (as it was later to be), known as the *orchêstra* (lit. 'dancing-floor'), and used by both actors and chorus. The dimensions of the *orchêstra* were perhaps of the order of some twenty metres in diameter and eight in depth, and to either side of it was an entrance/exit (*eisodos*, pl. *eisodoi*) for the performers.[86] The stage building had a main central door (which could change its identity in the course of a play: see *Women at the Thesmophoria* and *Frogs* in this volume), a usable roof (e.g. *Wasps* 136 ff., *Birds* 267 ff., *Lysistrata* 829 ff., and perhaps *Clouds* 275 ff.), windows (cf. *Wasps* 156 ff., 317 ff., *Assembly-Women* 884 ff.), and, when required (*Acharnians*, *Clouds*, *Assembly-Women*), a second door. It is possible that there was a low wooden stage in front of the stage building, connected to the *orchêstra* by two or three steps; if so, it did nothing to impede the physical interaction between characters and chorus which is often evident in Old Comedy, for example in the confrontational parodoi of plays such as *Knights* (247 ff.) and *Birds* (352 ff.). Also available, though employed by Aristophanes purely for the purposes of paratragedy, were both the *mêchanê* ('machine'), a sort of crane which suspended characters in simulated flight (see Sokrates' entry at *Clouds* 219 ff., plus *Peace* 174, *Birds* 1199 ff., and, just possibly, *Women at the Thesmophoria* 1009–14), and the *ekkuklêma* or wheeled platform, which represented interior scenes (*Acharnians* 407–79, *Women at the Thesmophoria* 101–265).[87]

Most comedies were performed by three main actors, taking more than one role each when necessary, but occasionally supplemented by a fourth and even fifth actor for smaller parts; mute parts were

[85] For the scale of Assembly attendance, see M. G. Hansen, *The Athenian Democracy in the Age of Demosthenes* (Oxford, 1991), 130–2.

[86] The term *parodos* (as for the chorus's entry: see 'Formality and Performance'), though common in modern books, is post-classical usage; *eisodos* (Aristophanes' own term at *Clouds* 326, *Birds* 296) is to be preferred.

[87] It is also possible, but less likely, that the *ekkuklêma* was used for the bedroom scene at the start of *Clouds* and the later view into Sokrates' school (see note on *Clouds* 184) and for the contest of tragedians in *Frogs* (see note on *Frogs* 830).

additional. Masks, typically exaggerated and often grotesquely so, were always worn. All roles were played by males, and this probably held even for silent female figures such as the pipe-girl at *Wasps* 1326 ff., Reconciliation at *Lysistrata* 1114 ff., or Euripides' Muse at *Frogs* 1308 ff. Even when such roles were notionally 'naked', as with the first two of those just mentioned, the body-stockings which formed a standard part of comic actors' costumes would simply be designed to represent bare flesh and the appropriate anatomical externals.[88] A body-stocking also allowed for the padding of the actor's belly and rump, which seems to have been a frequent practice augmenting the general sense of grotesqueness. A visible phallus was a conventional appendage for male characters; it could be more or less prominent (cf. *Clouds* 537–9) and lent itself to stage business of various kinds (e.g. *Women at the Thesmophoria* 62, 239–48, 638–48, 1187–8). Those three accoutrements of the comic performer—(grotesque) mask, padding, and phallus—must have created a pervasive and inescapable sense of vulgar absurdity for Athenian audiences, ensuring that the action of a play was always visually suspended in a kind of misshapen world of its own.

The chorus, as mentioned in previous sections, consisted of twenty-four singers/dancers, including a chorus-leader who spoke and declaimed certain sections solo, especially when in dialogue with individual actors.[89] Many of the choral dance-sections took symmetrical strophic form, involving the musically and rhythmically matching pairing of strophe and antistrophe, as indicated in the margins of my translation. Musical accompaniment was provided by a piper, whose instrument was a pair of *auloi* or reed-pipes (akin to oboes). Comedy sometimes draws the piper temporarily into the sphere of the dramatic action, as with the sounds of Prokne at *Birds* 209 ff., Euripides' use of Teredon as part of his ruse at *Women at*

[88] Body-stockings are regularly depicted in fourth-century vase-paintings of comic actors from Magna Graecia: see the illustrations in Rusten, *The Birth of Comedy*, 434–54. They are also conspicuous on the important Athenian vase widely known as the 'Getty Birds' (formerly but no longer in the Getty Museum): see Rusten, *The Birth of Comedy*, ill. 72A, Csapo and Slater, *The Context of Ancient Drama*, pl. 5, Revermann, *Comic Business*, pl. 8, O. Taplin, *Comic Angels* (Oxford, 1993), pl. 24.28.

[89] We cannot always be confident whether particular choral utterances were collective or the leader's alone, but I have tried to follow a reasonably consistent practice of attribution in this respect.

the Thesmophoria 1176 ff., or the old hag's address to the player at *Assembly-Women* 890–2.[90]

When the plays of Aristophanes were written down, they contained, like virtually all ancient dramatic texts, no stage directions. We are therefore left to make our own inferences about the kind of staging which they could or would have been given, guiding ourselves, wherever possible, by other sources of information about the Athenian theatre. So the reader of this, as of any other, translation of Aristophanes (or of Greek tragedy) should keep in mind that all stage directions are a matter of interpretation, not independent fact, even though a fair number of them can be established uncontroversially, and more still can be persuasively justified from clues in the text. Readers should themselves cultivate the habit of picturing the realization of the script in an open-air theatrical space, and by a cast of grotesquely attired players, of the kind described above.

Aristophanes and Posterity

The works of Aristophanes have often aroused the curiosity of writers, readers, and audiences of comedy, but they have rarely influenced the later history of the genre to an appreciable extent. The fundamental explanation of this state of affairs lies in two kinds of difficulty: the difficulty of understanding, and ethical difficulty. The former arises from linguistic challenges (colloquial idioms, stylistic parodies, an immense range of imagery), topical references (to people, places, objects, and institutions), and imaginative exoticism. Ethical difficulty, though no longer prevalent, stemmed historically from Old Comedy's scurrilous and even seemingly vicious personal satire, irreverence in the treatment of religious matters, and a degree of obscenity, visual as well as verbal, not paralleled elsewhere in ancient literature: all three of these elements have regularly troubled readers committed to the long-dominant, indeed orthodox, view of comedy as a morally decent and edifying genre (see below). Yet these two sets of features, when seen from a different angle, can also be regarded as a large part of what makes Aristophanes' plays

[90] Additional musicians are sometimes involved: see e.g. the Theban pipers at *Acharnians* 862; a Spartan 'bagpiper' has often been posited at *Lysistrata* 1242, but the reference is probably to the ordinary piper.

special and therefore worth having. The story of 'Aristophanes and Posterity', of which this section can provide only a partial sketch, is therefore one of rather delicately balanced considerations, in which factors of attraction and repulsion have often operated side by side.

Old Comedy was so closely tied to the society and culture of fifth-century Athens that it could never have had a fully sustained afterlife even in the ancient world. Unlike the New Comedy of Menander and other playwrights in the late fourth and early third centuries, which was transported to Rome about a century later by Plautus, Terence, and others, and was subsequently to be a fertile ground for the development of theatrical comedy in the Renaissance and beyond, Old Comedy's interest and importance do not lend themselves to ready imitation or emulation. Until recently it was thought likely that no Aristophanic play ever received a performance after the poet's own lifetime. Serious doubt has now been cast on that claim, since vase-painting has given us near-certain evidence for the transference of Old Comedies to the theatres of fourth-century Magna Graecia (South Italy and Sicily). The most compelling single item of such evidence is a South Italian depiction of the moment from *Women at the Thesmophoria* where, in parody of Euripides' lost play *Telephos*, the Kinsman threatens Mika's 'baby', in reality a wineskin, with a sword.[91] In this particular instance it is germane that we are dealing with a comedy built around the (fictionalized) tragedian Euripides, whose works themselves received productions in the Greek theatres of South Italy and Sicily. It remains hard to imagine how, without considerable adaptation at any rate, some of Aristophanes' other comedies could have been transplanted to cities where their detailed references to matters Athenian would not have been fully intelligible. So there remains no good reason to suppose that Old Comedy's performance-life was much extended in this way.

For the rest of Graeco-Roman antiquity the works of Aristophanes were to be known only as texts, and then mostly to very small numbers of highly educated readers. The survival of eleven plays (out of more than forty) to the age of printing was, as with many other works of

[91] The vase (Würzburg, Antikensammlung, H5697) is illustrated in e.g. Taplin, *Comic Angels*, pl. 11.4, Revermann, *Comic Business*, pl. 2, R. Green and E. Handley, *Images of the Greek Theatre* (London, 1995), ill. 27, as the frontispiece to C. Austin and S. D. Olson, *Aristophanes Thesmophoriazusae* (Oxford, 2004), and at <http://www.iconiclimc.ch/visitors/imageview.php?source=138&image_id=10582&tree_id=60311>.

ancient literature, the result of a long and complex process, part cultural and part accidental. *Clouds*, for example, was preserved largely because of the lasting fascination of its central character, Sokrates; and a similar factor may have obtained in the cases of *Women at the Thesmophoria* and *Frogs*, in both of which Euripides, the most popular tragedian throughout antiquity, is so prominent.[92] It was for very different reasons, however, that *Wealth* not only survived but became established as the most commonly read of Aristophanes' works in antiquity and the Byzantine period. *Wealth* was valued as the least taxing, both historically and linguistically, of the poet's plays, but also for the apparently clear-cut morality of its plot. The second of those factors became increasingly active during the medieval centuries, when pagan literature was subjected to judgement—though hardly ever, it seems, to censorship—in the light of Christian values.

Clearly, though, such criteria were not applied consistently. Otherwise, works such as *Knights*, with its dense texture of contemporary political allegory, or *Wasps*, with its detailed references to and travesty of the Athenian judicial system, would not have been preserved and copied. In instances like these it is tempting to suppose, though impossible to show, that survival partly depended upon the interest of certain readers, especially scholars, in precisely this rich element of historical allusiveness. Be that as it may, it was *Wealth*, *Clouds*, and *Frogs* which became standard 'set texts' in the schools of Byzantium. Equally, and surely not accidentally, the three 'women plays'—*Lysistrata*, *Women at the Thesmophoria*, and *Assembly-Women*—were the least studied of the eleven during the Byzantine centuries.

Among ancient readers of Aristophanes probably belong the Roman authors of poems in the genre of *satura*, 'satire'. By the time of Horace, whose own *Satires* were composed in the 30s BC, the idea had acquired some currency that fifth-century Athenian Comedy was a precursor of, or partial model for, Roman satire. Horace refers to this idea at the beginning of *Satires* 1.4, where he claims that the creator of the Latin genre of verse satire, Lucilius, was heavily indebted

[92] But the case of *Women at the Thesmophoria* also illustrates the importance of chance: the play survived the Middle Ages in only a single manuscript; if that one copy had been destroyed at any point between around 1000 and 1500, the play would now be on our list of lost works.

to the Old Comedy of Kratinos, Eupolis, and Aristophanes.[93] The connection, according to Horace, takes the form of a shared concern for the public chastisement of vice and crime. Horace's claim, which exemplifies a view of Aristophanic satire which has had a long history (see 'Satire and Seriousness', above), can best be interpreted as a mock-formal arrogation of Greek pedigree for his own literary genre. But the view itself became a kind of academic orthodoxy, represented, for example, in the statement by Quintilian, rhetorician and educationalist of the first century AD, that Old Comedy had been 'pre-eminent in the persecution of vice' (10.1.65).

The fullest critical reaction which we have from any one ancient reader of Aristophanes is that of Plutarch in the later first and early second century AD. It is a hostile reaction. Plutarch complains of Aristophanes' vulgarity, linguistic artificiality, confusions of tone, failures of consistent characterization, and acrid malice; in all respects he compares him unfavourably with Menander.[94] Plutarch's points suggest nothing so much as a chasm of taste between his own rather dry, academic leanings and the earthy scurrilities which had evidently answered to a genuine Athenian sensibility (and need) in the Dionysiac festivities of the classical period. It is an interesting index of the special status of Old Comedy within its culture that even so well-informed an antiquarian as Plutarch is essentially nonplussed about its original significance.[95]

A greater and more creatively fruitful insight into the genre's qualities can be traced in the Greek writer of comic dialogues, Lucian (second century AD), whose own combination of fantasy and satire self-consciously owes something to Aristophanic precedent. Lucian's writing is, however, much blander, less sharply contemporary, and more reliant on generalized, stereotypical images of human vice. For that very reason, Lucian himself was to exercise greater influence than Aristophanes on the classicism of the Renaissance.[96] While Lucian's works were quite widely translated into several European languages in the sixteenth century, the plays of Aristophanes were very rarely tackled in this context. The contrast with the Roman poets of New

[93] Horace, *Satires* 1.4.1–6; cf. 1.10.16–17, Persius, *Satires* 1.123–4.

[94] Plutarch, *Moralia* 853–4.

[95] This did not stop Plutarch from citing Aristophanes, in his *Lives* and elsewhere, as though his plays were a straightforwardly reliable source of historical information.

[96] See C. Robinson, *Lucian and his Influence in Europe* (London, 1979), part II.

Comedy is even starker. The works of Plautus and Terence dominated both the theory and the practice of comedy in the Renaissance. They supplied scenarios, characters, and themes which could be so much more easily staged, imitated, and adapted than the peculiarities of the Aristophanic imagination, whose grotesque contortions were so much harder to reconcile with the prevailing notion of comedy as a 'mirror of life'.

That situation was to hold good throughout the various phases of neoclassical drama, right up to the eighteenth century. For the whole of this period Aristophanes was a 'name' to be brandished in various contexts, the prime example of this, as mentioned earlier (see 'Satire and Seriousness'), being the repeated indictment of *Clouds* by puritans and moralists concerned about uncontrolled or malicious laughter. But the reading of Aristophanes, in any language, was the preserve of a few. In the sixteenth century Erasmus' wide knowledge of the author emerges from the frequency with which he cites him in his *Adages* and elsewhere. In England, we know that Ben Jonson possessed two editions of Aristophanes and read at least some of the plays in the original; Jonson's own works, both his plays and his notebook *Timber*, contain references to Aristophanes and Old Comedy. Jonson was undoubtedly intrigued by the ancient playwright, and occasionally indebted to him: perhaps the best instance is the mock-trial of the dogs, an idea taken from *Wasps*, in Act V of *The Staple of News*. Yet even Jonson was nonetheless typical in knowing Lucian better than he knew Aristophanes, and modern claims about Aristophanic influence on his work have sometimes been exaggerated.

Later creative writers to have exhibited a fascination with Aristophanes include Racine, whose only comedy, *Les Plaideurs* (1668), adapts its basic scenario and several motifs from *Wasps*, blending these with the style of *commedia dell'arte* characters to produce a result (as Racine acknowledged in the Preface) rather remote from the dominant Terentian model of comedy at the time; and Goethe, who read a good deal of Aristophanes at more than one point in his life, and staged a loose imitation of *Birds*, as the basis for a satire on German literary culture, at Weimar in 1780. Productions of Aristophanes had, up to this date, been even more of a rarity than translations. In England, to which I shall largely confine my attention, we know for certain only of two before the nineteenth century, both of them in sixteenth-century Cambridge. The first, at St John's

College in 1536, was almost inevitably of *Wealth*, which was likewise later to be the first play to be translated into English (by Thomas Randolph, adopted son of Ben Jonson).[97] The second, *Peace*, produced at the newly founded Trinity College in 1546, seems at first sight an odd choice, until we note the involvement in it of John Dee, later notorious as an astrologer at the courts of Elizabeth and James I. The one recorded fact about this production is that Trygaios' ascent to heaven on his dung-beetle was effected illusionistically, a fact which points, I think, to Dee's familiarity with continental techniques of stage-machinery and an interest in re-creating the ancient use of the 'machine' or crane, *mêchanê*, which is mentioned in *Peace* itself (174: see 'Stage Directions', above). It is conceivable that the whole production was built around Dee's aspiration to merge modern theatrical technology with antiquarian experimentation.

Not long after those late Renaissance productions the chances of staging any Aristophanic comedy in England must have diminished steadily, first under the pressure of puritanical attitudes to the theatre,[98] and later because of the eighteenth century's predominant favouring of benign, humane laughter over more ribald, indecent varieties of humour. The eighteenth century was not a propitious time for the appreciation of Old Comedy. It is rather revealing that the title of 'the English Aristophanes' or 'the modern Aristophanes' was sometimes given to a dramatist of farces, Samuel Foote, who had very probably never read a word of his supposed model. Even practising satirists such as Swift and Pope ostensibly repudiated comparison with Aristophanes.[99] It was hard anywhere in Europe, in fact, to provide a publicly respectable justification of Aristophanic humour at this date, given the still-strong sway of neoclassical canons of taste and decorum.

A more far-reaching interest in Aristophanes starts to develop only

[97] Randolph's version may itself have been acted in Cambridge at some point before 1628: for this possibility, within the general context of performances of classical plays in this period, see B. R. Smith, *Ancient Scripts and Modern Experience on the English Stage 1500–1700* (Princeton, 1988), 168–77.

[98] One of the largest of puritan tracts on the stage, William Prynne's *Histriomastix*, refers to Aristophanes as 'that scurrilous, carping comedian . . . [who] personally traduced and abused virtuous Socrates' (1633 edn., p. 121).

[99] See the ironic couplet in Swift's 'A Letter to the Rev. Dr. Sheridan', 5–6 ('But as to comic Aristophanes, | The rogue's too bawdy and too prophane is.'), Pope's 'Epistle to Henry Cromwell', 102–4.

in the later eighteenth century, and builds up during the nineteenth, with the growth of a more historically informed attempt to understand Old Comedy in its original cultural context and spirit. There was certainly no instant or total change of attitudes in this period, for in England, at least, the Victorian age saw a continuing concern over the moral dangers of too close a familiarity with the playwright: it is not surprising, for example, that the scholar who remarked that *Lysistrata* 'turns upon a proposal so gross, that we shall not insult our readers with it' subsequently published perhaps the most heavily bowdlerized translations of Aristophanes ever produced.[100]

Yet around this same time there are signs of a potential change of climate. In 1820, for example, Shelley wrote a savage satire, entitled *Oedipus Tyrannus, or Swellfoot the Tyrant*, on the contemporary royal *cause célèbre* of George IV's attempted divorce of Queen Caroline. Shelley, living in Italy at the time, was partly inspired by Aristophanic precedents: the work's animal chorus (of pigs) and its scurrilous and grossly fantastic political allegory, as well as a number of smaller details (such as compound Greek names: Wellington is Laoktonos, 'People-Slayer'), are undoubtedly reminiscent of Aristophanes, whom we know that Shelley had recently been reading.[101] Shelley's experimental work, which owed much to the radical traditions of English visual satire, is hardly part of a trend; nor was it successful (only seven copies were sold before a threat of prosecution led to its withdrawal). But it is nonetheless a harbinger of new possibilities opened up by Romanticism's more 'liberated' attitudes to ancient Greece.

In the course of the nineteenth century there was a growing recognition in some quarters that Old Comedy, like so much else from antiquity, could not be instinctively appreciated from a standpoint of modern taste. By 1871 John Addington Symonds was able to write: 'The time has come at which any writer on Greek literature, if not content to pass Aristophanes by in silence, must view him as he is.' Symonds warned that ordinary canons of comedy were of no use in interpreting the author; he described the plays as 'Dionysiac day-dreams', utterly alien to the expectations bred by Christian ideas,

[100] The scholar was Thomas Mitchell: the quotation is from an anonymously signed review in *Quarterly Review*, 9 (1813), 139–61, at 142. Even Mitchell had a sense of new priorities: on the preceding page he had warned against coming to the plays 'with English feelings and English ideas'; but he just could not practise what he preached.

[101] See F. L. Jones (ed.), *The Letters of Percy Bysshe Shelley*, ii (London, 1964), 468.

both ethical and religious.[102] Whatever reservations one might have about details of Symonds' essay, its direction of thought is clear and incisive. It represents an appeal for a fresh, informed, and unmoralistic appraisal of Aristophanes and his genre. The work of such an appraisal had, in fact, been under way for some time. We can find a major contribution to it in George Grote's great *History of Greece*, which started to appear in 1846, where amazement is expressed at the traditional tendency to treat the freely inventive materials of Old Comedy as though they could be made the basis of either historically or morally secure inferences. Like Symonds, though in rather more scholarly fashion, Grote perceived a cultural distance which could only be bridged by a careful combination of information and imagination; and in this fundamental respect he was concerned to create a framework of interpretation which holds good to this day.

Certain aspects of Aristophanes' work remained inescapably problematic, of course, for most nineteenth-century readers. In particular, the obscenity of Old Comedy continued to be bowdlerized[103] or tamed in both translations and productions (which, as with Greek tragedy, became increasingly common from the 1880s onwards). Aubrey Beardsley's priapic illustrations to *Lysistrata*, produced in 1896, are an exception that proves the rule: they were printed in a small limited edition 'for private distribution', and confiscations of copies by the police, on grounds of obscenity, are recorded in England as late as 1966. At the same time the late Victorian period fostered the curious idea, which still has currency, that the light operettas of Gilbert and Sullivan were close in spirit to Aristophanic comedy. Although Gilbert was undoubtedly influenced by a few Aristophanic motifs, and more especially by the rhythmical translations of the author which had become standard in the nineteenth century,[104] the gulf between the two forms of drama, and between their cultural associations, makes any attempt to assimilate them a historically very questionable enterprise. To turn the earthy, profane brio of

[102] Symonds' essay originally appeared in the *Westminster Review*, 39 (1871), 291–322, and was reprinted in *Studies of the Greek Poets*, 1st ser., vol. 2 (London, 1873), ch. 18.

[103] For a contrast between English and continental practices in this respect, see K. J. Dover, 'Expurgation of Greek Literature', in his *The Greeks and their Legacy* (Oxford, 1978), 270–86.

[104] Gilbertian verbal mannerisms were in turn influential on the widely known translations by B. B. Rogers, published between 1902 and 1915.

Aristophanes into the arch tweeness of Gilbert is to emasculate the former's energy.

Despite the risk of taking excessive self-satisfaction in modern standards of sophisticated reading, it is reasonable to claim that the twentieth century saw a steady improvement in our understanding of Aristophanes. Scholarship has made enormous progress in the interpretation of Athenian culture as a whole in the classical period, and resulting benefit has accrued to our grasp of the city's politics, social life, festival culture, and theatrical resources, among much else besides. While older controversies over Aristophanes' point of view as an observer and satirist of his world have continued to elicit polarized disagreement, criticism of the plays more generally has learnt to take their theatricality and their Dionysiac background into account, at every level, much more successfully than was the case in earlier periods. Rehabilitation has been implicit in these developments; George Bernard Shaw's repeated inclusion of Aristophanes in a 'great tradition' of comedy, and of theatre *tout court*, is a salient illustration of the new level of esteem for the playwright. An escape from (in historical terms) the unduly moralistic concerns of neoclassicism has of course been facilitated by wider patterns of change in ethical and social attitudes. Where he previously appeared dangerously licentious (though his power to shock has certainly not yet been lost), Aristophanes has come to appear enjoyably bawdy and scurrilous to democratic audiences which flatter themselves that they are peculiarly well attuned to his outspokenness and licentiousness.

There is, however, a subtle risk of misunderstanding lurking here. Classical Athens was not a 'liberated' society in (our) sexual, social, and ethical terms. To grasp the special nature of Old Comedy, we need a historically circumspect approach to the plays, not a reliance on peculiarly modern intuitions or assumptions. There may be a price to pay in other respects too. Twentieth-century translators of Aristophanes eschewed the somewhat mannered verse which had been the norm with their predecessors; but the predominant use of either prose or free verse has arguably tended to erase a sense of the playwright's distinctive combination of formality with invention, virtuosity with vulgarity (see 'Translating Aristophanes', above). Here, as elsewhere, one might be wise to conclude that there is something too multifarious about Aristophanes and his genre to be wholly or comfortably encompassed by our own cultural responses.

The first commercial (as opposed to university and school) stagings of Aristophanic plays go back to the first decade of the twentieth century, when at least two productions of *Lysistrata* were put on in London. They were, naturally, still far from faithful to the sexual details of the original, and it was not until the 1990s that productions appeared, such as the one directed by Peter Hall in London in 1993 (with its attempt to recapture the spirit of the original phallic and padded costumes), of which this was no longer true. It is arguable that appreciation of Aristophanic humour, in principle at least, has benefited from the pluralism of modern styles of entertainment: to some extent a contemporary audience is disposed to find in his work elements of, say, stand-up comedy, farce, pantomime, cabaret, topical satire, variety or vaudeville shows, and even theatre of the Absurd,[105] all synthesized into a rich theatrical kaleidoscope. Similarly, it is possible to find recent works which, whether coincidentally or not, have a broadly Aristophanic ethos. Tom Stoppard's *Jumpers* (1972) is a case in point, with its central philosophical character, its quasi-animal chorus, its dialectical verbal wit, and its pervasive mixture of fantasy and reality.

Direct influence, on the other hand, was no more common in the twentieth century than in the past. T. S. Eliot's *Sweeney Agonistes*, drafted in 1924 and subtitled 'Fragments of an Aristophanic Melodrama', is a peculiar hybrid of music-hall routines combined with ritualistic overtones derived from theories of comedy's origins propagated by the 'Cambridge School' of anthropologists: echoes of the comedies are few, and the so-called agon, with its rather morbid blurring of life and death, is remote from the Aristophanic form whose name it borrows (see 'Formality and Performance', above). At a rather different point on the comic spectrum, Tony Harrison's *The Common Chorus* (first published in 1988), a version of *Lysistrata* set in the women's anti-nuclear peace-camp at Greenham Common, contains obscenities which remarkably outdo even the original. The piece

105 There are, at any rate, passages in Samuel Beckett which remind one subtly of Aristophanes: compare, for example, the combination of suggested suicide, sexual humour, and exaggerated politeness in *Waiting for Godot* (*Samuel Beckett: The Complete Dramatic Works* (London, 1986), 18–19) with the prologue to *Knights*, where similar routines all occur. A short comparison of *Waiting for Godot* and *Birds* is offered by C. Segal, 'Aristophanes and Beckett', in A. Bierl and P. von Möllendorff (eds.), *Orchestra: Drama, Mythos, Bühne* (Stuttgart, 1994), 235–8.

is extensively related to its Greek model, but the view of both war and sexuality it projects is grimmer and more disturbing than anything to be found in Aristophanes' play.

I have tried in this final section of my Introduction, albeit in a highly selective manner, to convey some sense of the fluctuating responses to Aristophanes' work between antiquity and the present. For the post-Renaissance period I have concentrated largely on anglophone examples, partly for obvious reasons of convenience and partly because in certain respects these represent a more complicated, often contradictory, set of attitudes than were sometimes found on the continent.[106] But one overarching point, which I stress in conclusion, could have been made just as well by reference to other European countries. Aristophanes has never been central to literary or artistic forms of (neo-)classicism, yet his peripheral status in this respect has always been counterpoised by an underlying recognition of his importance as the sole survivor of an extraordinary phenomenon of classical Athens. It is not hard to see here a two-sided moral: if Old Comedy has proved to be largely inimitable, and therefore an elusive model for classicizing writers and artists, that is for precisely the same reasons as those which tied it so intimately to its original time and place. But since understanding the past must embrace the experience of what is unlike as well as what is like ourselves, the plays of Aristophanes will always remain fascinating and rewarding material for anyone who wishes to come seriously to terms with the history of theatre, the possibilities of comedy, and the relationship between both these things and the culture of democracy.

[106] Outside Greece itself, at any rate, where Aristophanic revivals have sometimes carried a special political charge: see Gonda A. H. van Steen, *Venom in Verse: Aristophanes in Modern Greece* (Princeton, 2000).

NOTE ON THE TRANSLATION

In accordance with the principles explained in the general Introduction, 'Translating Aristophanes', my translation follows the structure of the Greek text closely: for the editions on which the translations are based, see the Bibliography. However, because the marginal numbers in the translation refer to the standard modern numeration of the Greek text, and since this numeration is sometimes (mostly in lyric passages) slightly anomalous, readers should be warned that the sequence occasionally does not match exactly the printed lines of the translation itself. For consistency of reference, line numbers in the General Introduction, the Introductions to individual plays, and the Index of Names refer to the strict Greek numeration. However, line numbers as given in the lemmata to Explanatory Notes have, where necessary, been slightly adjusted for the convenience of the user of the translation.

SELECT BIBLIOGRAPHY

These suggestions for further reading are reluctantly restricted to items written in, or translated into, English. Preference has generally been given to more recent and more accessible publications, through which, for those interested, older and more specialized secondary literature can be traced. I have tried, none the less, to give guidance to a reasonably wide range of publications, suitably flagged so that readers can follow up as much or as little as suits their interests. References to works which contain untranslated Greek have been minimized but not altogether excluded. Full publication details of books are given only at the first citation.

General Works

For a compact and stimulating overview of Greek (and Roman) comedy see:

Lowe, N. J., *Comedy* (*Greece & Rome* New Surveys in the Classics, no. 37: Cambridge, 2007).

Also helpful are:

Handley, E. W., 'Comedy', in P. E. Easterling and B. M. W. Knox (eds.), *The Cambridge History of Classical Literature*, i. *Greek Literature* (Cambridge, 1985), 355–425.

Rusten, J., 'A Short History of Athenian Comedy', in J. Rusten (ed.), *The Birth of Comedy: Texts, Documents, and Art from Athenian Comic Competitions, 486–280* (Baltimore, 2011), 16–38.

Three up-to-date sets of essays covering various aspects of the genre are:

Dobrov, G. W. (ed.), *Brill's Companion to the Study of Greek Comedy* (Leiden, 2010).

Fontaine, M., and Scafuro, A. C. (eds.), *The Oxford Handbook of Greek and Roman Comedy* (New York, 2014).

Revermann, M. (ed.), *The Cambridge Companion to Greek Comedy* (Cambridge, 2014).

The best general books on Aristophanes include the following (the last of which is the least introductory):

Cartledge, P., *Aristophanes and his Theatre of the Absurd* (London, 1990).

Dover, K. J., *Aristophanic Comedy* (Berkeley and Los Angeles, 1972).

MacDowell, D. M., *Aristophanes and Athens* (Oxford, 1995).
Robson, J., *Aristophanes: an Introduction* (London, 2009).
Silk, M. S., *Aristophanes and the Definition of Comedy* (Oxford, 2000).

Three other books which contain thought-provoking ideas but are more free-wheeling are:

McLeish, K., *The Theatre of Aristophanes* (London, 1980).
Reckford, K., *Aristophanes' Old-and-New Comedy* (Chapel Hill, NC, 1987).
Whitman, C. H., *Aristophanes and the Comic Hero* (Cambridge, Mass., 1964).

Various aspects of Aristophanes' literary technique are lucidly discussed in:

Harriott, R., *Aristophanes Poet and Dramatist* (London, 1986).

A vigorous discussion of all the plays, whose angle of approach (often stimulating, sometimes strained) is indicated by its title, is:

Bowie, A. M., *Aristophanes: Myth, Ritual and Comedy* (Cambridge, 1993).

A collection of essays, several of which are cited separately below, is:

Segal, E. (ed.), *Oxford Readings in Aristophanes* (Oxford, 1996).

Another interesting collection, this one single-authored (and relatively technical in places), is:

Sommerstein, A. H., *Talking about Laughter and Other Studies in Greek Comedy* (Oxford, 2009).

Old Comedy is set within one (superficial) vision of the larger sweep of comedy's history by:

Segal, E., *The Death of Comedy* (Cambridge, Mass., 2001).

Aspects of Aristophanic Comedy

On the origins of comedy, see especially:

Rusten, 'Proto-Comedy', in Rusten (ed.), *The Birth of Comedy*, 45–58.

On Old Comedy's use of traditional elements of 'sub-literary' entertainment, see:

Murphy, C. T., 'Popular Comedy in Aristophanes', *American Journal of Philology*, 93 (1972), 169–89.

Some basic physical aspects of Aristophanic humour are dealt with by:

Dobrov, G., 'The Dawn of Farce: Aristophanes', in J. Redmond (ed.), *Farce* (Themes in Drama 10, Cambridge, 1988), 15–31.
Kaimio, M., 'Comic Violence in Aristophanes', *Arctos*, 24 (1990), 47–72.
MacDowell, D. M., 'Clowning and Slapstick in Aristophanes', in Redmond (ed.), *Farce*, 1–13.

A sensitive discussion of the discontinuities of Aristophanic characterization in terms of 'imagist' logic (an alternative to what I have called the 'improvisatory' quality of many protagonists) can be found in:

Silk, M., 'The People of Aristophanes', in C. B. R. Pelling (ed.), *Characterization and Individuality in Greek Literature* (Oxford, 1990), 150–73; repr. (without Greek) in Segal (ed.), *Oxford Readings*, 229–51.

Aristophanes' own (mostly parabatic) statements about his poetic values are discussed, not always with sufficient nuance, in:

Bremer, J. M., 'Aristophanes on His Own Poetry', in J. M. Bremer and E. W. Handley (eds.), *Aristophane* (Vandoeuvres-Geneva, 1993), 125–65.

The rhetoric of Aristophanic self-presentation, as found (chiefly) in the parabasis, is also discussed by:

Goldhill, S., *The Poet's Voice* (Cambridge, 1991), 188–205.
Hubbard, T., *The Mask of Comedy: Aristophanes and the Intertextual Parabasis* (Ithaca, NY, 1991).
Murray, R. J., 'Aristophanic Protest', *Hermes*, 115 (1987), 146–54.

A radical case for Aristophanes as a 'literary critic' more interested in highly educated *readers* than in mass audiences is made by:

Wright, M., *The Comedian as Critic* (London, 2012).

Some suggestive remarks on deceptiveness, both in Aristophanes' presentation of himself and in his characters, are offered by:

Heath, M., 'Some Deceptions in Aristophanes', *Papers of the Leeds International Latin Seminar*, 6 (1990), 229–40.
Salingar, L., 'The Trickster in Classical Comedy', in *Shakespeare and the Traditions of Comedy* (Cambridge, 1974), 88–104.

A detailed but often naive use of Aristophanes as sociological evidence is made by:

Ehrenberg, V., *The People of Aristophanes* (2nd edn., Oxford, 1951).

For those interested in details of Aristophanic language, it is impossible to avoid works which require knowledge of Greek. Two illuminating articles are:

Dover, K. J., 'The Style of Aristophanes', in his *Greek and the Greeks* (Oxford, 1987), 224–36.

——'Language and Character in Aristophanes', *Greek and the Greeks*, 237–48.

Essential for advanced study of the plays from a sociolinguistic perspective is:

Willi, A., *The Languages of Aristophanes* (Oxford, 2003).

Aristophanic obscenity receives a full analysis (but marred by errors), whose introductory chapters are partly accessible to the Greekless, in:

Henderson, J., *The Maculate Muse: Obscene Language in Attic Comedy* (New Haven, 1975; repr. with addenda: New York, 1991).

On the same subject in relation to Aristophanic humour more generally see:

Robson, J., *Humour, Obscenity and Aristophanes* (Tübingen, 2006).

An interesting attempt to explain the workings of comic nonsense is:

Kidd, S. E., *Nonsense and Meaning in Ancient Greek Comedy* (Cambridge, 2014).

On the development of 'Middle Comedy', during Aristophanes' later years and beyond, see

Arnott, W. G., 'From Aristophanes to Menander', *Greece & Rome*, 19 (1972), 65–80.

Aristophanes' Career

Different views of the problems of Aristophanes' early career are taken by:

Halliwell, S., 'Aristophanes' Apprenticeship', *Classical Quarterly*, 30 (1980), 33–45; repr. with Greek translated in Segal (ed.), *Oxford Readings*, 98–116.

MacDowell, D. M., 'Aristophanes and Kallistratos', *Classical Quarterly*, 32 (1982), 21–6.

Slater, N. W., 'Aristophanes' Apprenticeship Again', *Greek, Roman, and Byzantine Studies*, 30 (1989), 67–82.

A broader (but partly technical) argument for collaboration between comic poets is put by:

Halliwell, S., 'Authorial Collaboration in the Athenian Comic Theatre', *Greek, Roman, and Byzantine Studies*, 30 (1989), 515–28.

Aristophanes' relationship to his greatest comic predecessor (Kratinos) and contemporary (Eupolis) is selectively examined in:

Heath, M., 'Aristophanes and his Rivals', *Greece & Rome*, 37 (1990), 143–58.

The relationship of Aristophanes to his rivals is explored more elaborately, if sometimes in too contrived a manner, by:

Biles, Z. P., *Aristophanes and the Poetics of Competition* (Cambridge, 2011).

Festivals and Festivity

The outstanding work on festivals, audiences, actors, etc., but containing untranslated Greek and rather technical for the general reader, is:

Pickard-Cambridge, A. W., *Dramatic Festivals of Athens*, 2nd edn., rev. J. Gould and D. M. Lewis (Oxford, 1968; repr. with addenda, 1988).

Much of the same ground is more accessibly covered by an excellent sourcebook in translation:

Csapo, E., and Slater, W. J., *The Context of Ancient Drama* (Ann Arbor, Mich., 1995).

The relevant documentary evidence is presented in translation by:

Rusten (ed.), *The Birth of Comedy*, 93–132.

On the composition of theatre audiences, see (with some caution on details):

Roselli, D. K., *Theater of the People: Spectators and Society in Ancient Athens* (Austin, Tex., 2011).

For comedy's festive status, and effective exemption from legal and other norms of decency, see:

Halliwell, S., 'Comic Satire and Freedom of Speech in Classical Athens', *Journal of Hellenic Studies*, 111 (1991), 48–70.

The general place of dramatic festivals in the culture of Athens is explored by:

Osborne, R., 'Competitive Festivals and the Polis: A Context for Dramatic Festivals at Athens', in A. H. Sommerstein *et al.* (eds.), *Tragedy Comedy and the Polis* (Bari, 1993), 21–38.

That the City Dionysia, the oldest dramatic festival, was of democratic (not Peisistratid) origin, and represented a celebration of civic freedoms, is argued by:

Connor, W. R., 'City Dionysia and Athenian Democracy', *Classica et Medievalia*, 40 (1989), 7–32.

The relationship between tragedy and comedy is interestingly explored by:

Taplin, O., 'Fifth-Century Tragedy and Comedy: A *Synkrisis*', *Journal of Hellenic Studies*, 106 (1986), 163–74; repr. with Greek translated in Segal (ed.), *Oxford Readings*, 9–28.

For the application to Aristophanes of the idea of 'carnivalesque' laughter as developed by the Russian theorist Mikhail Bakhtin, see (but with caution about his simplified view of comic poets as 'conservatives'):

Edwards, A. T., 'Historicizing the Popular Grotesque: Bakhtin's *Rabelais* and Attic Old Comedy', in R. Scodel (ed.), *Theater and Society in the Classical World* (Ann Arbor, Mich., 1993), 89–117.

Formality and Performance

The three modes of dramatic poetry/delivery (speech, recitative, song) are technically analysed in:

Pickard-Cambridge, *Dramatic Festivals*, 156–67.

Formal structures are discussed, with schematic analyses of the plays, by:

Pickard-Cambridge, A. W., *Dithyramb Tragedy and Comedy*, 2nd edn. rev. T. B. L. Webster (Oxford, 1962), 194–229.

On the genre's formal conventions, see also e.g.:

Dover, *Aristophanic Comedy*, 49–53, 66–8.
Harriot, *Aristophanes Poet and Dramatist*, esp. chs. 2–3.

For the entry of the chorus (*parodos*) as manifesting Aristophanes' creative adaptation of formal conventions, see:

Zimmermann, B., 'The *Parodoi* of the Aristophanic Comedies', *Studi Italiani di Filologia Classica*, 2 (1984), 13–24; repr. with Greek translated in Segal (ed.), *Oxford Readings*, 182–93.

The parabasis (see also under 'Aspects of Aristophanic Comedy', above) is analysed in detail, though from rather different angles, in:

Hubbard, *The Mask of Comedy*.
Sifakis, G., *Parabasis and Animal Choruses* (London, 1971).

The evidence of the comic fragments for formal structures in other poets was analysed by:

Whittaker, M., 'The Comic Fragments in their Relation to the Structure of Old Attic Comedy', *Classical Quarterly*, 29 (1935), 181–91.

An analysis of Aristophanic plots in terms of narrative patterns and functional elements akin to those of folktale is attempted by:

Sifakis, G. M., 'The Structure of Aristophanic Comedy', *Journal of Hellenic Studies*, 112 (1992), 123–42.

Satire

Good surveys of the issues and controversies in this area are provided by:

Carey, C., 'Comic Ridicule and Democracy', in R. Osborne and S. Hornblower (eds.), *Ritual, Finance, Politics: Athenian Democratic Accounts Presented to David Lewis* (Oxford, 1994), 69–83.
Storey, I., 'Poets, Politicians, and Perverts: Personal Humour in Aristophanes', *Classics Ireland*, 5 (1998), 85–134; online at <http://www.ucd.ie/cai/classicsireland/1998/ClassIre98.html>.

A much-cited older work, spirited but actually rather muddled, is:

Gomme, A. W., 'Aristophanes and Politics', *Classical Review*, 52 (1938), 97–109; repr. in his *More Essays in Greek History and Literature* (London, 1962), 70–91.

An influential but extremely dogmatic modern reading of Aristophanes as a committed critic of radical democracy is:

Croix, G. E. M. de Ste, *The Origins of the Peloponnesian War* (London, 1972), appendix XXIX, 355–71; repr., in abridged form with Greek translated, in Segal (ed.), *Oxford Readings*, 42–64.

A sophisticated and demanding reinterpretation of Aristophanic comedy in relation to Athenian politics is:

Ruffell, I., *Politics and Anti-Realism in Athenian Old Comedy: The Art of the Impossible* (Oxford, 2011).

The views of scholars cautious (in various ways) about the possibility of inferring the poet's own political and social values from his plays can be found in:

Chapman, G. A. H., 'Aristophanes and History', *Acta Classica*, 21 (1978), 59–69.

Halliwell, S., 'Aristophanic Satire', *Yearbook of English Studies*, 14 (1984), 6–20; repr. in C. Rawson (ed.), *English Satire and the Satiric Tradition* (Oxford, 1984), 6–20.

Heath, M., *Political Comedy in Aristophanes* (Göttingen, 1987).

Redfield, J., 'Drama and Community: Aristophanes and Some of his Rivals', in J. J. Winkler and F. I. Zeitlin (eds.), *Nothing to Do with Dionysos?* (Princeton, 1990), 214–335.

A conception of comedy as embodying the power of the democracy to humble individuals, and remind elite leaders of the sovereignty of the people, is developed by:

Henderson, J., 'The *Dêmos* and the Comic Competition', in Winkler and Zeitlin (eds.), *Nothing to Do with Dionysos?*, 271–313; repr. with abridgements in Segal (ed.), *Oxford Readings*, 65–97.

——'Comic Hero Versus Political Élite', in Sommerstein *et al.* (eds.), *Tragedy Comedy and the Polis*, 307–19.

For the relationship of the festive traditions of comic satire to larger Greek ideas about the nature of laughter, see:

Halliwell, S., *Greek Laughter: A Study of Cultural Psychology from Homer to Early Christianity* (Cambridge, 2008), 215–63.

On the combination of honours and mockery in the traditions of Dionysiac festivals (but without reflections on the pertinence of this to comedy), see:

Cole, S. G., 'Procession and Celebration at the Dionysia', in Scodel (ed.), *Theater and Society*, 25–38.

Arguments against the idea of Old Comedy as either a reliable reflector of, or a potent influence upon, the currents of Athenian publicity are put by:

Halliwell, S., 'Comedy and Publicity in the Society of the Polis', in Sommerstein *et al.* (eds.), *Tragedy Comedy and the Polis*, 321–40.

For an old but interestingly negative case on the question of influence, see also:

Stow, H. L., 'Aristophanes' Influence on Public Opinion', *Classical Journal*, 38 (1942), 83–92.

Old Comedy's satirical and obscene connections with the older, semi-dramatic genre of iambos are discussed by:

Rosen, R. M., *Old Comedy and the Iambographic Tradition* (Atlanta, Ga., 1988).

Translating Aristophanes

For discussion of the problems, and the history of attempts to tackle them, see:

Dover, *Aristophanic Comedy*, 230–7.
Halliwell, S., 'Aristophanes', in O. Classe (ed.), *Encyclopedia of Literary Translation* (London, 1998), i. 77–8.
Robson, *Aristophanes*, ch. 10.
Silk, M., 'Translating/transposing Aristophanes', in E. Hall and A. Wrigley (eds.), *Aristophanes in Performance 421 BC–AD 2007* (Oxford, 2007), 287–308.
Sommerstein, A. H., 'On Translating Aristophanes: Ends and Means', *Greece & Rome*, 20 (1973), 140–54.
Walton, J. M., *Found in Translation: Greek Drama in English* (Cambridge, 2006), 145–61, 253–67.

A challenging treatment of Aristophanic lyrics, arguing that their strength lies in the use of a 'low', popular idiom, is offered by:

Silk, M., 'Aristophanes as a Lyric Poet', in J. Henderson (ed.), *Aristophanes: Essays in Interpretation*, *Yale Classical Studies*, 26 (Cambridge, 1980), 99–151.

Stage Directions

On the Theatre of Dionysos, performers, etc., see:

Csapo and Slater, *The Context of Ancient Drama*, 79–81.
Rusten (ed.), *The Birth of Comedy*, 399–433.

The most substantial work on Aristophanic comedy in relation to its original theatrical context (and including special study of *Clouds*) is:

Revermann, M., *Comic Business: Theatricality, Dramatic Technique, and Performance Contexts of Aristophanic Comedy* (Oxford, 2006).

A lively reading of all the plays as performance texts is provided by:

Slater, N. W., *Spectator Politics: Metatheatre and Performance in Aristophanes* (Philadelphia, 2002).

Some distinctively comic features of theatricality are analysed with insight by:

Lowe, N. J., 'Greek Stagecraft and Aristophanes', in Redmond (ed.), *Farce*, 33–52.

—— 'Aristophanic Spacecraft', in L. Kozak and J. Rich (eds.), *Playing Around Aristophanes* (Oxford, 2006), 48–64.

Selected theatrical aspects of the plays are treated, but in an irritatingly cluttered and disjointed way, by:

Russo, C., *Aristophanes an Author for the Stage*, Eng. trans. (London, 1994).

Other useful works on theatrical matters include:

Dover, K. J., 'The Skene in Aristophanes', *Proceedings of the Cambridge Philological Society*, 12 (1966), 2–17; repr. in *Greek and the Greeks*, 249–66.

——'Portrait-Masks in Aristophanes', *Greek and the Greeks*, 266–78.

Handley, E. W., 'Aristophanes and his Theatre', in Bremer and Handley (eds.), *Aristophane*, 97–123.

Stone, L. M., *Costume in Aristophanic Poetry* (Salem, Mass., 1984).

A well-illustrated book for the general reader is:

Green, R., and Handley, E., *Images of the Greek Theatre* (London, 1995), esp. chs. 4–5.

Aristophanes and Posterity

An interesting range of observations on the ancient evidence for knowledge of Aristophanes can be found in:

Dover, *Aristophanic Comedy*, 221–9.

Sommerstein, A. H., 'Aristophanes in Antiquity', in D. Barrett and A. H. Sommerstein (trans.), *Aristophanes: The Knights, etc.* (Harmondsworth, 1978), 9–20.

Evidence for fourth-century restaging of Aristophanes and other Old Comedy in Magna Graecia is presented and illustrated in:

Taplin, O., *Comic Angels* (Oxford, 1993).

——'Do the "Phlyax" Vases have Bearings on Athenian Comedy and the Polis?', in Sommerstein *et al.* (eds.), *Tragedy Comedy and the Polis*, 527–44.

On Lucian's work, including some of its Aristophanic features, see:

Branham, R. B., *Unruly Eloquence: Lucian and the Comedy of Traditions* (Cambridge, Mass., 1989).

A lively summary of some aspects of the reception of Aristophanes' plays, especially from the point of view of translation, can be found in:

Griffith, M., *Aristophanes' Frogs* (New York, 2013), 220–57.

A wide-ranging set of studies on the performance history of Aristophanes' plays, including England, is:

Hall and Wrigley (eds.), *Aristophanes in Performance*.

There are also numerous essays on the modern reception of Aristophanes' plays in:

Olson, S. D. (ed.), *Ancient Comedy and Reception: Essays in Honor of Jeffrey Henderson* (Berlin, 2014).

Further items dealing with particular aspects of Aristophanes' reception and influence:

Atkins, S., 'Goethe, Aristophanes, and the Classical Walpurgisnacht', *Comparative Literature*, 6 (1954), 64–78.

Gross, N., 'Racine's Debt to Aristophanes', *Comparative Literature*, 17 (1965), 209–24.

O'Sullivan, N., 'Aristophanes and Wagner', *Antike und Abendland*, 36 (1990), 67–81.

Segal, E., 'Aristophanes and Beckett', in A. Bierl and P. von Möllendorff (eds.), *Orchestra: Drama, Mythos, Bühne* (Stuttgart, 1994), 235–8.

van Steen, G. A. H., *Venom in Verse: Aristophanes in Modern Greece* (Princeton, 2000).

Clouds

My translation is based, with just occasional exceptions, on the Greek text edited by:

Dover, K. J., *Aristophanes Clouds*, repr. with corrections (Oxford, 1970).

See also, for an edition with facing translation:

Sommerstein, A. H., *Clouds* (Warminster, 1982).

On the incompletely revised state of the text, see:

Dover, *Aristophanes Clouds*, pp. lxxx–xcviii.
Storey, I., 'The Dates of Aristophanes' *Clouds II* and Eupolis' *Baptai*', *American Journal of Philology*, 114 (1993), 71–84.
Revermann, *Comic Business*, 326–32 (with 179–235 for his fuller treatment of the play).

A range of views on the treatment of Sokrates in the play, including some very different from mine, can be found in:

Konstan, D., 'Socrates in Aristophanes' *Clouds*', in D. R. Morrison (ed.), *The Cambridge Companion to Socrates* (Cambridge, 2011), 75–90.
Guthrie, W. K. C., *History of Greek Philosophy*, vol. 3 (Cambridge, 1969), 359–77; repr. in id., *Socrates* (Cambridge, 1971), 39–57.
Nussbaum, M. C., 'Aristophanes and Socrates on Learning Practical Wisdom', in Henderson (ed.), *Aristophanes: Essays in Interpretation*, 43–97.
Vander Waerdt, P., 'Socrates in the *Clouds*', in id. (ed.), *The Socratic Movement* (Ithaca, NY, 1994), 48–86.

Against the orthodox view that Plato's *Apology* treats *Clouds* itself as having contributed to the condemnation of Sokrates, see:

Halliwell, *Greek Laughter*, 254–6.
Heath, *Political Comedy in Aristophanes*, 9–10.

On the depiction of Sokrates' special concern with self-scrutiny see (with some caution):

Havelock, E., 'The Socratic Self as it is Parodied in Aristophanes' *Clouds*', *Yale Classical Studies*, 22 (1972), 1–18.

On the play's finale see:

Harvey, F. D., '*Nubes* 1493 ff.: Was Socrates Murdered?', *Greek Roman and Byzantine Studies*, 22 (1981), 339–43.

Other items of interest on the play include:

Segal, C., 'Aristophanes' Cloud-Chorus', *Arethusa*, 2 (1969), 143–61.
Sommerstein, A. H., 'The Silence of Strepsiades and the *Agon* of the first *Clouds*', in *Talking about Laughter*, 176–91.

Women at the Thesmophoria

My translation is based, with only a few small divergences, on the Greek text edited by:

Austin, C., and Olson, S. D., *Aristophanes Thesmophoriazusae* (Oxford, 2004).

For the lost plays of Euripides (*Andromeda*, *Palamedes*, *Telephos*) most important for the scenes of paratragedy, see:

Austin and Olson, *Aristophanes Thesmophoriazusae*, pp. lvi–lxiv.

Text and translation of all the relevant fragments can be conveniently found in:

Collard, C., and Cropp, M., *Euripides: Fragments*, 2 vols., Loeb Classical Library (Cambridge, Mass., 2008).

Discussions of various aspects of the play include:

Hall, E. M., 'The Archer Scene in Aristophanes' *Thesmophoriazusae*', *Philologus*, 133 (1989), 38–54.
Hansen, H., 'Aristophanes *Thesmophoriazusae*: Theme, Structure, Production', *Philologus*, 120 (1976), 165–85.
McClure, L., *Spoken Like a Woman: Speech and Gender in Athenian Drama* (Princeton, 1999), ch. 6.
Stehle, E., 'The Body and its Representations in Aristophanes' *Thesmophoriazousai*', *American Journal of Philology*, 123 (2002), 369–406.
Zeitlin, F. I., 'Travesties of Gender and Genre in Aristophanes' *Thesmophoriazusae*', in *Playing the Other: Gender and Society in Classical Greek Literature* (Chicago, 1996), 375–416.

Frogs

With one important exception (the transmitted order of lines from 1442 to 1466: see n. on *Frogs* 1436) my translation is based on the Greek text edited by:

Dover, K., *Aristophanes*: *Frogs* (Oxford, 1993).

Other editions of *Frogs*, with useful commentaries, are:

Sommerstein, A. H., *Frogs* (Warminster, 1996).
Stanford, W. B., *Aristophanes: The Frogs*, 2nd edn. (London, 1963).

For a wide-ranging general book on the play see:

Griffith, *Aristophanes' Frogs*.

The play's relation to mystery religion and ritual (esp. initiatory) symbolism is treated, sometimes too earnestly, by:

Edmonds III, R. G., *Myths of the Underworld Journey: Plato, Aristophanes, and the 'Orphic' Gold Tablets* (Cambridge, 2004), 111–58.
Lada-Richards, I., *Initiating Dionysus: Ritual and Theatre in Aristophanes' Frogs* (Oxford, 1999).

For a reading of the contest of tragedians which emphasizes Dionysos's conflicting and irresolvable impulses as connoisseur and 'critic' of poetry, see:

Halliwell, S., *Between Ecstasy and Truth: Interpretations of Greek Poetics from Homer to Longinus* (Oxford, 2011), 93–154.

For a selection of other work on *Frogs* see:

Konstan, D., '*Frogs*', in id., *Greek Comedy and Ideology* (New York, 1995), 61–74.
Lowe, N., 'Aristophanes' Books', *Annals of Scholarship*, 10 (1993), 63–83 (esp. 74–8).
Rosen, R., 'Aristophanes' *Frogs* and the *Contest of Homer and Hesiod*', *Transactions of the American Philological Association*, 134 (2004), 295–322.
Scharffenberger, E., 'δεινὸν ἐριβρεμέτας: The Sound and Sense of Aeschylus in Aristophanes' *Frogs*', *Classical World*, 100 (2007), 229–49.
Sommerstein, 'Kleophon and the Restaging of *Frogs*', in *Talking about Laughter*, 254–71.

Lost Plays

The definitive edition (variously abbreviated in the secondary literature as K–A and *PCG*) of all the surviving fragments of Aristophanes, but without translation and with scholarly notes in Latin, is:

Kassel, R., and Austin, C. (eds.), *Poetae Comici Graeci*, vol. III.2 (Berlin, 1984).

A bilingual text (Greek with facing English translations), based on the preceding, is provided by:

Henderson, J., *Aristophanes: Fragments*, Loeb Classical Library (Cambridge Mass., 2007).
Henderson's (partly revised) translations, but only of selected fragments, are also used in: Rusten (ed.), *The Birth of Comedy*, 273–327.

For commentary (with translations) on a selection of fragments of Greek comedy, but only a few by Aristophanes, see:

Olson, S. D., *Broken Laughter: Select Fragments of Greek Comedy* (Oxford, 2007).

An enterprising set of essays dealing with the lost plays of other comic poets, but touching on many of Aristophanes' as well, is:

Harvey, D., and Wilkins, J. (eds.), *The Rivals of Aristophanes: Studies in Athenian Old Comedy* (London, 2000).

CHRONOLOGY

This chronology contains the dates of (*a*) Aristophanes' surviving plays (and a few of his lost works), (*b*) certain prominent events mentioned in the plays themselves, and (*c*) a small selection of other important events in Athenian/Greek history.

*c.*525 Birth of Aischylos, tragic playwright.

514 Assassination of Hipparchos, brother of the Athenian tyrant Hippias, by Harmodios and Aristogeiton.

510 Expulsion (with Spartan help) of the Athenian tyrant Hippias.

508 Kleomenes, Spartan king, occupies Athenian Akropolis but is forced to withdraw.
Kleisthenes' democratic reforms of Athenian politics, including creation of demes.

*c.*496 Birth of Sophokles, tragic playwright.

490 First Persian invasion of Greece, under Dareios. Battle of Marathon.

486 Comic drama introduced into the official programme of the City Dionysia festival (spring).

480 Second Persian invasion of Greece, under Xerxes. Battles of Artemision, Thermopylai, and Salamis.

*c.*480 Birth of Euripides, tragic playwright.

478 Founding of Delian League of Greek states against Persia, under Athenian leadership; subsequently evolves into Athenian empire.

472 Aischylos' *Persians*.

469 Birth of Sokrates, Athenian philosopher.

467 Aischylos' *Seven against Thebes*.

462 Further democratic reforms at Athens, promoted by Ephialtes and Perikles.

458 Aischylos' *Oresteia* trilogy.

456 Death of Aischylos.

*c.*455 Birth of Thucydides, Athenian historian.
Athenian system of democratic law-courts strengthened; on Perikles' proposal, payment for jurors instituted.

451 Athenian citizenship law (requiring both parents to be Athenian) introduced by Perikles.

c.450 Birth of Aristophanes.

447 Building of Parthenon starts: financed by Athenian imperial revenues; completed in late 430s. Cult statue of Athena Polias designed by sculptor Phidias.

446–445 Thirty-year peace treaty concluded between Athens and Sparta.

c.440 Comic drama introduced into the official programme of the Lenaia festival (midwinter).

438 Euripides' *Telephos*.

c.432 Megarian decree passed by Athenians, on Perikles' proposal, prohibiting Megarian trade/business with Athens and her allies.

431 Thirty-year peace collapses: friction between Athenian and Spartan spheres of influence erupts into major conflict ('Peloponnesian War', spanning 431–404).
First of annual series of Spartan invasions of Attika, to damage crops and property.

430–429 Major outbreak of plague at Athens. Death of Perikles.
Ascendancy of Kleon as democratic leader: he proposes increase in rate of jury pay.

428 Euripides' *Hippolytos*.

427 Aristophanes' first play, *Daitales* (*Banqueters*), probably placed second; produced by either Kallistratos or Philonides.
Gorgias, Sicilian rhetorician, visits Athens.

426 Aristophanes' *Babylonians* (Dionysia), produced by Kallistratos, probably 1st prize: leads to official backlash by Kleon (see Appendix).

425 Aristophanes' *Acharnians* (Lenaia), 1st prize; produced by Kallistratos.
Athenian capture of Spartans on island of Sphakteria near Pylos; military kudos for Kleon.

425–424 Kleon elected as general.

424 Aristophanes' *Knights* (Lenaia), 1st prize.

423 Aristophanes' *Clouds*, first version (Dionysia), 3rd place.

423–422 Kleon re-elected as general.

422 Aristophanes' *Wasps* (Lenaia), probably 2nd place behind another Aristophanic play, *Proagon*: one of the two plays was produced by Philonides.
Death of Kleon at battle of Amphipolis.

421 Aristophanes' *Peace* (Dionysia), 2nd place.
Peace of Nikias between Athens and Sparta.

419–417 Gradual breakdown of peace, and renewal of outright war, between Athens and Sparta.

c.416 Ostracism of Hyperbolos, leading 'demagogue'.

415 Athens sends major expedition to Sicily; scandalous mutilation of herms takes place on eve of fleet's departure. Alkibiades, suspected of involvement, flees into exile.

414 Aristophanes' *Birds* (Dionysia), 2nd place; produced by Kallistratos.

413 Sparta occupies fort at Dekeleia in N Attika.
Sicilian expedition ends in catastrophic defeat.

413–412 Athenian Council (Boule) temporarily replaced by group of Commissioners (Probouloi).

412 Euripides' *Andromeda* and *Helen*.
Defection of Miletos and other cities from Athenian empire.

411 Aristophanes' *Lysistrata* (Lenaia, probably), result unknown; produced by Kallistratos.
Oligarchic coup at Athens, led by Peisandros and others (the Four Hundred).
Aristophanes' *Women at the Thesmophoria* (Dionysia, probably), result unknown.

410 Democracy restored at Athens.

408 Aristophanes' *Wealth* I (lost play/version; see 388 below with Appendix, s.v. *Ploutos* I).

407–406 Return of Alkibiades to Athens, later followed by his second exile.

406 Athenian victory in naval battle at Arginousai, followed by trial and execution of several generals.
Deaths of Euripides and Sophokles.

405 Aristophanes' *Frogs* (Lenaia), 1st prize; produced by Philonides.
Athenian defeat in battle of Aigospotamoi; effective destruction of the city's military capacities.

404 Final surrender of Athens to Sparta; Spartans destroy city's Long Walls and impose rule of Thirty Tyrants.

403 Expulsion of the Thirty from Athens; restoration of democracy.

*c.*400 Agyrrhios proposes introduction of pay for attendance at Athenian Assembly.

399 Sokrates executed on charges of impiety and corrupting the young.

396–395 Athens and Thebes form anti-Spartan league, later joined by Korinth and Argos.

395 Athens begins rebuilding its Long Walls.

394 Battle of Knidos: Spartan fleet destroyed by Persian fleet under Athenian leadership.

*c.*393 Aristophanes' *Assembly-Women* (festival and result unknown).

388 Aristophanes' *Wealth* II (surviving version); festival unknown, possibly 1st prize.

*c.*387 Plato opens philosophical school, the Academy.

*c.*385 Death of Aristophanes.

CLOUDS

INTRODUCTION

The old man is sorely vexed. He cannot sleep yet he has to endure the sound of his slaves snoring. Things used to be different, he assures himself. But the war has changed all that:

> Damnation on you, war! Not least because
> We've reached the point where I can't even punish my slaves.
> (6–7)

For just a few lines at the start of *Clouds*, the audience of the original performance in 423 could have been forgiven for supposing it was watching a play whose themes would be linked to the dominant fact of contemporary life, the war with Sparta. Some spectators might even have suspected that the character whose monologue they were hearing, and whose mask and costume would have revealed him to be old and rustically decrepit, would turn out to be, like Dikaiopolis in *Acharnians*, a victim of the particular hardships inflicted on Attica's rural population by the war. But Aristophanes is a master of the teasing and misleading opening.[1] Both presumptions, as it happens, would have been false: *Clouds* is not a war play, and Strepsiades' situation is not that of any ordinary peasant-farmer, still less one whose problems stem from the war itself.

After the success of *Knights* at Lenaia 424, and possibly the performance of another play on political themes at the Dionysia of the same year, Aristophanes opted to write a comedy of a very different kind—one which would return to the intellectual and cultural realms from which he had taken the materials for his very first play, *Banqueters*, in 427.[2] The parabasis of *Clouds* itself draws a connection with that earlier work, implying (through an elusive veil of authorial self-justification at 528–36) that both plays were aimed at the most sophisticated kinds of spectators and did not cater for vulgar tastes—a point I shall discuss in more detail later. Moreover, the huge contrast between the ethos of *Knights* (scabrously vitriolic)

[1] Several plays make a point of explicitly teasing the audience about their ignorance of the plot: see esp. *Wasps* 54–87, *Peace* 43–8, with my general Introduction, 'The Dynamics of Fantasy'.

[2] On *Banqueters*, see the Appendix, s.v. *Daitales*; see there also for the possibility that *Georgoi* ('Farmers') was performed at Dionysia 424.

and of *Clouds* (obsessed with ideas) is something highly significant for Aristophanes' values and development as a comic playwright. It did not, of course, represent a decisive turning-away from either the war or contemporary Athenian politics; on the contrary, *Wasps* and *Peace*, as well as other comedies of the later 420s, are emphatically political comedies. Ironically, however, the political plays which followed *Clouds* may themselves have been a reaction to the 'failure' of *Clouds* itself at its first performance in 423. The play came third out of three, the first time Aristophanes had experienced such a fate.

The failure of *Clouds*, if that is what we are entitled to call it, is only one of a number of unusual and problematic facts about the work. Another—the (incompletely) revised state of the text[3]—is itself arguably a consequence of that failure: if *Clouds* had come first, or even second, Aristophanes might not have revised the play and we would probably now possess the original version. But it is not clear that the same explanation applies to three further peculiarities which have a major bearing on how we read the play: first, the dissembling function of the chorus as supposedly 'new' Sokratic deities who turn out (at 1454 ff.) to be guardians of traditional morality; second, the central character's failure to achieve anything like the goal (of cheating his creditors) which he originally set himself; and, most important of all, the curious relationship—forming the comic fulcrum of the work—between this central character and the figure of Sokrates.

The critical literature on *Clouds* has been overwhelmingly dominated by concern for the play's relevance to the so-called 'Sokratic question', the question of just what sort of person and intellectual the historical Sokrates amounted to (and, equally, of just how we should interpret the various sources for his life). In this connection, something needs to be said about the two notorious references to *Clouds* in Plato's *Apology*, since these have often been read in a distorting light.[4] The orthodox view is that Plato represents Sokrates as making

[3] The revision was probably undertaken between *c.*420 and 416: see the works cited in the Bibliography. For information about the first version of *Clouds*, see the Appendix, s.v. *Nephelai* I.

[4] We cannot know whether Sokrates actually mentioned *Clouds* at his trial; for what it is worth, Xenophon's *Apology* contains no such reference (though Xenophon, *Symposium* 6.6–8 makes the Syracusan impresario allude to *Clouds* in a way which gives an impression of its retention in 'popular' cultural memory). *Clouds* is ignored in one of the best reconstructions of the trial: M. H. Hansen, 'The Trial of Sokrates—From the Athenian Point of View', in M. Sakellariou (ed.), *Démocratie athénienne et culture* (Athens, 1996), 137–70.

Clouds itself partly to blame for the existence of animosity towards him and for his eventual prosecution. But can that be right? Sokrates' first mention of *Clouds* in the *Apology* occurs when he is complaining that for many years he has had a false reputation for two types of interest: first, esoteric and perhaps 'metaphysical' questions ('things up in the sky and under the earth'); secondly, 'making the weaker argument into the stronger' (a slogan for rhetorical facility known to have been used by Protagoras).[5] He says it is impossible to name those who have spread these slanders (because, by implication, there were too many of them and they did so in general social intercourse), 'unless one of them happens to be a comic poet'. The unmistakable allusion to Aristophanes and *Clouds* is immediately followed, however, by this: 'But as for those who tried to persuade you [*sc.* of these things] *with animus and malice* . . ., there is no way of putting any of *them* on the witness stand or cross-examining them; I am simply compelled to shadow-box with them . . .' (18d). In other words, Sokrates draws a strong contrast which indicates that *Clouds* itself is *not* part of the serious social forces of 'animus and malice' which have corroded his reputation over the years.

The second reference to *Clouds* occurs soon afterwards, where Sokrates, still preoccupied with serious slanders made against him, tells the jurors: 'you yourselves have seen these things in Aristophanes' comedy, where a character called "Sokrates" swings around, asserting that he walks in the air and spouting a lot of other nonsense on matters about which I know nothing whatsoever' (19c). The idea of 'nonsense' or 'drivel' here refers specifically to the ethos of the comedy, not to the subject-matter of certain philosophical questions per se—as Sokrates underlines by saying immediately that he intends no disrespect for anyone who really does possess knowledge about such things. So, once again, while Plato makes Sokrates use *Clouds* to illustrate the kind of image that many Athenians (allegedly) had of him, he does so in a way which separates comic 'nonsense' from the damaging social forces of 'animus and malice'.

There are, in any case, three large problems with Plato's perspective on *Clouds* in the *Apology*. First, it is questionable whether Sokrates' total denial of interest in speculative forms of philosophical enquiry is the whole truth about him. In Plato's own *Phaedo*,

[5] See my note on *Clouds* 113.

Sokrates admits that he *was* interested in such things when young.[6] Secondly, the references in the *Apology* pick out only certain 'headline' themes of *Clouds*; they have nothing to say about other details of the play, including an interesting depiction of Sokrates' methods of self-examination at 695 ff. (to which I shall return). Thirdly, later in the *Apology* Sokrates states that when those who accuse him of 'corrupting the young' are challenged to say exactly how he has this deleterious effect, they fall back on clichés used against *all* philosophers, namely being interested in 'things up in the air and under the earth', 'not believing in [or recognizing] gods', and 'making the weaker argument into the stronger' (23d).[7] But if such slogans were used against *all* philosophers, it becomes harder to see why their application to Sokrates should have led to such an exceptional degree of resentment against him, let alone to his eventual prosecution: the *Apology* itself certainly does not explain this.

It remains highly dubious, therefore, whether Plato's *Apology* should be read as ascribing to *Clouds* a genuinely influential role in arousing hostility towards the historical Sokrates. Plato cites the play, rather, as a *reductio ad absurdum* of popular falsification of Sokrates' intellectual character. It is, in any case, intrinsically implausible that a play which was performed (probably) just once, almost a quarter of a century before the trial of Sokrates, and which, as we have seen, was not favourably received by the judges on that occasion, could have been a significant causal element in the processes that led to the eventual condemnation and execution of Sokrates. Whatever Plato's intent in making Sokrates twice refer to *Clouds* in the *Apology*, he does not supply an adequate basis on which to assess the comedy's ambiguous relationship to the intellectual domain represented by Sokrates. *Clouds* exploits, for sure, some of the popular stereotypes of 'the philosopher' to which Plato's *Apology* itself refers. But it does not do so one-sidedly. Instead, it builds them into a polarized encounter between Strepsiades, the naive bumpkin, and Sokrates, the lofty head of the Thinking Institute (*phrontistêrion*). The results, I shall suggest, oscillate with a kind of comic instability between different points of view. It may even be that this was a contributory factor in the original 'failure' of *Clouds*.

6 See *Phaedo* 96a–99d, in the so-called 'intellectual autobiography' which has been a source of much disputed interpretation.

7 For the phrase 'things up in the air and under the earth', cf. my note on *Clouds* 188.

The plot of *Clouds* begins from, and in a sense never leaves, the realm of popular perceptions of abstract thinkers or 'philosophers' (a term, however, which is not part of the play's own vocabulary).[8] But it does not provide its audience with a fixed relationship to such perceptions. Not everything that goes on in the Thinking Institute is a mere reflection of Strepsiades' expectations: what he expects and what he gets from Sokrates is, in fact, both complex and teasing. Strepsiades originally (and naively) describes the School to his son as combining, in essence, 'scientific' and rhetorical pursuits (94–9); it is the latter he hopes to harness to his own immoral ends (cheating his creditors). But once he himself is introduced to the Thinking Institute and to Sokrates, Strepsiades is confronted with a new religion (centring on the Clouds themselves as nature deities), forced to undergo a 'ritual' of self-scrutiny and mental exercises (more on this later), and exposed to a much wider range of intellectual subjects than he had anticipated. On top of all this, the school's eventual education of his son Pheidippides rebounds disastrously against Strepsiades' plans. To a degree unparalleled in Aristophanes' other surviving plays, Strepsiades turns into (or, rather, both starts and ends as) a *failed* comic protagonist. We need to consider this point further as a means to understanding the play's ambiguous relationship to the intellectual world of Sokrates.

All Aristophanic protagonists are strange creatures. But Strepsiades is peculiar in ways mostly unique to him in the extant comedies. Above all, and much more than any other comic protagonist, he is a victim, not a controller, of events.[9] Not only does he fail to achieve the (fantasized) success of, say, Dikaiopolis in *Acharnians*, Trygaios in *Peace*, or Peisetairos in *Birds*, he also largely lacks the compensating resilience and irrepressibility of a partially baulked protagonist such as Philokleon in *Wasps*. Though he shares various features with such figures (he is elderly like all of them, rustic like the first two, and in debt like Peisetairos), his position is made quirkily different from all theirs by his quasi-morganatic marriage

[8] *Philosophos* (with its cognates) was at this date still relatively rare; *Assembly-Women* 571 (as adjective), some thirty years later, is its only Aristophanic occurrence. *Clouds* itself makes general use of the vocabulary of *phrontistai*, 'thinkers' or 'intellectuals' (from the same Greek root as *phrontistêrion*, the Thinking Institute).

[9] Euripides in *Women at the Thesmophoria* is also a kind of 'victim' and suffers a series of setbacks in the course of the play. But he does get what he wants (a truce with the women) in the end.

to a (marginal) member of the aristocratic clan of the Alkmaionidai (46–7, 60–72). This fact about Strepsiades is, at the very least, an extravagant caricature of the sort of marital mismatch or unfortunate *mésalliance* (from the woman's family's point of view) that might just conceivably have occurred from time to time in classical Athens. But it is more likely that it represents a bizarrely implausible conjunction of extreme social contrasts (aristocratic/peasant, urban/rural, luxurious/parsimonious) between the partners and their families. Either way, Strepsiades' marital circumstances—which cause him to become the father of a horse-crazy son, a member of the knight class (120), whose habits have created a mountain of paternal debts—turns the protagonist into a hybrid, far-fetched oddity of a kind which by definition clashes with the social norms of contemporary Athens.

But Strepsiades also differs from other Aristophanic protagonists in his ethical character as well as his sociological profile. Others sometimes exhibit gross egotism in various ways (though several actually aim to achieve civically beneficial ends), but in no other case do we encounter a motivation which by its very nature involves outright injustice or immorality.[10] Strepsiades' ambition to cheat his creditors is unequivocally nefarious. No other comic protagonist *thinks* quite like Strepsiades, and no other is brought to the point of an eventual confession of guilt (1462–4, to which I shall return). The combination of a socially freakish marriage with the espousal of an immoral purpose makes it hard to regard Strepsiades as a 'sympathetic' character capable of channelling the feelings of, or attracting comic 'affection' from, many spectators. A misfit as both husband and father; reduced to the desperation (and absurdity) of a self-deceiving hope of never paying back a single obol of his debts (116–18); and repeatedly shown to be incapable of learning anything ('I've never in all my life met a bumpkin like this,' as Sokrates exclaims at 628)—given all this, who could possibly *want* to be like Strepsiades or afford to think that they *are* like him?

That question can be seen to have further ramifications when we start to trace Strepsiades' experience with the Thinking Institute and its implications for the audience of *Clouds*. His attitude to Sokrates' school is, from the outset, a paradoxical mixture of ignorance and

[10] On Aristophanic protagonists, see the general Introduction, 'The Dynamics of Fantasy'.

admiration. He tells Pheidippides he does not know the right name for the inhabitants of the school (100), but that they are people who call the sky a 'baking-lid' and humans the 'charcoal' underneath it (95–7): he thereby simple-mindedly translates something which spectators might recognize as a kind of cosmological *analogy* into a literal statement.[11] Later in the play he will show an even grosser failure to grasp a variety of scientific and technical points, yet his faith in intellectuals will remain (until near the end) undiminished. That faith is a matter, in part, of the conviction that people like Sokrates also possess a rhetorical expertise which could guarantee you success in any court case, no matter how blatantly unjust your position. This is equally a matter of literal-mindedness: he treats a formula encapsulating the amoral versatility of rhetorical technique (turning the weaker argument into the stronger) as a sure recipe for achieving his own immoral ends (112–18). In both these respects—the scientific and the rhetorical elements in Strepsiades' expectations of Sokrates' school—Aristophanes is doing something more than simply satirizing intellectuals; he is (also) mocking Strepsiades' own incomprehension. The plot of the play will demonstrate, in particular, the consequences of Strepsiades' failure to realize that if a morally bad case could always be guaranteed to win an argument, any individual, including himself, would be just as liable to be a *victim* as a beneficiary of that fact. Aristophanes' play requires spectators who can see what Strepsiades himself cannot see.

The comic paradox of Strepsiades' attitudes is that they represent a gullible trust placed in intellectuals by a supremely unintellectual man. The very clichés picked out by Plato as characterizing popular prejudice *against* philosophers (p. 6 above) are the basis of Strepsiades' attraction to Sokrates' school. This is highlighted by contrast with Pheidippides' view of the school: he regards Sokrates and Chairephon as socially despicable impostors, notable above all for their physical pallor and asceticism (102–4). Pheidippides' worldly contempt draws attention to a contradiction within his father's position between the idea of the philosopher-intellectuals as both pursuing abstruse ideas *and* as possessors of a key to practical success. But this contradiction is important for the play as a whole, and we shall need to return to it.

[11] See my note on *Clouds* 97.

As the plot of *Clouds* unfolds, those factors in the protagonist's situation I have so far emphasized conspire to create a predicament from which it seems less and less likely that he will escape. To an extent unique in the surviving plays, Strepsiades is a character who is virtually never in control of events (even when he *thinks* he is: note the ironies of his self-encomium at 1201–13)—not, at any rate, until the abrupt and problematic ending of the work (of which more in due course). He is precipitated from his original financial difficulties, via a miserable failure to influence his son's behaviour (119–25), into gradual humiliation at the hands of the intellectuals in whose special powers he believes. The entire stretch of the play between his first approach to the school at 126 and his return to the school with Pheidippides at 888 is a process of prolonged frustration and repeated *deferral* of the one thing he hoped to acquire from the school. His mounting impatience at this experience twice breaks out expressly: first at 655–7, where he reacts to Sokrates' exasperation at his stupidity with a reaffirmation of his desire to learn 'that immoral way of debating', and again at 738–9, where he says to Sokrates, 'I've told you a million times what I really want'. On neither occasion, significantly, does Sokrates offer to satisfy Strepsiades' desires. On the first, in fact, he deliberately postpones satisfaction by assuring him, 'But you need to learn other things first' (658). Sokrates—and this is a problem for some readings of the play—is much less ready to transmit rhetorical expertise to Strepsiades than the latter had naively hoped.[12] The plot of *Clouds*, till its final twist, is about the thwarting of the protagonist's wishes.

Strepsiades' expectations of the school comprise, as we saw, two main elements: natural philosophy/science and (cynically amoral) rhetoric (94–9). This combination of interests was not completely inconceivable for a contemporary intellectual: Hippias of Elis boasted competence in both these fields in his advertised range of competence.[13] But Hippias was, or claimed to be, exceptionally polymathic. Strepsiades' conception of the school runs together spheres of

[12] Only once in the play, at 874–6, does Sokrates unequivocally acknowledge a kind of rhetoric that might be put to immoral purposes; but that passage has a raison d'être of its own as a typically Aristophanic joke-form (at Hyperbolos' expense).

[13] See Plato, *Hippias Major* 285c, *Hippias Minor* 367e–8a, *Protagoras* 315c, 318e. But all these passages contain some satirical irony at the expense of Hippias's self-vaunted polymathy.

thought which were *not* typically pursued by the same individuals. Most 'natural philosophers', including the Hippon who may have been responsible for the baking-lid analogy alluded to at *Clouds* 96–7, did not teach rhetoric. Similarly, most teachers of rhetorical theory or practice did not engage in cosmological speculation or in technical subjects.[14] When Strepsiades voices his expectations of the Thinking Institute at 94–9, therefore, at least some members of the audience are likely to have seen him as ludicrous precisely in virtue of his ignorant reliance on some of the clichés used, as we saw Plato attesting (*Apology* 23d), against philosophers in general—except that Strepsiades, to reiterate the crucial point, is supposedly *pro*, not *contra*, Sokrates' school.

In fact, Strepsiades' initial conception of Sokrates' establishment greatly underestimates its range of interests. As the play develops, we are given a picture of the Thinking Institute as housing at least five types of intellectual/philosophical enquiry: first, cosmology, astronomy, 'meteorology', and physics of the kind particularly ascribed to the Ionian tradition of early Greek philosophy; second, a further group of scientific subjects, including geometry, zoology, and geography; third (though overlapping with the first category), a kind of philosophical theology which critiques traditional religion and sets up a new, more abstract conception of the divine (even if it also shows signs of being able to *dispense* with the divine altogether); fourth, language-related matters ('proto-linguistics', one might say), including systems of grammatical and metrical classification; fifth, rhetorical debating skills, as enacted in the play's showpiece contest between the two personified arguments, Moral and Immoral. We can see that Aristophanes has taken (and distorted) material related to a large range of thinkers, among them the early Milesians (Thales, Anaximander, Anaximenes), Empedokles, Anaxagoras, Diogenes of Apollonia, Hippon of Samos, Protagoras, the music-theorist Damon, the Pythagoreans(?), as well as the historical Sokrates himself (especially in hints of his one-to-one dialectical methods and his concern for intense self-scrutiny or 'the examined life').[15] The effect

[14] Compare, likewise, the rhetorician Isokrates a generation later: see his attitudes to scientific and technical subjects at 12.26, 15.261, 265.

[15] See the questioning of Strepsiades at *Clouds* 478 ff. and the emphasis at 695 ff. on Strepsiades' need to find a solution to his problems by a kind of introspective self-examination. For the other figures mentioned in my text, see the notes to the translation.

is a shifting kaleidoscope of ideas and motifs, which we should not simplify by taking *Clouds* to be targeted against a particular group of people later known as 'the sophists'.[16]

There are two important implications of that last point which need to be drawn out. First, the depiction of intellectuals and philosophers in *Clouds* lacks a single, unified focus, despite the comic fiction that they live together in their own community, the Thinking Institute.[17] Whatever else Aristophanes wishes his audience to infer about Sokrates and his school, he must expect them to have at least a rudimentary awareness of the diversity of ideas and interests associated with the inhabitants of the *phrontistêrion* at various points in the play, and not to take the comic portrait literal-mindedly as corresponding to any specific thinker or thinkers.[18] Secondly, and relatedly, if spectators did not possess some ability to recognize the play's manipulation and mixing of different intellectual types, they would be in precisely the same position of ignorance as Strepsiades himself, and would accordingly be unable to appreciate the comedy of his ineptitude and mental incompetence. Again and again in *Clouds*, the humour of particular passages, many of them with something like a marked 'joke-form', presupposes that the hearer can understand what the protagonist himself *misunderstands*: this is true, with varying nuances, of Strepsiades' bafflement over, for example, the symbolic nature of maps (206–17); Sokrates' materialist 'theory of mind' (227–36); meteorological causation (369–411); or the nature of poetic metres (638–56).[19] This is tantamount to saying that, if there are many elements in *Clouds* which mock the pretensions of intellectuals (including the abstruseness and pointlessness of abstract forms of

[16] The term *sophistês* originally meant a skilled specialist; it only gradually developed a pejorative sense in the later fifth and early fourth centuries, and it was chiefly Plato who cemented the term as a label for a certain *type* of intellectual. *Clouds* uses the term (331, 360, 1111, 1309) to poke fun at intellectual pretentiousness, but without implying that there is a clearly defined group of people who can be called 'sophists'.

[17] The *phrontistêrion* is a kind of amalgam of (a) an ordinary school, (b) a Pythagorean 'sect' or closed society, and (c) the centre of a mystery cult (cf. 143, 254 ff.).

[18] There is nothing implausible in supposing that a fair number of Athenians could have known *something* about Sokrates' specific ways of thinking and, equally, about what distinguished him from other intellectuals: Plato, *Apology* 19d certainly posits such familiarity for many of the jurors in 399.

[19] On the last of these topics, it is obvious that theatre audiences by definition could appreciate poetic metres and must have had some awareness of basic rhythmic classifications.

speculative thought), there are at least as many passages which mock Strepsiades' utter dimwittedness and lack of sophistication. It is this factor which produces the play's recurrent ambiguity in relation to the two main characters and to the opposing extremes of airy intellectualism and crass obtuseness which they embody. In short, the comic dynamic of *Clouds* cannot be aligned one-sidedly with the satire or mockery of just one of these extremes: it depends on its audience's ability to savour the interlocking absurdities of both.

But did Aristophanes succeed in finding an audience of that kind? The revised version of *Clouds* we possess provides us with some intriguing evidence on this point, in its parabatic complaints about the 'failure' of the first (and only) performance in 423. I shall return to those complaints at the end of this introduction. Before that, however, I need to say something about the play's set-piece debate (the first 'agon', 949–1104) between the personified 'arguments' Moral and Immoral, since it is this which, for many critics, forms the climax of the work's satire of Sokrates' school as a place which harbours deeply dangerous and subversive ways of thinking. Prima facie, the agon acts out the notion contained in Strepsiades' original expectations (98–9, 112–15), namely the defeat of the 'stronger' argument by the 'weaker'—in effect, the capacity of manipulative rhetorical skills to fight and win cases which appear, by moral (and other) standards, to be at a distinct disadvantage. But is the result of the agon sufficient to make it, for Aristophanes' audience, a compelling critique of contemporary intellectual developments? My contention is that such a view of the agon ceases to be convincing once we recognize the degree of thematic multiplicity and inconsistency built into the debate. What's more, the contest actually draws our attention to a paradox which, I shall suggest, helps to support some of my preceding comments on the comedy's ambiguities.

One highly pertinent feature of the agon of *Clouds* is the disparity it creates between the persona of Immoral and the general depiction of Sokrates and his pupils. Immoral is an advocate of sybaritic softness and sensuality (warm baths, drinking parties, sexual indulgence), whereas the ethos of the Thinking Institute was earlier depicted as one of ascetic deprivation and endurance—qualities which, if anything, are much closer to the values urged by the educational traditionalism of Moral. This disparity highlights an underlying comic contradiction in the play as a whole: its treatment of intellectuals as (supposedly) living apart from normal society *and* as teaching the key to material success in life! But there are other divergences too between the agon and earlier elements of the play. Immoral expresses no direct atheism nor espouses 'new' deities in the way that Sokrates himself had;[20] he shows no interest whatsoever in metaphysical, scientific, or technical subjects of the sorts Sokrates was earlier associated with; and the debate between the two arguments puts an emphasis on 'junior' schooling (what/how young adolescents should be taught) which played virtually no part in the earlier sections of the play. This misalignment between the agon and the preceding Sokratic scenes adds its own weight to the case I have already made about the lack of a coherent or stable focus in *Clouds*' composite image of intellectuals.[21]

But there is a further, and equally fundamental, observation to be made about the agon. Not only does it shift the ground from the kaleidoscopic array of ideas associated with the Thinking Institute to a clash of broader educational and cultural value-systems ('tradition' versus 'the modern'). It also connects the values at stake less to the thought-world of intellectuals than to the state of Athenian society in general. This is evident near the start, when Immoral happily agrees to show himself to the audience: '. . . the bigger the crowd | The more I'll argue you into the ground,' he asserts (891–2), thereby proclaiming himself some sort of *populist*. When he goes on to claim that his novel arguments will bring him success, Moral retorts by blaming the prevalence of such things on 'these idiots sitting in front of us here' (897–8), that is, the audience itself (whom Immoral immediately woos as '*clever*', 899) as notionally representative of Athenian democratic culture and its supposed susceptibility to corrupt rhetorical techniques. This is underscored by Moral's later exclamation about the madness of 'the city | That nurtures you | To drip poison into the minds of the young' (926–8). The spectators themselves are

[20] The denial of the existence of Justice at 902 might seem germane; but if Aristophanes had wanted to make Immoral sound 'theologically' just like Sokrates, he would hardly have written 903–5 in the way that he has.

[21] It would certainly be a mistake to suppose that the sharply opposing attitudes displayed in the agon represented invariable mentalities within contemporary culture: the mistake is easier to see if we consider Isokrates 7.43–9, where many of Moral's views are paralleled (e.g. the need to avoid the agora, pipe-girls, and disrespect for elders) yet in an argument which ascribes devotion to *philosophia* to the older ideals of Athenian education!

treated as implicated in, and thoroughly tainted by, the kind of decadence, iconoclasm, and rhetorical shamelessness in which Immoral glories and which Moral denounces.[22] It is indeed Immoral's clinching argument at the end of the debate that, like everyone else, the audience watching the play consists largely of 'wide-arsed' degenerates (1096–1104).

The first agon of *Clouds*, then, puts its contemporary audience in a paradoxical position which is hardly compatible with allowing it to feel 'seriously' on Moral's side, especially when we add that Moral himself is patently subjected to satirical treatment for his exaggerated nostalgia and sexual hypocrisy. That is not to say, however, that the debate invites the audience to feel positively on Immoral's side either, in his slick opportunism and cynicism. The comic dynamic of the scene calls, fairly transparently, for a capacity to relish the caricatured mentalities of *both* antagonists: the reactionary conservatism of one, the rebellious radicalism of the other. But if that is right, it forms a parallel to the earlier parts of the play, where spectators need to be able to relish from both sides, as it were, the polarized contrast between the abstruse intellectual and the obtuse rustic. Standard interpretations of *Clouds* as an anti-intellectual critique of 'new' thinkers founder on the basic ambiguity of the play's comic perspective.

There is, moreover, another layer to that ambiguity. It has often been noted—it is, in fact, hard *not* to notice—that in the (revised) parabasis of *Clouds*, where Aristophanes (ventriloquized by the chorus) discusses the comedy's failure at its first performance in 423 and discusses the kind of audience it was intended for, he repeatedly applies to his own work some of the key vocabulary of 'cleverness' and 'newness' which is used elsewhere in the play for Sokrates, Immoral, and the whole realm of intellectual ideas. Aristophanes wishes to be thought a clever or skilful poet (520) and *Clouds* to be thought the 'cleverest' of his comedies (522). He claims to shun the trite routines of comic vulgarity and offers constant dramatic inventiveness, originality, and sophistication (537–48). Furthermore, his work appeals to, and calls for, spectators who are themselves sophisticated and clever (521, 526–7, 535, cf. 575). The key terms in these claims

[22] Cf. my introduction to *Frogs* for an analogous point about the audience of that play in relation to the supposedly decadent 'Euripidean' values of contemporary Athens.

can all be traced elsewhere in the work as leitmotifs in the depiction of intellectuals.[23]

Authorial statements in an Aristophanic parabasis can never be taken simply at face-value. The parabasis has its own scope for comic rhetoric and even fantasy, and we know that Aristophanes was not alone in exploiting it for self-aggrandizement and corresponding denigration of his rivals.[24] But that does not remove all significance from the conspicuous 'coincidence' in *Clouds* between the values which the playwright boasts about in relation to his own work and the key value-terms which run through the verbal fabric of the comedy in relation to Sokrates, the Thinking Institute, and Immoral. Aristophanes' choice of the language of cleverness, sophistication, and novelty in the parabasis of *Clouds* is no accident (he also uses it, in referring back to this play, in the parabasis of *Wasps*).[25] It ironically highlights the fact that *Clouds* itself is a rather *intellectualizing* comedy, a work which makes intricate, knowing use, for its own purposes, of philosophical, scientific, and other intellectual ideas and motifs, and which is accordingly locked into a comically incestuous relationship with the materials of 'new' thinking. In addition, it is a play which, as Aristophanes insists, came looking for—but had trouble finding—a clever *audience* (535), spectators with the knowledge and sophistication to appreciate how cleverly the poet was manipulating his themes and to laugh at the rustic dimwittedness of Strepsiades himself. Hence, as I have emphasized, the ambiguity which underlies the play's relationship to the sphere of modern intellectualism from which it extracts its comic materials.

But there is one remaining problem to address, and that is the play's ending. After suffering violence at the hands of Pheidippides, who has learnt from Immoral that showing respect to one's parents is an outmoded value, Strepsiades complains to the chorus, but is told by

23 Cleverness/sophistication (adjs. *sophos* and *dexios*, with their cognates): esp. 94, 148, 331, 360–1, 412, 418, 428, 489, 757, 834, 895, 1111, 1309, 1399. Newness (the adj. *kainos*): esp. 480, 896, 937, 943, 1032, 1397, 1399. Inventiveness (from the root *heur-*, 'find', 'discover'): 137, 228, 232, 447, 728, 737, 896.

24 On the parabasis, see further in the general Introduction, 'Formality and Performance'. For other comic poets' boasts and gibes, cf. A. H. Sommerstein, *Talking about Laughter* (Oxford, 2009), 118–25; NB 124 for the uniqueness of Aristophanes' claim to 'intellectual sophistication'.

25 *Wasps* 1044–59: this passage was composed in late 423 or early 422; it therefore pre-dates the revisions to the parabasis of *Clouds* itself.

them that the situation is his own fault, the result of his wicked desires (1452–62). In a manner unique for an Aristophanic protagonist, he admits the charge (1462–4)—but decides, nonetheless, on revenge against Sokrates' school (1464–6). When Pheidippides refuses to help his father, Strepsiades prays to Hermes for advice and purports (in what is probably framed as ludicrous self-deception)[26] to receive sanction for setting fire to the Thinking Institute (1478–85), which he proceeds to do with the help of his slaves.

Critics often claim that the end of *Clouds* shows Sokrates and his disciples being 'burned to death' inside the building. Neither the text nor the conventions of comedy support that reading.[27] The 'fire' (with no more than one or two brandished torches to stimulate the comic imagination) will have been a kind of pantomime fiction; it is essentially no different in kind—though critics often conveniently overlook this—from the precipitate and crazy comic aggression of the old men at *Lysistrata* 269–70 or the similar belligerence of the women at *Women at the Thesmophoria* 726–7. In any case, *Clouds* 1508 clearly suggests that the philosophers escape from the house and are chased off by an angry Strepsiades in the rumbustiously frantic final lines. Even so, one might think, this is surely no indeterminate conclusion but some sort of endorsement for the outright rejection of subversive, anti-traditional ideas of the kinds projected onto the Thinking Institute—perhaps even an 'invitation to violence' against intellectuals such as Sokrates.[28]

Making sense of the end of *Clouds* is not so straightforward.[29] Why should we assume that the stage action in any clear sense advocates, or expresses approval of, the kind of wilful aggression into which the protagonist now launches himself? If the end of the play could be simply 'translated' into a didactic message, as some suppose, it would

[26] Athenians did not normally believe they could hear specific advice from statues. Ironically, Strepsiades' behaviour, in its comic way, has something in common with Sokrates' own 'divine' voice/sign as described by sources such as Plato, *Apology* 31c–d, Xenophon, *Memorabilia* 1.1.2–4.

[27] See F. D. Harvey, '*Nubes* 1493ff: Was Socrates Murdered?', *Greek, Roman and Byzantine Studies*, 22 (1981), 339–43.

[28] The phrase 'an invitation to violence' is used by K. J. Dover, *Aristophanes Clouds* (Oxford, 1968), p. lvi, of the last part of the play more generally.

[29] For one great scholar's strange uncertainty on the point, see E. R. Dodds, *The Greeks and the Irrational* (Berkeley, 1951), 188: having stated that the audience was expected 'to care little if Socrates were burnt with [his school]', he immediately draws back and suggests that it might all just be 'Aristophanes' friendly fun'!

be a very strange and contradictory message: immediately after confessing that it is wrong to try to cheat his creditors, Strepsiades becomes convinced that it is acceptable to set fire to people's property! So much for the restoration of 'traditional' moral standards. In any case, Strepsiades has been an abject failure and a specimen of naive stupidity throughout the play: can he now really become an effective vehicle of 'moral' punishment against the inhabitants of the Thinking Institute? Even when he is confronted with the results of the education in cynically manipulative rhetoric that he had selfishly wanted all along for his son, and is made to admit his own responsibility, he still falls back on blaming Sokrates and his friends.

In terms of its dramatic impact, moreover, it is also important that Strepsiades' action receives no support from others (his slaves apart). He is a comic loner. Admittedly, the refusal of Pheidippides to join his father in attacking the school is not itself meaningful; indeed, it is the occasion for some further Aristophanic irony with the moral upheavals of the plot: 'I'm not prepared to *wrong* [or 'do injustice to'] my former teachers' (1467), states Pheidippides (just moments after advocating beating up his own parents)—as though, preposterously, he still had a traditional sense of right and wrong! But far more tellingly, the chorus itself, despite revealing their 'true' and previously disguised identity as defenders of traditional piety (1458–61), do not utter a word of guidance or encouragement to Strepsiades. They fall completely silent after line 1461, and we have to picture them moving back to the perimeter of the performance area to take no further part in proceedings (till their perfunctory exit line at the very end, 1510). If Aristophanes was as keen as many critics suppose to turn the finale into a moral(istic) message about the perniciousness of contemporary intellectuals like 'Sokrates' and the desirability of somehow suppressing them, why does he leave the chorus so glaringly silent? It is hard to avoid the inference that he wants the final scene to stand out as an impulse of reckless violence, stemming wholly from the frustration of the protagonist and every bit as 'immoral' (if also unrealistic: no competent arsonist would go about the job so blatantly and loudly) as his original desire not to pay back his debts.

Aristophanes does something at the end of *Clouds* which we find in none of his other extant plays: he leaves his protagonist with the same problem he started with (Strepsiades' debts have not gone away), a problem further compounded by the rift with his son.

Every other surviving Aristophanic comedy ends with a joyous celebration, whether for the protagonist alone (*Acharnians*, *Wasps*, *Birds*) or for a larger group (*Knights*, *Peace*, *Lysistrata*, *Women at the Thesmophoria*, *Frogs*, *Assembly-Women*, *Wealth*). *Clouds*, by contrast, ends in Strepsiades' failure, which finds an expressive outlet in, but is not cancelled out by, his wild act of arson. It is as if Aristophanes has created a challenge for himself by bending the rules of his genre: how do you extract the usual comic finale of high spirits and self-satisfied revelry from a situation in which the central character remains a failure? (The two earlier scenes with the creditors had underlined that by displaying Strepsiades' *premature* self-satisfaction.) How, moreover, do you do so in a way that can induce a sort of vicarious pleasure for the audience, when that same character has been treated throughout as dimwitted and ineffectual, thus rendering him a poor candidate for much 'sympathy' or indulgence from spectators?

Aristophanes' attempted solution is to whip up an atmosphere of animated stage action. There is plenty of theatrical scope here for visually burlesque antics: commotion with a ladder, the tossing of a few simulated roof-tiles, the brandishing of mattock and torches, a hubbub of figures rushing in and out of the stage building. But the text indicates no scope for a coherent dramatic point—nothing more coherent than the frustration-driven revenge of a simpleton against intellectuals he had never had any hope of understanding. If it is true, as the ancient commentators reported, that the ending of *Clouds* was one of the parts which was changed in the (unfinished) second version, it is reasonable to infer that Aristophanes was trying to rescue some dramatic control for Strepsiades, belatedly converting him from a passive failure into at least a frenetically energetic agent. But by doing so, the playwright arguably exposes the dramatic 'deficit' involved in seeking one-sided closure for a work which has depended so heavily on the counterbalancing of opposite comic extremes.

CLOUDS

Speaking Characters

STREPSIADES: an elderly rustic Athenian
PHEIDIPPIDES: his son
SLAVE: of STREPSIADES
STUDENT[A]: a pupil of SOKRATES' school
SOKRATES: Athenian intellectual, head of the Thinking Institute
CHORUS (24 dancers/singers): of Cloud deities
LEADER: of the CHORUS
MORAL: personification of just and traditionally 'stronger' arguments
IMMORAL: personification of unjust and therefore supposedly 'weaker' arguments
CREDITOR[A]: from whom STREPSIADES borrowed money for his son's horses
CREDITOR[B]: ditto
STUDENT[B]: another member of SOKRATES' school

Silent Characters

STUDENTS: various pupils of the Thinking Institute
WITNESS: accompanying CREDITOR[A]
SLAVES: further members of STREPSIADES' household

[*The stage building has two doors in its façade: next to one of them* (A) *stands a herm (see note on 1478); next to the other* (B), *which will turn out to be* SOKRATES' *school, there is a large round pot (note on 1473). Door* A *belongs to* STREPSIADES' *house, but at the outset the space in front of it has to be imagined as inside his bedroom.* STREPSIADES *and* PHEIDIPPIDES *are discovered (after the removal of screens?) lying in bed, the son fast asleep while the father tosses and turns. The two side entrances* (eisodoi) *connect the onstage locations with other parts of Athens.*]

STREPSIADES [*loudly*]. Oh blast! Oh blast!
Zeus, king of the gods, how I hate the dead of night.
The time feels endless. Will daylight never arrive?
Yet I'm sure I heard a cock crow ages ago.
The slaves are snoring. They never used to do.
Damnation on you, war! Not least because
We've reached the point where I can't even punish my slaves.*
And of course this splendid young fellow lying next to me here
Never wakes in the night—oh no, he just farts away
With five blankets, no less, to bury his head beneath.
Okay, I'll try the same: cover up and snore.

[*He pulls up a blanket, tries briefly to sleep, but soon re-emerges with frustration.*]

I just can't sleep! What a miserable life, being bitten
By the debts I've incurred for keeping a stable of horses
For this son of mine. He lets his hair grow long*
And his life's an obsession with horses and chariot-racing*—
He even *dreams* of horses. Meanwhile I'm distraught
As I watch the moon reach the twentieth day of the month.*
All that interest mounting up! [*Sits up and shouts.*]
Hoy, slave, a lamp!
And bring me out my accounts. I want to read
How many my creditors are and work out the interest.

[*A* SLAVE *appears from door* A, *carrying a lamp and a set of wax tablets. He stands and holds the lamp while the old man starts to read.*]

What's this first debt here? Twelve minas to Pasias.*
Twelve minas to *Pasias*? But what was that for?

Of course, when I bought that dashing racer.* Oh fool!
[*Sarcastically*] I'd rather have lost an eye—*dashed* out with a stone!

[*As* STREPSIADES *continues to examine his accounts*, PHEIDIPPIDES *starts talking animatedly in his sleep*.]

PHEIDIPPIDES. Philon, you're a cheat! Just stick to your chariot lane!
STREPSIADES. There you are, the very affliction that's blighted my life.
He can't even sleep without dreaming equestrian dreams.
PHEIDIPPIDES. How many laps do the war-carts drive in this race?*
STREPSIADES. Well I'm the one you're *driving* crazy, that's sure!
[*Gloomily*] 'What burden next was mine'—after Pasias' loan?*
[*Reading*] Three minas, chariot base and wheels: Ameinias.
PHEIDIPPIDES [*still dreaming*]. Get my horse rolled clean in the dust, then take him home.*
STREPSIADES. Well, mate, it's *me* you've taken to the cleaners!
I've got several convictions for debt, and now other lenders
Say they'll seize my goods.*
PHEIDIPPIDES [*waking*]. What's wrong with you now, then, father?
Why spend the whole night fretting and tossing and turning?
STREPSIADES. There's a thing in my bed that bites me—a debt enforcer!*
PHEIDIPPIDES. For goodness' sake, just allow me to get some sleep.
STREPSIADES. Go on then, carry on sleeping. But mark my words:
These debts will all be on *your* head one day.

[PHEIDIPPIDES *wraps himself up once more under his blankets. His father groans.*]

What calamity!
How I wish that matchmaker woman had been wiped out,*
The one who urged me on to marry your mother.
[*Nostalgically*] I used to enjoy such a lovely *rustic* life:
I wallowed in seedy abundance, not a care in the world,
My existence teeming with bees and sheep and olives.
Then I married a niece of Megakles, son of Megakles!*
Yes, me a rustic and her a true city girl,

So haughty, so classy—*Koisyra* from head to toe.*
On my wedding day, when I got into bed beside her,
I smelt quite strongly of wine, dried figs, and wool,
While *she* smelt of perfume, saffron, sexy kisses,
Conspicuous consumption, and women's cults!*
She wasn't exactly lazy; she worked the loom hard.
But I'd take this cloak of mine to show her and say:
'You're using too much wool, my spendthrift wife.'

SLAVE. There's no more oil to keep the lamp alight.

STREPSIADES. Oh no! But why did you light such a thirsty lamp?
Come here, you need a thrashing.

SLAVE. But what have I done?

STREPSIADES. You inserted one of those big fat wicks, that's what!

[*The* SLAVE *slips away through door* A. STREPSIADES *recomposes himself.*]

Then, when this son of ours right here was born,
The son of me and my high-and-mighty wife,
We started to wrangle at once about his *name*.
She wanted a name with a horsey-hippo ring:
Xanthippos, Chairippos, Kallippides, or the like.
I wanted Pheidonides, his grandad's name.*
Well we argued away for a while, till in the end
We compromised and agreed—'Pheidippides'.
His mother would pick up the child and pamper him rotten:
'When you're big and drive your chariot up the Akropolis,*
Like Megakles did, in a flowing robe . . .' *I'd* counter:
'No, wait till you're herding goats on the rocky hillside,
The way your father does, in a farmer's jerkin . . .'
He never paid any attention to what I said.
He just left my property ailing from horse-disease.
So I've spent the whole night pondering how to escape.
I can think of just one way but it's rather special;
If only my son will agree, it'll be my salvation.
But the first thing I need is to rouse him out of his sleep.
Now, what's the *nicest* way to do it? Let's see.
Pheidippides, Pheidippi*diddles*—

PHEIDIPPIDES [*stirring*]. What now?

STREPSIADES. Give your father a kiss and clasp my hand in yours.

PHEIDIPPIDES [*sitting up*]. Okay. What's wrong?
STREPSIADES. Please tell me you really love me.
PHEIDIPPIDES. I swear by Poseidon Hippios I do!*
STREPSIADES. No, please, not *him*: don't swear by the god of horses.
He's the very god who's left my life in ruins!
But if your love for me is true and heartfelt,
Please do what I ask, my child.
PHEIDIPPIDES. Well *what* do you want?
STREPSIADES. I want you to change your way of life at once
And to go and learn the things I tell you to.
PHEIDIPPIDES. What things do you mean?
STREPSIADES. Will you promise?
PHEIDIPPIDES. All right, I'll promise,
I swear by Dionysos!
STREPSIADES. Then look over here.

[*Father and son get up and leave their beds, which are now removed by* SLAVES. *The setting implicitly shifts: the part of the stage building with door* B *is referred to by Strepsiades in what follows as though it were a nearby house observed from the street.*]

Do you see that little house there, the one with that door?
PHEIDIPPIDES. Yes I see it. But what's the point you're making, father?
STREPSIADES [*with naive awe*]. Clever *souls* live here: it's their Thinking Institute!*
Inside this building are men who say the sky
Is not what it seems—no, it's really a baking-lid
Which curves all round us here, so we're the charcoal.*
These people will teach anyone who pays them a fee
How to argue and win, regardless of right and wrong.
PHEIDIPPIDES. Who *are* these people?
STREPSIADES. I'm not quite sure of their name.
But they're deep-thought-cogitators of highest standing.
PHEIDIPPIDES. Yuck! A load of swine, you mean. They're charlatans,

That pale-faced, shoeless crowd you're referring to—
Like wretched Sokrates and Chairephon!*

STREPSIADES. Shh, shh! Keep quiet! Enough of such childish talk.
If you care at all how your father feeds the family,
Agree to join these men and give up your horses.

PHEIDIPPIDES. Not a chance, by Dionysos! No, not if you gave me
Every one of the pheasants Leogoras rears for himself.*

STREPSIADES. I beg you, please, since you know how dearly
I love you.
Go and be their pupil.

PHEIDIPPIDES [*puzzled*]. But *what* do you want me to learn?

STREPSIADES. It's said they possess a pair of arguments:
The stronger, whatever that is, and also the weaker.*
They say that one of this pair, the weaker, that is,
Can always win a debate with its immoral claims!
So if you learn this immoral way of debating,
Of all the debts I've incurred because of *you*
I'd never repay a single person one obol!*

PHEIDIPPIDES. I'm not prepared to do it. I'd be ashamed
To face the cavalry men with a scoured complexion.*

STREPSIADES. I swear, then, by Demeter I won't be paying
For any more food for you or your fancy horses.*
You can go and rot—you're barred from my house for good!

PHEIDIPPIDES. So what? Uncle Megakles won't allow me to live
Without horses. I'm off. I couldn't care less about *you*. [*Exits through door* A.]

STREPSIADES. Well I've no intention of letting this knock me down.
[*Approaching door* B] I'll pray to the gods then become a student myself
By going to join the Thinking Institute.
[*Hesitating*] Then again, I'm old, forgetful, and rather slow:
Can I really learn their hair-splitting, quibbling speech?
I'm determined to do it. What's keeping me hanging back here?
I'll bang on the door right now. [*Knocks and shouts.*] Hello there! Slave!*

[*A pale-faced figure emerges from door* B.]

STUDENT[A]. To hell with this banging! Who's knocking like this at the door?

STREPSIADES. It's Strepsiades, son of Pheidon—deme Kikynna.*
STUDENT[A]. And an idiot too, by Zeus! You kicked the door
So hard and without any trace of self-reflection
You *aborted* a thought my mind had just discovered!*
STREPSIADES [*naively*]. I'm terribly sorry—I live in the country, you see.
But tell me, please, what it was that was just aborted.
STUDENT[A] [*gravely*]. It's a ritual secret that none but the students may know.
STREPSIADES. It's safe to tell me then: that's why I'm here,
To join the Thinking Institute as a student.
STUDENT[A]. I'll tell you—[*confidentially*] but treat it all as a sacred mystery.
Just the other day, Sokrates asked Chairephon
How many times its foot-length a flea can jump.*
A flea had bitten the eyebrow of Chairephon
Before jumping across, you see, to Sokrates' head.
STREPSIADES [*absorbed*]. Well how did he measure it then?
STUDENT[A]. Oh, *so* astutely.
He melted some wax, then picked up the flea with his hand
And dipped both its feet straight into the puddle of wax:*
When it cooled, there they were—Persian slippers, no less, for the flea!*
He took them off and used them to measure the space.
STREPSIADES. Zeus, king of the gods, such delicate mental powers!
STUDENT[A]. Would you like to hear *another* extraordinary thought
Of Sokrates'?
STREPSIADES. What kind? Yes please, do tell me.
STUDENT[A]. He was asked by Chairephon, of the deme of Sphettos,*
Which view he held on the humming sound of gnats:
Do they sing through the mouth, or is it the rump that they use?
STREPSIADES. And what was Sokrates' answer about the gnat?
STUDENT[A]. He said that the gnat's intestine's extremely narrow
And through this delicate passage the air is forced
Until it makes its way to the animal's rump:
That's where the hollow space at the end of the gut,
The anus that is, releases a forceful blast.

STREPSIADES. A *trumpet* then for an anus, that's what gnats have!
[*Naively*] He's a happy man who knows their innards so well.
He'd find it easy to get acquitted in court
If he knows a gnat's intestines inside out.
STUDENT^{A}. Two days ago Sokrates lost a big idea
Because of a lizard.
STREPSIADES. A lizard? I'd like to hear that.
STUDENT^{A}. He was puzzling over the curving paths of the moon
Across the heavens and gawping up at the sky
When down from the roof in the dark came—a gecko's shit.
STREPSIADES [*laughing*]. I love it! A gecko that shitted on Sokrates!
STUDENT^{A}. Just yesterday we had no food for dinner.
STREPSIADES. I see. What scheme did he use to find you grain?
STUDENT^{A}. He sprinkled a layer of ash across the table
Then bent a spit to serve as compasses—
Then stole a cloak from the gym to pay for the food!*
STREPSIADES [*animated*]. Then why do we think so highly of ancient Thales!*
Open up, open up the Thinking Institute,
Show me Sokrates himself without delay.
I'm longing to be his student. Please open the door.

[STUDENT^{A} *opens door* B, *through which emerges not* SOKRATES, *as anticipated, but a group of* STUDENTS*: engaged in various 'scientific' activities, they take up positions in a kind of tableau.** STREPSIADES *walks round among them.*]

By Herakles, what on earth are these creatures I see?
STUDENT^{A}. Why be so amazed? What d'you think these people look like?
STREPSIADES. Like the captured men from Pylos, the Lakonian lot!*
But why is this group over here staring down at the ground?
STUDENT^{A}. They're seeking the things under ground.*
STREPSIADES. Ah, looking for onions!
No need to continue to worry yourselves about that.

I know where to find some great big lovely ones. [*They ignore him.*]
And what is this group doing here, the ones bent double?
STUDENT[A]. Taking Erebos probes down under Tartaros' realm.*
STREPSIADES [*examining their buttocks*]. Then why is their anus gazing right up at the sky?
STUDENT[A]. It's learning to do astronomy all on its own.
[*Gesturing to group*] Come on inside, in case the master finds you.*
STREPSIADES. Not yet, not yet. Let them stay a moment longer.
I'd like to share with them a problem of mine.
STUDENT[A]. But they're not allowed in the open air like this
Or to hang around outdoors any length of time.

[*The* STUDENTS *go back inside, leaving behind on the ground various pieces of equipment which* STREPSIADES *proceeds to examine.*]

STREPSIADES. In the name of the gods, what's all this stuff? Please tell me.
STUDENT[A]. Well this is astronomy here.
STREPSIADES. And what about this?
STUDENT[A]. That's geometry.
STREPSIADES. What's the *use* of a thing like that?
STUDENT[A]. To measure the earth.
STREPSIADES. For cleruchies, you mean?*
STUDENT[A]. No no, the *whole* of the earth.
STREPSIADES. I like what you're saying!
An ingenious way of helping the people at large.*
STUDENT[A] [*picking up papyrus*]. And this is a map of the whole wide world, you see?*
This is Athens right here.
STREPSIADES [*peering*]. Surely not, I don't believe you:
I can't see *jurors* sitting in court on benches!*
STUDENT[A]. I assure you, look, this is Attika's territory here.
STREPSIADES. Well where are my fellow Kikynnian demesmen then?*
STUDENT[A] [*pointing*]. Somewhere round here. And there's Euboia, you see,*
This long flat strip laid out along the coast.

STREPSIADES. I remember we flattened them once with
Perikles' help!*
But what about Sparta? Where is it?
STUDENT[A]. It's *here*, of course.
STREPSIADES. That's far too close to us! Please change your minds
And move it as far away as you possibly can.
STUDENT[A]. You can't just move it!
STREPSIADES. You'll regret it, by Zeus, if you
don't.

[*At this point a figure whose mask has particularly large, bulging eyes appears over the roof of the stage building suspended from the theatrical 'crane'* (mêchanê) *in a kind of swing.*]

STREPSIADES. Oh, who's this then, this man who's swinging
there?
STUDENT[A]. It's the master!
STREPSIADES. The master?
STUDENT[A]. Yes, Sokrates.
STREPSIADES. *Sokrates*!
Please shout and summon him down on my behalf.
STUDENT[A]. You can call him yourself. I'm far too busy for now.
[*Exits through door* B.]
STREPSIADES [*excited*]. O Sokrates!
[*Ingratiating*] O Sokra*tiddles*!
SOKRATES [*portentously*]. Whose mortal call is that?
STREPSIADES. Tell me first what exactly you're doing. I'd love
to know.
SOKRATES. Air-walking and spinning my thoughts around the sun.*
STREPSIADES. You mean you look down on the gods from up on
your perch?
Why not stay here on the ground?
SOKRATES. I'd never be able
To investigate all higher matters correctly*
Without elevating my intellect and thought
And mixing my delicate mind with the kindred air.
If I studied the things above from down on the ground
I would never have made discoveries, since the earth
Draws down by force the moisture of our thoughts.*
[*Banally*] The phenomenon's just the same with watercress.

STREPSIADES [*baffled*]. You what!
Our thought draws moisture into watercress? [SOKRATES *ignores him.*]
But please come down to see me, o Sokra*tiddles*.
I need you to teach me the things I've come to learn.
SOKRATES. And *what* would that be?
STREPSIADES. I want to learn to *argue*.
I've so many debts, and creditors wild with rage.
They're plundering all I've got and seizing my goods.*
SOKRATES. But how did you fail to *notice* your debts were mounting?
STREPSIADES. A consuming disease—of horses!—afflicted my mind.
Please teach me one of those arguments of yours,
The one that doesn't pay back. And whatever the fee
You charge, I swear by the gods that I'll pay it in full!
SOKRATES. The gods! Which ones will you swear by? We *have* no gods
In the currency of our speech.
STREPSIADES. Then what do you swear by?
[*Joking*] Not *iron* coinage, the way Byzantion does?*
SOKRATES. Would you like to know in clear and rigorous terms
The truth about the gods—
STREPSIADES. By Zeus, if I may!
SOKRATES. And to speak, yes face to face, with the Clouds themselves,
Our own divinities?
STREPSIADES. Yes, I certainly would!

[*By this stage* SOKRATES *has been lowered to the ground; the crane swings back out of sight. The objects used in the following lines are taken from those earlier left behind by the* STUDENTS.]

SOKRATES. Sit down then here on the side of this holy couch.*
STREPSIADES. Right, there, I'm seated.
SOKRATES. Now place upon your head
This wreath.
STREPSIADES. A *wreath*! Why? Crikey, Sokrates,
Don't sacrifice me the way that Athamas was!*

SOKRATES. But these are the ritual acts we have to perform
With our new initiates [*starts sprinkling him with flour*].

STREPSIADES. What's the gain for me?

SOKRATES. You'll become an old hand at speaking—a *floury* talker!*
But please keep still.

STREPSIADES. By Zeus, you're not half right.
If I'm sprinkled all over, I'll soon be a heap of flour!

[SOKRATES *now intones like a priest, in recitative rhythms.*]

SOKRATES. Hold sacred silence now, old man, and hearken to my prayers.
[*Gesturing upwards*] O lord and master, measureless Air, who hold the earth up high!*
O radiant Aither! And goddess Clouds, awesome wielders of thunder and lightning!
Rise up aloft, o mistresses, appear to me—the *thinker*!

STREPSIADES. No, wait—not yet. Let me wrap myself up. I'm afraid of getting drenched!
What a fool I was to leave the house without bringing my dog-skin cap.

SOKRATES. Come to us, venerable Clouds, exhibit yourselves for this man here.
If now you rest on sacred, snow-capped peaks of mount Olympos,
Or plan the sacred dance of Nymphs in father Ocean's gardens,
Or if in vessels of gold you draw up moisture from the Nile,
Or hover above the Maiotian lake or the snowy peak of Mimas—
Receive this sacrifice, enjoy our rites, and heed our prayer.*

[*Part or all of the* CHORUS *of Clouds now appears on the roof of the stage building.** STREPSIADES *and* SOKRATES *can hear their song but not yet see them.*]

[PARODOS: 275–477]

CHORUS. Ever-floating Clouds, *Strophe*
Let us rise aloft, on clear display in our dewy glistening nature,
From deep-echoing waters of father Ocean*
To lofty mountains' pinnacles

Thick-grown with trees, our vantage-point
To see conspicuous hill-tops in the distance
Above the sacred land of irrigated crops
And to hear the numinous rivers' roaring sounds
And the booming roar of the sea.
There the undimmed eye of Aither fills with rays
Of brilliantly dazzling light.
Come, let us shed the rainy cloud-mass
From our immortal form and gaze upon
The earth with our far-seeing eyes.

SOKRATES. O Clouds of majesty immense, you heard my call, it's clear!

[*To* STREPSIADES] Did you hear their voices and how their thunder bellowed with godly power?

STREPSIADES. Oh yes I did, o venerable Clouds, and would like to echo with farts

The sound of the thunder! That's how very much I'm trembling with fear right now!

And if it's allowed, and even if not, I'm starting in fact to shit!

SOKRATES. Don't make crude jokes or fool around like those wretched comic poets.

Keep sacred silence. Our gods are stirring themselves in song again.

CHORUS. Rain-bearing maidens, *Antistrophe*
Let us go to Pallas' lustrous country, to see where stalwart men
Abound in Kekrops' lovely land.*
Where awe of secret rites abides,
Where the home in which the mysteries are housed
Is opened up in sacred ritual acts.*
The heavenly gods receive gifts there as well,
High-roofed temples and glorious statues,
Sacred processions for the blessed ones,
Garlanded sacrifices and feasts for the gods
At every season of the year,
Including springtime's Dionysiac joy
When mellifluous choruses compete
And the pipes' deep-resonant notes resound.*

[*The* CHORUS *members now disappear from the roof of the stage building. They will start gradually to move into view again from line 323 onwards, but this time from an* eisodos, *until they occupy the* orchêstra *behind and around the characters.*]

STREPSIADES. By Zeus, please tell me, Sokrates, who *are* these women I hear,
The ones whose awesome voices those were. Are they heroines from the past?

SOKRATES. Not at all. They're heavenly Clouds, great gods for people of leisure like me.
It's they from whom our intelligence comes, our debating techniques, and our wits,
Our portentous tricks, our circumlocutions, knock-down arguments, clinching retorts.

STREPSIADES [*excited*]. That must be why my soul, now it's heard their voices, starts to take wing
And desires to master subtle words, make vacuous talk about vapour,
Rebut every judgement with views of my own and contradict everyone else!
If you know how to make it happen, I want to behold them face to face.

SOKRATES [*gesturing*]. Look here towards Mount Parnes then.* I can see them floating down
In tranquil silence.

STREPSIADES. Where? Show me where?

SOKRATES. They're approaching in massed formation
Through the wooded glades. Look here, from the sides.

STREPSIADES [*disorientated*]. What on earth are you talking about?
There's nothing to see.

SOKRATES. Through the entrance there.*

STREPSIADES. Ah *now* I can just about see them.

SOKRATES. They're staring you in the face, unless you've got pumpkins in your eyes!

STREPSIADES. There they are, by Zeus! O venerable ones! Now they're filling the place completely.

SOKRATES. Did you really not know or acknowledge before that these Clouds are goddesses true?

STREPSIADES. I had no idea! I used to think they were mist and moisture and steam.

SOKRATES. You don't know then that they keep alive great hordes of *clever* people:
Purveyors of prophecy, medical experts, long-haired signet-ring-wearers,
Composers of intricate dithyramb lyrics, and cheats with their heads in the clouds.
Layabouts like these they keep alive for treating the Clouds as their Muses.*

STREPSIADES. So *that*'s why they wrote 'from moist clouds flash zigzagging bolts of light',
And 'cloudy locks of hundred-headed Typhos', 'gale-blast storms',
And 'airy-moisty squalls', and 'crooked-taloned, air-swimming birds',
And 'floods of rain from saturated clouds'—and in return
They wolfed down gourmet mullet and slices of finest breast of thrush!*

SOKRATES [*pointing to* CHORUS]. And all because of *these*, of course.

STREPSIADES. But tell me, what's the reason
They look exactly like mortal women, if they're really and truly *clouds*?
[*Pointing*] Those ones up there don't look like women.

SOKRATES. Well what do you think they are?

STREPSIADES. I'm not quite sure. They look like pieces of wool that lie stretched out
And not like women, by Zeus! Not even remotely. [*Pointing at* CHORUS] *These* have noses!

SOKRATES. Come on then, answer whatever I ask.

STREPSIADES. Fire away then, ask what you like.

SOKRATES. Have you ever looked up and seen in the sky a cloud resembling a centaur

Or perhaps a leopard, a wolf, or a bull?

STREPSIADES. Yes of course, but why does it matter?

SOKRATES. The Clouds can become whatever they want. So suppose they spot down here

A long-haired brute of the shaggy brigade, like the son of Xenophantos:

In order to mock his crazy looks they assume the shape of centaurs.*

STREPSIADES. And what if they spot a person who filches the public funds, like Simon?*

SOKRATES. Their appearance reflects his nature at once: they take on the shape of wolves!

STREPSIADES. That's why when they saw Kleonymos yesterday, that shield-discarder,*

They thought he was such a colossal coward they turned themselves into deer!

SOKRATES. And when just now they saw Kleisthenes, that's why they turned into women!*

STREPSIADES [*to* CHORUS]. All hail then, goddesses great! Come now, vouchsafe your voice to me

In a crack of sound that will fill the heavens, o queens almighty above!

CHORUS.* Greetings, old man of ancient stock, who seeks out cultured words.

[*To* SOKRATES] And you too, priest of subtle drivel, do tell us what you want:

There's no other sage with head in the clouds whose requests we'd deign to answer—

Well, only Prodikos that's to say, on account of his wisdom and knowledge,*

While *you* we respect for that swaggering walk and the way you twist your eyes,

And your life of discomfort without any shoes and that solemn face in our honour.*

STREPSIADES. O goddess Earth, what sounds they make! So sacred, solemn, portentous!*

SOKRATES. Indeed, for these are the only gods. The rest are a load of old rubbish.

STREPSIADES. But please explain, in the name of Earth: is Olympian Zeus not a god?

SOKRATES. What, *Zeus*! Please stop that twaddle. He doesn't exist.

STREPSIADES. But what do you mean?

Who makes it rain, if it isn't Zeus? Explain that first to me.

SOKRATES [*pointing*]. *They* do, of course! I'll teach you how with some very impressive signs.

Now tell me this: have you ever seen rain that falls from a cloudless sky?

Yet if it was Zeus, he ought to make rain when these Clouds are nowhere around.

STREPSIADES. By Apollo, you've found a perfect way of making your argument fit.

And yet I really used to think it was Zeus who pissed through a sieve.*

But tell me who makes the thunder then, the sort that gives me the jitters.

SOKRATES. It's *these* who thunder by rolling round.

STREPSIADES. But how, audacious thinker?

SOKRATES. It's when they're soaked to the limit with water and compelled to move about

While sagging low all teeming with rain, and then in this heavy state

They collide with one another and make those sounds of cracking and rumbling.

STREPSIADES. But *who* is it then who compels them to move, well isn't it Zeus himself?

SOKRATES. Not at all! It's the swirl of the atmosphere.*

STREPSIADES. The swirl? It was lost on me

That Zeus just doesn't exist but instead it's Swirl that rules the world.

But you haven't yet taught me exactly how the rumble and thunder occurs.

SOKRATES. Are you deaf? I told you it's when the clouds are brimming full of water

Then bang into each other and rumble because they're so compressed.

STREPSIADES. But how do I know I can trust what you say?

SOKRATES. I'll explain from you yourself.
Have you ever been full of broth at the Panathenaia then felt your stomach*
Start churning round and a sudden roar goes whooshing through your insides?

STREPSIADES. By Apollo, not half! And straight away there's a furious churned up feeling
And just like thunder the lovely broth keeps rumbling in ominous tones.
It starts quite low, 'pah-pah pah-pah', then grows into 'pa-pa-pa-paaaah'!
By the time I *shit*, it's outright thunder, 'pa-pa-pa-PAAAAH', like them.

SOKRATES. Well think what a noisy fart is produced by this tiny stomach of yours.
But the air up there is endless, so how could thunder not be so loud?*
You must admit that the sounds themselves are remarkably like one another.*

STREPSIADES. But tell me now the source of thunderbolts that gleam with fire
And turn to cinders the people they strike, though a lucky few are just singed.
It's clear that *Zeus* wields thunderbolts against all perjurers here.

SOKRATES. What a fool you are! You reek of the age of Kronos, you blethering fool!*
If Zeus strikes perjurers, why has he never sent Simon up in flames,
And why not Kleonymos, why not Theoros, perjurers through and through?*
Instead he strikes his very own temple, and 'Sounion, headland of Athens',*
And very tall oaks—but *why* do that? No oak tree perjures itself!

STREPSIADES. I can't answer that. You seem to be right. But what *is* a thunderbolt then?

SOKRATES. Well, when a dry wind blows up on high and is locked inside these clouds,
It fills them with air just like a bladder and then with pure compulsion
Makes it burst back out with violent force on account of its great compression,
And because of the rushing, whirring motion the air ignites itself.*

STREPSIADES. By Zeus, I had this same experience once at the Diasia.*
I was roasting an animal's stomach for all my kinsmen but failed to slit it.
It had filled with air and all of a sudden it burst right down the middle
And squirted shit in both my eyes and left my face all burnt.

[*The* CHORUS-LEADER *now approaches* STREPSIADES.]

LEADER. O mortal man who's set your heart upon our greatest wisdom,
The people of Athens and all of Greece will deem you to be happy
If your memory's good and your intellect too and you're tough enough to endure
All manner of mental exercise without flagging or getting sore feet
And you don't much mind feeling cold or depend on a meal at the start of the day
And can do without wine and athletic pursuits and the rest of a life of folly
And you think, as the smartest people do, that the most important thing
Is to win every battle in life through action, through scheming, through use of your tongue!

STREPSIADES. As far as toughness of mind's concerned, or worries that trouble my sleep,
Or leading a stingy life with a stomach that's fed on no more than sour herbs,
You can count on me, don't worry—I'll take all the blows and the poundings you like!

SOKRATES. Will you undertake to recognize no other gods than we do,
So the Chaos of space, the Clouds, and Tongue—no others but just these three?*

STREPSIADES. I won't speak a word to the rest of the gods, even if I meet them in person!
I won't sacrifice or pour libations or burn incense on their altars.

LEADER. Be candid then and tell us what you'd like from us. You'll obtain it
If you show us honour and awe, and strive to be always a person who's *smart*.

STREPSIADES. O goddesses great, there's just one tiny thing I want from you:
To be the finest speaker in all of Greece by a million miles!

LEADER. You'll have this gift for sure from us. From now for all the future
There'll be no politician who wins more Assembly votes than you.

STREPSIADES. It's not Assembly proposals I want to make. That's not my wish.
I want to twist the law in court and evade my creditors' grasp.

LEADER. You'll receive, then, what you crave. This desire of yours is certainly modest.
You must place yourself with confidence in the care of our servants here.

STREPSIADES. I'll put my trust in you and do what you say. I've no real choice,
It's all because of those thoroughbred horses and a marriage that's worn me out.*
[*Excited*] Now let these people do what they want.
This body of mine I'll put in their hands:
They can flog me, starve me, subject me to thirst,
Make me shrivel and shiver and flay my skin,
Provided I'm free from my debts for good
And come to be thought by everyone else
As brash, slick-talking, audacious, assertive,
Revolting to deal with, deviser of falsehoods,
A spinner of words, an old hand round the courts,
A quoter, a yapper, a fox and a wriggler,
A schemer, duplicitous, oily and phoney,

A rogue and disgusting, a twister and cheat,
A lip-smacking creep!*
If these are the names I'm called everywhere,
Then let these people do what they must,
And if they want
By Demeter they're free to serve me up
As sausage for all these thinkers!

[*The whole* CHORUS *bursts into song and* STREPSIADES *responds in song*: 457–75.]

CHORUS. What spirited pride is his!
No shrinking back, all's ready for action.
[*To* STREPSIADES] Be sure of this:
If you learn from me, then sky-high glory
Will be yours among all mortals.

STREPSIADES. What will happen to me?

CHORUS. For ever with me
You'll lead the most enviable life
Of the whole human race.

STREPSIADES. Is it really the case that
I'll see this happen?

CHORUS. You'll actually find
Great crowds at your doors,
Sitting there day and night,
Wanting to consult you
And engage in discussion
About problems and lawsuits
With large sums at stake—
All well worth your thought
When they seek your advice!*

LEADER (*to* SOKRATES). You must now take steps to prepare the old man for the things you intend to teach him.
Make sure you activate his mind and test his mental powers.

[*The* CHORUS *now moves back to the edge of the* orchêstra*; the characters return to spoken dialogue.*]

SOKRATES. Right then, disclose the type of person you are.
Once I know what this is, I'll use new mechanisms
To bring to bear and break your defences down.*

STREPSIADES [*alarmed*]. What d'you mean? It sounds like a plan for siege warfare!

SOKRATES. Not at all but I need to ask you a few short questions. Is your memory good?

STREPSIADES. It depends, I've got two kinds.
If I'm owed some money, my memory couldn't be better.
But if I'm the miserable debtor, it couldn't be worse.

SOKRATES. Do you have any natural talent for using words?

STREPSIADES. No talent for words at all—but I'm good at *stealing*!

SOKRATES. Well how are you going to learn?

STREPSIADES. Don't worry, with ease.

SOKRATES. Let's see. If I toss you a clever conundrum to solve
About higher matters, then try to grasp it at once.

STREPSIADES. Do you mean I should gnaw it the way a dog does a bone?

SOKRATES. This man's a fool and a philistine all in one!
I suspect, old man, that a thrashing is what you need.
Let's see. What d'you do when you're hit?

STREPSIADES [*feebly*]. I accept the blows,
Then I wait a moment and start to shout for a witness.
Then I leave it a little while longer and bring a charge.*

SOKRATES. Well now, take off your cloak.

STREPSIADES. Have I done something wrong?

SOKRATES. It's just our custom to wear few clothes inside.

[*He starts a surreptitious body search under* STREPSIADES' *cloak*.]

STREPSIADES [*resisting*]. I'm not coming to look for stolen goods, you know.*

SOKRATES. Take it *off*! Stop all this chatter.

STREPSIADES. Just tell me this:
If I try my best and am eager to learn your teachings,
Which student of yours will I turn out to resemble?

SOKRATES. You'll be no different from Chairephon, that's who.*

STREPSIADES. That's *not* what I wanted, the prospect of being half-dead!

SOKRATES [*removing the cloak*]. Just stop this babble and follow me here inside
Without further delay.

STREPSIADES [*anxiously*]. But I need to protect myself
By holding a cake to placate any dangerous forces.
It's as scary as going inside Trophonios' cave!*
SOKRATES. Come straight inside. Stop hanging around at the door.

[*Both exit through door* B.]

[PARABASIS: 510–626]

CHORUS. Farewell to you
For the manly courage you're showing!

May all good fortune follow
This man. Despite the fact
Of advancing years
His nature's assuming
A youthful lustre
As he practises wisdom!

LEADER [*stepping forward to address the audience*].
Spectators, I'm going to speak my mind to you candidly
And truthfully, in the name of Dionysos who reared me!*
As surely as I wish to win the prize and be thought a clever poet,
It was because I believed you *sophisticated* spectators
And took this comedy to be the cleverest of all my plays
That I deemed it right for you to be the first to savour a work
That caused me so much effort. Yet I left the theatre defeated*
By vulgar rivals, an ignominious fate! That's why I blame you,
You 'clever' spectators, for all the trouble this caused me.
Even so, I'll never willingly betray the sophisticated among you.
Ever since in this theatre some men it's a pleasure to mention
Gave such acclaim to two figures (one bashful, the other an arsehole)
And I, like an unmarried girl not yet allowed to give birth,
Had to expose my baby and another girl took it for herself,
And *you* were the ones who reared and trained it so proudly*—
Since then, I've had a firm pledge of your intelligent judgement.
Well, just like the famous Elektra, this present comedy
Came on a quest in search of such clever spectators:
She'll recognize, if she ever sees it, the lock of her brother's hair!*

And consider how bashful this play of mine is. To begin with,
It didn't come before you with a leather appendage dangling
With a big red tip, the thickest sort, to make the small boys laugh.*
It didn't crack jokes about bald men, nor drag in obscene dances,
It didn't produce an old man who spoke his lines while using a stick
To strike somebody and stop you noticing the lousy humour.
It didn't rush on stage waving torches and shrieking 'alarm, alarm!'*
Instead it's come before you relying on its own poetic merits.
And although that's the sort of poet I am, I don't give myself airs and graces,
Nor do I try to cheat you by staging the same stuff again and again,
But I always display my cleverness by bringing you new forms of humour
No two of which are the same—and they're all so sophisticated.
I'm the one who, when Kleon was at his height, struck him hard in the belly
Yet couldn't bring myself to jump back on him once I'd knocked him flat.*
But these other poets, ever since they got hold of Hyperbolos,
Won't leave the poor sod alone: they keep trampling him and his mother.*
Eupolis started it, dragging his character Marikas on stage
And making a right botched job of reworking my own play *Knights*.
All for the sake of an obscene dance he added a drunk old woman:
But Phrynichos did this long ago in the scene with the hungry sea-monster.
Then Hermippos wrote another play making fun of Hyperbolos*
And by now all the rest are grinding out plays making fun of Hyperbolos
As well as copying an eel-fishing simile all my own invention.*
So, whoever laughs at such poets should take no pleasure in work of *mine*.
But if it's me and my comic inventions which give you delight,

You'll always be thought to have very high standards of judgement.

Strophe

High and mighty among the gods,
Zeus their ruler: he's the first I summon
In all his greatness to witness my dance.
Second the trident's powerful keeper,*
Who makes the earth and briny sea
Heave with his raw power.
I also call our father of great renown,
Aither the most majestic, life-giver for all.
And finally the celestial charioteer*
Who bathes in rays of unequalled light
The whole earth's surface—divinity great
Among gods and mortals.

LEADER. You clever spectators, concentrate and give us your full attention please.
We feel that we've been wronged by you and wish to make our grievance heard.
Of all divinities we're the ones who lend the city the maximum help
Yet we're the only ones to whom no sacrifice or libation comes,
Even though it's us who keep you safe. Suppose you send an expedition
That makes no sense, we let you know with thunder loud or pouring rain.*
Or when the Paphlagonian tanner, that god-forsaken man himself,
Received your votes to serve as general, we drew our eyebrows sharply down
And made our anger plain to all: 'the lightning and the thunder cracked'.*
The moon was seen to wander from its usual paths, the sun as well
Extinguished its lamp and drew itself abruptly into self-concealment:
It threatened its light would never more shine on you if Kleon became a general.
Yet you went ahead and elected him. They say this city's afflicted with

A habit of taking rash decisions, but nonetheless the gods themselves
Redeem your blunders and turn things round to make them always work out fine.
To show that's true in the present case too is easy for us to demonstrate.
If Kleon the cormorant glutton's found guilty of taking bribes and embezzlement too,
And if you fasten him into the stocks and tighten his neck as much as you can,*
There'll be a return to the good old days and you'll find your blunders have been reversed.
The city's affairs will turn out fine, its future fortunes will be assured.

CHORUS. All hail, in turn, Lord Phoibos, *Antistrophe*
Delian god, who occupies Kynthos,*
The island's high-horned rock.
You too, blessed deity whose golden dwelling*
Is on Ephesos, where the Lydian girls
Worship you unstintingly.
You too, our own local goddess,
Charioteer of the aigis, Athena of the Akropolis.*
And you who occupy Parnassos'
Rock and gleam amid pine-wood torches,
Conspicuous among the bacchants of Delphi,
Reveller Dionysos!

LEADER. We were just preparing to start our journey and come down here to visit this place
When the moon encountered us and asked us to bring you all a message from her.
She told us first to greet the Athenian people and all their allies as well.
But she also said she's angry with you. She claims you've made her suffer a lot
Despite the manifest ways in which she helps the lives of one and all.
For a start her light saves money for you, at least a drachma on torches per month,

So on leaving the house when evening comes you all look round and are able to say:
'No need to purchase a torch, my slave, since the light of the Moon is shining so bright'.
She helps you in other ways too, she insists, but you've let your calendar get out of joint.
You break the regular pattern of days and throw everything into total confusion.*
And then it's the Moon herself at whom the rest of the gods keep making their threats
When they turn up for dinner and find it's not there and have to go home on an empty stomach
Because their festivals haven't occurred on the days when the calendar states they should.
At the times assigned for sacrifice, you're torturing slaves and holding trials.*
But at *other* times, when we the gods decide to abstain from eating food
Because of our grief for fallen heroes, the likes of Memnon or Sarpedon,*
You pour libations in festive mirth. And that's the reason Hyperbolos
When allotted to sacred office this year was punished by us the gods above:
His garland was blown right off his head! That way he'll learn his lesson for good,
To obey the dictates of the Moon in the way she orders the days of life.*

[*The* CHORUS *moves back to the sides of the* orchêstra. SOKRATES *now re-emerges from door* B, *gesturing with frustration as he does so.*]

SOKRATES. In the name of Respiration, of Chaos, and Air!*
I've never in all my life met a bumpkin like this,
So helpless in every respect, so crass and forgetful!
When you try to teach him the merest little trifles
He forgets them in no time at all. But nevertheless
I'll ask him to come here outside back into the daylight.
[*Calling at door*] Hoy, Strepsiades! Come out, and bring your bed.

[STREPSIADES *emerges from door* B, *struggling with the same couch/bed he was made to sit on at 254 ff. He is now scantily clad, without the cloak and shoes he wore in the previous scene.*]

STREPSIADES. It's hard to carry, with so many bedbugs to fight!
SOKRATES. Get a move on there. Put it down. Pay attention.
STREPSIADES. Okay.
SOKRATES. Right then, what's the first thing you'd really *like* to learn?
Choose a subject you've never been taught before. Well, what?
Perhaps about metrical units, or verses, or rhythms?*
STREPSIADES. About units of measure. That's good. Just a few days ago
I was cheated of two whole units by a barley-seller.
SOKRATES. Not *that* kind of unit! I mean: what's your favourite *metre*?
Is it three-measure verses or four-measure verses you like?*
STREPSIADES. I'd choose half a bushel of barley—there's nothing to beat it.
SOKRATES. What on earth are you talking about?
STREPSIADES. I bet you I'm right.
What else is a four-measure unit if not a half-bushel?
SOKRATES. To hell with you! What a bumpkin and cretin you are!
[*Sarcastically*] You'll learn about rhythms in no time at all, that's clear.
STREPSIADES. But what use are rhythms to me, compared to barley?
SOKRATES. It'll help to make you modish on social occasions
If you show you know exactly what kind of rhythm
The 'military beat' or the 'bending finger' is.*
STREPSIADES. The bending finger? By Zeus, that's easy.
SOKRATES. Well tell me.
STREPSIADES. What else but making a naughty gesture like this?*
When I was a boy, all those years ago, we loved it!
SOKRATES. How crude and vulgar!
STREPSIADES. You seem to be missing the point.
It's not rhythms I want to learn.
SOKRATES. Well *what* is it, then?

STREPSIADES. What I mentioned before: that immoral way of debating.

SOKRATES. But you need to learn other things first. Now here's an example:
Which animals rightly belong to the masculine gender?*

STREPSIADES. I know all the masculine ones. Any fool knows that!
The ram, the goat, the bull, the dog, and the cock-fowl.

SOKRATES. You see what you're doing? The word for cock you've used
Is the same one you always use for hens as well.

STREPSIADES. Is that really so?

SOKRATES. But of course: you say 'cock' for both.*

STREPSIADES. By Poseidon, that's right! Well, what should I say then instead?

SOKRATES. Cock*ess*, you should say, and call the male a he-cock.

STREPSIADES. Cock*ess*? How I like that word, by your god the Air!*
You've taught me something already that makes me grateful:
I'll repay you by giving you grain for your kneading-trough.

SOKRATES. You're doing the same again. A kneading-trough
Is a feminine noun but the ending's wrong.

STREPSIADES. How come?
Am I making it masculine instead?

SOKRATES. Exactly.
It's just the same with Kleonymos.*

STREPSIADES. What? Explain.

SOKRATES. He's a feminine thing that's given a masculine name!

STREPSIADES. But you'll find Kleonymos used no kneading-trough.
[*Gesturing obscenely*] He used himself as a pestle inside a round mortar!*
Well how should I change my language in future?

SOKRATES. It's simple.
Say a 'kneading-trough*ess*', so it serves as a feminine noun.

STREPSIADES. A kneading-trough*ess*?

SOKRATES. Yes, that makes your grammar correct.

STREPSIADES. So it's kneading-trough*ess*—and Kleonym*ess* as well.

SOKRATES. But there's more besides you must learn on the gender of names,
Dividing masculine forms from the feminine ones.

STREPSIADES. I know all the feminine ones.

SOKRATES. Well tell me them then.

STREPSIADES. Lysilla, Philinna, Kleitagora, Demetria.

SOKRATES. Now give me the masculine ones.

STREPSIADES. There are thousands of those.
Philoxenos, Melesias, Ameinias.

SOKRATES. How hopeless you are! But *those* are not masculine names.

STREPSIADES. Do you people really not think so?

SOKRATES. We certainly don't.
Well how would you greet Ameinias if you met him?

STREPSIADES. It's obvious, isn't it? 'Hoy there, Ameinia!'*

SOKRATES. You see? That's a woman's name—Amein*ia*.

STREPSIADES. Well it serves him right for dodging military service!*
But what am I learning this for? It's all common knowledge.

SOKRATES. Never mind. But lie down here instead.

STREPSIADES. What for?

SOKRATES. It's time to think very deeply about your problems.*

STREPSIADES. No, please, I beg you, not here. If I really must,
Let me lie on the ground if I need to use deep thought.

SOKRATES. You've got no choice.

STREPSIADES. What a miserable prospect's in store.
These bedbugs will punish me here for the rest of the day!

[SOKRATES *goes back into the School.* STREPSIADES *lies down but immediately begins to writhe around in discomfort. The* CHORUS *moves forward into the* orchêstra *and surrounds his bed as it sings the following.*]

CHORUS. Use concentrated thought and vision. *Strophe*
In every way intensify yourself
Then let your mind spin. If you fall into

Perplexity, jump straight to a different
Train of thought. Make sure that sleep,
With its soothing sweetness, shuns your eyes.

STREPSIADES. Aaaaaaaaargh! Aaaaaaaaargh!
CHORUS. What troubles you? What ails you?*
STREPSIADES. I'm in deep distress and pain. Inside this bed
There's a horde of biting bugs—Korinthian ones!*
[*Chanting*] My ribs they're devouring,
My life-blood they're drinking,
My testicles they're lacerating,
My anus they're excavating,
And they're going to finish me off!
CHORUS. Don't let the pain wear you down too much.
STREPSIADES. But how can I not when
My property's gone, my complexion's gone,
My soul has gone and my shoes have gone,*
And piled on top of all these woes
Awake all night like a singing watchman
I'm almost a total goner!

[*The* CHORUS *steps back again, apart from the* LEADER. SOKRATES *now re-enters and stands menacingly over* STREPSIADES' *bed.*]

SOKRATES. Well what are you up to? I hope you're *thinking*.
STREPSIADES. What me?
By Poseidon, I am!
SOKRATES. Then tell me what thoughts you've had.
STREPSIADES. I've been asking myself if the bedbugs will leave me alive.
SOKRATES [*turning aside*]. You deserve to die!
STREPSIADES. But I'm already dead in this bed.
LEADER. You mustn't give up. Just cover yourself with the bedding.
You need to discover the mental techniques to cheat
And defraud.
STREPSIADES. I can't! Who'd find clever thoughts of cheating
While lying beneath a pile of sheepskin covers?

[STREPSIADES *disappears under the bedding.* SOKRATES *ponders the bed for a moment before speaking again.*]

SOKRATES. Right then, let me make a fresh start and see what he's doing.*
Hey you, are you sleeping?

STREPSIADES [*peering out*]. By Apollo I'm certainly not.

SOKRATES. Have you *grasped* anything?

STREPSIADES. Not at all.

SOKRATES. What, nothing whatever?

STREPSIADES. The one thing I've grasped is my prick—under here in my hand!

SOKRATES. Well cover your head, get on with it: start some *thinking*.

STREPSIADES. Start thinking of what? Please give me some hints, Sokrates.

SOKRATES. Discover the subject yourself and say what you want.

STREPSIADES. I've told you a million times what I really want—
To avoid ever having to pay back the money I borrowed!

SOKRATES. Well cover yourself, then release and refine your thoughts
Before gradually thinking your way around the problem,
Making careful divisions and probes.

STREPSIADES [*wriggling around*]. Oh no, please help me!

SOKRATES. Keep still. If you find your ideas have reached a dead end,
Let them go, turn back round. Then using your full mental powers
Reactivate your thought and weigh up the problem.

STREPSIADES [*popping up*]. Dear Sokratiddles, I've got it!

SOKRATES. Got what, old man?

STREPSIADES. A thought that will cheat my creditors out of their interest.

SOKRATES. Explain it to me.

STREPSIADES. Well give me your view.

SOKRATES. Of what?

STREPSIADES. Suppose I hire a Thessalian sorceress*

And get her to draw down the moon from the sky at night.
Then I'd lock the moon away in a big round case,
Just like a mirror, and guard it with all my care.

SOKRATES. What possible good would this do you?

STREPSIADES. The point, you see,
Is that if the moon never rose in the sky again,
I'd never pay back all the interest.

SOKRATES. But why ever not?

STREPSIADES. Because the money is lent on a monthly basis!

SOKRATES. What a wonderful trick! Let me give you another conundrum.
Suppose you were taken to court for the sum of five talents.*
Tell me how you'd manage to have the charge wiped out.

STREPSIADES. How to have it wiped out? I don't know. But I'll search for the answer.

SOKRATES [*encouraging*]. Don't always keep your mind cooped up inside you,
But release your thoughts to float in the air above
Like a beetle whose foot you've tied with a piece of string.*

STREPSIADES. I've found it, the cleverest way of annulling the charge!
I'm sure you'll agree yourself this is good.

SOKRATES. What is it?

STREPSIADES. Do you know that thing which medicine-sellers possess?
You've surely seen it—that lovely, translucent stone
With which they kindle fire?

SOKRATES. You're talking of glass?*

STREPSIADES. That's it! Well suppose I got hold of this object myself,
Then when the clerk of the court was writing the charge
[*gesturing*] I stood to one side like this and facing the sun
Used the glass to melt the writing which spells out the charge?*

SOKRATES. What cleverness, by the Graces!

STREPSIADES. And what a relief
That a five-talent charge against me has been wiped out!

SOKRATES. Let's see how quickly you grasp this too.

STREPSIADES. What is it?

SOKRATES. Think how you'd challenge a lawsuit with one of your own
If it seemed you were going to lose and you had no witness.
STREPSIADES. That's easy, no problem at all!
SOKRATES. Well how?
STREPSIADES. I'll tell you.
I'd wait till the very last case before my own
Then before I was called I'd—run off and hang myself!
SOKRATES. That's no answer at all.
STREPSIADES. I assure you it certainly is.
I won't be tried in court once they find that I'm dead!
SOKRATES. What nonsense! Get lost! I'm tired of trying to teach you.
STREPSIADES. But what's the matter? Please carry on, Sokrates.
SOKRATES. But you keep forgetting whatever you've started to learn.
Look: what was the *first* thing I taught you? Just tell me that.
STREPSIADES [*straining*]. Let me see, the *first*, what was it? Oh, what was first?
What's the thing in which we knead our barley grain?
Oh dear, what was it?
SOKRATES. Just go to the crows and rot!*
You're the most forgetful and stupid old man in the world!

[SOKRATES *moves away in frustration but remains within earshot*.]

STREPSIADES [*to himself*]. Oh no, I'm doomed! What's now in store for me?
I'm ruined for failing to learn all these tongue-twisting words.
[*To* CHORUS] Please, Clouds, I need you to give me some helpful advice.
LEADER. Our advice to you, old fellow, would be as follows.
If you happen to have a son you've reared at home,
Send *him* instead of yourself to learn in this school.
STREPSIADES. I certainly *do*—he's a fine and handsome young man.
But he simply refuses to learn, so what can I do?
LEADER. And you let him say no?
STREPSIADES. He's bigger and stronger than me,
And he comes from a line of preening Koisyra-like women.*

Still, I'll try to fetch him. And if he refuses to come,
I'll ban him for ever from living at home with me.
[*To* SOKRATES] So wait inside for a while till I come back here.

[STREPSIADES *exits through door* A. SOKRATES *stays on stage at first: the whole* CHORUS *comes into the* orchêstra *and addresses the following song to him.*]

CHORUS. Do you realize how many rewards *Antistrophe**
You're about to derive from us alone
Among the gods? This fellow's ready
To do whatever you instruct him.
Recognizing the man's deranged
And patently overexcited,
Be sure you fleece him as much as you can
And don't delay: things like this tend
To take an unexpected turn.

[*As the* CHORUS *moves back to the side of the* orchêstra, SOKRATES *now departs through door* B, *just a moment before* STREPSIADES *re-emerges from door* A, *angrily dragging* PHEIDIPPIDES *behind him.*]

STREPSIADES. By the goddess Mist, you're not staying *here* any longer!*
Go to Megakles' colonnades and live off *his* wealth.*

PHEIDIPPIDES. Good heavens above! I don't know what's wrong with you, father.
You're out of your mind, I swear by Olympian Zeus!

STREPSIADES [*laughing*]. Just listen to that, 'Olympian Zeus'! How stupid
To go on believing in Zeus when fully grown up!

PHEIDIPPIDES. What's making you laugh like this?

STREPSIADES. The thought of you
Being still such a baby and holding such primitive views.
[*Wheedling*] But come back here and learn some special knowledge.
I'll tell you a thing which will make you a *man* when you learn it.
[*Confidentially*] Only take great care not to share this with anyone else.

PHEIDIPPIDES. All right, what is it?

STREPSIADES. You swore by Zeus just now.

PHEIDIPPIDES. I certainly did.

STREPSIADES. Well I'll show you how useful is knowledge.
Zeus doesn't exist, Pheidippides!

PHEIDIPPIDES. He *doesn't*?

STREPSIADES. It's Swirl who's driven Zeus out and is ruling the world.*

PHEIDIPPIDES. What disgusting drivel!

STREPSIADES. I assure you it's all quite true.

PHEIDIPPIDES. Who claims all this?

STREPSIADES. It's Sokrates from Melos*
And Chairephon—who knows how to track fleas' feet.*

PHEIDIPPIDES. Have you gone quite out of your mind? You surely don't
Believe such crazy lunatics?

STREPSIADES. Watch your words!
Don't dare abuse these men: they're really clever
And full of intelligent thoughts. They don't waste money
On grooming their hair or rubbing themselves with good oil
Or going to wash in the baths.* Whereas you, by contrast,
Are washing my *life* down the drain with the money you waste.
[*Pointing to door* B] Please go in there and be taught for your father's sake.

PHEIDIPPIDES. But what could I learn from these men that would be any use?

STREPSIADES. Do you need to ask? They teach all human wisdom.
They'll lead you to know yourself—how you're stupid and thick!*
But wait for me here just a moment until I come back. [*Exits into door* A.]

PHEIDIPPIDES. What on earth should I do? My father's lost his wits.
Should I get a court order and have him declared insane?*
Or even prepare for his death and order his coffin?

[STREPSIADES *returns with a* SLAVE *who is carrying both a cock and a hen.*]

STREPSIADES. Let's see then. What do you call this bird? Please tell me.

PHEIDIPPIDES. It's a cock.

STREPSIADES. Okay, that's fine. But what about *this*?

PHEIDIPPIDES. It's also a cock.

STREPSIADES. The same? What ludicrous nonsense!
You need to know better in future. Call this one here
A cock*ess*, and refer to the other one there as a he-cock.

PHEIDIPPIDES. Cockess! Are *these* the ingenious things that you learnt
From your recent visit in there to those ancient clods?

STREPSIADES. They taught me lots more besides. But whatever I learnt
I kept forgetting at once because I'm so old.

PHEIDIPPIDES. And is that the reason you've lost your cloak as well?*

STREPSIADES. It's not true that I've *lost* it. It's just that I've *thought* it away.

PHEIDIPPIDES. And your shoes as well? What's happened to those, you fool?

STREPSIADES. As Perikles said—I lost them 'for special reasons'.*
But come along, please, let's go. Just humour your father,
No matter if right or wrong. [*Wheedling*] I humoured *you*
When you were no more than a lisping child of six.
With the very first obol I earned for jury service
I bought you a little toy cart for the Diasia.*

PHEIDIPPIDES. I assure you you'll live to regret this action one day.

STREPSIADES. Well done for obeying.
[*Calling into door* B.] Come out here, Sokrates,
Come out! I've brought this son of mine here with me.
It was hard to persuade him.

[SOKRATES *emerges and glances quickly at* PHEIDIPPIDES.]

SOKRATES. No wonder, he looks so childish!
It'll be hard work to teach him the ropes round here.

PHEIDIPPIDES. You could do with a rope yourself—to be strung up!

STREPSIADES. To hell with you! How dare you curse your teacher?

SOKRATES. Just listen, 'strung up'! What a babyish voice he's got:

He pronounces his words with his lips all hanging apart.
No hope he'll learn to win an acquittal in court
Or how to bring summons or use persuasive bluster.
Then again, *Hyperbolos* learnt these things—for a talent.*

STREPSIADES. Never mind, just teach him. You'll find he's an eager learner.
While still a tiny child, [*sentimentally*] no higher than this,
He used to make clay houses and carve little boats,
He also made little toy carts from pieces of fig-wood,
And frogs out of pomegranate peel, just imagine!
So get him to learn that pair of arguments here,
The stronger, whichever that is, and the weaker as well,
The one whose immoral claims can knock out the stronger.
If he can't learn both, it's the immoral one he must learn!

SOKRATES. He'll learn himself from the arguments in person.
I won't be here. [*Starts to exit through door* B.]

STREPSIADES. Well please remember this,
Make sure that he learns to rebut all rightful claims!

[*From door* B *there now emerges* MORAL, *soon followed by* IMMORAL. *From 889 to 948 they exchange short lines in 'recitative' mode, chanted to the accompaniment of the pipe-player.* STREPSIADES *and* PHEIDIPPIDES *observe the whole confrontation.*]*

MORAL. Come over here then! Show yourself
To the audience there. What an impudent thing!

IMMORAL. Go wherever you want! The bigger the crowd
The more I'll argue you into the ground.

MORAL. What *you*?

IMMORAL. With my words.

MORAL. But you're weaker than me.

IMMORAL. All the same I'll defeat
One who makes the claim that he's stronger than me.

MORAL. What's your clever trick then?

IMMORAL. I have *new* ideas I've discovered myself.

MORAL. Well such things only flourish
[*gesturing at audience*] On account of these idiots sitting in front of us here.

IMMORAL. But these people are *clever*.

MORAL. I'll tear you to shreds.

IMMORAL. And how will you do it?

MORAL. By making just claims.

IMMORAL. But I'll knock them all down and refute them as well.
I don't even admit that Justice exists!*

MORAL. You deny she exists?

IMMORAL. Show me where she is then!

MORAL. She lives with the gods.

IMMORAL. Well if Justice exists how is it that Zeus
Hasn't been destroyed for binding in chains
His very own father?*

MORAL. Ugh! Listen to this
Disgusting stuff. You make me puke!

IMMORAL. A deranged and senile wreck you are!

MORAL. A gaping, shaming arsehole you are!

IMMORAL. These names smell like roses to me.

MORAL. Buffoon!

IMMORAL. A garland of lilies.

MORAL. You father-beater!

IMMORAL. You bedeck me with gold but just don't know it.

MORAL. In the past this 'gold' was regarded as lead.

IMMORAL. But now such abuse is adornment to me.

MORAL. You impudent scoundrel!

IMMORAL. You archaic relic!

MORAL. It's all your fault
That the young won't go to normal school.
One day all Athens will recognize
The things you teach your foolish pupils.

IMMORAL. You're shrivelled and ugly.

MORAL. While *you* grow rich.
Yet in the past you were just a beggar,
Like Mysian Telephos, you claimed,
With a pouch from which
You nibbled the maxims of Pandeletos.*

IMMORAL. Ah yes, what wisdom—

MORAL. Oh no, what madness—

IMMORAL. . . . you're talking about.

MORAL. . . . is displayed by the city
That nurtures you
To drip poison into the minds of the young.

IMMORAL. An old dotard like you won't teach this young man.
MORAL. But he certainly needs to be protected
From learning no more than *your* sort of prattle.

[IMMORAL *and* MORAL *both try to draw* PHEIDIPPIDES *over to their side; a brief scuffle develops.*]

IMMORAL. Come here to me, leave this luny alone.
MORAL I'll make you suffer if you touch this boy.
LEADER. You must stop this fighting and all this abuse.
Expound instead
[*to* MORAL] The way you taught in olden times
[*to* IMMORAL] And you in turn
Your new education. He'll hear the debate
And go to the school he decides is the best.
MORAL. I'm willing to do this.
IMMORAL. And I'm willing too.
LEADER. Very well. Now which of you's going to speak first?
IMMORAL. I'll let *him* go first.
Whatever he chooses to say in his speech
I'll use locutions new and fancy
And clever thoughts to shoot him down.
By the end, if he dares to mutter a protest,
He'll find his face and both his eyes
Are covered in stings, as though by wasps.
My ideas will finish him off!

[AGON I: 949–1104]

CHORUS. They'll show us now, confident in *Strophe*
Their ever so clever
Arguments and deepest thoughts
And mind-shaped ponderings,
Which of the two will
Prove the superior speaker.
Now is the time and place
For a dangerous gamble with wisdom:
These friends of mine are facing
The greatest contest of all.

LEADER [*to* MORAL]. O you who crowned our ancestors with many noble virtues,
Break into speech of the kind you enjoy and describe your nature to us.

MORAL. I'll tell you then the kind of education that once prevailed
When I flourished for holding upright views and self-control was a virtue.
No child would ever be heard, for one thing, indulging in whining complaints.
When going to music lessons, moreover, they walked through the streets in good order,*
A group from each neighbourhood—lightly clad too, no matter how heavy the snow.
They were trained to learn their songs by heart (and no fooling around with their thingies!),*
Such as 'Pallas, fearsome sacker of cities' or 'Far-travelling cry of the lyre':*
They sang these songs to traditional tunes which their fathers had handed on down.
If a boy at that time ever monkeyed around and twisted a tune out of key
The way that they do everywhere these days, like Phrynis's frightful contortions,*
He would have been thrashed repeatedly for spoiling the work of the Muses.
In the wrestling school all boys were expected to sit on the floor with legs crossed*
To avoid giving onlookers even a glimpse of things that might cause their eyes torment.
When he stood up again, each boy was required to smooth the sand back over
To make sure he left no trace of his manhood for lovers to stand and observe.
No boy in those days ever rubbed with oil the parts beneath his navel;
They let their genitals glisten with down, all dewy, just like that on quinces.

And none of them used a sexy softness of voice in speaking to lovers
Or played the part of pimps for themselves with their eyes when walking along.
When eating dinner they weren't allowed to take the head of a radish
Nor to grab some dill or celery either, when these things were there for their elders,
Nor to choose any special foods or giggle or sit with their legs crossed over.

IMMORAL. What primitive tosh—like the Dipolieia or old cicada brooches
Or Kekeides that awful poet or ox-slaying rites!*

MORAL. But these things
Enabled my style of education to nurture those Marathon-fighters.*
Whereas *you* now teach the young to wrap themselves in cloaks like blankets.
It makes me choke to watch when they have to dance at the Panathenaia
And they hold their shields by their thighs with no care for Athena Tritogeneia.*
[*To* PHEIDIPPIDES] So listen, young man, stand firm, choose me, the *stronger* argument.
If you do, you'll hate the Agora's ways and keep away from the baths
And you'll feel ashamed of shameful things and blush when someone mocks you
And give up your seat on a public bench if an older man approaches
And you'll never misbehave at all or upset your very own parents
Or commit a single shameful deed that will tarnish your modest image.
Still less will you rush to a dancing-girl's house: if you do go and gawp at such things,
A prostitute may toss you an apple and then your good name will collapse.*
You'll always obey your father and never abuse him by mocking his age

Or make complaints about how you were treated when just a young bird in the nest.

IMMORAL. If you follow all *that* advice, young man, I swear by the god Dionysos
You'll resemble Hippokrates' sons and people will call you a big namby-pamby.*

MORAL. But your body will gleam with a youthful bloom, you'll spend all your time in the gym
Not round the Agora prattling recondite barbs in the current manner,
Nor dragged to court to take part in a piece of pointless, confused litigation.
Instead to the Academy's groves you'll go, with its sacred olive trees,*
And you'll race with another well-behaved boy, a crown of white reeds on your head.
You'll smell of yew, of a trouble-free life, and of fragrant poplar leaves;
You'll relish the days of spring, when plane tree and elm exchange their whispers.
If you do the things I urge you to,
And concentrate on sticking to these,
You'll be assured of
A gleaming chest and glowing skin,
Big broad shoulders, a minimal tongue,
The stoutest buttocks, a tiny willy.
But if you follow the *current* fashions
You're bound to develop
The palest skin and tiny shoulders,
A puny chest, a massive tongue,
A tiny haunch, a big *decree*!*
And *he*'ll persuade you that everything shameful
Is really good, and vice versa.
To cap it all, like Antimachos
You'll be a buggered arsehole!*

CHORUS. O you who build wisdom's edifice *Antistrophe*
To its beautiful towered heights,

How lovely to smell on your words
The fragrance of self-control.
Happy were those who lived in that former age!
[*To* IMMORAL] In reply, O you with the slickest of tongues,
You must find something novel to say.
Your opponent has proved impressive.

LEADER. You're going to need a resourceful scheme to make your case against him,
If you hope to defeat this man and don't want to appear a laughing-stock.

IMMORAL. But it's just this chance I've been waiting for, my guts were choking with rage!
I could hardly wait to contradict him and smash all his words to pieces.
It's not for nothing that intellectuals all call me by the name
Of the weaker argument: it's because I was first to have the idea
Of always choosing to contradict what the laws and justice expect.
It's worth a fortune in coins of gold to have a knack like mine,
To choose what seems the weaker case yet manage to win the debate!
[*To* PHEIDIPPIDES] Just watch me refute this education in which he puts such trust.
Let's start with his claim that he won't allow you to go and enjoy hot baths.
[*To* MORAL] What possible reason can you produce for finding fault with hot baths?

MORAL. It's because they're a truly terrible thing: they make a person spineless.

IMMORAL. Aha, stop there! I've got you at once in my grip and you'll never escape.*
Just tell me this: which son of Zeus do you think was the noblest man,
The one who had the finest spirit and toiled at the greatest labours?

MORAL. There's no one higher in my esteem than great Herakles himself.

IMMORAL. Well where have you seen *cold* baths that bear the name of Herakles, then?*
Yet no one's more a *man* than him.

MORAL. I knew it! I saw it coming!
It's arguments like these that make young men frequent the baths
To spend their days in idle chatter, deserting the wrestling-grounds.

IMMORAL. And spending time in the Agora's something else that you hate but I like.*
But if it was wrong, you wouldn't have found that Homer himself described
Old Nestor as being an agora-speaker, and other wise characters too.*
And next I'll address the role of the tongue: my opponent here says that it's bad
For the young to cultivate its use—but that's what I strongly advise!
He says, what's more, that self-control is needed: another great blunder!
[*To* MORAL] Can you name a single occasion when self-control has proved itself
Any use at all? Well, answer the question. Refute me, let's see you try.

MORAL. There are many cases—Peleus, for one: it was virtue that earned him his knife.*

IMMORAL. A *knife*! Well there's a handsome reward. Is that *all* the poor devil received?
Contrast the huge amounts of money Hyperbolos, seller of lamps,*
Has made from living a life of corruption—but no one gave him a knife!

MORAL. There was marriage to Thetis as well for Peleus because of his self-control.

IMMORAL. But later she left him and went away. He wasn't aggressive enough
And wasn't much fun when it came to spending the night together in bed.*
A woman likes nothing so much as rough treatment. But *you*'re a relic of Kronos.

[*To* PHEIDIPPIDES] Consider, young man, the implications of practising self-control,
And think of all the pleasures you'll lose if *that*'s the life that you choose:
Boys, women, and parties, food and drink, and the stuff of roaring laughter.
What point would there be in life at all if deprived of all these pleasures?
Right then, the next thing I need to address is the topic of nature's compulsion.
Suppose you conceived an adulterous passion, indulged it, but then you were caught.
You're doomed, you can't defend yourself—unless you make *me* your friend.
If you do, you'll indulge your instincts, cavort, laugh aloud, think nothing is wrong.
Then if you're caught in adulterous acts, you can tell the woman's husband
You haven't committed a crime at all! You can even refer him to Zeus,
Pointing out that even *he* succumbs to sexual passion for women,
So how can a mortal like you be expected to do what a god cannot do?

MORAL. But what if he takes your advice and receives retribution by radish and ashes?*
Will he have any argument then to prevent himself becoming wide-arsed?

IMMORAL. And suppose he does become wide-arsed, so what?*

MORAL. Well what could he suffer that's really worse than that?

IMMORAL. Then what will you say if I manage to win this point?

MORAL. I'll be lost for words, what else?

IMMORAL. Then tell me this:
What sort of people are advocates?

MORAL. They're all wide-arsed.

IMMORAL. I quite agree.
And what sort of people are tragic poets?

MORAL. They're wide-arsed too.

IMMORAL. You've got that right.
And the politicians? What sort are they?

MORAL. They're wide-arsed too.

IMMORAL. Then haven't you grasped
That your principles are nothing but tosh?
And look at the audience, what's the main sort you see?

MORAL. I'm looking at them.

IMMORAL. And what do you see?

MORAL. The great majority, by the gods,
Are wide-arsed types! [*Pointing*] This one over here
Is one, I can tell, and that one there,
And this long-haired one here as well.

IMMORAL. So what do you say?

MORAL. We've lost! And all you fucked ones,
I beg you by the gods to take my cloak:
I'm defecting now to your side!

[MORAL *drops his cloak at* IMMORAL*'s feet and rushes off through door* B *(or alternatively into the audience itself*). IMMORAL *now turns to* STREPSIADES, *who has watched the whole debate.*]

IMMORAL. Well, what do you want to do, take your son away
Or leave him here with me to be taught to argue?

STREPSIADES. Yes, teach him, don't spare the rod. And please remember
To train him well, so his tongue becomes a sword:
On one side sharp for dealing with minor lawsuits,
While the other side's ready to deal with the really big things.

IMMORAL. Don't worry, we'll give you him back as a quick-witted expert.

PHEIDIPPIDES. More likely all pale and woebegone, you mean!

[IMMORAL *leads the reluctant* PHEIDIPPIDES *into the Thinking Institute through door* B. STREPSIADES *turns and goes into his house, door* A, *as the* CHORUS *starts to perform.*]

CHORUS. Go on your way then! [*To* STREPSIADES] But you, I think,
Will soon regret these things.

[SECOND PARABASIS: 1115–30]

LEADER. Now's the time for us to state the benefits that await the judges
If they do the proper thing and show their favour to this chorus.

First of all, whenever you think the time is right to plough your fields,
Yours will be the ones we Clouds will rain on first, before the rest.
Next we'll take good care of all the fruit that hangs along your vines,
Making sure it suffers neither drought nor deluges of rain.
Woe betide that judge who as a mortal slights these goddesses.
Best for him to ponder closely all the harms he'll then endure:
Land of his will yield him neither wine nor anything else at all.
Once his olive trees and vines begin to sprout their annual shoots,
Off we'll chop the lot with downfalls just as hard as slingers' shots.
Should we see him making bricks we'll send a downpour on his roof
Smashing all his roof-tiles into bits with hailstones large and round.
Wedding-feasts suppose he plans, his own or for his kith and kin:
Rain will pour the whole night through, to make him wish for somewhere else—
Even Egypt he'd prefer, a lesson to learn for judging wrong!

[STREPSIADES *comes back out of his house*.]

STREPSIADES [*counting*]. The fifth, the fourth, the third, and then the second.
And then the day of all the days in the month
That I dread and makes me shudder and want to puke—
The 'old-and-new', the very last day of the month.*
That's when every one of my creditors swears he'll start
The legal procedure to tear my life to pieces.
The pleas I make are entirely modest and fair:
'I beg you, sir, don't ask for it all just now.'
'Defer this part, and waive that part.' No use:
They say they'll lose their money, they shout abuse,
They accuse me of crime and insist they'll take me to court.
Well *let* them take me to court. I couldn't care less,
Provided Pheidippides has learned to argue!
I'll knock on the Thinking Institute now and check. [*Bangs on door* B.]
Hoy, slave, open up!

SOKRATES [*opening abruptly*]. Ah, Strepsiades, hello.
STREPSIADES. Hello to you too. [*Handing him something*] I'd like you to take this first.
It's right to show the teacher a little respect.
And tell me about my son: has he managed to learn
That argument, the one you brought out before?*
SOKRATES. He's learnt it.
STREPSIADES. Hurrah! O Fraud, you queen almighty!*
SOKRATES. You can now evade any lawsuit you care to imagine.
STREPSIADES. What, even if witnesses saw when I borrowed the money?
SOKRATES. Yes, all the more! Who cares if a thousand were present!
STREPSIADES [*breaking into exuberant song*].
I'll raise a cry at the highest intensity
Of joy! Go hang, you moneylenders,
You and your loans and your compound interest!
You can no longer do me the slightest harm,
Such is my offspring,
The child within this dwelling,
His tongue a gleaming two-edged sword,*
My bulwark, my house's saviour, my enemies' ruin,
Liberator from his father's great woes.
Run inside and call him here to me! [SOKRATES *exits through door* B.]
O child, o son, come outside the house,
Heed the voice of your father!

[SOKRATES *returns with* PHEIDIPPIDES, *the latter now looking pale and emaciated*.*]

SOKRATES. Behold the man himself!
STREPSIADES. O loved one, o loved one!
SOKRATES. Take him and leave. [*Exits*.]
STREPSIADES. O joy, o joy, my child!

[STREPSIADES *embraces* PHEIDIPPIDES, *who does not reciprocate his emotions. We now return to spoken dialogue*.]

How wonderful!
What a pleasure, to start with, to see your new complexion.
Your look gives an instant impression of always denying

And contradicting. You've got that familiar scowl
That jumps right out at one—that 'what do you mean?',
That how to look wronged when you're *in* the wrong, it's plain!
It's such an *Attic* expression that's on your face.*
Now's the time to help me: you ruined me in the past.
PHEIDIPPIDES. But what are you anxious about?
STREPSIADES. The old-and-new day!
PHEIDIPPIDES [*argumentatively*]. But how can one day end the month and open another?*
STREPSIADES. It's the day they threaten to institute legal proceedings.
PHEIDIPPIDES. If they do, they'll lose their legal deposits for sure.*
It just can't be that one day turns into two.
STREPSIADES. It just can't be?
PHEIDIPPIDES. Well how could it be? It's like
A woman who's old and young at the very same time.
STREPSIADES. But my creditors follow the law.
PHEIDIPPIDES. I don't believe
They know what the law really means.
STREPSIADES. But what *does* it mean?
PHEIDIPPIDES. Solon of old loved the people right from the heart.*
STREPSIADES. But what's that got to do with the end of the month?
PHEIDIPPIDES. Well, Solon decided a summons should take two days,
The final day of the month and the first of the next,
So legal deposits be placed when the moon is new.*
STREPSIADES. But why did he add the last day too?
PHEIDIPPIDES. He wanted
Defendants to have the chance to turn up that day
And settle without litigation. Then if they didn't,
They'd find themselves in distress on the day of new moon.
STREPSIADES. Why then is it not on the day of the new moon itself
But the day before that the magistrates take deposits?
PHEIDIPPIDES. It's just like what happens, I think, with tasters of food.*
To give them the chance to embezzle the money at once,
They get their hands on the funds the previous day.

STREPSIADES. I like it! [*To audience*] But why are you wretches sitting like dummies,
Dupes of us clever people, as dumb as stones,
Mere masses, moronic sheep, a pile of old jars?
I feel it's time to sing a song of praise
For myself and my son, to celebrate our success.

'What happiness, Strepsiades,
Is yours for being so clever
And rearing a son like this!'
That's what my friends and demesmen*
Will say with envy when you speak in court
And win the cases against us.
Let me take you indoors and serve you a feast.

[STREPSIADES *and* PHEIDIPPIDES *go back into their house through door* A. *As they do so,* CREDITOR[A] *enters from one of the* eisodoi *in mid-conversation with his* WITNESS.]

CREDITOR[A]. Is a man supposed just to kiss goodbye to his money?
I'll never do it! It would have been better back then
To suffer embarrassment rather than take on this trouble.
Look where things stand: for the sake of obtaining my money
I'm dragging you here as a witness, and in addition
I'll be locked in feud with a fellow-demesman of mine.
Still, as long as I live I'll never bring shame on my homeland.
I'll issue this summons to Strepsiades—
STREPSIADES [*emerging suddenly*]. Who's this?
CREDITOR[A]. —for the old-and-new day of the month.
STREPSIADES [*sarcastically*]. I call for a witness.
He referred just now to *two* days! And what debt do you mean?
CREDITOR[A]. Twelve minas: the sum you borrowed from me to buy
The dapple-grey horse.*
STREPSIADES. A *horse*! [*To audience*] Do you hear what he says?
When all of you know that I loathe equestrian matters.
CREDITOR[A]. But by Zeus you swore by the gods that you'd pay back the money.
STREPSIADES. But by Zeus that was so long ago, before my son

Pheidippides learnt how to argue and win any case.
CREDITOR[A]. You mean you intend to *deny* that you owe the money?
STREPSIADES. What else was the point of having Pheidippides taught?
CREDITOR[A]. Are you ready to swear a supporting oath by the gods
In a place of my choice?
STREPSIADES. By the gods? *What* gods do you mean?*
CREDITOR[A]. Zeus, Hermes, Poseidon, for instance.
STREPSIADES. Well yes, by Zeus,
I'd pay three obols for having the fun of an oath!*
CREDITOR[A]. I hope you'll rot one day for this shamelessness.

[STREPSIADES *nonchalantly pats the* CREDITOR*'s protruding belly.*]

STREPSIADES. You know, a good rubbing with salt is all that this needs.*
CREDITOR[A]. How dare you mock me!
STREPSIADES. Just right for a nice big wineskin.
CREDITOR[A]. I swear by great Zeus as well as the rest of the gods
You won't get away with this.
STREPSIADES [*guffawing*]. How hilarious, 'gods'!
And to those in the know it's absurd to swear by Zeus.
CREDITOR[A]. You'll pay for this in court, you mark my words.
But do you intend to return the money or not?
I need an answer before I leave.
STREPSIADES. Stay calm:
I'm going to give you a very clear answer at once.

[STREPSIADES *dashes into his house.* CREDITOR[A], *baffled, turns to his* WITNESS.]

CREDITOR[A]. What d'you think he's going to do? Will he give me the money?

[STREPSIADES *comes back out carrying a kneading-trough.*]

STREPSIADES. Well where's this fellow who wants the return of his loan.
Do you know what this is?

CREDITOR[A]. Of course, it's a kneading-trough.
STREPSIADES. So you don't even know such things, yet you ask for your money!
I'm not prepared to return a single obol
To someone who gets their basic grammar all wrong.*
CREDITOR[A] [*bemused*]. So you won't repay the loan?
STREPSIADES. Not as far as I know!
Come on now, time to hurry along, buzz off
From my door.
CREDITOR[A]. I'm going, but let me assure you of this:
I vow on my life that I'll start a legal procedure.

[*He starts to leave with his* WITNESS. STREPSIADES *shouts the following lines mockingly after him before turning towards the house door.*]

STREPSIADES. Then you'll lose your deposit as well as the money I borrowed!*
It's a shame, though—not what I want you to suffer at all
Just because you appeared a grammatical ignoramus!

[*Enter from the opposite* eisodos *the bruised and battered figure of* CREDITOR[B]. STREPSIADES *pauses at his house door.*]

CREDITOR[B]. Oh woe, oh woe!
STREPSIADES. What now?
Who on earth have we got here crying in loud lament?
[*Ironically*] Did I hear the voice of a god from old Karkinos' plays?*
CREDITOR[B] [*melodramatically*]. Does the world really want to know who stands before it?
An ill-fated man.
STREPSIADES. Then keep yourself out of my way!
CREDITOR[B]. Harsh destiny's mine! O chariot-wrecking fortune
That befell my horses! O Pallas, my ruination!
STREPSIADES [*ironically*]. What evil has Tlempolemos made you bear?*
CREDITOR[B]. Don't mock me, old chap. I just want my money, that's all.
Tell that son of yours to repay the loan that I gave him,
Especially now that I've fallen on such hard times.
STREPSIADES. What money is that?

CREDITOR^{B}. The money he borrowed
from me!
STREPSIADES. You're in real distress, unless I'm badly mistaken.
CREDITOR^{B}. My chariot crashed and threw me out, that's why.
STREPSIADES. The nonsense you're talking suggests you're out of
your mind!
CREDITOR^{B}. What nonsense is that—just because I want my
money?
STREPSIADES. It's all too clear you're just not sane.
CREDITOR^{B}. Why's that?
STREPSIADES. I think your brain must have had a right old bashing.
CREDITOR^{B}. By Hermes, you'll soon be facing a legal charge
If you don't repay my money.
STREPSIADES [*mock-earnestly*]. Please tell me something.
Do you think that when Zeus rains he always sends
A fresh supply of water, or does the sun
Draw up the same water from earth to be reused?
CREDITOR^{B}. I haven't the faintest idea—and couldn't care less!
STREPSIADES. What makes you entitled then to reclaim your
money
If you don't have an inkling about such *higher* matters?
CREDITOR^{B}. Look, if you're short of money just pay the interest
That's due.
STREPSIADES. The 'interest'? What kind of thing is *that*?
CREDITOR^{B}. The amount, of course, that with every month and day
Makes the sum of money that's owed grow bigger and bigger
As time flows by.
STREPSIADES. Well thanks for the explanation.
But tell me this: do you have any reason to think
The sea's now bigger than in the past?
CREDITOR^{B}. No, the same.
It wouldn't be right for its size to increase.
STREPSIADES. Then how
Can it be that the sea, you wretch, doesn't get any bigger,
Even though all the rivers flow into it all the time,
While *you* are trying to make your money grow bigger?
Get out of here! Go on! Get away from my house.
[*Shouting inside*] Bring my horse whip out!
CREDITOR^{B}. I call for witnesses!

[*A* SLAVE *comes out of door* A *with a large horsewhip.* STREPSIADES *starts to whip* CREDITOR[B] *with exaggeratedly equestrian gestures.*]

STREPSIADES. Giddy up! What's wrong? Pull my chariot, pedigree horse!

CREDITOR[B] [*fleeing*]. This is brutal assault!

STREPSIADES. Get going! I'll have to goad you
With a good sharp stab in the anus, you sluggish trace-horse.*
Are you running away? I knew I'd make you scarper
With all those chariot wheels and horses of yours.

[*As* CREDITOR[B] *exits by a side entrance,* STREPSIADES *goes back inside his house.*]

CHORUS. Ah, folly to set one's heart on sordid things! *Strophe*
This old man's passion
Is to cheat his creditors,
Steal the money he borrowed.
It's inevitable on this very day
He'll find himself involved
In a turn of events
That despite his clever designs
Will make the crime he's started
Abruptly become his undoing!

I think he's about to find the very thing *Antistrophe*
He's long been seeking—
A son resourceful enough
To come up with ideas
That contradict what's right
And can win every argument
In which he's entangled
No matter how wicked his words.
But maybe just maybe he'll wish
His son couldn't speak after all!

[STREPSIADES *comes rushing out of his house, clearly in physical distress and followed almost immediately by a swaggering* PHEIDIPPIDES.]

STREPSIADES. Help! Help!
My neighbours and kinsmen and fellow-demesmen of mine,

I need you to come and protect me. I'm being attacked.
I'm in terrible pain all over my head and my face.
You loathsome thing, are you hitting your father?

PHEIDIPPIDES. Yes, father!

STREPSIADES [*to audience*]. Does everyone see he admits that he's hit me?

PHEIDIPPIDES. Too true!

STREPSIADES. You loathsome father-beater, you utter delinquent!

PHEIDIPPIDES. Feel free to go on calling me names like those.
Don't you know how much pleasure I get from being abused?

STREPSIADES. You cavernous arsehole!

PHEIDIPPIDES. A name that smells like roses!*

STREPSIADES. You're prepared to hit your father?

PHEIDIPPIDES. By Zeus, I'll show I was *right* to hit you.

STREPSIADES. Your loathesomeness knows no limits!
But how could it ever be right to beat your own father?

PHEIDIPPIDES. I'll give you the proof and win the debate between us.

STREPSIADES. Win *this* debate?

PHEIDIPPIDES. There's nothing I'd find so easy.
Choose which of the pair of arguments is yours.

STREPSIADES. What arguments?

PHEIDIPPIDES. The stronger or the weaker.*

STREPSIADES. So it's really the case, by Zeus, that I had you trained
In contradicting what's right, if you're going to try
To argue the case that it's wholly just and proper
For a son to use his fists on his very own father.

PHEIDIPPIDES. But I think you'll find I'll convince you yourself in fact:
Once you've heard my argument stated, you'll have no reply.

STREPSIADES. Well I'd certainly like to hear what you're going to argue.

[AGON II: 1345–1451]

CHORUS. It's your job now, old man, to think out a way *Strophe*
To defeat this opponent.
If he didn't have something to make him confident,

He wouldn't be so outrageous.
There's something that makes him brash: just look
At his arrogant pose!

LEADER. Go back to the start and to how this fight broke out in the very first place.
The chorus needs to hear your account and I'm sure you'll oblige us now.*

STREPSIADES. I'll go back, then, to the very beginning and how our quarrel broke out.
It came about when we feasted at dinner, the way that you all understand.*
The first thing I did was to tell him to take up the lyre and sing a song
By Simonides—the one that tells 'How Krios the Ram was shorn'.*
But straight away he called it old-fashioned to take up the lyre like that
And to sing while drinking, the way a woman would do while grinding barley.

PHEIDIPPIDES. Right then at the start you deserved to be thrashed and be pounded into the ground
When you told me to sing as though you were holding a feast for a group of cicadas!*

STREPSIADES. It's sentiments the same as these that he uttered while still in the house,
And he kept on claiming Simonides was a really appalling poet.
I found it hard but all the same I endured this behaviour at first.
Then I urged him instead to take a branch of myrtle and holding it up*
To recite some Aischylos to me. That made him retort at once:
'Yes of course, what else, since I take the view he's the *greatest* of all the poets—
All that noisy ranting, that incoherence, that bombast, those boulder-like words!'*
At that my heart was palpitating so much, you can surely imagine.

Still I bit back my anger and said to him, 'Well, in that case, I'll let you choose
Whatever you think are the cleverest things that those *modern* poets now write.'
His immediate choice was Euripides; he recited a speech about how
A brother was screwing his very own sister—o Herakles, save us from this!*
I couldn't endure any longer but started at once to assault him with words,
Heaping up lots of filthy abuse. After that, it is hardly surprising to tell,
We traded word for word like blows. And *then* he jumped from his seat
And bashed me and punched me and throttled me too and wanted to beat me to pulp.

PHEIDIPPIDES. Well wasn't I justified? You refused to praise Euripides,
The cleverest poet.

STREPSIADES. The 'cleverest poet', what *him*! Oh, what can I call you?*
I'm bound to get beaten again.

PHEIDIPPIDES. And by Zeus you're bound to deserve it again!

STREPSIADES. Deserve it? How? You've lost all shame. I brought you up as my child.
[*Sentimentally*] I always tried to understand what your babyish lispings meant.
If the word was 'wa-wa' I always held a drink to your lips for sipping.
If you asked for 'br-br' I always rushed to give you some bread to eat.
As soon as I heard the sound 'poo-poo' I took you straight to the door:
I would carry you out and hold you up. Yet just now you were *strangling* me.
Even though I shouted and cried aloud
That I needed a shit, you weren't prepared
To carry me out, you loathsome thing,

You kept on throttling all the time
Till I poo-pooed on the spot!

CHORUS. I imagine that younger spectators' hearts are throbbing *Antistrophe*
To hear his reply.
If after doing the things we've heard about
He persuades us with his words,
The skins of older men, we think,
Won't be worth a chickpea!

LEADER. It's your job now, o mover and engineer of novel words,
To find a means of persuasion to make your case seem wholly just.

PHEIDIPPIDES. How lovely it is to devote one's life to novel and clever affairs
And to have the power to show contempt for traditional laws and customs.
At the time when the only thing that mattered to me was riding horses,
I wasn't able to string together three words without some sort of error.
But since this man over here has himself put a stop to my former habits,
And my life's now one of subtle ideas and words and intricate thoughts,
I think I'll be able to demonstrate that it's just to chastise one's father.

STREPSIADES. By Zeus, I'd prefer you to ride your horses. Far better for me, for sure,
To pay for the upkeep of four big horses than be beaten and thrashed to pulp.

PHEIDIPPIDES. I'll return to the point where you interrupted, pursuing my case from there.
And first of all I'll ask you this: when I was a child did you beat me?

STREPSIADES. Of course I did, but I always had your best interests at heart.

PHEIDIPPIDES. Then tell me

Why isn't it right for me to have your best interests at heart as well
And to beat you too, if that's what follows from showing such care and concern?
Since why should *you* get immunity from blows for this body of yours
When *I* didn't get it? Yet I was born just as much a free man as you.
[*Poetically*] 'The children cry—do you really think the father can't cry as well?'*
You'll say, no doubt, that custom fixes such treatment as fit for children.
But my answer to that is to emphasize that old age is a *second* childhood.
And in addition, it makes more sense for the old, not the young, to be beaten:
There's less excuse, when they've lived so long, for the old to get things wrong.

STREPSIADES. Yet nowhere in the world does custom allow that a father be beaten.

PHEIDIPPIDES. But wasn't the person who made that law so long ago just a man
Like you and me, and didn't he use persuasion to win agreement?
So why shouldn't *I* be free to propose a new law in turn for the future,
A law that states where sons are concerned they can beat their fathers as well?
As regards all the blows we suffered ourselves before this law was in place,
We'll not count those: we accept those beatings require no compensation.
But consider the case of roosting cocks and the rest of the animal kingdom,
The way they fight against their fathers—yet why should there be any difference
Between the animal world and us, except that they don't make decrees?

STREPSIADES. Well if you're quite so keen to model yourself on roosting cocks,

Why don't you live on a diet of dung and sleep on a plain wooden perch?

PHEIDIPPIDES. But that's not the same sort of thing at all—and it wouldn't be *Sokrates*' view.

STREPSIADES. You'd be well advised to stop striking me blows. If not, you'll regret it one day.

PHEIDIPPIDES. Why's that?

STREPSIADES. Well just as *I've* the right to use chastisement against you

So *you* in turn can chastise any son you produce.*

PHEIDIPPIDES. But suppose I don't have one?

All those beatings I had will have been in vain and you'll be content in your grave.

STREPSIADES [*to audience*]. Well, all you men as old as me, I have to say he's right.

I think we ought to concede to the young that the points he's made are fair.

It stands to reason that *we* should be beaten for failing to do what's right.

PHEIDIPPIDES. And consider this further thought as well.

STREPSIADES. No more, it'll finish me off!

PHEIDIPPIDES. But perhaps it will stop you resenting the things you suffered a moment ago.

STREPSIADES. How's that? I'd like to know just how you'll supposedly do me good.

PHEIDIPPIDES. I'll beat my *mother* as well, like you.

STREPSIADES. But I can't believe my ears!

Another and still bigger evil!

PHEIDIPPIDES. But what if despite my weaker position

I can still defeat you in argument

And prove that my mother needs beating?

STREPSIADES. If that's what you do, there's nothing else left

But to take your own body and throw it into

The criminals' pit*—with Sokrates

And the Immoral argument too!

[*The formal debate over,* STREPSIADES *now turns towards where the* CHORUS *is standing in order to remonstrate with it.*]

STREPSIADES. It's all your fault, you Clouds—all the things I've suffered
Since I placed my affairs entirely in your control.

LEADER. Not at all. You've no one else but yourself to blame
For getting yourself involved in such nasty affairs.

STREPSIADES. Why didn't you tell me *that* at an earlier stage?
I'm just an old bumpkin—it's you who urged me on.

LEADER. But that's our usual behaviour, whenever we see
A person who's set his heart on nasty affairs.
We lead him on till we land him in serious trouble,
To make sure he learns to fear the gods in future. [*Turns away.*]

STREPSIADES. That's a really nasty method, you Clouds—but it's justice as well.
I was wrong to cheat my way out of what I'd borrowed.

[*The* CHORUS *now moves back to the edge of the* orchêstra. STREPSIADES *turns to his son.*]

But I beg you now to help me, my dearest child:
Please come with me to destroy vile Chairephon
And Sokrates—the men who deceived us both.

PHEIDIPPIDES. But I'm not prepared to wrong my former teachers.

STREPSIADES. You must, you must, 'in awe of paternal Zeus'.*

PHEIDIPPIDES. Just listen, 'paternal Zeus'! What a primitive mind!
You believe that Zeus exists?

STREPSIADES. He does!

PHEIDIPPIDES [*smugly*]. He doesn't,
'It's Swirl who's driven Zeus out and is ruling the world.'*

STREPSIADES. No, he *hasn't* driven him out. That's what I thought
Because of this pot over here.* What a wretched fool
To believe as I did that a pot like you was a god!

PHEIDIPPIDES. I'm off. You can stay and babble away insanely.
[*Exits into house.*]

STREPSIADES. What made me go out of my mind? I was simply crazy
To reject the gods themselves. It was Sokrates' fault.

[*He turns to the herm that stands outside his house door.*]

O Hermes, my friend, don't turn your anger against me,*
Don't rub me into the dust, please show some mercy:
It was foolish blather that sent me out of my mind.
I beg you to give me advice: should I take revenge
By pursuing a legal charge—or what else do you think?

[*He leans towards the statue as though it were whispering in his ear, then becomes animated.*]

That's good advice: all legal quibbling is pointless,
Much better to set alight the house that they're in,
These foolish blatherers here!
[*Shouting into his house*] Hoy, Xanthias,*
Come out with a ladder, and bring me a mattock as well.

[*A* SLAVE *emerges promptly from door* A *with ladder and mattock; he proceeds to follow* STREPSIADES' *instructions.*]

Climb up there on the Thinking Institute wall
And dismantle the roof, if you love this master of yours,
Until you make their house collapse on their heads.
And I want a burning torch for myself at once.

[*Another* SLAVE *rushes out from door* A *with the requested torch.*]

I'll exact revenge from the lot of them on the spot,
I'm determined to do it, no matter what bluster they use.

[*The action during the following lines is carried out in symbolic and pantomime-like fashion, not realistically: the first* SLAVE *dismantles the roof-tiles;* STREPSIADES *follows him up the ladder, using his torch to 'set fire' to the building and his mattock to help destroy the roof. In the hubbub, various characters appear at windows in the building and/or at door* B.]

STUDENT[A]. Help! Help!
STREPSIADES [*gleefully*]. It's up to you, my torch, to create a blaze!
STUDENT[A]. Hey you, what on earth are you doing?
STREPSIADES. What me? Can't you see?
Engaging in subtle debate with the building's roof-beams!

STUDENT[B]. What's happening, help! Who's setting our house on fire?

STREPSIADES. It's that fellow whose cloak you stole when I came to the school.*

STUDENT[B]. You'll kill us, you'll kill us!

STREPSIADES. Exactly the outcome I'd like,
If this mattock of mine doesn't disappoint all my hopes—
And if I don't fall down first and break my neck!

SOKRATES. Hey you, up there on the roof, what d'you think you're doing?

STREPSIADES. 'Air-walking and spinning my thoughts around the sun.'*

SOKRATES. I'm in desperate trouble, the smoke is making me choke.

STUDENT[B]. And I'm in danger of burning to cinders in here!

STREPSIADES. It serves you right for showing the gods contempt
And daring to scrutinize the moon's backside.*

[*At this point* SOKRATES *and other members of the school run out from door* B. STREPSIADES *and his* SLAVE *have come down off the roof by now. There is a brief mêlée before all the characters exit running by the two* eisodoi.*]

Pursue them, hit them, pelt them—for lots of reasons
But most of all because they wronged the gods.

LEADER. Let's file off now: we've done our full share of dancing for this performance.

WOMEN AT THE THESMOPHORIA

INTRODUCTION

Women at the Thesmophoria was probably first staged at the Dionysia festival of 411, at a time (late March, early April) of exceptional significance in the history of classical Athens. This was the very period when a political faction was plotting radical, anti-democratic changes in the government of the city, changes that would materialize that summer as the short-lived oligarchic revolution of the Four Hundred.[1] Athens had been in a state of heightened political tension ever since the calamitous failure in late summer 413 of the expedition to Sicily and the various consequences of that failure (including the revolt of several allied cities in 412). But the situation had become acute in late 412, when the conspiratorial faction in question was beginning seriously to mobilize itself both at Athens and among leading figures stationed with the Athenian fleet at Samos in the eastern Aegean.[2] Before long, events took a sinister turn: a number of political assassinations in the city helped to fuel a general mood of fear and anxiety. Not a context, one might think, which would lend itself readily to the creation of comic drama.

Yet, rather remarkably, Aristophanes actually had *two* plays in rehearsal during late 412 and early 411.[3] One, *Lysistrata*, was prepared for performance (at the Lenaia, in early February 411) by Kallistratos, who had produced several of Aristophanes' earlier plays as well; the other, *Women at the Thesmophoria* itself, was presumably under the control (as *didaskalos*: chorus-trainer and director) of Aristophanes in person. Is it coincidence that both plays, unlike all the poet's earlier surviving works, have scenarios in which female characters—though not, of course, female performers (since chorus-members as well as actors were all male)—have prominent roles? Is it

[1] For the chronology of the period in relation to the writing and staging of *Women at the Thesmophoria*, see C. Austin and S. D. Olson, *Aristophanes Thesmophoriazusae* (Oxford, 2004), pp. xxxiii–xliv.

[2] Thucydides 8.47–69 gives the main sequence of events, but Aristotle, *Athenaion Politeia* 29–32 contains some significant differences of emphasis. For one modern reconstruction, see P. J. Rhodes, *A History of the Classical Greek World*, 2nd edn. (Oxford, 2010), 169–75.

[3] Plays selected for Athenian dramatic festivals were rehearsed over a period of months, during which some changes could be made: cf. n. 3 to my Introduction to *Frogs*.

possible that this fact represents a strategy for a kind of comic 'flight from politics' during the mounting tension and uncertainty of the period?

Matters cannot be quite so simple. *Lysistrata* is, on one level, a highly political play: indeed, rather ironically, a play about a kind of 'oligarchic' conspiracy in the city (and, supposedly, in all the cities of the Greek world), only a conspiracy where the plotters are *women* and their primary levers of power are sexual.[4] The result, from a political point of view, is an ambiguous tease. There is, on the other hand, something to be said for the idea that *Women at the Thesmophoria* is a decidely non-political comedy—arguably, in fact, the least politically engaged of all Aristophanes' surviving works. There is just one section of the play which might be thought to carry some pointed resonance in the circumstances of early 411. This is where the women convene their special meeting at the Thesmophoria in a manner reminiscent of the meetings of the city's regular Assembly (*ekklêsia*). At 335–7 the chorus-leader's solemn proclamation includes a curse on anyone who 'plots against the community [*dêmos*, the 'people'] . . . or makes clandestine approach | To . . . the Medes . . .' (i.e. the Persians, an alliance with whom was part of the oligarchs' plan at this date).

Two things, however, mute the force of this passage: one, that it echoes the regular curses delivered at the start of Assembly meetings; the other, that the chorus-leader says '. . . the community | *Of the city's women*' and '. . . clandestine approach | *To Euripides* and the Medes . . .'. In other words, any allusion that might be detected here to contemporary oligarchic plottings is not only fleeting but instantly smudged, as it were, by the fantasy of the comic scenario. When the whole chorus reinforces their leader's curses by targeting those 'whose aim is that all decrees and laws | Be overturned and replaced' (361–2), there is further scope to catch a specifically contemporary resonance, though the oligarchs themselves did not in fact present their proposals in terms of a complete overturning of existing laws. But such resonance is in any case optional (spectators would vary in their sensitivity to it), and is heavily outweighed by the specifics of the Thesmophoria setting and the female ambience of the scene. Whatever Aristophanes' own views may have been in 412–411,

[4] Lysistrata herself, at 577–8, refers disparagingly to political 'clubs' of the kind which Thucydides 8.54.4 indicates were drawn into the planning of the oligarchic coup in 411.

he made sure that *Women at the Thesmophoria* almost entirely steered clear of the fraught political issues of the period.[5]

What he produced, instead, can be firmly located on the broad spectrum of his comic repertoire. The play is nothing less than the first surviving Western comedy to be centred on the dynamics of metatheatre, the self-conscious framing of 'life' as quasi-theatrical.[6] The scenario is built on the basic idea that the (supposed) nature of Euripides' tragedies has rebounded against the playwright in his own life. The women of Athens have taken offence at the alleged misogyny of Euripides' treatment of female characters and have resolved to discuss some kind of revenge against him when they meet at the women-only festival of the Thesmophoria. Somehow alerted to the danger in advance, Euripides has decided that he needs a *man* to infiltrate the Thesmophoria in disguise on his behalf. Accompanied (for what rapidly show themselves to be reasons of comic convenience) by an elderly and decidedly vulgar Kinsman, he turns first, in the play's opening scene, to his younger and allegedly effeminate fellow-tragedian Agathon to undertake this task for him. Although Agathon refuses, the idea allows a further level of comic metatheatricality to be introduced: dramatists, it is understood (and Agathon has something to say about this for his own reasons: see below), are adept at conjuring up imaginative worlds, so why should they not be good at using their fictionalizing skills to manipulate the 'real' world as well?

After Euripides' Kinsman has reacted to Agathon's refusal by offering to be the secret infiltrator himself, Agathon is at any rate willing to lend some female attire and appurtenances for the role, thereby simultaneously underlining his credentials as both a feminine man (who really *uses* such things himself) and a dramatist (who needs them for his stock of costumes and theatrical props). Reliance on the Kinsman, who shows himself in the opening scene to be shamelessly vulgar and buffoonish, will inevitably prove disastrous. But it will also provide an excuse for both him and Euripides to close the circle of

[5] One other passage, at 962–4 (see my note there), might even be taken as an explicit signal that the play will avoid political comment at a time of heightened tensions in the city.

[6] Aristophanes' older rival Kratinos had earlier (in 423) gone a step further and written a play, *Wine-Flask* (*Putine*), in which he metatheatrically made a plot out of his *own* life as comic playwright: full discussion in E. Bakola, *Cratinus* (Oxford, 2010), esp. 59–64, 275–85.

metatheatricality, so to speak, by enacting parts of Euripides' plays 'in life' in an attempt to bring about the Kinsman's rescue. *Women at the Thesmophoria* turns into a work in which Euripides' life becomes a scripted drama amalgamated from several of his own tragedies. Yet that process of scripting is also an ironic transformation of tragedy into comedy.

The 'Euripidean' plot through which that is achieved unfolds in a sequence of gradually intensifying stages: first, the disguised Kinsman's misdirected attempts to defend Euripides' reputation with the women and his consequent unmasking as a man (466–654); then, his Telephos-like 'kidnap' of a woman's baby (689 ff.; see below) and his resort to motifs from Euripides' *Palamedes* (765 ff.) and *Helen* (849 ff.); finally, a series of interventions by Euripides in person with the aim of rescuing his relative (868–1231). As a way into all this, as well as a kind of preamble to it, Aristophanes takes full advantage, just as he does in *Lysistrata*, of the opportunity to generate comedy from the notion of opening up a secret female gathering to the prying eyes of men (i.e. the overwhelming majority of his audience).[7] The resulting cast of humour is—once again as in *Lysistrata*—double-sided: it involves exaggeratedly cynical male stereotypes of female behaviour, but also the simultaneous assimilation of women to *men* in certain respects. In consequence, there is no simple or consistent 'gender politics' to be inferred from this aspect of the play, or of Aristophanic comedy more broadly.

The quintessentially Aristophanic blurring and confusion of categories, in this case male and female, is set in train by the fluctuating tone and style of the women's meeting. We have already seen that part of the section of ritual prayers (298–371) which initiates the festival gathering simultaneously echoes and travesties prayers for the welfare of Athens which formed part of the ritualized preliminaries of Assembly meetings. By, for instance, bracketing together Euripides and the Persians as though they were similar types of threatening enemies (337), or by similarly swerving from fears of tyranny to a string of scenarios involving surrogate babies, adultery, and

[7] As it happens, *Women at the Thesmophoria* itself contains a prime piece of evidence that Athenian women did not normally attend the theatre: 395–7, though a joke, takes for granted that most husbands attended without their wives (cf. *Birds* 793–6). See the general Introduction, n. 32.

cheating innkeepers (338–49), the chorus-leader speaks in a hybrid register. Shortly afterwards, the women start to hold their business meeting—more precisely, start to conduct their business (on the absurd motion of what kind of punishment is to be pronounced on Euripides) in a manner blatantly modelled on a session of the city's political Assembly or *ekklêsia*, with an 'agenda' set by a prior meeting of the (women's) Council (372–77) and an invitation to speak (379) of the kind which the Herald formulaically announced in the Assembly. The first speaker, Mika, comes forward and prepares to speak, no doubt with parodic gestures, just like 'real orators' (382), launching herself into an attack on Euripides for his supposed misogyny with a vehemence and accumulation of devices (e.g. the rhetorical questions of 389–94) that do have something in common with the habits of contemporary oratory.

Such points, however, form only the most obvious components of comic gender-jumbling. More subtly, when Mika complains that Euripides depicts women as adulterers, drinkers, and schemers, part of the humour consists in toying with men's own suspicious stereotypes (hence, for example, the ludicrous vignette of husbands coming home from the tragic theatre and searching the house for hidden lovers, 395–7), and part in the gradual, unconscious admissions by Mika herself of women's (supposedly) secret vices (398, 407–9, 419–25). How can one extract a consistent viewpoint from these comically intersecting premises? What's more, all this is mixed together, even more self-contradictorily, with a growing sense of metatheatricality. Mika finishes her speech on one level like a male public speaker (undertaking to consult with the scribe on the precise wording of a decree, 432), but on quite a different level with the suggestion that the women should consider *poisoning* Euripides (430)—itself a motif found in several Euripidean plays!

This layered humour, which adds up to a rich texture that an audience in the theatre would intuitively appreciate without a need for analysis, is cemented once the Kinsman comes forward to speak (466–519). We now have (i) a male character impersonating a woman who (ii) both complains about Euripides and, as Mika had done, ironically admits female faults, but (iii) also presents a persona which reflects exaggeratedly male stereotypes and jokes (e.g. an obscene anecdote of the very young bride and her nocturnal tryst with a lover, 478–89; or a preposterous folktale-like story of the wife hiding a lover behind a cloak, 499), and, finally, (iv) all this in a speech which borrows from one of Euripides' own plays, *Telephos* (see below).

Once Aristophanes has activated these various comic elements, he continues to combine and recombine them in shifting ways. Several are present in the 'slanging match' (cf. 571) into which the confrontation between the Kinsman (still purportedly a woman at this point) and Mika degenerates (531–73). They are then given a new embodiment in the figure of Kleisthenes, who rushes onto the scene at 574 to warn the women of a rumour that a man has infiltrated their festival. Kleisthenes had already been the butt of a passing joke at 235, a miniature anticipation of things to come. Satirized in all three plays in this volume, he was a favourite target of Aristophanes' mockery over many years.[8] How and why he came to be so readily available for jokes about effeminate appearance and passive homosexual habits, we cannot now know. But since he was probably in life no mere object of ridicule but a socially and politically active figure of at least a minor kind, he suits the present context perfectly: adding his own contribution to the gender-confusions of the play, he behaves *both* as a 'friend' of women (574–6) *and* as someone who knows how to liaise urgently with the Council (654) and operate the mechanisms of democracy. He even helps sustain the play's metatheatrical dimension, since the urgency of his entrance and information carries overtones of the conventions of tragic messenger-speeches.

The upshot of Kleisthenes' intervention and the subsequent interrogation of the Kinsman is a 'mirror-scene' corresponding to the latter's original shaving and cross-dressing by Euripides. In a sense this forms the climax of the first half of the play. It brings to a head the whole business of gender-blurring by reducing it to its most basic (comic) constituent, the actor's phallus (643 ff.). (So much for Aristophanes' supposed boast at *Clouds* 537–9 that he was not the sort of playwright to resort to vulgar phallic humour for the sake of making the boys in the theatre audience laugh.) Nor is this the last moment in the play at which the phallus will be brought into action: the Skythian Archer points to the Kinsman's phallus again at 1114, and the Archer's own phallus will spring lewdly into life in the very last scene (1187).

But the exposure of the Kinsman's manhood is not the end of his play-acting. On the contrary, his capture by the women is the cue for the

[8] See the entry on him in the Index of Names.

comedy's metatheatricality, and with it the Kinsman's shifting identity, to assume enlarged proportions. From now on, starting with the *Telephos* parody at 689 ff. (see below), almost everything in the dramatic action is filtered through quasi-Euripidean frames of reference. Comedy is now 'rescripted' as (pseudo-) tragedy, and vice versa: the second half of *Women at the Thesmophoria* turns into Aristophanes' most elaborate (surviving) exercise in paratragedy, the comic adaptation and burlesquing of tragic materials. It is not for the most part productive to try to distinguish paratragedy from parody of tragedy, if only because parody itself is a notoriously elastic and slippery category of humour. The workings of paratragedy necessarily deflate the tragic originals from which they take their bearings, stripping them of their solemnity and seriousness, not to mention their darker moments. But whether or how far Aristophanes' manipulation (on a spectrum running from verbatim quotation to extravagant distortion) of Euripidean language, characters, and situations should be taken to direct mockery against those originals themselves is not a question that admits of an easy answer: maybe not even a question one can meaningfully pose at all. One thing we can say for sure is that paratragedy on the scale and in the detail practised by Aristophanes could only have been produced in a theatrical culture where tragedy and comedy existed side by side for overlapping (though not identical) festival audiences. In other words, the rich and extensive paratragic colouring of *Women at the Thesmophoria* presupposes spectators who, as also in the case of the second half of *Frogs*, were highly knowledgeable about, and appreciative of, tragedy in its own right: both plays would be largely stultifying for audiences of whom that was not true. We are dealing here with paratragedy for connoisseurs of drama.

That does not mean, however, that Aristophanes could have expected his audience to have uniform familiarity with the particular Euripidean sources he draws on in this play. He must have allowed for mixed experience on the part of spectators: some would have seen (some of) the plays in question performed, others might have heard reports of them, and a few might even have had access (as Aristophanes himself clearly did) to texts.[9] The two prerequisites for appreciation of paratragedy which he could depend on a majority of

[9] The size of the 'reading public' for tragedy in the late fifth century remains impossible to calculate. Cf. Dionysos as reader at *Frogs* 52–3, with the (disputed) reference to play-texts at *Frogs* 1114 and my notes on both passages.

spectators possessing are, first, an accumulated stock of familiarity with tragedy in general as a theatrical and poetic genre, and therefore a ready attunement to the various games which he plays with its conventions and stylistic registers; secondly, a reasonable knowledge of (or an ability to pick up quickly) at least the core mythological subject-matter of the scenarios which he 'borrows' from Euripides (and/or makes Euripides 'borrow' from himself).

We can apply those basic points by considering briefly in turn the four main blocks of paratragedy in the second half of *Women at the Thesmophoria*.[10]

(I) 689–761. Parody of a scene from Euripides' Telephos[11]

Several features of this case are thought-provoking. *Telephos*, originally staged in 438, was by far the oldest of the four Euripidean plays concerned here: even spectators who had seen that production twenty-seven years earlier would have struggled to remember it well. Yet the play is the only one of the four which is not actually *named* in Aristophanes' text but is still expected to be readily identifiable. The essentials of Telephos's story must have been quite widely known; several other tragedians of the period had based plays on the myth. Moreover, the particular Euripidean scene in question, where Telephos seized the baby Orestes as 'hostage' while defending himself against the Greeks, could have been a memorable *coup de théâtre* in its own right, and certainly lent itself to visually striking burlesque in the form of the Kinsman's kidnapping of Mika's 'baby' (which turns out to be a wineskin, symbol of the stereotype—the theme of numerous jokes in the play—of Athenian wives as secret drinkers).[12] We certainly know that the plot of *Telephos* appealed strongly to Aristophanes' imagination, since he had already parodied it much earlier in his career at several places in *Acharnians* (with the seizure of the Acharnian chorus's coal-scuttle at 325–34 corresponding to the Kinsman's present action with the wineskin). But in contrast to both *Acharnians* and the further blocks of paratragedy discussed below, the

[10] Fuller information on all this material can be found in Austin and Olson's edition (n. 1), pp. lvi–lxiv. [11] Cf. the Index of Names, s.v. Telephos.

[12] See the depiction of this scene on a fourth-century Apulian vase cited in my general Introduction, 'Aristophanes and Posterity', with n. 91 there.

current passage contains no verbally close borrowings or adaptations from Euripides' text: it is the visual-cum-thematic features of the scenario which constitute the main vectors of humour.

For the more acute (and well-informed) members of Aristophanes' audience, there would be additional nuances to appreciate. We can see in retrospect that the *Telephos*, as a source of paratragedy, has been lurking in the background for some time: the Kinsman's disguise and infiltration of the women's meeting is analogous to the Mysian king's disguised infiltration of the Greeks' assembly at Argos. The analogy came closer to the foreground at 466 ff., as several resemblances to Dikaiopolis' Telephos-speech at *Acharnians* 497 ff. confirm. So when the Kinsman seizes Mika's baby at 689 and takes refuge at the altar, paratragedy fuses with metatheatre: it is as if the Kinsman's paratragic engagement with the *Telephos* reflects his dependence on Euripidean plot-resources for self-defence in a moment of crisis. The pattern will soon be repeated. And the metatheatrical dimension will increasingly assume an ironic slant: despite all his buffoonery and maladroit impersonation of a woman, it turns out that the Kinsman has the instincts of a tragic actor! Even so, his resort to the *Telephos* does not save him: he is now trapped at the altar under the guard of the women.

(II) 765–84. Parody of a scene from Euripides' Palamedes

The Kinsman's Telephos-like role with Mika's baby did not give him a means of escape; it merely staved off the immediate reprisals of the women and helped him seek 'sanctuary' at the altar. Now, apparently warming to his function as a vehicle of Euripidean metatheatricality, he consciously ponders a means of rescue and recalls the scene from *Palamedes* in which the eponymous hero's brother, Oiax, scratched a message on oars which he threw into the sea at Troy in the hope that they would find their way to his father. Aristophanes bases this next phase of paratragedy on a much more recent play; *Palamedes* had been staged only four years earlier, in 415, though that by no means implies that all spectators of the comedy would have seen it. Once again, however, he focuses on a peculiar dramatic moment, and one which lends itself to visual absurdity and hence a degree of comic effectiveness even for those who did not know Euripides' original play in any detail. Spectators need only be capable of grasping the story of Oiax's message (which may or may not have been unique to Euripides' version) once they are told about it, which happens explicitly at 769–71.

What follows may in fact have had no exact equivalent in Euripides' play, since we do not know that Oiax's action was staged rather than simply described.[13] In any case, the paratragic reworking of the scene combines two clear strands: first, the clumsy physical action with which the Kinsman carves a message on wooden dedicatory tablets with his knife (the one with which he had killed Mika's 'baby') and then flings the tablets as though he were sending them as messengers through the streets (cf. 783–4); secondly, the short solo song he sings, in pseudo-tragic self-consciousness (776–84), while doing so. Adding song to speech expands the Kinsman's performative repertoire as a would-be tragic actor; it also makes all the more ironic the distance he has travelled since his original mockery of the poet Agathon's tragic songs in the first scene of the play (130 ff.). In an unusual technique of suspension, Aristophanes keeps his audience waiting for the duration of the parabasis (785–845) to discover the outcome of the Kinsman's attempt to make contact with Euripides.

(III) 849–922. Parody of parts of Euripides' Helen

After a nice metapoetic joke at 848 (Euripides has not shown up because 'He must be ashamed of that boring work, *Palamedes*'—as though the whole situation revolved around the poetic qualities of the playwright's works rather than the need for a practical solution to the Kinsman's predicament) Aristophanes now intensifies his paratragic technique by making more extended and verbally specific use of the source play.[14] It is no coincidence that this more detailed, intricate form of paratragedy exploits, as also with the *Andromeda* (below), a play produced just a year earlier (Dionysia 412), thus maximizing the chances of recollection on the part of a fair number of spectators. Even so, the alternative myth of Helen's stay in Egypt during the Trojan War, and her subsequent reunion there with Menelaos, must

[13] Oiax's action was nonetheless dramatically salient: among other things, it used one of the very arts, writing, of which his now dead brother Palamedes was the inventor; cf. Euripides fr. 578 for Palamedes' own boasts about this in the same play (with specific mention, lines 4–5, of writing carrying information across the sea).

[14] See n. on 855–7 for the relevant cross-references.

have been well-enough known to most people for some pleasure to be derived from the travesty of it in the present scene.[15] It helps that the parody starts (as neither the *Telephos* nor the *Palamedes* passages did) at the very beginning of the source play (855–6 ~ *Helen* 1–2), thereby evoking the setting in a pointedly framed way.

As elsewhere too, in fact, Aristophanes employs paratragedy in a sort of stratified manner which allows different kinds of spectators to relish the comedy of the scene at various levels of sophistication. The best-informed can savour closely the individual verbal borrowings, as well as the mixing-in of tragic language (e.g. 872–3) that does not belong to the *Helen* itself or even comes from other sources (870 is partly based on a line of Sophokles). Such spectators would also have some sense of the neat way that Aristophanes telescopes together three main moments in the original (Helen's prologue and conversation with Teucer, Menelaos's companion; the arrival of Menelaos himself; and the recognition-scene between husband and wife) and would be alert to other subtleties, such as the irony of the Kinsman's echo at 850–1 ('I'll act out that recent play, the *Helen*. | At least I'm already wearing a female costume) of precisely the notion of mimetic role-playing that Agathon had originally espoused, to the Kinsman's derision, at 154–6. But anyone with only minimal knowledge of Euripides' play, provided they possessed a general familiarity with tragedy's style and ethos, could appreciate the grotesque clashes of register and perspective (exotic, mythological Egypt versus everyday Athens) between the worlds of the play-acting Kinsman and Euripides on the one hand, and the baffled but pugnacious Kritylla on the other—not to mention, as in the previous cases, some colourfully visual humour, such as the no doubt exaggeratedly seaweed-swathed appearance of Menelaos-Euripides (cf. 910).

(IV) 1009–1135. Parody of parts of Euripides' Andromeda

As Euripides beats a hasty retreat at 924, he promises his Kinsman something further from his 'ample stock of schemes', where the term *mechanê*, 'scheme', can simultaneously denote both general craftiness and dramatic plot-devices, but may additionally hint at use of the

[15] On the origins of the myth, which pre-dated Euripides' play of 412, see T. Gantz, *Early Greek Myth* (Baltimore, 1993), 574–6; cf. esp. Herodotos 2.112–20.

theatrical 'machine' or crane.[16] Once again, there is a delay (during which the chorus performs while the Kinsman is taken off-stage to be shackled to a plank) before we see Euripides' next attempt to perform one of his plays as a means of rescuing his Kinsman.

The last major phase of the play's paratragic sequence begins at 1009, when the Kinsman, now tied up, gets a signal from Euripides that he must enact the role of the enchained Andromeda as counterpart to Euripides' own impersonation of the hero Perseus. Euripides' *Andromeda* had been staged at the same festival as the *Helen* in 412; several points already made about the latter in relation to Aristophanes' audience apply equally, therefore, to the former. The story of Andromeda's enchainment to rocks on the coast of 'Ethiopia' by her father Kepheus as appeasement to a sea-monster (sent by Poseidon to punish an offence by Kepheus's wife), and her rescue by Perseus on his return from a mission to kill the Gorgon Medusa, was very well known. Aristophanes relies on many spectators' ability to appreciate not just the basic scenario but his specific burlesquing of Euripides' treatment of the myth, which started with Andromeda singing a lament in her chains and hearing some of her words echoing back to her from a cave in the rocks.[17] However, instead of following the order of events in the original (as he did, if selectively, with the *Helen*), Aristophanes mischievously reconfigures them. He starts the parody (1015 ff.) with material taken from Andromeda's response to the appearance of the sympathetic female chorus (an ironic contrast to the hostile chorus of the comedy itself) at the end of the tragedy's opening scene. Next, he moves back to the beginning of that scene and to Andromeda's lament itself (1065 ff.), though not before introducing Echo as a personified character (1056–64). Finally, he jumps forwards to the arrival of Perseus-Euripides (1098 ff.)—'flying' on the theatrical crane in the original but here probably walking on the ground—and his erotic attraction to Andromeda, whom the hero goes on to rescue in the tragedy itself, though not in its present botched adaptation.

Much of this parodic version, from midway through the Echo scene (1082 ff.), is in comic counterpoint to the presence of the

[16] The same noun was used at both 87 and 765 by the Kinsman and will be used again by Euripides at 1132: so 'scheming' becomes a leitmotif of Euripides' clever character/plays.

[17] For specific references to the fragments of Euripides' play, see my note on 1015.

irredeemably vulgar, dim-witted, but aggressive Archer. The Archer is the only character in the surviving plays of Aristophanes to speak 'bad' Greek over an extended stretch; his involvement widens to a maximum the incongruity between the stylized elevation of tragic poetry, as adopted by Euripides and the Kinsman, and the sordid circumstances of the latter's predicament. One aspect of this dramatic polarization is that the Kinsman, who as Andromeda now has to perform more *sung* poetry (and therefore behave like a highly virtuoso tragic actor), to some extent yields the role of prime comic buffoon, which he had occupied from the start of the play, to the Archer: hence, for example, the fact that the Archer's obscenities at 1114–20 are reminiscent of some of the Kinsman's own earlier jeers at the effeminate Agathon. Only, though, 'to some extent': the Kinsman's physical abasement and humiliation (pinned to the plank in the remains of his female costume, 943) leave him central to the ridiculous nature of the situation—all the more so given the way in which he cannot sustain his paratragic identity as Andromeda without lapsing into betrayals of his underlying masculinity (esp. 1020, 1042–5). That last detail would in performance give a further edge to the comedy of paratragedy: the actor playing the Kinsman would convey the confusions of genre, register, and reference by variations in pitch and timbre of voice, as well as by his general (though constrained) body language.

One final observation is worth making on the Echo section of the *Andromeda* parody. It is not hard to see the attractions to Aristophanes of this personified character: the comic potential of 'echo effects' is self-evident. We would dearly like to know how Euripides had given Echo and her voice tragic dignity in his own play, but however he handled the motif its aim must have been to add pathos to Andromeda's isolation. In terms of the present scene, by contrast, what is notable is that the contributions of Echo seem simply redundant. Within the context of the *escape* plot, it makes no sense for Euripides to 're-enact' this part of his play (with the conspicuously metatheatrical reference at 1060–1), especially since his echo effects not only wake up the sleeping Archer but take on a momentum of their own, like a mechanism stuck in gear. By highlighting Echo's role, Aristophanes underlines what I have suggested is the *raison d'être* of paratragedy: not to critique or devalue tragedy as such, but to *convert* it into the stuff of comedy. Euripides is trying to follow his own script, yet finds his words being translated into a very different form of drama.

Four substantial blocks of Euripidean paratragedy, then, have served Aristophanes well but have 'failed' Euripides: after even his appearance as Perseus gets him nowhere (1098–1125), the tragedian still needs a way to rescue his kinsman. Yet, in a sense, Euripides' problem is Aristophanes' as well: namely, how to find an ending. Whether Aristophanes manages this entirely successfully is something about which critical disagreement is possible (though the quality of performance would obviously be a crucial factor in the theatre). But what is clear is that the denouement involves an abrupt and double shift of direction. The first shift is arguably a disappointing short-cut. Euripides simply proposes a permanent truce with the women, backed up by one more instance of the play's characteristically double-layered humour: the tragedian will stop 'slandering' the women—but if they remain hostile, he will continue to tell *the truth* about their nefarious secret lives (1160–9). That is not enough, however, to solve Euripides' (or Aristophanes') problem, since the Kinsman remains fastened to the plank and the Skythian Archer, acting on the orders of the Council, remains a stumbling-block.

Euripides' final solution takes him out of tragic mode altogether (though still within the realm of 'schemes', 1132: cf. n. 16) and sees him fall back on the basic comic resource of the phallus. He thereby enables Aristophanes' play to move to a different part of the spectrum of comic styles from the large preceding section of paratragedy. Aware of the Archer's sexual vulnerability, Euripides lures him easily into a trap by assuming the role of a woman in charge of a dancing-girl (Elaphion: literally 'little deer') and a boy piper: the group supplies musical entertainment for private parties (1178) and the woman knows how to play the procuress and extend the musical into the sexual (for a price: 1195). The ensuing distraction of the Archer by the physical lure of the dancing-girl entails familiar comic routines. When Euripides arranges for the girl to strip naked and sit on the Archer's lap (1181 ff.), the situation has something in common with old Philokleon's sexual shenanigans with the pipe-girl he has 'stolen' from a drunken symposium at *Wasps* 1341 ff. There is also a degree of resemblance to the calculated exploitation by Lysistrata of the naked figure of Reconciliation at *Lysistrata* 1115 ff.

But there is a little bit more to the dynamics of the present scene. Euripides' character in this passage, as well as his manipulation of his two young companions, would have reminded Aristophanes' audience of what might be called an alternative form of comedy. The woman Euripides impersonates is a female equivalent to the (more respectable) male Syracusan impresario who supplies the entertainment for the drinking-party in Xenophon's *Symposium*—entertainment which includes music, song, dance, juggling, and a short choreographed sketch (with kissing and brief dialogue) about the love of Dionysos and Ariadne.[18] Such small performing troupes clearly existed in the contemporary social world, and they no doubt varied in their degree of cultural sophistication. Euripides deliberately pitches his own group at the vulgar end of the scale in order to work the necessary effect on the Archer. The little scene he scripts and directs is the sort of self-contained, low-life drama which Greeks called 'mime' (including words, contrary to modern usage of this term), and of which the Dionysos–Ariadne sketch in Xenophon's *Symposium* is a more decorous variant.[19] Aristophanes' ultimate trick of metatheatre in *Women at the Thesmophoria*, therefore, is to incorporate a mime-like revue within the poetically elaborate and ambitious framework of his own genre—but to do so, in a delicious paradox, through the figure of none other than a tragic playwright.[20]

[18] Xenophon, *Symposium* esp. 2.1, 2.7–8, 2.11, 9.2–6. Note that at 9.4 Dionysos sits on the knees of Ariadne: the reverse of *Women at the Thesmophoria* 1182–4!

[19] For a useful outline (but with untranslated Greek) of the various kinds of things covered by the term 'mime' in Greek antiquity, see I. C. Cunningham, *Herodas Mimiambi* (Oxford, 1971), 3–11. Mime is usually called 'subliterary' because it was not part of the standard system of ancient genres; but Aristotle, *Poetics* 1.1447b10–11 does mention mime in passing when mapping out his own classification of mimetic art-forms.

[20] For another case where Aristophanes probably echoes typical mime scenarios, see my introduction to *Assembly-Women* (in *Aristophanes: Birds and Other Plays* in this series).

WOMEN AT THE THESMOPHORIA

Speaking Characters

KINSMAN: of EURIPIDES
EURIPIDES: tragic playwright
SERVANT: of AGATHON
AGATHON: tragic playwright
LEADER: of the CHORUS
CHORUS (24 dancers/singers): of women attending the Thesmophoria
MIKA: an Athenian woman, wife of Kleonymos
KRITYLLA: another (older) Athenian woman
KLEISTHENES: an effeminate Athenian citizen
PRYTANIS: one of the standing committee of the city Council
ARCHER: a Skythian slave, official armed attendant of the PRYTANIS

Silent Characters

NURSE: wet-nurse of MIKA's child
WIVES: various women present at the Thesmophoria
ELAPHION: a dancing-girl
TEREDON: a young male piper

[*The stage building has a single door which will serve in the opening scene as the house of* AGATHON, *later as a store-room related to the women's festival, later still as an indeterminate building on the Akropolis. In the centre of the* orchêstra *stands an altar, and over to one side, somewhere near the door, a statue of Apollo. From one of the two side entrances* (eisodoi), *which connect with other parts of the city, enter* EURIPIDES, *neatly dressed and with grey hair and beard, and, trudging along some way behind him, his* KINSMAN, *also elderly but more scruffily dressed.*]

KINSMAN. O Zeus, when on earth will a swallow appear in the sky?*
I'm about to drop dead. This fellow's been frantic since dawn.
Do you mind if I ask, before my spleen bursts open,
Where it is you're dragging me to, Euripides?

EURIPIDES [*earnestly*]. You're not permitted to hear what you'll soon find out
With your very own eyes.

KINSMAN. What d'you mean? Please tell me more.
I'm not permitted to hear?

EURIPIDES. Not the things that you'll see.

KINSMAN. And mustn't I see them then?

EURIPIDES. Not the things you should hear.

KINSMAN. I'm certainly missing your point—though it sounds very clever.
Do you mean I should neither hear nor see at all?

EURIPIDES. Why would you? The nature of each is quite distinct.

KINSMAN. Not hearing or seeing, you mean?

EURIPIDES. Precisely my point.

KINSMAN. But why distinct?

EURIPIDES [*abstractly*]. That's how they once split apart.
When Aither in the beginning took separate form
And started to breed living creatures inside itself,
It first contrived as our instrument of vision
The eye that mimics the wheel of the sun itself,
And it drilled the ears to serve as a funnel of hearing.*

KINSMAN. Through a funnel, you mean, I should neither hear nor see?
[*Ironic*] By Zeus, I *love* to learn new things like this:
How special it is to keep company with the wise!

EURIPIDES. There are many such things you could learn from me.

KINSMAN. But how
In addition to all this wonderful stuff could I find
A way to lose the use of both my legs?

EURIPIDES. Come on, catch up, and pay close attention.

KINSMAN. All right.

EURIPIDES. Do you see this house door here?

KINSMAN [*warily*]. Well by Herakles
I *think* so.

EURIPIDES. Now silence.

KINSMAN [*obtusely*]. I'm silent about the door!

EURIPIDES. Now listen.

KINSMAN. Okay—I'm silent about the door!

EURIPIDES. It's here the well-known Agathon happens to live,
The tragic poet.

KINSMAN. Which Agathon's that one then?

EURIPIDES. He's the Agathon who—

KINSMAN. Not the swarthy, muscular one?

EURIPIDES. No, a different one.

KINSMAN. Well I've never set eyes on him.
Not the one with the big bushy beard?

EURIPIDES. Have you really not seen him?

KINSMAN. No I haven't, at least as far as my memory serves me.

EURIPIDES. Well I'm sure you've *fucked* him—but maybe you still don't know him!

[*The stage door now starts to open.*]

But let's step back out of sight this way: here comes
One of Agathon's servants. He's carrying fire and myrtles,
To sacrifice, I think, for poetry's sake.

[*Enter the* SERVANT *carrying a brazier and myrtle wreath; he places both on/by the altar, adopts the posture of a priest, and begins to chant, observed by* EURIPIDES *and his* KINSMAN *standing back to one side.*]

SERVANT. Let sacred silence hold all the people!
Let all mouths be locked, since present inside

These halls of ours is a band of Muses
Engaged, our mistresses, in making song!
Let windless Aither check the breezes,
Let the waves of the sea now cease to crash,
The grey-green sea—

KINSMAN. What bullshit!

EURIPIDES. Keep quiet!

SERVANT. Let feathered creatures fall into slumbers,
Let the feet of wild beasts that run through forests
Be immobilized.

KINSMAN. More bullshitty bullshit!

SERVANT. This man of beautiful words, Agathon,
Our leader, prepares—

KINSMAN. Surely not to be fucked?

SERVANT. Who uttered those words?

KINSMAN. It was windless Aither.

SERVANT. He lays his groundwork, his play's foundations,
He bends fresh timbers as wheel-rims of words,
While others he smooths and fastens together.
Ideas he mints, creating new terms.
He pours his wax and rounds the model,*
Then injects the bronze—

KINSMAN. And gives a blow-job!

SERVANT. What rustic comes nigh to this enclosure?

KINSMAN. Someone who's ready, with you and your poet
Of beautiful words, to breach your enclosure
And rounding you and turning you over
[*Holding phallus*] To inject this prick of mine!

[*The* SERVANT *stops chanting and confronts the* KINSMAN *directly.*]

SERVANT. I suppose when young you must have been violent, old man.

EURIPIDES. Please pay no attention to *him*, my friend, but go
And ask Agathon without delay to come out.

SERVANT. No need to beseech: he'll appear himself in a moment.
He's just beginning to compose his lyrics. In winter
It's hard to bend the timbers to make his verses*
Unless he comes out of doors and stands in the sun.

KINSMAN. What am *I* supposed to do?
SERVANT. Just wait, he's coming.

[*The* SERVANT *goes back inside the stage building.* EURIPIDES *starts to pace around nervously, followed by his increasingly exasperated* KINSMAN.]

EURIPIDES. O Zeus, what plans do you have for me today?
KINSMAN. Well by the gods I'd certainly like to know
What's going on here. Why these groans and all this angst?
You're a kinsman of mine—you shouldn't be keeping secrets.
EURIPIDES. There's a really big problem about to come to the boil.
KINSMAN. What sort of problem?
EURIPIDES. A decision's about to be made
On whether my life continues or comes to an end!
KINSMAN. But how can that be? The courts aren't sitting today
To hear any trials, and there won't be a session of Council:
The Thesmophoria's still underway today.*
EURIPIDES. That's precisely why I'm afraid there's a threat to my life!
All the women have formed a conspiracy aimed at *me*:
In the Thesmophorion shrine they've agreed to hold*
An assembly today with a view to my ruin.
KINSMAN. But *why*?
EURIPIDES. On the grounds that my tragedies give them a bad reputation.*
KINSMAN. Oh I see—well by Poseidon they're *right* about that!
But what's your scheme to find an escape from this?
EURIPIDES. I want to persuade Agathon, my fellow-playwright,
To enter the Thesmophorion.
KINSMAN. And do *what*?
EURIPIDES. To attend the women's assembly and if need be
Defend me.
KINSMAN. But in his own person or in disguise?
EURIPIDES. He'd be in disguise, dressed up in the clothes of a woman.
KINSMAN. An ingenious ploy—entirely your style of things.
Our family takes the biscuit for crafty scheming!*

[*At this point the door of the stage building starts to open; during the following lines* AGATHON *comes into view on a wheeled platform, the* ekkuklêma*: he is a beardless young man, reclining on a couch, wearing female attire and surrounded by an array of women's garments and accessories. As he emerges, he starts to hum and to tune a lyre he is holding.*]

EURIPIDES [*turning*]. Shh, shh!

KINSMAN. What's wrong?

EURIPIDES. Look, Agathon's coming out now.

KINSMAN. But where?

EURIPIDES. Can't you see? He's the man being wheeled out here.

KINSMAN. Have I lost my sight altogether? I simply can't see
Any *man* over here—that's surely Kyrene there.*

EURIPIDES. Keep quiet. He's on the point of starting a song.

KINSMAN. Are those anthill tunnels or *what* that he's crooning about?*

[AGATHON *now starts to sing out loud, taking alternately—with suitable inflections of performance style—the lyric voices of a chorus-leader* [solo] *and a chorus of Trojan maidens* [group]. *The song is poetically compressed and rhythmically mannered.*]

AGATHON. [*Solo*] The chthonic goddesses' holy*
Torch receive, you maidens, with our free*
Fatherland, and dance with voices loud.
[*Group*] For which deity the revel?
Tell his name! My spirit is ready
To hold the gods in reverence.
[*Solo*] Come now celebrate in music
The one who draws the golden bow,
Phoibos, who founded the spaces of
Our land on the banks of the Simoeis.*
[*Group*] Hail, in our loveliest songs,
Phoibos, and in our melodious worship
Display your sacred privilege!
[*Solo*] The goddess on oak-breeding mountains,
Artemis, maiden of the wild—of her too sing!
[*Group*] I follow you, acclaiming
And extolling Leto's solemn offspring,
Artemis who shares her bed with no one!

[*Solo*] Sing of Leto too, with twangs of Asian lyre,
Keeping clashing rhythms in time with your dance
To the beat of the Phrygian Graces.*
[*Group*] I revere mistress Leto
And the lyre, mother of hymns
That resound with manly voice.
[*Solo*] The lyre makes a beam flash in divine
Eyes, as does our sudden song-cry. Wherefore
Glorify lord Phoibos!
[*Group*] Hail, blissful child of Leto!

[AGATHON *remains reclining on his couch while* EURIPIDES *and his* KINSMAN, *the latter twitching with ironic excitement, step forward to speak with him.*]

KINSMAN. What a gorgeous song, o gods of the female domain!*
It reeked of feminine odours, lascivious kisses,
And tongued endearments! Just listening made me feel
A tickling sensation creep right down under my bottom.
As for you, my girly young man: using Aischylos' words
From his *Lykourgeia*, I'd like to ask you some questions.*
[*Mock-poetically*] Whence comes this sissy? What country is yours? What dress?
What confusion of life is this? What can fancy lyre
Say to saffron dress, or ordinary lyre to hairnet?
Why athlete's oil-flask and woman's breast-band together?*
What have mirror and sword to do with one another?
And you, my child, are you being brought up as a man?
Then where's your prick? Your cloak? Your Lakonian shoes?*
But perhaps you're really a woman? Then where are your tits?
What's your answer? Why this silence? Do I have to seek you
From the song that you sang, since you won't explain yourself?

AGATHON [*loftily*]. Old sir, old sir, your envious complaints
I hear, but inside I feel no tribulation.
[*More prosaically*] I'm wearing the clothes that match my state of mind.
The task of a poet requires assimilation
Between his traits and the plays he has to write.
If, for instance, he's writing plays with female roles,
His body must also share in the traits involved.

KINSMAN. You have kinky sex when writing a part for Phaidra?*

AGATHON [*ignoring him*]. When writing for masculine roles, the body already
Has its natural features. But as for the things we lack,
We must use role-playing to help us pursue what we need.*

KINSMAN [*holding his phallus*]. Remember to call for *me* when you write satyr-plays:
I'll stand behind you and help—with a large erection!*

AGATHON. Besides, it's such an uncultured sight to see
A poet who looks like a peasant and is shaggy all over.
Take famous Ibykos and Anakreon of Teos,
Alkaios too: their lyrics have piquant flavours
And they wore head-scarves and displayed Ionian softness.*
Or take Phrynichos—[*patronizingly*] you've surely heard of *him*:*
He had beautiful looks, his clothes were beautiful too;
That's why his plays were beautiful works as well.
A poet is bound to write what's like his nature.*

KINSMAN. That's why ugly Philokles writes such ugly stuff,
And rotten Xenokles writes such rotten things too,
And Theognis as well: he's boring and so are his plays!*

AGATHON. There's no escaping the link. I've recognized this
And have pampered myself accordingly.

KINSMAN. But why?

EURIPIDES [*to* KINSMAN]. Stop yapping away. I used to be just the same
When *I* was the age he is and was starting to write.

KINSMAN. By Zeus I'm glad I wasn't brought up like *you*!

EURIPIDES. But let me explain the reason I've come.

KINSMAN. Yes, tell him.

EURIPIDES. Agathon, 'it's the mark of a skilful man to know how
To compress a long speech with a fine concision of words'.*
I've been struck down by a blow of fresh misfortune
And have come to you in supplication.

AGATHON. What for?

EURIPIDES. The women have plans to destroy my life today
At the Thesmophoria, because I slander them.

AGATHON. What kind of help do you think that *I* can give?

EURIPIDES. Every kind that I need! If you infiltrate the meeting
That the women are holding and look like a woman yourself,

You can speak in defence of me and save my life!
Only you can speak in a style that's worthy of *me*.

AGATHON. Why can't you go and present your own defence?

EURIPIDES. I'll tell you. For one thing, my face is known to all.
For another, my hair is grey and I'm bearded as well.
But *your* face is pretty, as pale as a woman's and shaved,
You've a woman's voice, you're soft-skinned, and lovely to look at.

AGATHON [*hesitating*]. Euripides—

EURIPIDES. What's the matter?

AGATHON. Did you write the line:
'You're happy alive, don't you think that your father is too?'?*

EURIPIDES. I certainly did.

AGATHON. Then don't expect that I
Will face your problems for you. I'd be insane!
You must shoulder the burden yourself, it's no one else's.
'When disaster strikes it's no time for ingenious schemes.
Submission alone is the way to bear the pain.'*

KINSMAN [*to* AGATHON]. Well *you're* an arsehole that's gaping for all to see
Not because of your words but because of submission all right!

EURIPIDES. What makes you afraid to go and do this for me?

AGATHON. My fate would be worse than yours.

EURIPIDES. How's that?

AGATHON. Must you ask?
They think I want to usurp their nocturnal work
And to steal for myself the sex that belongs to women.

KINSMAN. 'Usurp', you say? By Zeus, you want to be fucked!
Still, I take your point, by Zeus—it makes good sense.

EURIPIDES. Well will you or won't you do it?

AGATHON. No chance at all.

EURIPIDES. Thrice godforsaken plight!

KINSMAN [*apparently moved*]. Euripides,
You're my dearest relative, please don't let yourself down.

EURIPIDES. Well what do you think I should do?

KINSMAN [*pointing to* AGATHON]. For a start tell *him*
To go to hell. And make use of *me* instead.

EURIPIDES. Come on then, since you're making this offer of help,
Remove this cloak you're wearing.

KINSMAN [*obeying*]. I've thrown it aside.
But what are you going to do?

EURIPIDES. Shave off your beard
And singe all this hair down here.

KINSMAN [*nervously*]. Feel free, if you want.
But I shouldn't have offered my services after all!

EURIPIDES. Agathon, I know you always carry a razor,
Be so kind as to lend us one.

AGATHON. Please help yourself
From this razor-box down here.

EURIPIDES. That's decent of you.

[EURIPIDES *opens the razor-box lying with many other accessories by* AGATHON*'s couch and finds a suitable implement in it. He then turns back to his* KINSMAN, *whom he moves to the end of the couch and sets about shaving.*]

Sit down and start by puffing your right cheek out.

KINSMAN. Ouch, ouch!

EURIPIDES. Shut up! I'll force a peg in your mouth*
If you don't keep quiet.

KINSMAN [*jumping up*]. Aargh, aaaaaaaaaaaaaaaaaaargh!

EURIPIDES. Hey, where are you running?

KINSMAN. The Awesome Goddesses' shrine!*
In Demeter's name I'm not hanging round here any longer
To be cut to shreds.

EURIPIDES. But you'll be a ludicrous sight
With just one half of your face being shaved like that.

KINSMAN. I couldn't care less.

EURIPIDES [*wheedling*]. But I beg you, by all the gods,
Don't betray me. Come back.

KINSMAN [*reluctantly returning*]. Why on earth did I ever agree?

EURIPIDES. Keep still and hold your head up. Stop wriggling around!

KINSMAN. Oh, oh.

EURIPIDES. Stop moaning. The job's been nicely finished.

KINSMAN [*feeling his cheeks*]. What a wretch I am. You've stripped me of manliness.*

EURIPIDES. Don't worry about it, you'll now look extremely pretty. Do you want to see yourself?

KINSMAN. If you like—pass me that.

[EURIPIDES *hands him a mirror from* AGATHON*'s belongings.*]

EURIPIDES. Do you see yourself?

KINSMAN. No I don't! I see Kleisthenes!*

EURIPIDES. Stand up to allow me to singe you. And now bend over.

KINSMAN. I find this revolting. You'll turn me into a piglet.*

EURIPIDES [*calling*]. Can someone bring me a torch or a lamp from inside?

[*The* SERVANT *re-enters from the stage building, bringing a large torch. As* EURIPIDES *puts the* KINSMAN *in the appropriate position, he notices the latter's phallus hanging between his legs.*]

Bend over, and watch out there for your piglet's tail!

KINSMAN. You can bet that I will—though I think that I'm now on fire!
[*Parodically*] Help, help, I'm in trouble! Bring water at once, my neighbours,
Before the flames spread next to a nearby arsehole!

EURIPIDES. Keep calm.

KINSMAN. But how keep calm when I'm burnt to cinders?

EURIPIDES. There's only the tiniest bit still left. You're through
The worst by far.

KINSMAN [*standing up*]. But just look at the soot you've produced!
The whole area under my bottom's completely black.

EURIPIDES. Don't worry, it's someone else's job to sponge it.

KINSMAN. If anyone tries to wash my anus, he'll cop it!

[EURIPIDES *now gives the torch back to the* SERVANT, *who exits with it back into the stage building.*]

EURIPIDES. Agathon, as you weren't prepared to help in person,
At least please lend us a suitable cloak for him
And a breast-band too. You can't deny that you've got them.

AGATHON. You're welcome to take what you want.

KINSMAN. Well what should I take?

[EURIPIDES *examines* AGATHON*'s possessions and then proceeds to help dress his* KINSMAN *in the garments selected, both characters taking some care over the whole process.*]

EURIPIDES. Take this saffron dress and drape it over yourself.

KINSMAN. By Aphrodite, what a lovely smell of willy!*
Now tighten the belt for me.

EURIPIDES. Next the breast-band.

KINSMAN. There.
But please adjust the hang of the dress round my legs.

EURIPIDES [*to* AGATHON]. He needs a hairnet and headscarf too.

AGATHON. No, look,
Take this *wig* instead; I sometimes wear it at night.

EURIPIDES. By Zeus, a perfect suggestion. Exactly what's wanted.

KINSMAN. Will it fit my head?

EURIPIDES [*arranging it*]. Of course. It couldn't be better.
[*To* AGATHON] Please give us a cloak.

AGATHON. Take this one here from the couch.

EURIPIDES. And shoes as well.

AGATHON. You can take this pair of mine here.

KINSMAN. Will they fit me too? I know you like things *loose*!

AGATHON. That's for you to decide. But now that you've got what you need
I'd like to be wheeled back inside without further delay.

[*The* ekkuklêma *platform (see 96) is now wheeled back into the stage building.* EURIPIDES *takes a step back to inspect the appearance of the* KINSMAN.]

EURIPIDES. Well, well, this fellow's appearance has been transformed
To a woman's. But if you *speak*, adjust your voice
And be sure to sound like a woman.

KINSMAN [*in falsetto*?]. I'll try my best.

EURIPIDES. Let's see your style of walk.

KINSMAN. By Apollo, not yet!
I want you to swear—

EURIPIDES. Swear what?

KINSMAN. That you'll use every means
To *rescue* me, if the plan goes badly wrong.

EURIPIDES. I swear by Aither, the dwelling-place of Zeus.*

KINSMAN. As good as an oath by Hippokrates' tenement house!*

EURIPIDES. I swear by *all* the gods without exception.

KINSMAN. Remember, then, that your mind has sworn the oath
But your tongue is not what's sworn—and *I* didn't make you!*

EURIPIDES. Well it's time for you to hurry. The assembly's starting:
I can see the signal inside the Thesmophorion.*
I'd better be off myself.

[EURIPIDES *hurries off by one of the side entrances* (eisodoi). *His* KINSMAN *slips into the role of a woman attending the Thesmophoria: using his falsetto voice, he addresses an imaginary slave.*]

KINSMAN. Come this way, Thratta.*
O Thratta, look at those torches burning away
And the crowds coming up the hill beneath the smoke.*
You glorious gods, Thesmophoroi, welcome me,*
May my journey here and home bring me good fortune.
O Thratta, put down the basket and get out the cakes
For me to sacrifice to the two goddesses.

[*He goes through a charade of taking cakes and putting them on the altar before starting to pray.*]

O mistress dear, Demeter, most venerable goddess,
And Pherrephatta, grant me huge wealth from which*
To sacrifice—[*sheepishly*] if not, let no one notice!
And may my daughter, Piglet, find a husband*
Who's stinking rich—but otherwise stupid and dim.
And may my son, little Willy, be clever and bright.*

[*The* KINSMAN *bustles around like a woman settling herself at the festival.*]

Now where, oh where should I sit to hear the speakers
Without any trouble? You'll have to go now, Thratta:
Slaves aren't allowed to hear the women's speeches.

[*During the latter part of the* KINSMAN*'s speech a crowd of women has gradually entered, imagined as making their way up the Akropolis to the festival. Twenty-four of them now take up formation as the* CHORUS, *ready to sing and dance in what follows.*]

[PARODOS: 295–371]

LEADER [*in prose*]. Let sacred silence prevail! Let sacred silence prevail! Pray to the two Thesmophoroi and to Ploutos and to Kalligeneia and to Kourotrophos and to Hermes and the Graces that we may hold this assembly and meeting in the finest and most excellent manner, bringing multiple benefits to the city of the Athenians and good fortune to us women ourselves. And may the woman who does and speaks the best for the community of the Athenians and of the women here as well win the debate! Pray for these things and for everything good for ourselves. Hail paion, hail paion, hail paion! Let us rejoice!*

CHORUS. We accept your instructions and beseech
The race of the gods to respond to these prayers
By joyously showing themselves to us.
Zeus of immense renown, and you of the golden lyre
Who own Delos, sacred island,
And you all-powerful maiden,
Grey-eyed goddess of the golden spear who
Inhabits this envied city, come here to us.*
And you too, many-titled slayer of beasts,
Offspring of golden-visaged Leto.*
And you, awesome marine god Poseidon,
Ruler of the seas,
Leave the fish-abounding recesses
Where the waters swirl furiously,
With you, maiden daughters of the sea-god
Nereus,
And you mountain-roaming Nymphs.
May the golden phorminx of Apollo*
Resound in response to these prayers
Of ours. May perfection belong

To this assembly convened by Athens'
Women of good birth.

[*The* LEADER *continues in the elevated tones of a formal proclamation somewhat reminiscent of the start of a meeting of the city's political Assembly.*]

LEADER. Pray now, I enjoin you, to all the Olympian gods
And Olympian goddesses too, and the Pythian gods
And Pythian goddesses too, and the Delian gods
And Delian goddesses too, and the rest of the gods,*
That if anyone plots against the community
Of the city's women, or makes clandestine approach
To Euripides and the Medes to cause some harm
To the women's interests, or schemes to become a tyrant*
Or restore a tyrant from exile, or betrays a woman
Who uses a surrogate baby, or if a slave-girl
Acts as a go-between but then tells the master*
Or falsifies a message she's sent to deliver,
Or if an adulterer cheats and lies to a woman
Or doesn't give all the presents he promised he would,
Or if a crone wins an adulterer with gifts
Or a courtesan is bribed to take two lovers,
Or if an innkeeper, whether man or woman, corrupts
The standard measures they use for serving drinks—
Call down on such people, and on their houses as well,
Total ruin! But pray that the rest of us women receive
Every possible blessing the gods know how to bestow.

CHORUS. We join in praying for fulfilment
In the interests of city and people
For all these wishes of yours,
And that all those women who offer the best advice
May prevail in their speeches. But as for those others
Who deceive us and contravene
The oaths tradition prescribes,
For private profit and to cause us harm,
Or whose aim is that all decrees and laws
Be overturned and replaced,
Or who disclose our secrets

To those who are our enemies,
Or who enlist the Medes*
In harming our country –
All *those* are impious people and wrong the city.
O all-powerful
Zeus, ratify these things to ensure
That the gods stand beside us,
Mere women though we are.

LEADER. Pay attention, one and all. A decision was taken
By the women's Council: Archikleia presided,
Lusilla was scribe, the proposer was Sostrate.
We must hold assembly at dawn on the middle day
Of the festival, the day we're most at leisure.
The first item of business concerns Euripides:
His punishment needs deciding; his crimes are clear
To all of us. Who wishes to speak to the motion?*

MIKA [*stepping forward*]. I do!

LEADER. Then put on this garland before you speak.
Silence all round, pay attention. She's clearing her throat
Just like real orators. Clearly she'll speak at length.

MIKA. I swear by the two goddesses it's no pretension*
That makes me stand up to speak, you women. It's this:
I've felt oppressed and angry for ages now
At seeing the vilification we women endure
At Euripides' hands, the son of a vegetable-seller,*
And at all the different slanders he makes against us.
Well, hasn't he smeared us in every conceivable way?
He's maligned us without exception wherever you find
Spectators with tragic actors and choruses too.*
He calls us adultery-addicts and man-seducers,
Wine-swillers, betrayers, with tongues that never stop wagging,*
An utterly worthless lot and a bane to all men.
So when they return from watching his plays on the benches,*
They give us suspicious glances and start a search
In case an adulterer's hidden somewhere in the house.
We can no longer do all the things that we *used* to do.
He's made it impossible—such are the terrible views

That he's taught our husbands to hold. So if, for instance,
A woman should weave a garland, they say she's in love.*
If she's wandering round the house and drops a pot,
Her husband asks her: '*Who* is this breakage for?
There's only one person, "the Korinthian guest" himself.'*
Or suppose a girl is sick, her brother will say:
'This pale complexion's strange; it makes me suspicious.'
Or another example: a woman who can't get pregnant
Wants to smuggle a surrogate child. But how can she hide it?
The men of the family sit round her bed at the birth.*
In the past there were older men who'd marry young girls
But they've heard his slanders as well, so none of them's left
Who's prepared to marry a wife because of this line:
'If an old man marries, his wife will become his ruler.'*
It's also Euripides' fault that in women's quarters*
The men put seals and bars on all the doors
To maintain surveillance. What's more, they keep fierce dogs
To scare adulterers off from coming inside.
Well, some of these things are understandable.
But we used to have total control over household stocks
And could take some barley or oil or wine unnoticed.
No longer! The men now carry the keys themselves
Or hide them away. And they're always that awful kind
They call Lakonian keys, the sort with three teeth.*
In the past we could secretly open the storeroom doors
By getting a cheap signet-ring for stamping the seal.
But now Euripides, lousy slave that he is,
Has taught them to use more intricate types of seal
With the signet-rings they wear. Well here's my proposal:
His downfall has got to be plotted, one way or another,
Whether using poison or some other method instead.*
We've got to destroy him! So that's my public statement.
I'll draft the full decree with the woman who's scribe.*

[MIKA *removes the garland and steps back to join the general group.*]

CHORUS. Never before have I heard *Strophe**
A woman of craftier wiles
Or a more impressive speaker.
Everything she says is right.

Everything was fully examined.
Everything was weighed with thought, and shrewdly
She conceived her detailed arguments
And worked them out with care.
If you could compare her speech
With one from Xenokles, Karkinos' son,*
You'd all agree, I have no doubt,
He speaks the purest drivel!

[*Another woman now comes forward and puts on the speaker's garland.*]

KRITYLLA. I too would like to speak but I'll keep it brief.
The previous speaker's complaints were well expressed
But I want to tell you my own first-hand account.
My husband died some time ago on Kypros.*
He left behind five children, all young. I struggled
To rear them by weaving myrtle garlands for sale.
For a while I survived in this way, though only just.
But now this fellow, by writing all his plays,
Has persuaded the men that the gods don't exist at all:*
The result is that sales of garlands have fallen badly!
So I urge and propose before this gathering here
That this man should be punished for lots of different reasons.
The wrongs he does us, o women, are as rank and foul
As the vegetable plots in which his mother reared him.*
But I'm off to the Agora now: some men have placed
An order for twenty garlands—I need to weave them.

[*She removes the speaker's garland and rushes off by one of the* eisodoi.]

CHORUS. A second example, this, of fiery spirit
And even more subtle than the one before.
What a flow of verbiage
And all so timely, from a woman of sense
And wily intelligence, every word convincing!*
For his outrageous treatment of us this man
Must pay the penalty for all to see.

[*After glancing around, the* KINSMAN *now seizes his chance and steps forward to take the speaker's garland. He speaks in the quasi-female falsetto that* EURIPIDES *had instructed him to use.*]

KINSMAN. Let me start, o women, by saying this indignation*
At all Euripides' terrible slandering words
Is hardly surprising, and nor is your boiling bile!
I myself—I pledge what I say on my children's future—
Simply *hate* that man: I'd be mad to feel anything else.
But nevertheless we need to review these matters.
We're all alone and our words won't get reported.
Why is it we keep on making complaints against him
And feeling upset, when it's only a tiny handful
Of all our *numerous* misdemeanours he's mentioned?
Just to limit the point to myself, never mind other women,
I can tell you I've done many things that I shouldn't have done.
Worst of all was when I'd been married for only three days
And my husband was sharing my bed. But I still had a lover,
The man who'd deflowered me when I was only—seven.
He came that night, in lust, and scratched on the door.*
I knew the sound at once and crept off down.
'Well where are you going?' my husband asked. I said:
'My stomach's in painful spasms, my husband; I need
To go outside and use the latrine.' 'Go on then.'
He got up to grind some juniper, dill, and sage.*
I took some water and moistened the house-door hinge
And went out to my lover. He gave me a good hard bonking
While I bent and gripped the laurel by Apollo's statue.*
Euripides never told anyone *that*, you see.
Nor how we use our slaves and muleteers
To give us a shag when there's no one else to do it.
Nor how, when we spend all night being screwed by someone,
Next day at dawn we chew on lots of garlic
So that when our husbands come home from guarding the walls,*
They'll never suspect us of mischief. These things, you see,
Euripides never revealed. If he slanders Phaidra,
What's that to us? Moreover, he's never described
How a wife holds up a cloak to show her husband
What it's like against the light, while hidden behind it
Is the lover she lets from the house. No he's never told *that*!*
And I know a woman who claimed she was having contractions
For a whole ten days, till she'd managed to *purchase* a baby.
Her husband went shopping for things to help with the birth*

While an old hag smuggled the baby inside in a pot,
A honeycomb stuffed in its mouth to prevent it from bawling.
Then when the old hag gave a nod, the woman cried out
To her husband, 'Get out, get out! I think I'm about
To give birth!' The child was kicking inside the pot.
So the husband ran out in joy while the wife pulled out
The stopper from the baby's mouth and the baby yelled.
Then the filthy old woman who brought the baby along
Runs out with a grin to the husband and gives him the news:
'Your son's a lion, a lion! He's your spitting image
In all respects, including his dear little willy:
It's exactly the same as your own—all bent like a catkin.'
Don't we do these terrible things? By Artemis, yes
We certainly do! Should we rage at Euripides then,
Though all he inflicts on us are the things that we've done?*

[*The* KINSMAN *stays where he is while a reaction of shock spreads through the women and the* CHORUS.]

CHORUS. This leaves me quite amazed: *Antistrophe**
It came from out of the blue!
What place gave nurture to
So impudent a woman as this?
For this scoundrel to say these things
So publicly and shamelessly—
I thought it inconceivable,
Such outright recklessness.
There's nothing impossible now.
I endorse that familiar proverb:
Be sure to look under every stone
In case an orator bites you!*

[*The following exchanges, to 573, are in a longer 'recitative' metre, accompanied by the piper.*]

LEADER. Don't be surprised, we've always known there's only one thing worse
Than utterly shameless women, and that's—well, just more women, that's all!

MIKA. I swear in the name of Aglauros, o women, you must be out of your minds.*

You've either become the victims of drugs or suffered some other impairment
Allowing this woman, this damnable creature, to utter such vilification
Of all of us here. Well we've no other option, we'll have to take action ourselves.
With the help of our slaves what we need to find is a source of some very hot ashes,*
Then we'll burn away all the pubic hair from her pussy. That way she'll learn
As a woman she shouldn't abuse other women—a lesson she'll never forget.

KINSMAN. No, no, not my pussy, I beg you, o women! Please don't get carried away.
When we citizen women are gathered together we're allowed to say what we think.
So if I just said what I think is the truth in defence of Euripides
Do I then deserve to be punished by you by having my pubic hair cropped?

MIKA. And you think you *don't* deserve to be punished? You're the only one here who's dared
To speak in defence of a man who has done us so many intolerable wrongs.
He's deliberately sought out plots for his plays in which a bad woman appeared.
*Melanippe*s and *Phaidra*s, it's works of that sort he composes.* But no play at all
Called *Penelope*, no play about *her*. Why not? Because of her virtue.

KINSMAN. But that's not the reason, I know what it is. There isn't a woman alive
Who could be compared to Penelope—every one of them's some sort of Phaidra!

MIKA. Do you hear what she said, you women, this loathsome creature who stands before us?
Yet again she's slandered us one and all.

KINSMAN. But by Zeus I've nowhere near finished!
I haven't yet told all the secrets I know. Would you like me to tell you some more?

MIKA. What more could there still be left to describe? You've surely revealed all you knew.

KINSMAN. But I haven't recounted the tiniest fraction of all of the things that we do!
For instance, I haven't explained, you see, how we take an athlete's scraper*
And use it to siphon off wine for ourselves—

MIKA. Enough! Damnation upon you!

KINSMAN. Or how we filch Apatouria meat and use it to pay procuresses,
Then claim the weasel*—

MIKA. Too shocking for words! You're talking sheer nonsense about us.

KINSMAN. Or how one woman smashed open her husband's skull with the blow of an axe.
Nor the way that another used drugs to poison her husband and make him insane,*
Nor how yet another, an Acharnian woman, hid her own father's body . . .

MIKA. Confound you!

KINSMAN. . . . beneath the bathtub inside the house.*

MIKA. How on earth can we tolerate this?

KINSMAN. Nor how you yourself when your slave-girl gave birth to a boy decided to take it,
Passed it off as yours, and instead gave the slave-girl your own baby daughter to keep.*

MIKA. I swear by the two goddesses that you won't get away with talking like this.*
I'll tear out your tufty pubic hair!

KINSMAN. You won't lay a finger on me!

MIKA. We'll see about that.

KINSMAN. Yes we'll see about that.

MIKA [*to another woman*]. Here, take my cloak, Philiste.

KINSMAN. If you try to touch me you'll soon find out, by Artemis—

MIKA. What will you do then?

KINSMAN. I saw you gobbling a sesame cake—well I'll make you shit it back out!*

LEADER. You must both stop slanging each other like this. I can see there's a woman approaching.
She's running this way with an urgent look. Before she enters our midst,
Please stop the noise: we need decorum to hear what her message will be.

[*Enter in haste from one of the* eisodoi KLEISTHENES, *a beardless and generally effeminate-looking figure. The piper now stops playing and the metre returns to spoken iambics.*]

KLEISTHENES. Dear women, my kith and kin, who share my bent,
My cheeks make it easy to see that I'm one of your friends.
I'm *besotted* with women's affairs and I'm always your spokesman.*
Now I've heard about something important that matters to you:
It was all the talk in the Agora just this morning.
So I've come here to bring you this message and help make sure
You're vigilant, on your mettle, and don't allow
Something big and awful to catch you all off your guard.

LEADER. What is it, boy? It's right to call you a boy
So long as your cheeks are all smooth and hairless like this.

KLEISTHENES. Euripides, word has it, has sent a kinsman,
An old male inlaw, to come to this place today.

LEADER. With what end in view, what purpose behind the deed?*

KLEISTHENES. So that all your deliberations and plans today
Can be reported back. This man is a spy!

LEADER. But how could a *man* have infiltrated the women?

KLEISTHENES. Euripides singed and removed his pubic hair
And dressed him to look like a woman in all respects!

KINSMAN [*to the rest*]. Do you find these claims believable? What man's
So stupid he'd let his pubic hair be plucked?
I don't believe it, by the venerable goddesses two!*

KLEISTHENES. You're talking nonsense. I wouldn't have brought this message
If I hadn't found out from people who know it for certain.

LEADER. A grave and terrible matter is being reported.

Come, women, we cannot afford to procrastinate.
We must undertake a search and look for this man
Who is here somewhere concealed in our very own midst.
[*To* KLEISTHENES] You too must help us find him—that way you'll earn
Our thanks twice over, o spokesman of ours in the city.*

[*The women in general, with encouragement from* KLEISTHENES, *start to look at one another suspiciously. The* KINSMAN *is visibly alarmed but tries to avoid attention.*]

KLEISTHENES [*to* MIKA]. Let's start with you—who are *you*?
KINSMAN [*aside*]. Oh no, I'm trapped!
KLEISTHENES. You must all be scrutinized.
KINSMAN [*aside*]. I'm in serious trouble!
MIKA. You dare to ask who I am? I'm Kleonymos' wife!*
KLEISTHENES. Can you all confirm this woman's the person she says?
LEADER. Yes, we know her well. But examine the rest of them too.
KLEISTHENES. Well who's this one over here, the one who's carrying
A baby?
MIKA. My wet-nurse, that's who.
KINSMAN [*slipping away*]. I'm really done for!
KLEISTHENES. Hey you, where d'you think you're going? Come back. What's wrong?
KINSMAN. I need to urinate. Don't dare to stop me!
KLEISTHENES. Very well, go ahead if you must. But I'll wait for you here.

[*The* KINSMAN *goes over to one side and squats down as if to urinate like a woman.* KLEISTHENES *stands warily nearby.*]

LEADER. Be sure you wait and watch her like a hawk.
She's the only woman we don't recognize at all.
KLEISTHENES. This urination is very protracted.
KINSMAN. Yes, friend,
My bladder is sore from eating pungent cress.
KLEISTHENES [*grabbing him*]. Don't give me such twaddle.
Come over here with me.

KINSMAN. Why drag me like this? I'm not feeling well.

KLEISTHENES. Just tell me
Who your husband is.

KINSMAN [*blustering*]. What, the name of my husband, you mean?
You surely know what's-his-name from Kothokidai deme.*

KLEISTHENES. Which what's-his-name do you mean?

KINSMAN. What's-his-name, the one
Who with what's-his-name, son of what's-his-name—

KLEISTHENES. Pure baloney!
Have you come to this festival before?

KINSMAN. Of course!
For years and years.

KLEISTHENES. Then who shares your tent with you?*

KINSMAN. It's what's-her-name.

KLEISTHENES. I give up! It's more of your piffle!

MIKA [*intervening*]. Step aside. I'll test her better myself with questions
About last year's rites. [*To* KLEISTHENES] But *you* must move away
To make sure as a man you don't hear our secrets.

[KLEISTHENES *steps back.* MIKA *turns to the* KINSMAN.]

Now tell me
What sacred rite was the first we were told to perform?

KINSMAN. Let me see, what *was* it came first? [*Thinks.*] We started to drink!

MIKA. And what came next after that?

KINSMAN. We drank some toasts.

MIKA [*baulked*]. Someone *gave* you this information! But what was third?

KINSMAN. Xenylla asked for a bowl, as no piss-pot was there.

MIKA. You're talking rot! Come back here, Kleisthenes.
We've found the man you mean—it's *him*!

KLEISTHENES. What now, then?

MIKA. Remove all his clothes. He's telling a pack of lies.

KINSMAN. You mean you'll strip naked a woman who's had nine children?

[KLEISTHENES, *grappling with the* KINSMAN, *sets to work pulling off his woman's dress and revealing what is underneath it—including his phallus.*]

KLEISTHENES. Untie that breast-band quickly, you shameless person!*

MIKA. What a lusty, muscular body she seems to have.*
And by Zeus she hasn't got breasts like the rest of us women!

KINSMAN. That's because I'm barren and never got pregnant once.

MIKA. You say that now but you claimed that you'd had nine children!

KLEISTHENES. Stand upright! Where are you pushing your prick down there?

[*The* KINSMAN *makes increasingly desperate efforts to hide his phallus, pushing it backwards and forwards between his legs as the other characters keep moving to try to see it.*]

MIKA [*excited*]. Oh, I saw it peep out at the back! What a lovely colour!

KLEISTHENES. Well where is it now?

MIKA. It's come back out at the front.

KLEISTHENES. It's not visible here.

MIKA. No, it's round at the back once again.

KLEISTHENES. You've got your own isthmus, my fellow. You're pushing your prick
Back and forth more often than goods on the causeway at Korinth.*

MIKA. The filthy bastard! So *that*'s why he vilified us
For Euripides' sake.

KINSMAN [*aside*]. I'm a godforsaken fool!
What a terrible mess I've managed to get myself into.

MIKA. Well what should we do about this?

KLEISTHENES. Keep guarding him here,
Make sure he can't wriggle away and make his escape.
Meanwhile I'll inform the Prytaneis all about it.*

[*Exit* KLEISTHENES *by the same* eisodos *by which he entered. The*

CHORUS *now moves into formation, performing/miming the actions referred to by its* LEADER, *who chants to the piper's accompaniment.*]

LEADER. We ought to light our torches now and gather ourselves for action.
Let's gird our loins as men would do and remove our heavy cloaks.
We need to find if anyone else has infiltrated our meeting.
Let's sprint around the whole of the Pnyx and inspect the tents and pathways.*

[*The* CHORUS*'s movements continue with a rhythmically heightened impetus.*]

Onwards then! And first of all we need to dart with nimble feet,
Scour the place from top to bottom, but treading stealthily as well.
Vacillation's not allowed—no time for hesitation this.
I myself shall lead our action, running around in circles here.

[*The* CHORUS*'s movements of urgent investigation now continue in fully lyric form with choreographed dancing in a circle around the edges of the* orchêstra.]

CHORUS. Onwards, follow the tracks, search quickly everywhere
To see if lurking in this place
Some other man is hiding.
Turn your gaze in all directions, first this way,
Then over there, then here again,
Investigate with care in every corner!

If we catch a doer of impious deeds
He'll be fully punished, and in addition
We'll make an example of him to the rest
To show the price of outrage and injustice
And godless behaviour.
He'll then admit the gods are manifest,*
He'll show the need
For all the human race to reverence deities,
To observe traditional rituals
And be scrupulous in doing what's right.
If they fail to act like this, the consequence

For anyone caught in breach of piety
Will be to rage with madness, become unhinged,
And demonstrate to the world,
Both women and other mortals,
That infringements of law and piety
Are swiftly avenged by god!

LEADER. Everywhere has been explored as well as we could hope to do.
No one else has been exposed as hiding in our gathering here.

[*By this stage,* MIKA *is holding her baby again (cf. 608–9). As the* CHORUS *ends its dance, the* KINSMAN *moves towards* MIKA, *snatches her baby, and runs with it to the altar at the centre of the* orchêstra, *where he picks up a sacrificial knife and adopts a menacing posture.*]

MIKA. Eeek!
Stop! Where do you think you're going? Come back, come back!
Oh dear, please somebody help me! He's got my baby.*
He snatched it from my tits and is running away.

KINSMAN. Screech all you like! You won't get your baby back
If you don't let me go. [*Melodramatically*] Right here on this sacred surface
This sacrificial knife will open its veins
And the blood will drench the altar.

MIKA. O woe is me!
O women, please come to my aid! Raise the cry of battle,
Erect a trophy to mark our fight.* Don't stand
And watch me deprived of my only child.

CHORUS. Scandal, scandal!
O Fates* who rule us, what strange
Apparition do I behold?

[*The piper accompanies the following lines, which are chanted in 'recitative'.*]

LEADER. Everything in the world, it seems, abounds in brazen shamelessness.
Stunned we are, yes stunned, o women, by the further deed this man's performed.

KINSMAN. Stunned you'll be for sure until I knock your stubbornness out of your heads.

LEADER. Terrible then this situation, terrible like no other we've seen.

MIKA. Terrible in the extreme indeed—he's snatched my baby and grips it tight.

[*In the following lyric exchange, the* KINSMAN *too delivers his lines in song.*]

CHORUS. How could anyone disagree with that,
When this man's actions display no shame?
KINSMAN. But I haven't yet reached the limit!
CHORUS. However you came to be here
Don't think you can simply escape and boast
That you did this deed then slipped through our grasp.
A nasty fate awaits you!
KINSMAN. May no such outcome ever befall me—I pray that it won't.
CHORUS. But who of all the immortal gods would ever
Come down as your ally in such injustice?
KINSMAN. You blabber in vain! I'll never release this female child.
CHORUS. By the two goddesses, you won't carry on gloating about your violence
Or uttering your impious words.
For these godless actions we'll pay you back
In the way you deserve.
The winds have suddenly changed direction, your luck
Is carrying you towards big trouble.

LEADER [*to* MIKA]. Time for you and some other women to go and bring some logs out here,
Then light a blaze around this scoundrel and set him on fire without delay.*

[*During the following lines* MIKA *and her* NURSE, *followed by some other women, go inside the stage building and reappear with pieces of wood, which they proceed to place in a circle round the* KINSMAN.]

MIKA. Let's go inside to fetch some firewood, nurse.
[*To* KINSMAN] I'll soon reduce you to a lump of half-burnt charcoal!

KINSMAN [*defiantly*]. Go ahead and stoke a fire! But let's remove
This little dress from the child. Your death, o baby,
Is the fault of just one person—your very own mother. [*Removes the dress.*]
What's *this*? No baby girl after all but a leather wineskin!
It's full of wine too—and wearing Persian bootees!*
O dissolute women, taking bibulousness to extremes!
You go to such lengths to contrive your supplies of wine.
Good business for innkeepers—but bad for us husbands.
No wonder you smash your pots and spoil your weaving.*

MIKA. Pile up the firewood, nurse, all the way around him.

KINSMAN. Go ahead and pile it up! But answer me this:
Do you say you're this baby's mother?

MIKA. And for nine full months*
I carried it.

KINSMAN. Carried it, did you?

MIKA. By Artemis, yes!

KINSMAN [*holding it up*]. And filled with the cheapest plonk?

MIKA. But look what you've done!
You shameless thing, you've removed my baby's dress
Even though it's so tiny.

KINSMAN. So tiny? The poor little thing!
What's its age? Let me see: a vintage of three or four?*

MIKA. Roughly that—but born at a Dionysiac feast.*
Now give it me back.

KINSMAN [*gesturing*]. No I won't, by Apollo right here.*

MIKA. Then we'll set you alight.

KINSMAN. Go ahead then and set me alight.
But this baby girl here will be slaughtered the moment you do.

MIKA. No don't, I implore you! Do whatever you want to *me*
But spare this baby.

KINSMAN. What maternal instincts you have!
All the same this baby girl's about to be slaughtered.

MIKA. Oh no, my child! Quick, nurse, pass a ritual bowl—
I need to catch the blood of my child as it's spilt.

KINSMAN. Hold the bowl right there: I'll do you this favour at least.

[MIKA *holds up her bowl towards the* KINSMAN, *who takes his knife and carries out the 'sacrificial' deed but does not let* MIKA *catch as much 'blood'/wine as she was expecting. While this action is taking place,* KRITYLLA *re-enters from the* eisodos *through which she exited at 458. She is carrying a torch.*]

MIKA. Damnation on you! How mean and unkind you are.
KINSMAN. And the skin itself is the priestess's perk to keep.*
KRITYLLA. What's the priestess's perk?
KINSMAN. This skin. Here, take it yourself.
KRITYLLA. O poor, poor Mika, who's left you drained like this?
Who's taken your darling child away from you?
MIKA. This scoundrel here! But now that you're back with us,
I want you to guard him while *I* fetch Kleisthenes
And report to the Prytaneis everything this man's done.

[MIKA *exits by an* eisodos. KRITYLLA *stands guard over the* KINSMAN.]

KINSMAN [*aside*]. Let me see, what scheme can I find for getting rescued?
What attempt? What clever idea? The one who's to blame
And who managed to get me into this terrible mess
Is not to be seen—not yet. What messenger then
Could I send to him? I know a device of course
From his play *Palamedes*. Just like that man I'll write
A message on oars and throw—[*pausing*] but I don't have the oars.*
Well where could I find some oars? Where on earth could I get them?
[*Looking round*] Suppose I used these tablets instead of the oars?*
I could scratch a message then scatter them. That's much better!
They're made of wood after all and those oars were wooden.

[*He now breaks into song, like a tragic hero at a moment of great intensity. While singing he uses his knife to carve messages onto the votive tablets and then hurls them in various directions.*]

O hands of mine,
You must grasp an ingenious task!
Come, tablets of polished timber,

Receive the tracks of my chisel,
Heralds of my toils. Alas!
This letter *rho* is awkward.*
Go on, go on! What furrow do you cut?
Proceed, make haste, down every street,
This way, that way, without delay!

[*The* KINSMAN *remains at the altar, still guarded by* KRITYLLA, *while the* CHORUS *comes forward to take up formation for the parabasis.*]

[PARABASIS: 785–845]

LEADER. Step forward, then, let's praise ourselves: self-eulogy is called for.*
In contrast, every *man* has nothing but insults to speak about women.
They say we're a plague on the human race and the source of every evil:
Of quarrels and strife, of grievous discord, of grief and war. But tell us:
If we're such a plague, why *marry* us then, if you really think we're so bad,
And why forbid us to leave the house or even to peep from our doors,*
What makes you quite so eager to *keep inside* what you think is an evil?
And if some woman does leave her home and you find her outside the house,
You become insane with rage even though you ought to be filled with joy
At finding that something you think is evil has left and vacated your house.
Or suppose we visit each other's houses then fall asleep after dancing:*
Every male who finds us lying on couches prowls round and fancies this 'evil'!
Or suppose we peek from the door of our house, you all want a sight of this 'evil';
And if the woman's abashed and steps back, that only heightens the lust

That each of you feels for a further glimpse of this 'evil' you saw peeking out.*
We women are actually better than you, and here's a proof that reveals it.
Let's put to the test which group is *worse*. We women assert it's men,
But you say it's us. Let's examine the question by setting up contrasts between us,
In each case placing the name of a woman and man right side by side.
Take Nausimache and Charminos: he's inferior—what could be clearer?*
Here's a further example: take Kleophon—far worse than the tart Salabaccho!*
No man even tries to compete with Aristomache, Marathonian woman,
And the same is true where Stratonike's military might is concerned.*
But as for last year's Councillors, not one could match Euboule.
They abandoned office to somebody else: they couldn't deny it themselves.*
So that's why we boast that women are better, much better, than all you men.
No woman would steal vast sums of money from the city's public funds
Then ride a chariot up the Akropolis hill. The most she'd filch,
Say a basket of wheat from her husband's stores, she always pays back the same day.*

There are many men who steal like that:
We could name them if we wanted.
We could also prove that men outdo us
As greedy gluttons and violent muggers
And silly buffoons and kidnappers too.
And there's one other thing: men are worse than us
At conserving ancestral customs.
Right up to this day we women have kept
Our weaving equipment, our baskets of wool,
And our parasols too!*
But as for the menfolk we live alongside,
In numerous cases they've managed to lose

The spears their families handed down,
While quite a few others have thrown from their shoulders
While out on campaign—
Well, what else but their parasols too!*

Numberless complaints we women could find good grounds to bring against
All the men—yes numberless, but one that looms above the rest.
Think of a woman whose son grows up to become a person of serious note:
Army officer, general even—*she* herself should have prestige:
Front-row seating should be her right at the Stenia and the Skira too,
Every festival, in fact, which all we women can call our own.*
Women, however, whose sons grow up as wretched cowards—you know the sort:
Warship captains who shirk their duty or helmsmen who can't do their job—
They should sit with hair cropped close behind the mothers of citizens brave.*
After all, o city of Athens, what argument could justify
Seating at the front Hyperbolos' mother in robes of glistening white,
Hair left hanging down behind her, with Lamachos' mother right next to her,
Lending money, what's more, to others, when any woman who borrows from her
Ought to refuse to pay the interest Hyperbolos' mother demands from her,
Ought in fact to refuse to pay the loan at all, but instead should say:
'*You* deserve no fruit from your loans: how could you, given the fruit of your loins!'*

[*As the* CHORUS *steps back, the* KINSMAN *once again starts peering round anxiously from the altar.*]

KINSMAN. I've developed a squint, looking out for him. He's late!
I wonder what's holding him up. I know what it is:
He must be ashamed of that boring work, *Palamedes.*

Well which of his plays can I use to entice him here?
I've got it! I'll act out that recent play, the *Helen*.*
At least I'm already wearing a female costume.

KRITYLLA. What's this latest mischief of yours, this constant fretting?
You'll soon have a Helen that's more than you bargained for
If you don't keep quiet till one of the Prytaneis comes.

[*Ignoring the warning, the* KINSMAN *adopts the stylized posture and manner of a tragic actor and maintains it in the face of* KRITYLLA*'s hostility*.]

KINSMAN. Lo I behold the virginal springs of the Nile,
Which in the place of heaven's moisture bedew
Egypt's white plain, where black purge-lovers dwell.*

KRITYLLA. You're a scoundrel all right, I swear by Hekate's torch!*

KINSMAN. The land of my birth is one of high renown,
Sparta. My father was Tyndareos.*

KRITYLLA. You blackguard,
Claiming *him* as your father? Phrynondas more likely, that's who.*

KINSMAN. I was given the name of Helen.

KRITYLLA. What, a *woman* again,
Before you've paid for that earlier female charade?

KINSMAN. For my sake, numerous souls by Skamander's waters*
Met their death.

KRITYLLA. And I wish that had happened to you as well!

KINSMAN. Now I myself am here. But my wretched husband,
Menelaos himself, remains far out of sight.
Why, then, am I still alive?

KRITYLLA. 'Cos the ravens aren't hungry!*

[*Enter* EURIPIDES *from one of the side entrances: he is draped in rags and seaweed, supposedly in keeping with the plight of the shipwrecked Menelaos in his play* Helen. *In what follows* EURIPIDES *ostentatiously matches his* KINSMAN*'s paratragic manner in the face of* KRITYLLA*'s down-to-earth interventions*.]

KINSMAN. But I feel a kind of fluttering in my heart.
O Zeus, deceive me not—don't dash my hopes!*

EURIPIDES. To whose domain do these dark halls belong?
Is it one who might give shelter to shipwrecked strangers
Who've struggled in storms on the ocean's rolling swell?

KINSMAN. This palace belongs to Proteus.
KRITYLLA. Proteus, eh?
Godforsaken rogue! [*To* EURIPIDES] He's a liar, by the goddesses two!
It's a good ten years since Proteas dropped dead.*
EURIPIDES. What shore is this on which we've beached our bark?
KINSMAN. Egypt.
EURIPIDES. Alas, alas! How far off course.
KRITYLLA. Don't believe a single word from this scumbag here!
He's talking drivel. It's the Thesmophorion here.*
EURIPIDES. Is Proteus himself at home or far abroad?
KRITYLLA. Your journey's clearly left you seasick, stranger.
I told you before that Proteas is *dead*,
But you nonetheless ask if he's here at home or not.
EURIPIDES. O woe, he's dead! But where was his body entombed?
KINSMAN. His grave stands here, the very spot where I'm seated.
KRITYLLA [*to* KINSMAN]. You deserve to rot—and rot you will, I promise!
How dare you describe this altar as somebody's grave!
EURIPIDES [*to* KINSMAN]. Wherefore, o woman, do you rest where tombs are laid,
Your head enveiled in grief.
KINSMAN. Under duress
To link my bed in marriage to Proteus' son.
KRITYLLA. Still trying to fool this stranger here, you wretch?
[*To* EURIPIDES] This fellow came here, o stranger, with wicked motives.
He came to steal gold jewellery from the women.*
KINSMAN. Snarl all you like and hurl reproaches at me!
EURIPIDES [*to* KINSMAN]. O woman, what crone is this who denigrates you?
KINSMAN. Theonoe, Proteus's daughter.*
KRITYLLA. Strike me down
If I'm not Kritylla, Antitheos' wife, from Gargettos!*
And *you're* a scoundrel.
KINSMAN. Waste all the breath you want!
I shall never allow myself to marry your brother
And betray Menelaos my husband, who's still at Troy.
EURIPIDES. What did you say, o woman? Turn round your gaze.*

KINSMAN. I feel embarrassed: my cheeks have been defiled.*

EURIPIDES. What thing is this? I lose the power of speech.
Ye gods, what sight do I behold? Who are you?

KINSMAN. I ask you too: the same thought holds us both.

EURIPIDES. Are you Greek or are you a woman born in this land?

KINSMAN. A Greek. But I too wish to ask the same.

EURIPIDES. To me, o woman, you look like Helen herself.

KINSMAN. And you to me, in your seaweed, like Menelaos.

EURIPIDES. You've rightly identified your hapless husband.

KINSMAN. You've come, you've come at last to your spouse's hearth!
[*Breaking into song*] Hold, hold me, husband, clutch me in your arms,
Come, let me kiss you! Take, take, take, *take* me away
At once!

KRITYLLA [*blocking them*]. By the goddesses two, there'll be big trouble
In the form of a whack from this torch if anyone takes you!

EURIPIDES. Do you mean to prevent me from taking my very own wife,
The daughter of Tyndareos, back to Sparta with me?*

KRITYLLA. Oh no, you too are a scoundrel like him, now I see it.
You're hatching a plot between you. So that explains why
You were both Egyptians before! [*Glancing off*] But he'll still be punished:
Here's one of the Prytaneis coming, an Archer beside him.

[*Enter the* PRYTANIS *from one of the side entrances, accompanied by the Skythian* ARCHER, *whose equipment includes a bow and quiver of arrows, a whip, and a large knife.* EURIPIDES *starts to move away towards the opposite side entrance.*]

EURIPIDES [*to* KINSMAN]. This is looking bad—I've no choice but to slip away here.

KINSMAN. And leave me in the lurch? What then?

EURIPIDES. Stay calm.
I'll never betray you, so long as there's breath in my body,
Unless my ample stock of schemes should fail me. [*Exits.*]

KINSMAN. Well that was a ploy that failed to come up with the goods!

PRYTANIS [*to* KRITYLLA]. Is this the scoundrel that Kleisthenes told us about?

[*To* KINSMAN] Hey you, stop skulking there. [*To* ARCHER] Escort him inside,
Tie him up on the plank, then bring him back here outside*
And stand guard over him, making quite sure that no one
Gets anywhere near him. But keep your whip to hand
And strike anyone who approaches.

KRITYLLA. That's right! Just now
A man nearly grabbed him—an Egyptian sailor, I think.*

[*As the* ARCHER *starts to manhandle him towards the door, the* KINSMAN *takes the hand of the* PRYTANIS *in a supplicatory gesture.*]

KINSMAN. O Prytanis, please, I beg you by this right hand
Which you always hold cupped in the hope of receiving a bribe,
Do me one small favour although my death is near.

PRYTANIS. What favour is that?

KINSMAN. Please give the Archer instructions
To remove my clothes before I'm tied on the plank.
As an old man in a woman's dress and headscarf,
I'll prompt public derision by giving a feast to the ravens.

PRYTANIS. You've got to be bound as you are; the Council decided.
It's to show the passers-by what a scoundrel you are.

KINSMAN. Aaaaagh! [*Melodramatically*] O female dress, what deeds you have wrought!
All hope of rescue has vanished from sight for ever.

[*The* ARCHER *now pulls the* KINSMAN *into the stage building. The* PRYTANIS *and* KRITYLLA *exit by one of the* eisodoi.]

LEADER. Come, let us perform the usual dances expected upon this occasion
When we women maintain the sacred rites for the goddesses, mother and daughter.
Like us, Pauson keeps ritual fast,*
Frequently addressing these same gods
And praying to them that he like us
May observe these rites for ever.

[*The* CHORUS *comes forward and takes up formation for a dance whose first part is circular.*]

CHORUS. Step forward, advance!
With nimble steps come form a circle,
Make a chain hand by hand,
Each one of you joining the rhythm of dance.
Start moving with fleetest footwork.
Keep a watchful eye in all directions,
Glancing round and round, for the shape of the dance.

As you dance sing the race of Olympian gods, *Strophe*
Combine loud praise of them with ecstatic dancing.

But if anyone thinks we women will slander* *Antistrophe*
Male citizens while we're in this shrine, he's crazy!

Instead we need
To prepare for something new
By stopping the lovely movements of circling dance.

Step forward and celebrate the lyre-god, *Strophe*
Apollo, and bow-carrying
Artemis, our sacred mistress.
Hail, god who works from afar,
Confer victory upon us!*
And Hera, fulfiller of wedlock,
Let us rightly sing her praises too:
She joins with us in all our dances
And guards the keys of marriage.*

Hermes, god of pastures, I entreat, *Antistrophe*
With Pan and the friendly Nymphs,
To demonstrate heartily with laughter
The joy they take in all
The movements of our dances.
Each one of you heartily rouse
The joy of the dance for us and the gods.
Let's perform our usual steps, o women—
Why not, we're fasting in any case!

Come leap and twist with springy rhythm!
Embellish the song throughout!
And be our leader yourself,
O ivy-wearing Bacchic god,*
Master of ours! In revels
That love the dance I'll sing your name.

Euios, son of Zeus, *Strophe*
Bromios, Semele's child,*
Who delights in dances
On mountain slopes, with the Nymphs' lovely
songs,
O Euios, Euios, euoi!
You take pleasure in joining the dance!

And all about you resound *Antistrophe*
Kithaironian echoes,*
As the darkly forested mountains,
Deep in shade, rumble with their rocky glens.
Encircling your head the ivy
Blossoms with glistening tendrils.

[*The* ARCHER *comes out from the stage building dragging a large plank on which the* KINSMAN *is now shackled.*]

ARCHER. 'Ere den go cry away in open air.*
KINSMAN. I beg you, Archer—
ARCHER. No beggin' me na, ye dont.
KINSMAN. Please slacken the clamp.
ARCHER. Okay, I do de clamp.

[*The* ARCHER *roughly hits the metal clamp which attaches the* KINSMAN*'s neck to the plank.*]

KINSMAN. No, help, I'm dying! You're making it even tighter!
ARCHER. Ye want it more an' tight?
KINSMAN. Aaagh, aaagh! I'm choking!
Damnation on you!
ARCHER. Shut mouth, ol' man, ye dyin'.
I fetchy mat for me to guard ye den.

[*The* ARCHER *goes back briefly into the stage building and reappears with a mat on which he proceeds to lie down and fall asleep.*]

KINSMAN. Such a life of ease Euripides has brought me!

[*Bending his head as far as he can to one side, the* KINSMAN *shows sudden signs of excitement. From one of the side entrances* EURIPIDES *makes a sudden, brief appearance in the costume of Perseus, and gestures elaborately towards the* KINSMAN.]

But what? O gods! Zeus Saviour! There's hope after all.
It looks as though Euripides won't betray me.
He just jumped out as Perseus and gave a signal
That I need to play the part of Andromeda now.*
Well I've got the bondage at least! It's clear to me
That he'll come to rescue me. What else could he mean?

[*The* KINSMAN, *accompanied by the piper, now starts to sing an elaborate monody which oscillates between the role of Andromeda and the character's masculine identity.*]

Dear maidens dear,*
If only I might escape and
Elude the Skythian's watch!
Do you hear my voice, o you who sing out from the cave?*
Nod your agreement, allow me
To return to my wife.
Pitiless the one who bound me here
As the most woebegone of mortals.
I barely escaped the old woman's clutches,
The putrid hag, but I still came to ruin!
This Skythian has long stood guard
And has hung me here, wretched and unbefriended,
As a meal for the ravens.
As you see, I cannot join the dances
Nor with young girls of my own age
Do I stand in fine adornment,
But instead in heavy chains enshackled
I'm exposed as food for a sea-monster—Glauketes!*
With no wedding-song
Of joy, but a dirge of enchainment

Lament for me, o women,
For the miserable things I have suffered
In my misery, o woe, o woe!
And in addition from kith and kin more outrageous sufferings,
Though I, a woman, begged the man, pouring out
A tearful lament for my death,
Alas, alas, o grief, o grief,
Yet he shaved me first
And swathed me in saffron,*
And in addition sent me up here
To this shrine exclusive to women.
I sob for my fate
Brought to birth by a malign spirit.
Accursed I am!
Who will not look upon my
Suffering as unenviable, so full of evils?
If only for me a fiery star falling from the Aither—
Would annihilate this barbarian!
No longer is beholding the sun's immortal flame
Dear to me, since I was suspended here
In a state of throat-severing anguish, ready
For a rapid route to death.

[*Enter* EURIPIDES *from the stage building, dressed as an old woman and playing the part of Echo (n. on 1018) from his own play* Andromeda.]

EURIPIDES. Greetings, dear girl. But as for your father, Kepheus,
Who exposed you here—may the gods annihilate him!
KINSMAN. But who are *you* who pity this plight of mine?
EURIPIDES. Echo—who sings back your words in mocking voice.
Last year in this very same place where we're standing now
I too, like you, played a Euripidean role.*
But come, my child, you need to do your thing,
Cry pitiful tears.
KINSMAN [*sarcastically*]. And *you'll* be crying soon after!
EURIPIDES. Just leave that to me. But now begin your lines.

[*The* KINSMAN *starts to chant, initially in the persona of Andromeda—till the echoing of his words by* EURIPIDES, *now standing just inside the door of the stage building, increasingly exasperates him.*]

KINSMAN. O sacred Night
On how long a course you drive the horses
Of your chariot across the star-studded arc
Of the sacred Aither
And revered Olympos's spaces.*

EURIPIDES. . . . Olympos's spaces

KINSMAN. Why do I, Andromeda, beyond all others
Suffer such a woeful destiny?

EURIPIDES. . . . woeful destiny

KINSMAN. Forlorn facing death.

EURIPIDES. . . . forlorn facing death

KINSMAN. You'll kill me, crone, with your babbling.

EURIPIDES. . . . with your babbling

KINSMAN. By Zeus, your grating interventions
Are just too much.

EURIPIDES. . . . just too much

KINSMAN. Let me sing, good man, a solo song,
And do me a favour. Please stop.

EURIPIDES. . . . please stop

KINSMAN. To the crows with you!

EURIPIDES. . . . to the crows with you

KINSMAN. What's wrong?

EURIPIDES. . . . what's wrong

KINSMAN. You're crazy!

EURIPIDES. . . . you're crazy

KINSMAN. Hang yourself!

EURIPIDES. . . . hang yourself

KINSMAN. Get knotted!

EURIPIDES. . . . get knotted

ARCHER [*waking, to* KINSMAN]. Wot ye jabberin'?

EURIPIDES. . . . wot ye jabberin'

ARCHER. Me Pritanees call.

EURIPIDES. . . . me Pritanees call

ARCHER. Wot wrong?

EURIPIDES. . . . wot wrong

ARCHER. Wot de voice I 'ear?
EURIPIDES. ... wot de voice I 'ear
ARCHER [*to* KINSMAN]. More jabber?
EURIPIDES. ... more jabber
ARCHER. Ye'll be sore.
EURIPIDES. ... Ye'll
be sore
ARCHER. Ye mockin' mi?
EURIPIDES. ... mockin' mi
KINSMAN. It's not me speaking, it's this woman right here!
EURIPIDES. ... this woman right here
ARCHER. Where is dat bitch?
KINSMAN. She's running away.
ARCHER [*bewildered*]. Oy stop, where ye runnin'?
Ye pay for dis.
EURIPIDES. ... ye pay for dis
ARCHER. Won't ye shut your trap?
EURIPIDES. ... won't ye shut your trap
ARCHER. Get 'old o' de bitch.
EURIPIDES. ... get 'old o' de bitch
ARCHER. Ye just a jabberin' blasted wumman!

[EURIPIDES *disappears inside the stage building but soon reappears in a new costume—with winged boots and the decapitated Gorgon's head—that marks him as the hero Perseus.*]

EURIPIDES. O gods, what foreign land is this I've reached
With speed of sandalled feet? Straight through the Aither
I cut my path with movements of wingéd feet—
I Perseus who navigate my way to Argos
With the Gorgon's head.
ARCHER. Wot's dat? Ye got de 'ead
O' Gorgos de Council scribe?*
EURIPIDES. No, the *Gorgon*'s head
I'm talking about.
ARCHER. Me too, de 'ead o' Gorgos.
EURIPIDES. But ah! What crag is this I see, and a maiden
Just like a god in beauty yet moored like a ship?
KINSMAN. O stranger, take pity on me, a forsaken woman.
Release me from these bonds.

ARCHER. Shut up, no jabber!
Ye blasted ding, ye go to die but jabber?
EURIPIDES. I pity you, maiden, when seeing you hanging here.
ARCHER. No maiden diss but is very naughty ol' man
An' thievy an' wicked.
EURIPIDES. What rot, you Skythian slave!
This woman you see is Andromeda, Kepheus' child.
ARCHER [*pointing at* KINSMAN*'s phallus*]. Dat ding no cunty—no see wot whopper it is?
EURIPIDES. Come, give me your hand, young girl, and let me hold it.
Please, Skythian—don't forget, all human beings
Suffer some affliction. In my own case this girl
Has aroused intense desire.
ARCHER. I no envy ye.
But if de arse wa' facin' diss way round,
I let ye take an' bugga 'im on de plank.
EURIPIDES. Why won't you let me, Skythian, set her free
Then lie with her upon our nuptial bed?
ARCHER. If want very much to bugga de ol' man den,
Drill 'ole in plank and fuck 'is arse from back.
EURIPIDES. No, no, I'll free her bonds.
ARCHER. I whip ye den!

[*A brief scuffle takes place, with the* ARCHER *forcing* EURIPIDES *back, first with his whip and then with a large knife.*]

EURIPIDES. I'll not give up.
ARCHER. I got ye den,
I chop de 'ead right off wid diss big knife.
EURIPIDES. Ah, no! What next? What appeals can I turn to now?
Such things are lost on this barbarian's nature.
Bringing words of novel wisdom to bear on the stupid*
Is a vain and wasteful thing. But there's one more scheme
I can use against this fellow—this one will suit him.

[EURIPIDES *rushes off by one of the* eisodoi *before the* ARCHER *can apprehend him.*]

ARCHER. De nasti fox, 'e played me monkey trick!
KINSMAN. Remember, Perseus, you're leaving me all forlorn!
ARCHER. Ye want me whip ye den sum more?

[*The* ARCHER *lies back down on his mat and falls asleep again.*]

CHORUS. Pallas the lover of dances
I always summon to join our chorus—
Maiden unwed and youthful,
She protects our city,
Manifesting her power, and she alone
Is called the holder of the keys.*
Appear to us, goddess, rightful hater of tyrants!
The assembled women call upon you.
I pray you bring with you
The goddess Peace, festival-lover.
You too we bid come in benign kindness,
Our mistress deities, into our grove*
Where it is not permitted for men to behold
Our solemn rites, in the place where with torches
You reveal to us an immortal vision.
Come into our presence, we implore you,
O supreme mistresses of the Thesmophoria.
If ever in the past you answered our prayers and came,
Come now again, we beseech you, to this very place.*

[EURIPIDES *reappears, this time in the garments of an old woman but with his veil to one side. He carries a harp and is accompanied by* ELAPHION *and* TEREDON.]

EURIPIDES. If all you women would like to make a truce
That would last for ever with me, well now's the time,
On the basis you'll never again be slandered by me
In any respect. I'm happy to offer these terms.
LEADER. What's made you come to offer us this proposal?
EURIPIDES. This man on the plank's in fact a kinsman of mine.
So if he's returned to me, you'll never again
Be slandered by me. But if you refuse my offer,
I'll denounce to your husbands, as soon as they're back from campaign,
All the secret plans you devise inside your homes.*
LEADER. As far as *we're* concerned, your offer's accepted.
But you'll have to persuade this Skythian slave as well.
EURIPIDES. I'm about to do it. You too, Elaphion there,

Remember to do all the things that I mentioned before.
So tiptoe over and start to practise your moves.
And you, Teredon, strike up a Persian tune.

[*The group moves towards the sleeping* ARCHER. EURIPIDES *covers his face with his woman's veil,* TEREDON *(probably miming to the main piper) strikes up an exotically sensual tune, with some additional contribution from* EURIPIDES *on his harp, while* ELAPHION *starts to gyrate sexily. After a few moments the* ARCHER *wakes with a jolt and jumps up.*]

ARCHER. Wad ol diss buzzin' noise? A parti wake mi?
EURIPIDES. The girl was starting to practise some of her steps.
She's going to dance at a party some men are holding.
ARCHER. She dance an' practise more, I no want stop 'er.
She 'op nice quick like flea on fleecy blankit.
EURIPIDES [*to* ELAPHION]. Lift up your cloak, my child, and take it right off,
Then sit yourself on the knees of this Skythian here
And stretch out your feet—I'll remove your shoes.
ARCHER. Ya ya!
Sit 'ere, sit 'ere, ya ya, mi nice liddle girl.

[ELAPHION *removes her cloak and sits, now naked, on the knees of the* ARCHER, *who starts to fondle her; she stretches out her feet for* EURIPIDES *to remove her shoes.*]

Ee ee! Diss tit so nice, firm like a turnip!
EURIPIDES [*to* TEREDON]. Pipe faster—don't be afraid of this Skythian now.

[TEREDON *pipes with more urgency and* ELAPHION, *despite the* ARCHER*'s efforts to keep hold of her, gets up to dance again. As he watches her, the* ARCHER*'s phallus springs up from his groin.*]

ARCHER. Wot luvly buttock! [*To his phallus*] Oy back, ye stay inside.
Okay, dat look ol nice, diss shape o' mi dick.
EURIPIDES [*to* ELAPHION]. That's enough. Here, take your cloak. It's time for us
To be moving along.
ARCHER. But no she kiss me first?
EURIPIDES. Of course. [*To* ELAPHION] You can kiss him.

ARCHER. Oo-oo, oo-oo, so nice!
De tongue taste sweet as 'oney from Attika bees.
Why no she lie wid me?

EURIPIDES [*taking* ELAPHION]. Goodbye now, archer.
I'm afraid I can't oblige.

ARCHER. Ya please, ol' wumman!
Diss favour just for me.

EURIPIDES. Will you pay a drachma?*

ARCHER. Ya ya, I pay!

EURIPIDES. Come on then, give me the money.

ARCHER. But dont 'ave money. Ye take diss quiver instead.

[EURIPIDES *takes the* ARCHER*'s quiver from him and releases* ELAPHION *again.*]

EURIPIDES. You can have this back when you pay.

ARCHER [*to* ELAPHION]. Den follow me, child.
[*To* EURIPIDES] Stay 'ere, ol' wumman, an' guard ol' man for me.
But wot ye name?

EURIPIDES. My name is Artemisia.*

ARCHER. Me rememba den diss name: Artamouxia.

[ARCHER *and* ELAPHION *exit into the stage building;* EURIPIDES *now springs into action, removing his female cloak before setting about unfastening the* KINSMAN *from the plank.*]

EURIPIDES. Hermes, god of stealth, you're making the plan work well.
[*To* TEREDON] Here, run along, boy, and take this cloak with you.
Now at last I'll free this man. [*To* KINSMAN, *ironically*] Please show your spunk
And once you're untied run away with all your might
Back home to where you belong with your wife and children!

KINSMAN. You can count on me for that once I've been untied.

EURIPIDES. There you are, you're free—run away before
The Archer comes back to find you.

KINSMAN. I'm off right now!

[EURIPIDES *makes a speedy departure by a side exit, with* KINSMAN *running immediately behind him. Only a moment later,* ARCHER *reappears from the stage building with* ELAPHION.]

Ol' lady, diss daughter o' yours is really sweet,
No nasti at all, so soft. But where's de wumman?
O no, I done for! Where gone de ol' man from 'ere?
Ol' wumman, ol' wumman! I no like dat ol' wumman.
Artamouxia!
De wumman played trick on me! [*To* ELAPHION] Ye run away now.

[ELAPHION *leaves by one of the side exits.*]

Mi quiver is lost—is really fucked to pieces!
Aaaaagh!
Wot I do now? Where's wumman den? Artamouxia!

LEADER. Are you asking about the old woman who carried a harp?

ARCHER. Ya ya! Ye see 'er?

LEADER [*pointing*]. She went away down there,
The woman you mean—and an old man went with her too.

ARCHER. De man wear yellow dress?

LEADER. He certainly did.
[*Pointing the wrong way*] You'd probably catch him up if you chased that way.

ARCHER. De lousy bitch! [*Confused*] Which way I run den now?
Artamouxia!

LEADER [*gesturing*]. Chase straight up there. Not that way! Back over here.
It's *this* direction here. You're getting it wrong.

ARCHER. I done for but run diss way. Artamouxia! [*Exits in wrong direction.*]

LEADER. Run in pursuit—and we hope you're blown to the crows!

[*The whole* CHORUS *now reassembles before chanting its parting words.*]

CHORUS. We've played our games for long enough.
It's time for us to go our way,
Each woman back home.
May the two Thesmophoroi goddesses*
Repay our worship with joy.

[*Exit* CHORUS.]

FROGS

INTRODUCTION

Frogs is a work of theatrical, literary, and comic brilliance. It brings together a fascinating set of thematic strands—poetic, religious, mythological, political—and intertwines them into a complex plot that is unlike any other surviving Aristophanic play in its dramatic shape and dynamics. Its overriding claim to fame lies in the extended contest between the tragic playwrights Aischylos and Euripides which occupies the second half of the work—a contest which stands not only as one of Aristophanes' most bravura pieces of comic theatre but also as a remarkable 'document' in the history of Western poetics. But the first half of *Frogs* has its own riches to offer as well. These include the treatment of the god Dionysos as a sort of burlesque substitute for his brother Herakles on a journey down to Hades; Dionysos's famous encounter with the frog chorus of the play's title in the form of a competition for rhythmic supremacy between the god's clumsy rowing and the amphibians' insistent croaking; the appearance of the chorus of initiates whose activities in the underworld are a sort of mirror-image (though the mirror, as always, is comically distorting) of their Eleusinian celebrations on earth; and a series of episodes in which the threatened exposure of Dionysos as a pseudo-Herakles leads to a game of swapped identities between himself and his slave Xanthias.

In between the two halves of the plot, which are tied together by the dramatically improvisatory figure of Dionysos himself (first as Heraklean visitor to Hades, then as theatrical judge of the tragedians' contest), occurs the work's parabasis, which has attracted a great deal of attention for its comments on the contemporary political situation at Athens in 406–5. *Frogs* was first performed at the Lenaia festival (late January, early February) of 405; most of the play must therefore have been composed (and rehearsed, under the chorus-trainer Philonides) in the second half of 406. There is an ancient report that it was specifically the parabasis which was so admired by its first audience that Aristophanes was publicly honoured and *Frogs* specially awarded a re-performance (at Lenaia 404, it is normally assumed). If that was true, it is testimony to an extraordinary moment in Aristophanes' career. I shall return to this matter, and to the parabasis itself, at the end of this Introduction. But let us start by taking some account of the historical context in which Aristophanes composed *Frogs* in 406–5.

Two aspects of that context are of particular relevance, though it required Aristophanes' distinctive sensibility, with its love of comic paradox, to bring them together into elements of the same play. One was the perilous military condition of Athens after practically a quarter of a century of war with Sparta, and a concomitant sense (lurking in the background at various points in *Frogs* but brought into sharp foreground focus near the end of the contest at 1417–66) that the survival of the city was more than ever at stake. Athens faced both financial and manpower shortages in attempting to sustain its war efforts at this date. During 406 it actually melted down some golden statues of Athena Nike on the Akropolis in order to make new coins (*Frogs* 720 alludes to this), and faced with an acute shortage of rowers for its fleet, it went so far, in the summer of this same year, as to offer freedom and citizenship to slaves who rowed on the triremes at the battle of Arginousai (a point referred to several times in *Frogs*).[1] Athens had won that battle, but nonetheless suffered large further losses and was plunged as a result into a traumatic political controversy.[2]

While writing *Frogs*, Aristophanes could not have known that Athens was only a few months away from final defeat in the war (the crucial juncture being defeat in the sea-battle of Aigospotamoi in late summer 405). But he, like many of the spectators at the first performance of *Frogs*, might have realized that the city could hardly maintain the same level of military activity much longer. As so often in the past, however, Athenian attitudes to the war were divided; more than one Spartan offer of peace was rejected during the final years of the war. Within *Frogs* itself Aristophanes might be thought to be hedging his bets. In a sentimental flourish at the very end of the play, the chorus briefly appeal to a desire for an end to war and curse the likes of the demagogue Kleophon, who is presented as still on the side of all-out belligerence (1531–3). Yet this flourish is linked to the fantasy return to life of Aischylos, a poet who had earlier proclaimed himself author of 'warlike' plays which taught the Athenians 'always to want to defeat their opponents' (1021–7), and whose view on how

[1] See my notes on *Frogs* 33, 191, 693–4.
[2] See my notes on *Frogs* 541, 1196.

Athens might best survive in the circumstances of 405 itself appears to be predicated on a *continuation* of war (1463–5)! *Frogs* does not send out (and why should it?) consistent signals about what attitude Athenians ought to take to the war.

The other most significant part of the background to *Frogs* was the death of the tragedian Euripides (in Makedon) at some point in early 406. This event, followed a few months later by the death of Sophokles,[3] prompted thoughts on Aristophanes' part (though hardly on his alone) of 'the end of an era' in the Athenian theatre: all the good tragedians are now dead, as Dionysos tries to explain to Herakles, and just the riff-raff is left (71–95). It seems hard to resist the inference that it was specifically the death of Euripides in 406 which triggered in Aristophanes the fundamental impulse of inspiration for *Frogs*, and certainly gave him the initial idea of a scenario in which Dionysos, god (among other things) of drama/theatre, would descend to Hades with the intention of bringing back his 'favourite' tragedian. Curiously, however, we know that what ensues from Dionysos's journey, namely the great contest between Euripides and Aischylos, was far from being a completely new Aristophanic conception at this date.

Aristophanes had always been somewhat obsessed with Euripides, who already makes an appearance (393–489) in *Acharnians* of 425, and provides material for extended parody in that play. The obsession if anything grew stronger with time, as *Women at the Thesmophoria* (411), earlier in this volume, demonstrates. Even the specific premise of the contest in *Frogs*—the head-on confrontation between Euripides and Aischylos—had been germinating for some time in Aristophanes' imagination. This is revealed by the fact that as early as *Clouds* (and the scene in question probably belonged to the first version of the play in 423) we fleetingly meet the idea of treating Aischylos and Euripides as polar opposites, and representatives of incompatible values, within the poetics of tragedy. In one of their violent altercations, Strepsiades and Pheidippides fall out precisely over their relative estimates of these two tragedians. The elderly father thinks of the early poet as supreme in his genre, his young son expresses contempt for

[3] Aristophanes must have inserted references to the death of Sophokles into the text of *Frogs* (at 76–82, 787–94, 1516–19) when composition of the play was already well under way; see my notes on those passages.

Aischylos (as a bombastic figure from the past) and chooses Euripides as a clever, 'modern' poet whose work he seems to like partly for its taboo-breaking daring (*Clouds* 1364–72). That passage shows that Aristophanes had long thought of an Aischylos–Euripides clash as a framework within which to pit (supposedly) traditional and modern values against one another. In *Frogs*, he was ready to turn that idea into an elaborately sustained piece of comic theatre.

If we put together the two aspects of Athenian history outlined above—the question of the city's recent fortunes in the long, exhausting war against Sparta, and the idea that a whole era of tragic drama had come to a close in 406—what should we make of their conjunction in relation to *Frogs*? There is, of course, no necessary or obvious link between them. Athenians must mostly have debated and calculated the city's military policies without giving any conscious thought to tragic poetry. Equally, many Athenians who cared passionately about tragedy and/or attached importance to the death of Euripides are unlikely to have correlated their views on the history of the genre with the precise issues of the war in 406–5. Yet Aristophanes subtly and suggestively sets up in *Frogs* an interplay between these two areas of Athenian experience. He even perhaps allows his comedy fitfully to toy with a sense that Athens' greatness, equally in poetry and politics (including warfare), may be on the wane. What he does not do, however, is to offer any explicit formulation of what this combination of themes amounts to.

Instead, Aristophanes gives his comedy a design which enables it to find its way rather belatedly and ambiguously to the point at which war and tragedy become entwined. Dionysos sets off to bring Euripides back from Hades because he is (in comically hyperbolic form) a passionate devotee of the playwright's work who cannot bear to think of losing such a dramatist from the world. Indeed, he even suggests that Euripides' poetry matters to him, as the symbolic god of theatre, as much as food and drink matter to his philistine brother Herakles (58–67, 105–7; see further below). But it is only once he is in the underworld that he finds himself enlisted to judge an acrimonious quarrel that has broken out between Aischylos and Euripides over the 'throne' of tragedy (755–811). It is, moreover, only at a late stage of the contest that he *retrospectively* (re-)interprets his original intention as having been to bring back to life a tragedian who can help 'save the city' (1419): it is here that, almost despairing of reaching a verdict

(1433–4), he finally turns to war-related matters—first the controversial figure of Alkibiades (1422–34), then a more general question about the city's survival (1435–66)[4]—in an attempt (which turns out, even so, to be unsuccessful) to establish which of the playwrights has the most beneficial advice to give the city.

If Aristophanes has coloured *Frogs* with overlapping evocations of what we might call, for shorthand, the themes of 'the end of tragedy' and 'the threat to the city's survival', he has done so in a way which hardly communicates any kind of stable conviction, let alone a practical thesis, about the state of Athens in 406–5. I have already noted above that the victory of Aischylos in the contest brings with it contradictory implications on the war front: the poet whose work is allegedly suffused with the spirit of military heroism and prowess will somehow (there is not the slightest indication of *just* how) enable Athens to bring its hostilities with Sparta to an end. The victory and return to earth of Aischylos is hard to interpret as anything more than an exercise in comically hazy nostalgia.

The strengths of *Frogs* lie elsewhere than in the supposed solution to Athens' problems which some critics have taken its author to be advocating. It is a work which puts on display perhaps better than any other the whole spectrum of Aristophanes' verbal and dramatic repertoire: from the obscenely earthy (the slave who compares the pleasure of betraying the master's secrets to having an orgasm, 753; or Dionysos's obscene ditty at 542–8) to the lyrically ingenious (the jagged conflict of musical and visual rhythms as Dionysos rows against the frog-chorus's croaking, 209–67; or the wildly exaggerated parodies of each others' song-styles exchanged by Aischylos and Euripides at 1264–1363); from one-line gags (the sarcastic corpse that would 'rather come back to life' than carry Dionysos's luggage for too little payment, 177) to intricately constructed scenes that unfold in multiple stages (the dramatization of the Eleusinian initiates' processional rituals, 316–459; or the oscillating comic logic of the sequence of episodes in which Dionysos repeatedly sheds and reclaims his identity as 'Herakles', 460–673).

Nor do Aristophanes' preferred techniques and methods operate

[4] The order and attribution of lines in this last passage have been extensively debated and subjected to various textual reconstructions: see below on the putative revision of the play, together with my note on *Frogs* 1436.

discretely, one at a time; they are constantly combined and recombined in ways that produce a sort of layering of comic meanings. Appreciation of these qualities requires us, as modern readers, to exercise our visual and aural imaginations, in as historically informed a manner as possible, in order to compensate for the gap between words on the page and the vivid immediacy of theatrical performance. To bring out this point, let me comment illustratively on three sections from the first half of *Frogs*.

At the very start of the play, Aristophanes stages a wonderfully ironic and enigmatic mélange of visual and verbal elements. Many critics have dwelt on the metatheatrical paradox of the initial exchanges between Dionysos and Xanthias: they speak self-consciously as characters in a play, ostensibly drawing attention to the cheap, vulgar humour of other comic playwrights while simultaneously taking advantage of the joke-motifs in question for Aristophanes' own purposes. But that is only one of several strands woven together at the start of the play. For the original theatre audience, the scene's visually peculiar components would have been striking.[5] A 'master' (1) with Heraklean garb (lion-skin and club) superimposed over a woman's saffron dress and high boots is leading a donkey on which a luggage-carrying slave is riding: how make sense of such a bizarre configuration of features? Some spectators might have guessed, even before it is confirmed at line 22, that the master is Dionysos (in a pot-bellied, buffoonish form which reflects older comic traditions[6]), since the god, in his 'Asiatic' style, was often artistically depicted in quasi-female garments and was indeed thought of as a deity capable of blurring gender distinctions (cf. Euripides' *Bacchae*). Spectators alert enough to make that identification might additionally have spotted a mythological joke in the replacement of a fawn- or panther-skin (a badge of Dionysiac rituals)

[5] For one artist's (probable) depiction of this opening scene, presumably in connection with a later production of the play in Magna Graecia, see the fourth-century Apulian vase (formerly Berlin F3046, now lost) discussed and illustrated in O. Taplin, *Comic Angels* (Oxford, 1993), 45–7 and pl. 13.7, and E. Csapo, *Actors and Icons of the Ancient Theater* (Chichester, 2010), 58–61.

[6] Dionysos's fat belly is alluded to by Charon at 200. A buffoonish Dionysos had already been a character not only in Aristophanes' own *Babylonians* of 426 (see the Appendix to this volume) but also in earlier works by other comic poets, including Kratinos' *Dionysalexandros* and Eupolis' *Taxiarchs*: see J. Rusten (ed.), *The Birth of Comedy* (Baltimore, 2011), 181–4, 264–8, for the evidence.

with the lion-skin.[7] But they would still have been intrigued by the riding slave and also by the pseudo-Heraklean outfit, which, in a nice piece of comic self-reflectiveness, produces an outburst of mirth on the part of Herakles himself (42–5).

The Heraklean garb does get explained in due course, though in a way which helps to set up Dionysos as an absurdly naive deity in this context: costume alone can hardly equip one to face the terrors of Hades (as the subsequent episodes will bear out). In the text itself the riding-slave motif receives a rather casual, incomplete explanation (21–4: yet why *allow* a slave such indulgence?), but it has the capacity to stimulate the audience's minds with further comic implications and associations. One possibility is to take the apparently inverted master–slave hierarchy as preparing the way for later references to the recent emancipation and enfranchisement of slaves who fought in the navy at the battle of Arginousai.[8] Another is to see it as forming a witty visual 'pun' on a myth that many spectators would remember well, namely how Dionysos eventually brought back Hephaistos to Olympos after he had been flung away at birth by his mother Hera. That scene was often depicted with Hephaistos riding on a donkey, Dionysos on foot.[9] The full irony of this oblique allusion to the Hephaistos story at the start of *Frogs* only transpires once we learn that Dionysos is en route to *Hades*, not Olympos.

The play's opening, then, involves a plurality of comic ingredients, managing to fuse together metatheatre, scatology, master–slave banter (including the play on semantics at 25–30), and mythological confusion into a lively concoction that gives the work an initial burst of comic energy. One specific detail of the passage—a glimpse of Dionysos's strong reactions as a theatrical spectator himself (16–18)—helps to sow the seed for the subsequent conversation between Dionysos and his brother Herakles (38–72). Once again, it would be possible to analyse that conversation in terms of

[7] It is conceivable, if one thinks of spectators who liked trying to interpret clues at the start of a comedy (cf. Aristophanes' joke on this very idea at *Peace* 43–8), that some might have wondered about the Herakles who was made to dress as a woman while enslaved to the Lydian queen Omphale, though we do not know how early this 'transvestite' motif was invented: cf. T. Gantz, *Early Greek Myth* (Baltimore, 1993), 439–40.

[8] See my note on *Frogs* 33.

[9] See e.g. T. H. Carpenter, *Art and Myth in Ancient Greece* (London, 1991), 13–17 with ills. 2–13 (various), for the myth and its depiction in visual art. Cf. I. Lada-Richards, *Initiating Dionysus* (Oxford, 1999), 132–4, 156–7.

Aristophanes' typical liking for combining different techniques and registers of humour in a rich dramatic mélange. But I would like here to concentrate on just one aspect of this encounter between the 'real' Herakles and Dionysos's poor imitation of him—the aspect which anticipates what will turn out to be the play's main subject-matter, the values of tragic theatre. Via a rather zigzagging process, which includes jokes about warfare, sex, and food (47–65), Dionysos eventually reveals to Herakles the yearning passion he has for the recently deceased Euripides and his plan to descend to the underworld and bring him back to life.[10] What emerges from this is a comically spiced clash of values between the sensuous, poetry-loving Dionysos and the bluff, philistine Herakles.

Like most Greek gods and heroes, Dionysos and Herakles traditionally possessed multiple traits and qualities that could be developed in different narrative forms. Aristophanes deftly chooses just those attributes which are conducive to a disagreement about whether poetry is one of life's supreme pleasures and goods.[11] Dionysos, as god of theatre (as well as a deity associated with intense states of rapture), represents the allegiances and impulses of those who love poetry: he speaks in quasi-erotic vocabulary of the intense desire and longing aroused in him by Euripides' works. Herakles, by sharp contrast, as a supremely practical hero who primarily seeks fuel for his bodily appetites, just cannot understand his brother's attachment to such cultural activities. Dionysos is nervous of his brother's views (58–60), especially after the latter has mocked him several times (42–58). Although Herakles knows the names of tragic playwrights (73–87), he conveys a sense of insouciance about such matters: 'if you really *must* fetch someone' (77) sets the tone, which is expanded by the reference to hordes of young poets 'with more gift of the gab than Euripides' (89–91) and the description of Euripides' own poetry as 'a great big con-trick' and 'a load of rubbish' (104–6). As Dionysos insinuates with his neat put-down, 'Don't try to inhabit my mind . . .

[10] For another Aristophanic play which involved poetry and a visit to the underworld, see the Appendix on *Gerytades*.

[11] The mythological tradition in fact made Herakles an ambiguous figure vis-à-vis poetry and music: in some art/poetry he is an accomplished musician who can even play for the gods; in other places he is depicted as a failed student who kills his own music-teacher!

I'll take your advice on *food*' (105–7), Herakles stands for the sort of person who simply could not care less about good poetry.[12]

This exchange between god and hero (or, perhaps, two gods) is entertaining in its own right for the piquant back-and-forth of its dialogue. But it has further implications for the play as a whole: it points towards key issues of 'poetics', and above all, towards the depth of feelings experience of poetry can involve and the life-significance to be attached to those experiences. Now, on one level there is an underlying and teasing self-referentiality about the clash of values between Dionysos and Herakles. Aristophanic comedy itself abounds in ideas of (and characters who pursue) the pleasures of both food and sex, but what it actually *gives* its own audience is neither of those experiences but instead the pleasures of dramatic poetry. So comedy, in a sense, is necessarily on the side of Dionysos more than that of Herakles. At the same time, however, Dionysos is going to Hades with a passionate longing for a tragic, not a comic, poet, and that is something which allows Aristophanes to activate his penchant for a sort of 'inter-generic' rivalry with tragedy. Comedy, in other words, has a vested interest in questions of poetic value—but it can also, ambiguously and ironically, treat those questions at the arm's length of humour, exploring their inbuilt potential (and *everything*, in Aristophanes' universe, has such potential) for comic uncertainty and instability.

Before I turn to the sustained treatment of (tragic) poetry's values in the second half of *Frogs*, consider briefly one final illustration of the range and inventiveness of Aristophanes' dramatic repertoire from the first half of the play. This is the long sequence of songs, dances, and interactions between chorus and characters which forms the parodos of the Eleusinian initiates (316–459). There are many angles one might take on this fascinating passage. What I want to highlight is the irresistible manner in which Aristophanes turns the initiates' Iakchos procession into an enactment of comic festivity itself, allowing images and evocation of the Eleusinian occasion to merge with the expectations of comedy's own practices of revelry and ridicule.[13]

[12] Compare my comments on Euripides' Kinsman in the Introduction to *Women at the Thesmophoria*.

[13] Compare the treatment of the Rural Dionysia at *Acharnians* 241–79 and of the Choes at *Acharnians* 1000–1234: in both cases, the festival in question becomes an enactment of comedy's own festive values.

Even within Eleusinian terms, there is a slippery doubleness about the setting: the chorus are, at the same time, performing their earthly procession from Athens to Eleusis (though the parodos conflates different stages of the festival)[14] *and* celebrating their privileged afterlife in Hades, the reward for initiation into the Mysteries.[15] Throughout the parodos particular emphasis is placed on the theme of 'play': the Greek vocabulary in question (involving the verb *paizein* and its cognates) is a leitmotif of the scene, occurring no fewer than ten times in around 150 lines. The theme of 'play' brings with it a cluster of associations: hence it appears in my translation in the form of, and/or in conjunction with, 'celebration' (319), 'dance' (334, 388, 408, 411, 415), 'making merry' (376, juxtaposed with 'ridicule' and 'mocking humour', as also at 392), and general high spirits (444, 452). While this borrows something from the atmosphere of the Eleusinian procession itself, which undoubtedly made room for a number of ribald rituals of laughter,[16] it also inescapably stamps the occasion with the distinctive ethos of Old Comedy, a mixture of perpetual mirth and derision. And a similar point applies to subordinate themes such as the attractions of food (337–9), a sense of rejuvenation (345–53), and the pleasures of sex (409–13).

As always with Aristophanes, we need to read with an eye for concrete theatricality. When Dionysos and Xanthias hear, see, and even *smell* (314, cf. 338) the initiates approaching, they decide to hide out of sight and observe the procession (315). But their subsequent comments (318–22, 337–9) support the hypothesis that they remain visible to the *audience* throughout the scene, huddled together at one corner of the stage building. If so, this means that the whole scene has both foreground and background, with the god and his slave no

[14] Line 320 refers to the Agora at Athens, close to where the procession to Eleusis started, but the torches (313, 340 ff.) fit the night-time arrival at Eleusis itself, while the proclamation at 354 ff. reflects a stage of the festival four or five days earlier (as, probably, does the smell of sacrificial pigs, 338); meadows (e.g. 326, 343) evoke a traditional underworld topography, not Eleusis itself. For details of the actual Eleusinian festival, cf. R. Parker, *Polytheism and Society at Athens* (Oxford, 2005), 347–50.

[15] For the promise to Eleusinian initiates of a happy afterlife, see Parker, *Polytheism and Society*, 361–2.

[16] See S. Halliwell, *Greek Laughter* (Cambridge, 2008), 161–72, for details of the evidence. I take the serio-comic model of *Frogs* 389–90 ('. . . many jokes | But many serious things as well'), addressed to Demeter (384), to convey something of the mixed moods of the Eleusinian procession; it should not be treated as an 'authorial' Aristophanic agenda.

doubt reacting physically, with gestures and the like, to what they see before them. The parodos, in other words, is not detached from, but remains very firmly embedded in, Dionysos's experience of his descent to Hades. And the entirety of what the audience would witness, including the antics of the two 'hidden' characters, helps to throw into relief the eventual intrusion of those characters into the singing and dancing at 413 ff. Rather than introducing themselves first, they rush forward impulsively, overcome by an excited desire to join in with the general celebratory spirit of the occasion (which immediately turns into a satirical song, including some of the obscenest lyrics found anywhere in Aristophanes). That climax to the scene confirms that the fundamental matrix of the parodos is comedy's own realm of festive laughter. A nice indication of this is the description of the whole supposedly ritual context, in the proclamation at 357, as 'the cult of Kratinos the bull-eating god'. Through the symbolic figure of Kratinos, the most successful comic playwright of the generation before Aristophanes, comedy turns itself into an imaginary 'mystery religion' in its own right, but one whose 'ancient rites' (cf. 368) are unmistakably rooted in irreverence and hilarity.

By looking at selected details from the very start of *Frogs*, from the conversation between Dionysos and Herakles, and from the parodos of Eleusinian initiates, we have been able to see something of the heterogeneous styles of humour on which Aristophanes constantly plays variations. Dionysos's descent to Hades is in fact notable for its loosely episodic form and for the correspondingly multifarious comic modes which the play encompasses as the action twists and turns through the encounters with Herakles, a corpse, the ferryman Charon, the croaking frog chorus, the (probably) unseen monster Empousa, the Eleusinian initiates, a pair of underworld innkeepers, and various servants of Plouton, god of Hades. But this diversity of characters and situations adds up to only a temporary set of digressions and distractions from the trajectory on which Dionysos had set himself by going down to Hades to bring Euripides back to life.

Dionysos returns to that trajectory, though with a subtle shift of direction, when he finds himself invited to judge the dispute that has broken out between Aischylos, reigning occupant of the underworld 'throne' of tragedy (761–9), and the newly arrived Euripides. The resulting contest of tragedians turns into one of the most concentrated and ambitiously 'architected' stretches of action anywhere in the surviving plays of Aristophanes. Its engagement with the poetics of tragedy is so extensive that the second half of *Frogs*, for all its comic absurdities, stands as our most substantial piece of evidence for ways in which Athenians might have thought, felt, and argued about tragedy in the late fifth century. This part of the play has, indeed, acquired the semi-autonomous status of a 'document' in the evolution of literary and dramatic criticism.[17] But what kind of achievement does it represent on Aristophanes' part, to have created a comic text that has become a primary point of reference for the history of tragedy?

To orientate ourselves towards the structure of the contest, we can usefully think of it as organized along two axes. The first involves the series of theatrical topics, themes, and issues addressed in the various stages of the debate—a kind of 'anatomization' of tragedy.[18] In the 'agon' proper (895–1098),[19] the traditional comic form of head-to-head argument, the two playwrights introduce a mixture of considerations (*pro* themselves and *contra* one another) concerning dramaturgy, poetic styles, characterization, educational and ethical value, and the general relationship between their plays and the wider trends of Athenian society. In the following scene (1119–1250) they analyse each other's prologues, here focusing on a number of small-scale linguistic points. After that (1261–63) they undertake scathingly negative and elaborately parodic treatment of each other's choral songs. Since none of these stages of the contest yields a clear outcome in the eyes of the judge Dionysos, we then proceed to the 'weighing' of words at 1365–1410—an exercise which translates into preposterously mechanistic terms the nonetheless significant idea of evaluating the comparative worth of different pieces of poetry. Finally, and as noted earlier, Dionysos approaches the two playwrights as potential sources of insight for the benefit of Athens as a whole: he asks them for their views on subjects important to the politics of the city, first the controversial figure of Alkibiades (1422–34), then the general question of how the city can best ensure its survival (1435–66). In the

[17] Hence its inclusion in e.g. D. A. Russell and M. Winterbottom (eds.), *Ancient Literary Criticism* (Oxford, 1972), the standard anthology on the subject.

[18] Anatomization: in this connection, note the metaphorical 'sinews' of tragedy at 862, which may reflect larger conceptions of poetic form in terms of a quasi-organic 'body', as later attested at e.g. Plato, *Phaedrus* 264c, Aristotle, *Poetics* 7.1450b37–51a4.

[19] See the general Introduction, 'Formality and Performance'.

course of these various sections of the contest, we can trace several types of critical assumptions and methods at work, from the minute analysis of individual words and phrases to larger claims about whole plays, along with fluctuating appeals—in the judgement of tragedy's cultural value—to pleasure, technical craft, emotional expressiveness, and socio-political influence.

That first axis, then, is one along which we can plot the critical divisions of tragedy's poetic and dramatic artistry. But the second axis is one which exposes the extent of the differences between the poets themselves in all the features and aspects of their works. The tragedians' contest is pervaded by a strong sense of the two poets as authors whose entire personalities are imprinted on, and revealed by, their work. The resulting polarization can be broken down into a set of stark contrasts along the following lines.

Aischylos	*Euripides*
portentous grandeur	quotidian realism
heroic ethos	'democratic' ethos
larger-than-life characters	characters 'like us'
brooding silences	loquacious rhetoric
'Achillean' (in anger)	'Odyssean' (in craftiness)[20]
opaque language	quibbling word-chopping
masculine vigour	female eroticism
warlike spirit	banal vulgarity
inspiring uplift	encouragement of 'suspicion'
toughens through fear	softens through pity
long, obscure choral odes	neurotic solo songs
mysterious openings	mechanically explanatory prologues
affinity with Eleusinian Mysteries	abstract deities (Tongue, Astuteness)

It is very hard, in the absence of other forms of evidence, to say how far the conception of poetic authorship as a matter of constant *self*-expression (which supposedly allows us to read back from text to author at every point) was shared by audiences and readers in

[20] Aischylos is given explicit associations with Achilles at 912, 992, 1264; cf. 1020. Euripides is never explicitly called Odyssean, but cf. his craftiness at e.g. 957–8.

fifth-century Athens.[21] But it is certainly a highly convenient conception for Aristophanes' purposes, since it allows him to convert all the contest's issues of language, style, character, dramaturgy, and so forth into facets of the colourful comic figures presented to the audience directly onstage (and no doubt suitably embodied in their costumes and physical deportment). This means that, as with so much else in Aristophanes, we are dealing with 'multi-layered' constructions: the two tragedians take on an immediate dramatic life of their own, but they are also symbols and representatives of their theatrical careers and oeuvres as a whole—and even, on another level again, of the whole putative 'spirit of the age' (the era of the Persian Wars in Aischylos' case, and of the radical democracy of late fifth-century Athens in Euripides') to which each of them belonged.

That last point alerts us, however, to a basic asymmetry in the framework of the contest: an asymmetry in the relationship between *Frogs*' own audience and the phases of Athenian culture which the two tragedians allegedly epitomize. Aischylos was born 120 years before the production of *Frogs* in 405: his career started around 500, he died in 456. Any spectators of *Frogs* who had seen even the late plays of Aischylos as adults would have been in their mid-seventies in 405; if they had seen the first performance of *Persians* in 472 (mentioned at *Frogs* 1026), that figure would rise to around ninety. There cannot have been more than a few such spectators, and although we know that some of Aischylos' plays were re-performed after his death, this is unlikely to have given most spectators of *Frogs* a detailed familiarity with many of his works. In other words, most of the audience of *Frogs* were by definition part of the 'era' of Euripides; and since *Frogs* presents that era as one corrupted by Euripides' plays, the audience of the comedy was itself notionally implicated in Euripidean decadence.[22] The point is made explicitly by both tragedians: Aischylos condemns contemporary Athenians en masse (see especially 807–9, 1014–15, 1069–70, 1088), while Euripides claims that his plays have indeed

[21] Remember that Dionysos, as god of drama, is characterized as both a *spectator* (16–18, with immediate reference to comedy; cf. e.g. 1028–9) and a *reader* (52–4). The whole contest presupposes tragedy's status as a performance genre while at the same time treating it, through its reliance on constant *quotation*, as something that can be critically analysed as 'text'.

[22] There is an analogous point about the audience of *Clouds* in relation to the agon between Immoral and Moral: cf. my Introduction to that play.

shaped the mentality of this same generation (954, 960, 972). This does not, of course, compel individual spectators to feel in any particular way about the terms of the debate: individuals could dissociate themselves from the faults of their times. But it does add another layer of comic complexity to the whole competition, making it an intrinsically unbalanced clash between a nostalgically idealized past and a necessarily flawed 'modernity'.

But what are we to make of the *judge*, the 'critic',[23] of this elaborate contest, Dionysos himself? He starts out as a passionate devotee of Euripides but ends up bringing back Aischylos instead. Does that mean he gradually (or eventually) learns something about the standards of the best tragedy and its link to the best state of Athenian society? Many scholars have thought so. But the text of *Frogs* completely belies all such 'teleological' interpretations. At lines 1411–12 Dionysos states that he does not *want* to choose between the two playwrights (he wants them both as his 'friends'), and as late as line 1433 he professes himself simply unable to choose a winner. When forced by Plouton to pick one of them, he does so without giving a single *reason* (1468–78). It is hard to see how Aristophanes could have done any more to display Dionysos's inability (and unwillingness) to find a coherent critical basis on which to judge one style of tragic drama superior to another. Dionysos is the god of drama/theatre; he is also, as we saw, a lover of poetry, someone for whom good poetry is a thrilling life-value. Yet he cannot rationalize the critical judgements he is called upon to make: he feels that poetry matters, but cannot translate his feelings into a coherent, reasoned account. And part of what he feels (with, admittedly, an admixture of ludicrous buffoonery: he remains, after all, a quintessentially comic character) is that both Aischylos and Euripides are capable of fascinating him. If there is an underlying 'message' at all to the contest in *Frogs*, it is a message not about which of the two playwrights is really superior but about the problem of poetic *criticism* itself.[24]

[23] The whole vocabulary of 'judging' in *Frogs* uses the same Greek terms from which we derive the language of 'critic', 'criticism', etc.: i.e. the noun *krisis* ('judgement', 'competition') at 779, 785, 1467, and the cognate verb ('judge', 'choose between' etc.) at e.g. 805, 873, 1411, 1473.

[24] For a fuller version of this approach to the contest, see S. Halliwell, *Between Ecstasy and Truth: Interpretations of Greek Poetics from Homer to Longinus* (Oxford, 2011), 93–154; cf. the shrewd remarks of N. Lowe, 'Aristophanes' Books', *Annals of Scholarship*, 10 (1993), 63–83 (at 74–8).

That conclusion, I suggest, has further subversive implications for all attempts—and there have been many of them—to extract from *Frogs* an authentically Aristophanic 'poetics': a model of what makes poetry, comic as well as (or even instead of) tragic, good. After all, if the contest of tragedians seems to show that the quest for consistent, rational, and definitive criteria for judgements of poetic value is an unfulfillable goal in the case of tragic poetry (and we have seen that this point was already anticipated in the gap between Dionysos's love for Euripides and Herakles' view of the latter's poetry as 'a load of rubbish'), why should it be any different in the case of comedy itself? Can Aristophanes really have his cake and eat it, exposing the contestability of standards of value in another dramatic genre while laying claim to canonical standards in his own work? Those who think that he *can* are inevitably caught in a paradox: namely, that the play's conversion of deeply serious tragedy into extravagant absurdity is at the same time the vehicle of a claim to some kind of 'seriousness' on the part of comedy itself. But is this paradox a pointer to something important or merely an illusion produced by a desire on the part of critics to find in comedy (just as Dionysos does with tragedy) something of lasting value?

Those who believe that *Frogs* has a clear and positive poetics of its own, and that this poetics underpins Aristophanes' intention to 'teach' his audience something of direct relevance to the life of the city, unsurprisingly attach considerable significance to the play's parabasis, where the chorus—in a traditional parabatic pose—purport to 'give the city | Best advice and best instructions' (686–7), and proceed to urge that Athens should restore full citizen rights to those previously punished for anti-democratic activities. There is no doubt that this 'advice' reflects a realistic political option for the city: something very like it was implemented, through the decree of Patrokleides, later in 405.[25] But that point needs qualifying in two respects. First, Aristophanes makes his chorus echo a sentiment which, as Patrokleides' decree confirms, must have been gradually winning support in Athens under the pressure of the city's increasingly acute shortage of manpower for the war against Sparta (see above). To that

[25] Our main evidence for that decree is Andokides, *On the Mysteries* 73–80, though the text of the decree is spurious: see M. Canevaro and E. M. Harris, 'The Documents in Andocides' *On the Mysteries*', *Classical Quarterly*, 62 (2012), 98–129 (at 100–10).

extent, the parabasis is probably an attempt to strike a chord in tune with a growing mood of 'solidarity' in a time of political and military crisis (near-terminal crisis, as the defeat at Aigospotamoi later in 405 demonstrated). Secondly, whatever kind of gesture we might take the parabasis to be, it does nothing to determine the 'meaning' of *Frogs* as a whole. I noted earlier in this Introduction that *Frogs* sends out inconsistent signals about Athens' policy in the war, not least in relation to the stance of the victorious Aischylos. What's more, it seems that in the contest of tragedians it is actually Euripides who, at 1446–50, comes closest to sounding a note that chimes with part of the parabasis.[26] If we want to ascribe a 'poetics' to Aristophanes in *Frogs* (or beyond), we had better make plenty of room in it for comic caprice and incongruity.

There is a final point to be touched on in regard to the parabasis of *Frogs*. An ancient source, going back to Aristotle's pupil Dikaiarchos, reports that the play received a second performance; it also states, though we cannot be at all sure that Dikaiarchos himself said this, that the second performance was the specific result of a favourable reaction to the play's parabasis.[27] Great caution is called for in interpreting this testimony. It is one thing to accept that Dikaiarchos could have had evidence for a second performance of *Frogs* at some date. It is quite another to suppose, as a modern consensus does, that this was at one of the dramatic festivals of 404. By then, Athens' navy had been definitively defeated, the city was being besieged into starvation, and negotiations with Sparta were under way for the terms of surrender. If *Frogs* had been re-performed at that date, several passages of the play would have been jarringly anachronistic. These include various references to the war as an ongoing naval enterprise (e.g. 362–4, 1065–6, 1437–41, 1465), but above all the parabasis itself, with its

[26] Some editors give these lines (or at least 1446–8) to Aischylos; the issue is entangled with larger questions about the state of the text in this part of the play. But if we retain the transmitted order of lines (see my note on *Frogs* 1436), the lines in question have to be spoken by Euripides.

[27] *Hypothesis* I(c) (Dover) to *Frogs* says 'the play was so admired for its parabasis that it was re-performed, as Dikaiarchos says'. The 'Life' of Aristophanes (test. 1.35–9, Kassel–Austin) says Aristophanes was crowned with olive for the parabasis of *Frogs*. An attempt is made by A. H. Sommerstein, *Talking about Laughter* (Oxford, 2009), 254–71, to combine these sources into evidence for the hypothesis of re-performance at the Lenaia of 404. But his argument is highly speculative and does not properly address the point made in my text about jarring anachronisms.

suggestion that the previously disenfranchised should be given their rights back precisely on condition that they fight in the navy (701–2). How could a re-performance in early 404 have *celebrated* such ideas, when by that stage all attempts to sustain Athens' war effort had been tried and failed? If we want to believe that *Frogs* received a second performance, it is safer to infer that this was some time later, well after the end of the war (when the play's originally topical references could be received from a historical 'distance'), and that the supposed linkage with the parabasis was the result of idle later speculation.[28]

Frogs is an Aristophanic masterpiece, composed and performed during a period when Athenian fortunes in the long Peloponnesian War were threatening to become desperate. The play acknowledges that historical background by some of its references to contemporary circumstances and the perilous 'survival' of the city. But that does not warrant us in treating *Frogs* as itself somehow purporting to have the key to that survival (which, as Aristophanes well knew, depended on ships, manpower, money, and complex diplomacy), still less as issuing an invitation to think of comedy as a genre properly suited to solve such problems. What Aristophanes offers his fellow-Athenians instead is a dazzling fiction in which fantasized versions of past and present, gods and humans, poetry and politics are melded together into a world that no one could inhabit outside the imagination of the theatre. Comedy cannot make much difference to the course of a military conflict, but it can lift the spirits of its audience with temporary exhilaration, and perhaps some consolation, even in the dark days of war.

28 The claim about Aristophanes' olive crown (n. 27 above) is part of conspicuously flimsy generalizations about how he was cherished by the Athenians for his pro-democratic sentiments.

FROGS

Speaking Characters

XANTHIAS: slave of DIONYSOS
DIONYSOS: god of theatre, wine, and ecstasy
HERAKLES: famous hero and brother of DIONYSOS
CORPSE: anonymous, recently deceased person
CHARON: ferryman of the Acherousian lake in Hades
FROGS: singing/dancing group in amphibian costumes
CHORUS (24 dancers/singers): of Eleusinian initiates in Hades
LEADER: of the CHORUS
DOORKEEPER: of PLOUTON's palace
SLAVE[A]: of PLOUTON and Persephone (Pherrephatta)
INNKEEPER (female): in Hades
PLATHANE: a second Innkeeper
EURIPIDES: tragic playwright
AISCHYLOS: tragic playwright
PLOUTON: god of the underworld
SLAVE[D]: another slave of PLOUTON

Silent Characters

CARRIERS: of the CORPSE's bier
SLAVES([B] and [C]): accompanying INNKEEPER and PLATHANE
ATTENDANTS: under the command of the palace DOORKEEPER
EURIPIDES' MUSE: a castanet-playing female figure

[*The stage building has a single central door which will serve at 35 ff. as the house of* HERAKLES *and later as the palace of* PLOUTON *in Hades. The two side entrances* (eisodoi) *connect the on-stage scenes with loosely defined off-stage locations, both on earth and in the underworld. From one* eisodos *enter* DIONYSOS *and* XANTHIAS, *the former leading a donkey on which the latter, holding assorted baggage on a pole over his shoulder, is riding. The god, a portly and elderly figure, is dressed in long boots and a saffron dress, with,* à la *Herakles, a lion-skin on top and a large club in his hand. The two characters make their way falteringly towards the centre of the* orchêstra.]

XANTHIAS [*nonchalantly*]. Shall I tell them some of the usual gags then, master,
The things spectators *always* find so funny?
DIONYSOS [*wearily*]. Say what you like—except 'I'm all hard-pressed'.*
Steer clear of *that*: it's trite and makes my gorge rise.
XANTHIAS. But something else that's witty?
DIONYSOS. Except 'I'm squashed'.
XANTHIAS. Well then, should I tell them an excellent joke?
DIONYSOS. Go ahead,
Feel free. But avoid that old routine—
XANTHIAS. Which one?
DIONYSOS. Where you shift your load and say that you need a shit!
XANTHIAS. But can't I say that I'm carrying such a weight
That unless it's removed I'll release an explosive fart?
DIONYSOS. Please don't, I beg you—unless you want me to vomit!
XANTHIAS. Well what was the point of making me carry this baggage
If I can't make the jokes you hear in Phrynichos' plays
Or the kind that Lykis and also Ameipsias writes?*
Their comedies always have these baggage-slave scenes.
DIONYSOS. But just don't do it. I know that when I'm watching
And see that kind of 'sophisticated' humour,
I've aged by more than a year when I leave the theatre.*
XANTHIAS. This neck of mine is damned to perdition in that case.
It's getting *squashed* but is being denied its jokes.

[DIONYSOS *halts and looks up at* XANTHIAS *in disgust before delivering the following lines directly to the audience.*]

DIONYSOS. But look at this outrage here—just look how he's pampered!
I'm the god Dionysos himself, the son of Wine-jar,
Yet here I'm struggling on foot while letting him *ride*,
To make sure he's not worn out by the weight of his load.
XANTHIAS. But aren't I carrying still?
DIONYSOS. Not when you're riding!
XANTHIAS [*pointing to his pole*]. I'm carrying this!
DIONYSOS. How come?
XANTHIAS. Because it's so heavy!
DIONYSOS. But isn't the donkey bearing the weight that you've got?
XANTHIAS. Not the weight that I'm carrying here, no he's certainly not.
DIONYSOS. But how can you carry a thing when you're being carried?
XANTHIAS. I really don't know—except that this shoulder's *hard-pressed*!
DIONYSOS. Well if you're saying the donkey is lending no help
Try picking it up yourself and see what that's like!
XANTHIAS. Oh misery me! If only I'd served in that sea-fight*—
I'd tell you to go and get stuffed, I really would!
DIONYSOS. Dismount, you rogue. This door you can see over here
Is the very first place this journey of mine was meant
To bring me to. [*Knocking*] Hoy, slave, open up, open up!

[*While* XANTHIAS *gets down from the donkey and leads it to the corner of the stage building, where it disappears from view, the door of the stage building opens abruptly and* HERAKLES, *also wearing a lion-skin, steps out aggressively—but soon starts to crack up at what he sees.*]

HERAKLES. Who battered the door just now? Like a violent Centaur,*
Whoever it was who crashed—[*seeing* DIONYSOS] oh, what have we here?
DIONYSOS [*to* XANTHIAS]. Look, slave.
XANTHIAS. What is it?

DIONYSOS. Well didn't you see?

XANTHIAS. See what?

DIONYSOS. The way he took fright at me.

XANTHIAS. Yes, in case you were mad!

HERAKLES. In Demeter's name, I just can't stop myself laughing.
I'm biting my lip but it's just no use—I must laugh! [*Guffaws.*]

DIONYSOS [*to* HERAKLES]. Old chap, please come over here. I need a favour.

HERAKLES. But I just can't stifle this laughter that's overcome me
At the sight of this lion-skin here with your saffron dress.*
[*In mocking tone*] What's your state of mind? Why these boots and club combined?*
Where on earth have you been?

DIONYSOS [*blustering*]. I was sailing on Kleisthenes' boat.*

HERAKLES. You were in the sea-fight?

DIONYSOS. That's right, and we must have sunk
A dozen or more of the enemy's fleet of ships.*

HERAKLES. The pair of you?

DIONYSOS. That's right!

XANTHIAS [*sarcastically*]. And then I woke up!

DIONYSOS. In fact it was on board ship as I read to myself
That play *Andromeda*, all of a sudden it happened:*
The most intense desire took hold of my heart.

HERAKLES. A desire? How strong exactly?

DIONYSOS [*coyly*]. Quite small—like Molon!*

HERAKLES. Desire for a woman?

DIONYSOS. No, no.

HERAKLES. Then a boy?

DIONYSOS. Not at all.

HERAKLES. For a *man*?

DIONYSOS [*shuddering*]. Oh dear!

HERAKLES. Ah, you *did* it with Kleisthenes!

DIONYSOS. Don't mock me, brother. I'm really not feeling too well.
It's a terrible longing that's piercing me through and through.

HERAKLES. What kind, little brother?

DIONYSOS. It's rather hard to describe.

I'll have to explain in a somewhat roundabout way.
Have you ever been struck by a sudden desire for—soup?*
HERAKLES. For soup? You bet! At numerous times in my life.
DIONYSOS. Am I making my point quite clear? Do you need more hints?
HERAKLES. Not as far as soup's concerned. I know it too well.
DIONYSOS. Well it's just as strong a desire that cuts right through me
For Euripides!
HERAKLES. *Euripides*, dead and buried?
DIONYSOS. Yes, no one at all could persuade me not to go
And bring him back.
HERAKLES. You intend to go down to Hades?
DIONYSOS. By Zeus I do, and further down too, if need be.
HERAKLES. But what's your motive?
DIONYSOS. I need a skilful poet.
The best are all now dead and the rest are no good.
HERAKLES. Isn't Iophon still alive?
DIONYSOS. That's the only bit
Of quality left, and even then there's some doubt.
I'm not quite sure what to make of Iophon's case.*
HERAKLES. Well don't you want to bring Sophokles back instead
Of Euripides—if you really *must* fetch someone?
DIONYSOS. I can't do that till I've tested Iophon more
To see how he writes now Sophokles can't give help.
And Euripides, what's more, he's such a rogue
He'd be happy to try to escape back here with me,
While even-tempered Sophokles won't mind death.*
HERAKLES. And Agathon—where's he now?
DIONYSOS. He's gone and left me—
He's a good poet, true, and someone his friends all miss.
HERAKLES. But *where's* the poor thing gone?
DIONYSOS. To a land of plenty!*
HERAKLES. And what about Xenokles then?
DIONYSOS. He can go and hang!
HERAKLES. Pythangelos?* [DIONYSOS *shrugs*.]
XANTHIAS [*aside*]. But no one cares about *me*,

While my shoulder chafes and chafes beneath this burden.

HERAKLES. Aren't there lots of other young kids around the place
Composing tragic plays—huge numbers of them,
And all with more gift of the gab than Euripides has?

DIONYSOS [*animated*]. But they're shrivelled grapes, producers of empty prattle,
And haunts of twittering swallows. They damage the art,
And as soon as they've staged a single play they vanish,
Content to have pissed on tragedy just the once!
You'll search in vain for a poet of *fertile* mind,
The kind who's able to voice great noble expressions.

HERAKLES. What d'you mean by 'fertile'?

DIONYSOS. The sort whose language contains
Such bold, ambitious utterances as these:
[*airily*] 'Aither, bedroom of Zeus', 'the foot of time',
Or 'a mind that refuses to swear a sacred oath
But a tongue that perjures itself without the mind'.*

HERAKLES. You actually *like* this stuff?

DIONYSOS. It sends me crazy!

HERAKLES. It's a great big con-trick: you know very well that it is.

DIONYSOS. Don't try to inhabit my mind—just live in your own.

HERAKLES. Everyone can see these things are a load of rubbish.

DIONYSOS. I'll take your advice on *food*.

XANTHIAS [*aside*]. But what about me?

DIONYSOS. Well, the reason I came here wearing these clothes you see,
In impersonation of you, was so you could tell me
The names of people whose help I could call upon,
The ones you used when you went to fetch Kerberos.*
So tell me the hosts you stayed with, the harbours, the bread-shops,
The brothels, the resting-places, the springs, the roads,
The cities, accommodation, and the women whose inns
Have the fewest bedbugs.

XANTHIAS [*aside*]. But no one cares about *me*!

HERAKLES. Are you really fearless enough to make the descent?

DIONYSOS. Don't try to object. Just tell me the fastest road

By which I'll find my way right down to Hades.
And I don't want a route that's hot, nor too cold either.

HERAKLES. Let's see then, which is the way that I'd recommend first?
[*Ponders.*] There's one that starts with a rope and a bench to stand on.
You could hang yourself!

DIONYSOS. No more of that—too stifling!

HERAKLES. There's another path that's direct and widely used.
You pound it in a mortar.

DIONYSOS. You mean drink hemlock?

HERAKLES. I certainly do!

DIONYSOS. That's too chilly and wintry a way:
It immobilizes your legs by freezing them cold.*

HERAKLES. Do you want me to tell you a quick and downhill route?

DIONYSOS. By Zeus, yes please! I'm not very good at walking.

HERAKLES. Then take a stroll to the Kerameikos.*

DIONYSOS. What then?

HERAKLES. Climb up the tower, that high one.

DIONYSOS. And what after that?

HERAKLES. Look down from there when they're going to hold a torch-race.*
Then when you hear the spectators all shout 'Go then!',
At that point go yourself.

DIONYSOS. Go where?

HERAKLES. Straight down!

DIONYSOS. But that would make mincemeat of both halves of my brain!*
That's not the way I want to go.

HERAKLES. Which one then?

DIONYSOS. The route you took yourself.

HERAKLES. That involves a long voyage.
Right at the start you'll come to a very large lake
Of unfathomed depth.

DIONYSOS. Then how will I manage to cross it?

HERAKLES [*gesturing*]. In a boat no bigger than this, a very old man
Will take you across if you pay him a fare of two obols.*

DIONYSOS [*sighing*]. Good gracious!
How much two obols will buy wherever one goes!
How come this price reached Hades?

HERAKLES. It came with Theseus.*
After that you'll see great numbers of serpents and beasts,
The most frightening kinds.

DIONYSOS. But don't try to scare me like that:
You won't put me off.

HERAKLES. Then you'll come to a huge stretch of mud*
And a river of shit. That's where you'll see submerged
Any person who's ever done terrible wrong to a guest,
Or has screwed a boy and stolen his money as well,
Or has thrashed his mother or broken his father's jaw,
Or has sworn an oath and perjured himself in the act—
[*with mock horror*] Or has had a speech copied out from Morsimos' plays!*

DIONYSOS. By all the gods they ought to add to those
Any person who's learnt Kinesias' military dance!*

HERAKLES. After that the breath of pipes will waft around you
And you'll see the most beautiful light, just like on earth.
There'll be myrtle groves and groups of men and women
Ecstatic in celebration with clapping hands.

DIONYSOS. But who are *they*?

HERAKLES. Initiates of the Mysteries.

XANTHIAS [*aside*]. Well *I'm* the proverbial donkey in the Mysteries!*
I refuse to hold this baggage a moment longer.

[XANTHIAS *starts belatedly to take the various bundles off his pole, and has almost finished by line 165.*]

HERAKLES. These people will tell you everything else that you need.
They live right next to the road that you'll walk along
And close to the doors of Plouton's palace itself.
Goodbye, my brother. [*Exits into house.*]

DIONYSOS. Many thanks. Take care of yourself
As well. [*To* XANTHIAS] And you pick up this bedding again.*

XANTHIAS. Before I've put it all down?

DIONYSOS. And make it sharpish.

XANTHIAS. But please don't make me. Why not hire one of the people
Who are joining the dead—there's surely someone who'll do it?

DIONYSOS. Suppose I can't find one?

XANTHIAS. Then use me again.

DIONYSOS. It's a deal.
They're actually bringing a corpse along here now.

[*From one of the* eisodoi *two* CARRIERS *come into view with a* CORPSE *on a bier. They start to make their way across the* orchêstra. DIONYSOS *watches for a moment then hails the* CORPSE *as the group comes near.*]

Hey you! Yes it's you I mean, the one who's dead.
My man, are you willing to carry my baggage to Hades?

CORPSE [*sitting up*]. How much do you have?

DIONYSOS [*pointing*]. This much.

CORPSE. Will you pay two drachmas?*

DIONYSOS. I certainly won't. Much less.

CORPSE [*to* CARRIERS]. Please move on quickly.

DIONYSOS. Just wait a moment, my fellow—let's reach agreement.

CORPSE. If you won't pay the fee that I've stated, you're wasting your breath.

DIONYSOS. I'll offer nine obols.

CORPSE [*sarcastically*]. I'd rather come back to life!

[*The* CORPSE *is carried away and off by the opposite* eisodos.]

XANTHIAS. What an arrogant bastard he was! Good riddance to him!
[*Picking up the baggage*] I'll do the job.

DIONYSOS. You're an absolute gentleman then.
Let's head to the boat.

[DIONYSOS *and* XANTHIAS *resume their journey. As they do so,* CHARON *on his ferry-boat (on wheels, pulled by a rope mechanism) starts to come into view from the same* eisodos *by which the* CORPSE *has just left. The boat moves into the* orchêstra.]

CHARON. Pull in, bring her up to the jetty!
DIONYSOS. What's this?
XANTHIAS. Do you need to ask? It's the lake, by Zeus,
The one that Herakles mentioned—[*pointing*] I see the boat!
DIONYSOS. So do I, by Poseidon! It's Charon himself right here.
[*Giddily*] Hello, Charon! Hello, Charon! Hello!
CHARON. Is there anyone here for the resting-place from troubles?
Anyone for the Plain of Forgetting or Hopeless Task,
Or Kerberos Town, Crows' End, or Tainaron Point?*
DIONYSOS. Yes me!
CHARON. Get on board then quickly.
DIONYSOS. But where are you heading?
CHARON. To the crows!
DIONYSOS. What, really?
CHARON. As far as *you're* concerned!
Get onto the boat.
DIONYSOS [*to* XANTHIAS]. Slave, over here!
CHARON. No slaves!
Not unless he took part in the sea-fight to save our bacon.*
XANTHIAS [*shiftily*]. Not me, I couldn't—my eyes were giving me trouble.
CHARON. Get on with it then, you'll have to run round the lake.
XANTHIAS. But where shall I wait?
CHARON. By the stone of Shrivelling Place.
There's a resting-point there.
DIONYSOS. Understand?
XANTHIAS. Yes, only too well.

[*As* XANTHIAS *starts to trudge off and exits by the nearest* eisodos, DIONYSOS *moves towards* CHARON*'s boat.*]

What a wretched existence! I was cursed by someone today.
CHARON [*to* DIONYSOS]. Sit down at the oar. [*Calling.*] If there's anyone else, hurry up.
What the heck are you doing?
DIONYSOS. What's wrong? I've done what you said.
I've sat on the oar—that's where you told me to sit.

[CHARON *now moves* DIONYSOS *so that he is sitting in a position to row the boat while* CHARON *steers it from the stern.*]

Get up and sit here instead, pot-belly!
DIONYSOS. Okay then.
CHARON. Now stretch out both of your hands in front.
DIONYSOS. Okay then.
CHARON. Stop fooling around! You have to *push* with your feet
And pull the oar with real force.
DIONYSOS. But how can I do it?
I'm not a sailor, still less a Salamis type,*
And yet you expect me to row?
CHARON. It's easy: you'll hear
Some beautiful songs when you start.
DIONYSOS. Whose songs are those?
CHARON. The frog-swans' amazing songs.
DIONYSOS. Then give me my stroke!
CHARON. Pull—up—push! Pull—up—push!

[*As* DIONYSOS *starts to row and the boat moves back in the direction it came from, the* FROGS *appear from both sides of the stage, jumping in comically amphibian fashion and croaking loudly around* DIONYSOS, *who struggles to fit his rowing rhythm to their sounds and sings in competition with them.*]

[PARODOS I: 209–67]

FROGS. Brékekekex ko-ax ko-ax!
Brékekekex ko-ax ko-ax!
You children of marshes and springs,
With the pipe-tuned cries of our hymns
Let's proclaim our fine-voiced song.
Ko-ax ko-ax!
The same song which for Dionysos,
Son of Zeus and god of Mount Nysa,
We cried out in the marshes
When the hungover revellers
On the sacred day of Pots
Go in crowds through my precinct.*
Brékekekex ko-ax ko-ax!

DIONYSOS. But *I'm* beginning to feel an ache
Right under my arse, ko-ax ko-ax!
FROGS. Brékekekex ko-ax ko-ax!
DIONYSOS. But *you*, I suppose, don't care at all.
FROGS. Brékekekex ko-ax ko-ax!
DIONYSOS. I hope you rot with your croak 'ko-ax'!
This croak 'ko-ax' is your constant refrain.
FROGS. Why be surprised, old busybody?
I'm adored by the Muses who love good music
And by goat-hoofed Pan, who plays the reed-pipes.
Apollo the phorminx-player delights in me too
For the reed-stalks which strengthen the frame of the lyre
And grow in my watery marshes.*
Brékekekex ko-ax ko-ax!
DIONYSOS. But *I'm* developing blisters here
And my anus has long been oozing sweat.
Any moment now it will peep out and say—
FROGS. Brékekekex ko-ax ko-ax!
DIONYSOS. But o you song-loving species,
Please stop these sounds.
FROGS. On the contrary
We'll raise our voices, the way in the past
On sun-drenched days
We leapt through galingale
And tufty reeds, taking great pleasure
In songs of copious splashings,
Or when to escape the rain from Zeus
We performed deep-water dances
With brilliant flashes of sound
And bubbling, spluttering poppings.
DIONYSOS. Brékekekex ko-ax ko-ax!
I've borrowed this cry from you.
FROGS. In that case now we're heading for trouble.
DIONYSOS. Not as much as *I* am, if rowing like this
I split myself asunder!
FROGS. Brékekekex ko-ax ko-ax!
DIONYSOS. You can go and hang. Just see if I care.

FROGS. Well then we'll continue to shriek
As much as our throats
Can manage the whole day long.
DIONYSOS. Brékekekex ko-ax ko-ax!
You'll never defeat me this way.
FROGS. And nor will *you* defeat us either!
DIONYSOS. And nor will *you* defeat me either!
You'll never do it. I too will shriek
All day if I have to, until I succeed
In proving supreme with my own ko-ax!
Brékekekex ko-ax ko-ax!

[*In what follows, as* CHARON*'s boat reaches the edge of the* orchêstra, *the* FROGS *hop back off-stage. After* DIONYSOS *has disembarked, the boat continues till it is out of sight. Shortly afterwards* XANTHIAS *reappears from the opposite* eisodos *to the one by which he left. The piper stops playing here and we return to spoken dialogue.*]

DIONYSOS [*shouting*]. I knew I was bound to stop your croaking at last.

CHARON. Stop rowing, stop rowing. Steer in to the shore with the oar.
Get out now. Pay me your fare.
DIONYSOS. Right, here are two obols.*
[*Looking round*] Now, Xanthias! Where's Xanthias! Hey, Xanthias!
XANTHIAS [*appearing*]. Ho there!
DIONYSOS. Come over here!
XANTHIAS. Hello then, master.
DIONYSOS. Well where exactly is this?
XANTHIAS. It's darkness and mud.
DIONYSOS. So *did* you see the father-beaters round here
And the perjurers too, the way he described?
XANTHIAS. Didn't *you*?
DIONYSOS. By Poseidon I certainly did—[*peering at audience*] and I still see them now!
Right, what are we going to do?
XANTHIAS. It's best to move on,
Since this is the place where he told us that beasts are lurking,
The frightening ones that he mentioned.

DIONYSOS. He'll pay for such talk!
That was all pure bluster in order to make me afraid.
He's knows I'm a fighter but feels he needs to compete.
[*Loftily*] 'There's nothing as self-important as Herakles is!'*
I actually wish I could face a foe down here
And achieve some feat that's worthy of the journey.

XANTHIAS [*ironically*]. Of course you do! And indeed I can hear a noise.

[*In the following lines* XANTHIAS *peers and points, with mock-terror, into the supposed darkness, while* DIONYSOS *becomes increasingly agitated.*]

DIONYSOS [*startled*]. Where, where?

XANTHIAS. Behind you.

DIONYSOS. Then get behind me quickly!

XANTHIAS. No, it's now in front.

DIONYSOS. Then get in front of me quickly!

XANTHIAS. In fact I can see, by Zeus, a very large beast!

DIONYSOS. What kind?

XANTHIAS. A terrible kind. It's changing shape.
It was first a cow, then a mule, and now it's—a woman,
A ravishing beauty.

DIONYSOS. *Where*? Let me go and approach her.

XANTHIAS. She's no longer a woman. She's now turned into a dog.

DIONYSOS. It's Empousa then!*

XANTHIAS. There's a fire that's lighting up
The whole of her face.

DIONYSOS. Does she have a bronze leg too?

XANTHIAS. By Poseidon she does! And the other is made of dung.
It's true.

DIONYSOS [*panicked*]. Then where should I run?

XANTHIAS. I'm thinking the same!

DIONYSOS [*towards front row*]. O priest, protect me—I want to drink with you later!*

XANTHIAS [*as if to* DIONYSOS]. We're going to die, lord Herakles!

DIONYSOS. Don't call *me*,
I beg you please, good fellow, or mention my name.

XANTHIAS. Dionysos, then.

DIONYSOS. That's even worse than the other!

XANTHIAS [*as if to beast*]. Avaunt thee now! [*To* DIONYSOS] Come over here, my master.

DIONYSOS. What for?

XANTHIAS. Take heart. It's all turned out okay.
We can say, just like the actor Hegelochos did:
'After stormy waters I see once more—a weasel'!*
Empousa's vanished.

DIONYSOS. Do you swear it's true?

XANTHIAS. By Zeus!

DIONYSOS. And swear again.

XANTHIAS. By Zeus!

DIONYSOS. Once more.

XANTHIAS. By Zeus!

DIONYSOS. What a wretched business; the sight of her made me pale.

XANTHIAS [*pointing behind* DIONYSOS]. But this part here has turned a dark brown colour!

DIONYSOS. Well how have I found myself in so much trouble?
Which god's to blame for trying to ruin my life?

XANTHIAS. Blame 'Aither, bedroom of Zeus' or 'the foot of time'!*
[*Abruptly*] But hey!

DIONYSOS. What's wrong?

XANTHIAS. Well didn't you hear?

DIONYSOS. Hear what?

XANTHIAS. The breath of pipes.

DIONYSOS. Oh yes! And I feel warm air
That wafts from torches with mystic atmosphere.
Let's stand back over here out of sight and listen.

[*As* DIONYSOS *and* XANTHIAS *move back and stand at a corner of the stage building, the* CHORUS *processes in from an* eisodos *and starts to dance at 323 ff. They are a mixture of male and female: though dressed in ragged costumes, they represent ecstatic Eleusinian initiates who are celebrating in Hades in a similar manner as in the Mysteries themselves.*]

[PARODOS II: 316–459]

CHORUS. Iakchos, hail Iakchos!*
Iakchos, hail Iakchos!

XANTHIAS. Ah, now I know, o master. This must be where
The initiates that he mentioned are celebrating.
It's the Iakchos' chant they sing in the Agora too.*
DIONYSOS. You're right, that's who they are. Our best plan then
Is to keep entirely quiet and find out more.

CHORUS. Iakchos, venerable lord who dwells in this place, *Strophe*
Iakchos, hail Iakchos!
Come join our dance in this meadow,
Come among the pious followers of your cult,
Toss wildly a head that's crowned
With a wreath luxuriant in fruit
Of myrtle berries, and stamp your foot
In rhythms bold for this unbridled
Dance-loving act of worship,
An occasion full of the Graces,
A sacred dance for pious initiates.

XANTHIAS [*excited*]. O mistress venerable, daughter of Demeter,
What a lovely odour of pig flesh wafted this way!
DIONYSOS. Keep still then, please, if you want to get some sausage.*

CHORUS. Arouse the flaming torches you brandish aloft, *Antistrophe*
Iakchos, hail Iakchos,
Our light-bringing star for nocturnal rites!
The meadow blazes with flames of gleaming torches.
Even old men's knees flex in dance.
They shake off all their cares
And the heavy weight of copious years
To join the sacred worship.
Lighting the way with your torch
Lead on to the flowering marshy ground,
O blessed one, our dance of rejuvenation.

[*The* CHORUS *halts in the centre of the* orchêstra *and their* LEADER *steps forward to chant the following section.*]*

LEADER. I proclaim ceremonial silence now and demand all those should depart
Who have no knowledge of what's said here or whose minds are far from pure,
Or who've never seen our noble Muses' rites or joined in their dances
Or those who remain outside the cult of Kratinos the bull-eating god,*
Or who take great pleasure in vulgar jokes at a time when they're out of place.
And likewise with those who fail to avoid all forms of divisive faction
But stoke it up and fan the flames for the sake of private profit,
Or when the city's enduring a storm take bribes while holding office
Or betray our defences on land or at sea, or export contraband goods
From Aigina the way that Thorykion did, that damnable tax-collector,*
Transporting oar-pads and flax and pitch to enemy land, Epidauros.
Or the person who plots to furnish funds for the fleets of the foes that we're fighting,
Or the one who shits in Hekate's shrines yet composes dithyramb lyrics,*
Or the politician who tries to reduce the fees of dramatic poets*
Just because he's been mocked in the ancient rites that belong to the god Dionysos.
To all these people I now proclaim for a second and third time too:
Depart from our Eleusinian dances. But you who remain raise your song
And prepare to perform the nocturnal revels that suit our festival here.

[*The* CHORUS *moves into position for a further sequence of dance-songs.*]

CHORUS. Advance, each one of you, boldly *Strophe*
Into the blossoming bosoms
Of the meadowland. Stamp feet,
Aim shafts of ridicule,

Make merry with mocking humour.
We have eaten enough for the task.

Follow the dance-steps and raise *Antistrophe*
A noble cry for our Saviouress*
With voices of unison song,
For she promises us
She'll protect our land for ever,
Whatever Thorykion's wishes!

LEADER. Come now, undertake further hymns of joy for our grain-bearing queen herself,
The goddess Demeter. In loudest songs of worship give glory to her.

CHORUS. Demeter, mistress of holy rites, *Strophe*
Come stand amidst our ranks yourself,
Safeguard this chorus that is your own,
And grant that all day long in safety
We'll celebrate in play and dance.

And may we utter many jokes *Antistrophe*
But many serious things as well,
And may we serve your festival
In a worthy spirit of playful humour*
And win the ribbons of victory!

LEADER. Come again, I say,
And summon in song the handsome god to join us,
The one who makes this choral procession with us.

CHORUS. Iakchos the venerable, inventor of loveliest song *Strophe*
For this festival, accompany us
On our path to the goddess.
Show us how effortlessly
You complete this lengthy journey.
Iakchos, friend of dancers, escort me onwards!

It's you who to make us laugh (and keep things cheap) *Antistrophe* A

Gave us tattered sandals to wear
And nothing but rags.*
You found a cost-free way
For us to play and dance.
Iakchos, friend of dancers, escort me onwards!

I took a glance just now at a young girl here: *Antistrophe* B
She had the prettiest face you've seen,
And was dancing beside me.
Her dress was ripped down the side
And a tit bobbed out!
Iakchos, friend of dancers, escort me onwards!

[*For some time* DIONYSOS *and* XANTHIAS *have been becoming visibly excited by the* CHORUS*'s songs. They can now no longer restrain themselves but jump forward to make their own contributions to the increasingly high-spirited singing and dancing.*]

DIONYSOS. Well I myself like joining in!
I'd like to meet this girl
And play and dance with her.
XANTHIAS. Me too!

CHORUS. Would you like us then together
To lampoon old Archedemos,*
Who had neither teeth nor kin by the age of seven?

Yet now he leads the people
Up among the earthly corpses,
And holds first place in depravity up there.

I hear that Kleisthenes' son
Was seen among the tombstones
When plucking the hairs from his anus and tearing his cheeks.

He flailed away, bent double,
And wailed and shrieked aloud
For someone called Fuck-you from Anaphlystos.*

And Kallias, it's rumoured,
The son of one Horse-fucker,
Fought naval battles with cunts while dressed in lion-skin.*

[*The rhythms and steps of the preceding song continue even as* DIONYSOS *turns to more practical matters.*]

DIONYSOS. Could you give us some information?
We're looking for Plouton's palace.
We're visitors here who arrived not long ago.

LEADER. You don't have far to travel
And won't need to ask me again.
That's his very door you've reached just over there.

DIONYSOS. Get lifting then once more, slave.

XANTHIAS. What's that? You mean to say
It's the same old story again with all this baggage.*

[DIONYSOS *waits for* XANTHIAS *to pick up all the bags one last time. During the following lines they make their way round the* orchêstra *towards the door of the stage building.*]

LEADER [*to* CHORUS]. Advance then
Through the goddess's sacred precinct, the flowery grove,
In playful spirits, participants in festivities that please the gods.
I'll go to join the young girls and the women
In the goddess's all-night worship, and brandish this sacred torch.

CHORUS. Let's make our way to the rose-filled *Strophe*
Blooming meadows,
With our usual customs
Of lovely dances
In playful spirits, which the blessed
Fates organize.*

On us alone shine sunlight's *Antistrophe*

Sacred beams,
On us the initiated,
Who led pious lives
Attentive always to needs of strangers
And to ordinary folk.

[*The* CHORUS, *as though moving onwards in the underworld, now retires to the sides of the* orchêstra. DIONYSOS *and* XANTHIAS *have reached the door of the stage building.*]

DIONYSOS [*nervously*]. Let me think, what way shall I bang on this door before me?
I wonder how the locals round here do this.
XANTHIAS. Stop hesitating and just lay into the door
The way that Herakles would. Show some of his mettle!
DIONYSOS [*knocking*]. Hey, slave!
DOORKEEPER [*opening door abruptly*]. Who's this?
DIONYSOS. It's Herakles, the *tough* guy.
DOORKEEPER. You nauseating, shameless, audacious man,
You're loathsome—more than loathsome—as loathsome as hell!
It's you who kidnapped Kerberos, our dog.
You rushed away with your hands locked round his throat.
I was guarding him myself. But now I've caught you!

[DIONYSOS *collapses in a terrified heap; the* DOORKEEPER *declaims in melodramatic triumph over him.*]

The black-hearted rock of the river Styx itself
And the blood-dripping crag that looms over Acheron
Prevent your escape, with Kokytos' hotfoot hounds
And the hundred-headed viper who'll rend your guts
To pieces, while an eel from Tartessos
Will clamp itself on your lungs, and as for your kidneys
And the rest of your innards, they'll all be pulped to blood
And torn apart by Gorgons from Teithras deme!*
[*Stiltedly*] I'll guide my hasty foot to fetch them now.

[*The* DOORKEEPER *turns and rushes back into the stage building.*]

XANTHIAS. What's the matter with you?

DIONYSOS. I've shitted myself: call a god!

XANTHIAS. You ridiculous thing! Get back on your feet at once
Before a stranger sees you.

DIONYSOS. I can't, I'm fainting!
Please give me a sponge; I need it—[*coyly*] to cool down my heart.

[XANTHIAS *takes a sponge from the luggage;* DIONYSOS *starts to rub between his legs.*]

XANTHIAS. Here, take it and rub.

DIONYSOS. Where is it?

XANTHIAS. O golden gods!
Is *that* where you keep your heart?

DIONYSOS. It was so afraid
That it made its way right down—to my lower bowel.

XANTHIAS. You're the biggest coward among gods and men.

DIONYSOS. What, me?
How come I'm a coward? I managed to ask for a sponge.
No one else would have done such a thing.

XANTHIAS. Well what would they do?

DIONYSOS. A coward would just have stayed on the ground with the smell.
But *I* stood up and wiped myself down, what's more.

XANTHIAS. What courage, I say, by Poseidon!

DIONYSOS. Well that's what I think.
But weren't you frightened yourself by his booming words
And the threats that he made?

XANTHIAS. Didn't give them a moment's thought.

DIONYSOS. Right then, since you're keen to prove yourself so nerveless,
Let's see you play *my* role: you can take this club
And this lion-skin too, if you're such a fearless-guts!
Meanwhile I'll take your part and carry the bags.

XANTHIAS. Well hand me your things at once; I'm happy with that.

[*They exchange costumes and accessories.*]

And look at me now—this Herakles-Xanthias!
You'll soon see if I'm a coward and spineless like you.

DIONYSOS [*sarcastically*]. You'll serve as Herakles' double—and ready for whipping!
All right, I suppose it's my turn to carry this luggage.

[*As they prepare to move on, the* skênê *door opens and* SLAVE[A] *enters from the palace of the underworld gods, mistakenly rushing to embrace the disguised* XANTHIAS.]

SLAVE[A]. You've returned, o dearest Herakles! Come on inside.
As soon as the goddess learnt you'd arrived down here,
She arranged for loaves to be baked and had several pots
Of pea soup boiled for you, got a whole ox roasted,
And had various cakes and breads prepared. Come on in!

XANTHIAS [*embarrassed*]. That's terribly kind, do thank her.

SLAVE[A]. By Apollo, I won't
Just let you decline like this. She's also been stewing
Fine pieces of bird-meat and toasting lovely snacks
And mixing the sweetest wine for you to drink.
You really must join us inside.

XANTHIAS. No thanks.

SLAVE[A]. Don't be silly!
I simply won't let you go. There's a pipe-girl as well
In here, such a gorgeous young thing, and some other girls too
All ready for dancing.

XANTHIAS [*excited*]. What's that, some *dancing*-girls?

SLAVE[A]. They're in perfect youthful prime—[*gesturing*] and they've trimmed themselves!*
So come on inside. When I left just now, the cook
Was finishing off the fish and the table was laid.

XANTHIAS. Go on then, tell the dancing-girls in there
The important man they're expecting is now on his way. [*Exit* SLAVE[A].]
[*To* DIONYSOS] Pick up the baggage then, slave, and follow me in.

DIONYSOS. Hey, hold on there! You can't be serious now.

It was only a joke to dress you in Herakles' clothes.
So stop this fooling around now, Xanthias.
Pick up the luggage again and carry it all.

XANTHIAS. What d'you mean? You surely don't intend to take back
All the things you gave me before?

DIONYSOS. Just watch me now!
Take the lion-skin off.

XANTHIAS. I call the gods to witness
And ask them to lend me their help.

DIONYSOS. The gods? How funny!
You must be out of your mind to suppose that *you*
A mortal slave could become Alkmene's son!*

XANTHIAS. Okay, I suppose you win. Take them back. But remember
There may come a time, who knows, when you'll need me again!

[DIONYSOS *takes back the lion-skin and club and resumes the identity of* HERAKLES. *The* CHORUS*'s dance involves gestures/motions towards* DIONYSOS, *who responds by contribuing to the song himself.*]

CHORUS. This is the way a man should act whose *Strophe*
Mind and wits are all alert and
One who's sailed the seas a lot:
Always go with the list of the ship,
Keep to the side where things are safer,
Don't just stand like a painted image
Fixed in a pose that can't be changed,
Switch your side instead and always
Occupy the cushier station.
That's the role of a clever fellow—
Let's be blunt, it's *Theramenes*!*

DIONYSOS. Picture how ludicrous the scene if *Antistrophe*
Xanthias, the merest slave, should
Find himself on Milesian bedding,*
Supine and kissing a dancing-girl, then
Called for a chamber-pot while I was
Watching his antics and all the time was
Jerking away with my own little winkle!*
Say this scoundrel caught sight of me, he'd
Smash his fist right into my jaw and

Strike a blow that would knock right out
All the teeth from the front of my mouth!*

[*From one of the* eisodoi *two female figures enter:* INNKEEPER *and her colleague* PLATHANE, *accompanied by* SLAVE[B] and SLAVE[C]. *They immediately spot* DIONYSOS'S *lion-skin and club and approach him aggressively.*]

INNKEEPER. Plathane, Plathane, over here! Here's the scoundrel himself,
The person who came to our inn some time ago
And devoured those sixteen loaves without paying.

PLATHANE. By Zeus,
It's the very same man all right.

XANTHIAS [*ironically*]. Here's trouble for someone!

PLATHANE. There was more besides—all that stewed meat he managed to eat,
Twenty portions no less.

XANTHIAS. Then someone will pay for his crime!

INNKEEPER. And huge chunks of garlic.

DIONYSOS. Just stop all this prattle, you woman!
You're making no sense.

INNKEEPER. Yes I am! And you didn't expect
That I'd recognize you while you're wearing these boots on your feet.*
And I haven't yet mentioned the piles of fish that you ate!

PLATHANE. No you haven't, my dear. And what about all the fresh cheese
That he gorged himself on, even eating the baskets as well?

INNKEEPER. And when I tried to get him to settle the bill
He gave me the sourest look and started to bellow.

XANTHIAS. That sounds just like him! It's always the way he behaves.

PLATHANE. He started to pull out his sword—we thought he was mad!

XANTHIAS. I can just imagine, poor thing.

PLATHANE. We were so alarmed
That the pair of us jumped right up onto one of the roof-beams
While *he* rushed out, purloining some mats for good measure.

XANTHIAS. Oh yes, that's typical too.

INNKEEPER. Now it's time to act.
[*to* SLAVE^{B}] Hurry up and ask my patron, Kleon, to come.

PLATHANE [*to* SLAVE^{C}]. And you must fetch Hyperbolos, if you can find him,
To help us destroy this man.* [*Exit* SLAVE^{B} *and* SLAVE^{C}]

INNKEEPER [*to* DIONYSOS]. You filthy gullet,
How I'd love to take a stone and smash your molars,
The ones you used to devour all that food of mine!

PLATHANE. And *I'd* like to hurl you down in the criminals' pit!*

INNKEEPER. And *I'd* like to take a sickle and cut out your throat,
The one with which you gobbled my sausages down!
I'm off to get Kleon. He'll come back here today
And issue a summons and tear this man to pieces.

[*The two women exit in haste.*]

DIONYSOS. I swear on my life, I love Xanthias more than the world.

XANTHIAS. Ah yes, ah yes, I see your ploy! Just stop it.
I refuse to wear Herakles' outfit again.

DIONYSOS [*wheedling*]. Please don't,
Sweet Xanthias!

XANTHIAS [*sarcastically*]. But how could a 'mortal slave'
Like me become 'Alkmene's son'? No chance.*

DIONYSOS. I know that you're angry, I know it. You're right to be so.
I would even allow you to hit me—I couldn't object.

[DIONYSOS *starts to hand over the lion-skin and club a second time.*]

If I ever attempt to take back these things again,
I wish utter destruction for me and my wife and my kids—
And damnation on blear-eyed Archedemos to boot!*

XANTHIAS. All right, I accept your oath on the terms you've stated.

[XANTHIAS *exchanges costumes again with* DIONYSOS *while the* CHORUS *re-enters the* orchêstra *to sing and dance, this time gesturing towards* XANTHIAS, *who responds by contributing to the song himself.*]

CHORUS. Now's the time for further action, *Strophe**
Now you're wearing once again the
Costume that you had before.
Start to recover your dynamism,

Fix your face in a fearsome look that
Suits that hero, turned to a god, whose
Likeness you're adopting.
Don't betray yourself with nonsense or
Utter a word that suits a coward.
Any such lapse will mean one thing:
Lifting those bags on your back once more!

XANTHIAS. Wise advice you're offering, men. *Antistrophe*
Just this very same train of thought had
Formed itself inside my mind.
Even so it's clear to me that
Once he thinks it's in his interests, he'll
Try to take this costume back.
Nonetheless I'll do my best to
Let the world think I'm a hero and
See a menacing look in my eyes.
Time to adopt my pose—I hear the
Door behind me creaking open.

[*The* skêne *door opens and the* DOORKEEPER *enters again, this time with two* ATTENDANTS *carrying a rope. In the by-now familiar way, he inevitably identifies* XANTHIAS *by his costume as* HERAKLES.]

DOORKEEPER [*gesturing*]. Tie him up straightaway, this dog-thief over here.
He'll pay for his crime. Hurry up!
DIONYSOS [*chortling*]. Here's trouble for someone!
XANTHIAS [*waving his club*]. To hell with you! Keep off!
DOORKEEPER. So you'll put up a fight?
[*Calling inside*] Hoy there, Ditylas, Skeblyas, and Pardokas,
Come straight out here and use as much force as you like.*

[*Enter three more* ATTENDANTS. XANTHIAS *uses his club to resist arrest.*]

DIONYSOS. Well isn't this quite outrageous, to see this man
Using blows when he's caught as a thief?
DOORKEEPER. It's beyond the pale!
DIONYSOS. It's outrageous in the extreme.
XANTHIAS [*to* DOORKEEPER]. But I swear by Zeus
I've never been down here before—if I have, let me die—

Nor stolen a single thing of yours, not one crumb.
In fact I'll make you a rather generous gesture:
You can take and subject to torture this slave of mine.*
If you find I've committed a crime, you can put me to death.

DOORKEEPER. What way should I torture him then?

XANTHIAS. *Every* way: on a ladder,
Strung up, with bristle-whip lashings, or flaying alive,
Or tight on the wheel, pour vinegar into his nostrils
And crush him with bricks—any method you like! Just don't
Let him off with a smack from a leek or an onion-plant.

DOORKEEPER. What you say is fair. And if by using blows
I maim your slave, I'll promise you compensation.

XANTHIAS. No need to bother; just take him away for torture.

DOORKEEPER. I'll do it right here: you can see him answer the questions.
[*To* DIONYSOS] Put down your stuff at once. Make sure you don't
Try to tell any lies to me.

DIONYSOS. I hereby declare
You can't torture *me*: I'm a god. If you dare to try,
You'll have only yourself to blame.

DOORKEEPER. What nonsense is this?

DIONYSOS. I'm a *god*, I assure you: Dionysos, Zeus's son.
And this is my slave.

DOORKEEPER. Do you hear?

XANTHIAS. I certainly do.
That's all the more reason to give him a really good whipping.
If it's true he's a god, then he won't even feel the pain.

DIONYSOS. Well since you claim yourself that *you're* a god,
Why not accept a beating the same as mine?

XANTHIAS. That makes good sense. [*To* DOORKEEPER] Whichever of us you see
Start to shed tears first or flinching at all at the blows,
You'll be able to tell that this one can't be a god.

DOORKEEPER. That's very fair-minded of you, I can't deny it.
You're prepared to follow what's right. Well, both of you strip.

[DIONYSOS *and* XANTHIAS *both remove their upper garments to bare their backs. The* DOORKEEPER *takes a rope or whip from one of the* ATTENDANTS *with which to deliver the blows in what follows.*]

XANTHIAS. Now how will you test us fairly?

DOORKEEPER. That's easily done—
By giving alternate blows.

XANTHIAS. That sounds just fine.

[DIONYSOS *and* XANTHIAS *move slightly apart and bend forward in preparation.*]

Right then. Now wait and see if I flinch at all.
Have you struck me already?

DOORKEEPER. Not yet. [*He strikes now.*]

XANTHIAS [*faking*]. That's why
I feel nothing.

DOORKEEPER. Well I'll strike the other one now. [*He hits* DIONYSOS.]

DIONYSOS [*also faking*]. Will
you tell me when?

DOORKEEPER. I've done so already!

DIONYSOS [*nonchalantly*]. Then why did I not even sneeze?

DOORKEEPER. I can't explain. But I'll try the one here again.

XANTHIAS. Well hurry up please. [*The* DOORKEEPER *strikes harder.*] Agh, agh!

DOORKEEPER. Well what's that cry?
You surely weren't in pain?

XANTHIAS. Just getting excited
About the Herakles festival at Diomeia.*

DOORKEEPER. This man's got the gods on his side. Now to *this* one again.

[*He moves back to* DIONYSOS *and strikes a harder blow than before.*]

DIONYSOS. Eee, eee!

DOORKEEPER. What's wrong?

DIONYSOS. I'm cheering the sight of horsemen.

DOORKEEPER. But why are you crying?

DIONYSOS. There must be some onions round here.

DOORKEEPER. So you're not concerned by the blows?

DIONYSOS. Not the slightest concern.

DOORKEEPER. In that case I'll have to go back to this other one here.

[*He now strikes* XANTHIAS *again even harder.*]

XANTHIAS. Aagh, aagh!

DOORKEEPER. What's wrong?

XANTHIAS. I've trod on a thorn—pull it out.

DOORKEEPER. What's happening here? Back again to the other one then.

[*He takes his time and delivers the hardest blow yet to* DIONYSOS.]

DIONYSOS. Apollo, help!—[*solemnly*] 'from your home in Delos or Pytho'.

XANTHIAS. He yelped with pain! You must have heard.

DIONYSOS. No I didn't.
I was simply quoting a satire by Hipponax.*

XANTHIAS [*to* DOORKEEPER]. You're indecisive. What about a good whack to his ribs?

DOORKEEPER. I'll go one better—[*to* DIONYSOS] let's see that belly of yours. [*Hits him.*]

DIONYSOS. Poseidon, help!

XANTHIAS. There's someone in pain.

DIONYSOS [*suddenly singing*]. 'O you
Who control the Aegean headland
And rule in the grey sea's depths'.*

DOORKEEPER. In Demeter's name I'm quite unable to tell
Which one of you is a god. So come inside.
The master himself will know how to recognize you,
And Pherrephatta as well, since they're gods themselves.*

DIONYSOS. That's a good suggestion you've made. I only wish
You'd thought of it sooner, before I suffered these blows.

[*All the characters exit into* PLOUTON'*s palace.*]

[PARABASIS: 674–737]*

CHORUS. Muse, join us in our sacred dance-steps,

Come to be part of our song's delight,
Come where you'll behold great throngs of people,
Many thousands seated in their wisdom,
Every one more honourable than Kleophon*
On whose lips of muddled speech
Is heard the raucous sound
Of a Thracian swallow
Perched amid barbarian branches.
It shrieks a mournful nightingale's song,
Announcing Kleophon's destruction—
Even if the votes are equal!

LEADER. Right and proper it is for us, a sacred chorus, to give the city
Best advice and best instructions. First of all we think you should
Treat all citizens now the same and take away the fears of some.
Those who may have done some wrong when tripped in Phrynichos' wrestling-bouts,*
Now's the time to let them leave their previous lapses in the past,
Let them shed their former guilt and wipe away their old mistakes.
Next, we think no one should live amongst us with their rights curtailed.
That seems shameful when compared with those who fought in one sea-battle yet
Now, just like those old Plataians, are no longer slaves but masters instead.*
Not that we're purporting to say there's anything wrong with that, of course.
Praise we're happy to give you there: it's the only sensible thing you've done!
Surely, though, you should be fair to others who've fought in *many* sea-battles,
Those whose fathers did the same, whose families form ancestral stock?
They're the ones who ask your pardon: forgive them their misfortune now.

Come, relent, give up your anger, all you whose natures make you wise.
Let's agree to band together and count as kinsmen every one,
Give them all full citizen rights, provided they man our ships and fight!
Pride and hard disdain won't serve us well while things stand as they do.
'Tossed on stormy waves' our city's affairs hang in the balance now.*
Follow this good advice or else the future will show how foolish we were.

CHORUS. 'If my eye is a steady judge of the cast of life'*
And character of a man who's in for big trouble,
A certain monkey's mischief won't last much longer—
Kleigenes the diminutive,*
Foulest of all bath-keepers
Who mixing their washing-powders control
Adulterated soda
And earthy detergent.
He'll soon be done for! And knows it too,
Which makes him full of aggression,
Afraid he may be mugged when drunk
If he goes without a big stick!

LEADER. Many's the time we've noticed something strange about the city's ways,
Namely, how it treats those citizens who deserve to be thought the best
Just the same as it treats old coins as well as the recent gold ones too.
Those were coins of solid value, no counterfeits of them were found.
Nowhere has there ever been a finer currency, all agree.
Only they were minted pure and always proved their worth when tested;
All the world could count on them, Greeks and barbarians both alike.
Now, however, they're obsolete, replaced by lousy coins of bronze,

Recently minted, of no long standing, and stamped in the ugliest fashion as well.*
Just the same with citizens too: those we know to be true-born and decent,
Those whose conduct is always just, the ones who deserve to be thought the best,
Men brought up in wrestling-schools and taught to dance and play music too,
They're despised. Instead the ones of 'bronze', the foreign and flaming-haired,
Those who lack all breeding in every respect, it's *those* we choose to employ,
Recent arrivals of just the sort the city would once have rejected outright—
Even to play the part of scapegoats would once have been too good for them!
Please, you idiots listening now, it's not too late to change your ways.*
Choose to use the best men once again. If all then turns out well,
Praise will come your way. And if you fail, at least the wise will think
Swinging from a high-grade tree is consolation for the hanged!

[*The stage-door opens and* XANTHIAS *and* SLAVE[D] *enter in mid-conversation.*]

SLAVE[D]. By Zeus the Saviour, what a decent man he must be,
That master of yours.
XANTHIAS. But how could he fail to be decent?
He's the type who knows nothing except for drinking and fucking.
SLAVE[D]. I'm amazed he gave you no beating despite the fact
That you, the slave, purported to be the master.
XANTHIAS. A beating? He would have been sorry!
SLAVE[D]. Yes, that's the talk,
That's real slave spirit—the kind I like showing myself.
XANTHIAS. Do you really enjoy such things?
SLAVE[D]. It's a kind of rapture

When I'm able to curse my master behind his back.
XANTHIAS. And what do you feel as you mutter your private complaints
When he hits you then sends you outside?
SLAVE[D]. Oh I love that too!
XANTHIAS. And what about making *mischief*?
SLAVE[D]. There's nothing quite like it!
XANTHIAS. You're my own flesh and blood! And when you hear your masters
In private conversation?
SLAVE[D]. I'm crazy with joy!
XANTHIAS. Then dishing the dirt about them to others?
SLAVE[D]. Oh yes!
That's such a thrill it makes me ejaculate!
XANTHIAS. O Phoibos Apollo, please give me your hand to shake.
Let's kiss each other as well. [*Turns round.*] Please tell me now,
By Zeus who's the god of whipping-boys like us,
What's all this uproar and shouting I hear inside
Like a quarrel?
SLAVE[D]. It's Aischylos and Euripides.
XANTHIAS. Well I never!
SLAVE[D]. It's really a quite momentous affair
That's erupted among the dead in an outbreak of strife.
XANTHIAS. But what's the reason?
SLAVE[D]. A law exists down here
That for all the great sophisticated arts
The person who holds the highest esteem in his group
Should have special dining rights in the Prytaneion*
And a throne right next to Plouton.
XANTHIAS. I understand.
SLAVE[D]. Until, that is, a superior artist arrives,
Someone who's better than him. Then he has to give way.
XANTHIAS. But why's that caused any trouble for Aischylos?
SLAVE[D]. He held the throne for tragic drama, that's why.
He was deemed the best poet at that.
XANTHIAS. But who is it *now*?
SLAVE[D]. When Euripides came down to Hades, he started
To harangue the criminals here—the muggers and thieves,

The ones who'd beaten their fathers, the burglars as well:
There's a crowd of them all in Hades. And when they heard
His debating speeches, his verbal twists and turns,
They went quite crazy about him and called him the best.
He was so puffed up that he laid his claim to the throne
Where Aischylos sat.
XANTHIAS. But wasn't he pelted for that?
SLAVE^{D}. Not at all, the crowd cried out for a competition,
To decide which one has the finer poetic art.
XANTHIAS. The crowd of riff-raff you mean?
SLAVE^{D}. Yes, their shouts thundered out.
XANTHIAS. But weren't there others who sided with Aischylos then?
SLAVE^{D}. Superior taste's in short supply—[*gestures at audience*] like here!
XANTHIAS. Well tell me now what Plouton intends to do.
SLAVE^{D}. He's going to stage a contest and reach a judgement
By putting their artistry to the test.
XANTHIAS. But why
Didn't Sophokles too assert his right to the throne?
SLAVE^{D}. He's not like that.* He gave Aischylos a kiss
When he came down here, and grasped him by the hand.
He made it clear that he laid no claim to the throne.
But he said he was ready, just like Kleidemides,*
To wait as reserve: if Aischylos prevails,
He'll stay in his place; if not, he'll enter the contest
And pit his art against Euripides then.
XANTHIAS. So it's really going to happen?
SLAVE^{D}. It is, quite soon.
The whole tremendous commotion will take place here.
They'll actually weigh their art in a pair of scales.
XANTHIAS. What, you mean weigh tragedy just like chunks of meat?*
SLAVE^{D}. They'll bring out rulers and rods to measure their verses
And folding builders' frames—
XANTHIAS [*baffled*]. For making *bricks*?
SLAVE^{D}. Set-squares and wedges as well. Euripides says
He'll scrutinize word by word his opponent's plays.

XANTHIAS. I imagine that Aischylos must be fuming with rage.
SLAVE^{D}. With lowered head he glowered in bull-like aggression!
XANTHIAS. But who will *judge* these things?
SLAVE^{D}. An awkward question.
There's a shortage of expert men for them to choose from.
The Athenians weren't at all to Aischylos' liking—
XANTHIAS. I suppose he thought too many of them were scum!
SLAVE^{D}. And he took the view that the rest of the people were useless
At judging poets. So then they picked your *master*:
The tragedian's art is one that he knows very well.
Let's go back inside. Whenever our masters are busy,
It's bound to mean there's trouble in store for *us*.

[*They go back into the palace through the central stage door.*]

CHORUS. Fearsome the wrath the loud-thundering one will feel inside
When he sees his antagonist sharpening all his loquacious teeth.
At that moment a surge of terrible madness will make
His eyes start to swivel around in their sockets!

Great flashing-helmeted strife will follow among horse-crested words,
And screeching chariot axles will split into slivers of wood,
While one of these mortals, a craftsman of intellect, fights
Against the other's horse-galloping utterances.

Bristling the shaggy-necked hair of the mane flowing down from his head,
Contracting the fearsome skin of his forehead, he'll roar and release
Great bolt-fastened words which he's torn up like pieces of timber
With the force of a storm of gigantic proportions.

Then the mouth-manipulating assessor of verses, the smooth
Curling tongue that controls the horse's bit with envy,
Will dissect words and subtly reduce to nothing
The heaving efforts of the other's lungs.

[*The stage door opens: enter* PLOUTON, *who will observe from one side till 1414; behind him come a haughty* AISCHYLOS *and an overwrought* EURIPIDES, *rushing on in mid-conversation with* DIONYSOS.]

EURIPIDES [*to* DIONYSOS]. I refuse to let go of the throne, stop lecturing me.*
I claim that I'm better than him in this art of ours.
DIONYSOS. Why this silence, Aischylos? You hear what he says.
EURIPIDES. He'll start with this supercilious pose! It's like
The kind of pretentious bluster he used in his plays.
DIONYSOS. I suggest, my man, that you tone down your words a little.
EURIPIDES. I know what he's like; I saw through him long ago.
He's a poet who makes his characters wild and wilful,
His style's uncurbed, unruly, without any limits,
Devoid of slickness, verbosely vaunting its garbage.
AISCHYLOS. How dare you, 'son of a goddess who lives in the fields'!*
You abuse me like that, you collector of chatterbox talk,
Creator of beggars and rag-costume-stitcher to boot?*
You won't get away with such words.
DIONYSOS. Stop, Aischylos,
'Don't let your intestines become inflamed with choler.'*
AISCHYLOS. I've no intention of stopping before I've shown
The effrontery of this poet whose heroes are cripples.*
DIONYSOS [*melodramatically*]. Bring out black sheep, my slaves, bring out black sheep!*
A whirlwind's on the point of bursting upon us.
AISCHYLOS [*to* EURIPIDES]. You collector of monodies written in Cretan style,
And polluter of tragic art with stories of incest*—
DIONYSOS. Please stop, o Aischylos, revered by many.
And you, o wretched Euripides, hide from this hailstorm,

Pull back, keep out of the way, if you've got any sense:
There's a risk he'll strike your head with a word of anger
So it splits wide open and out pours—*Telephos*!*
And Aischylos, don't yield to anger, be mild.
Pose questions, be questioned in turn. But swapping abuse
Is not for poets but only for female bread-sellers.
You're roaring away like an oak-tree that's been ignited.

EURIPIDES. Well *I'm* quite ready—you won't see *me* pulling back—
To bite and be bitten in turn. If he wants, I'll go first.
There's tragedy's verses and songs and sinews to test.*
And by Zeus I'll offer my *Peleus* and *Aiolos* too,
And my *Meleager*—and on top of those, *Telephos*!*

DIONYSOS. And what do *you* propose, tell us, Aischylos?

AISCHYLOS. I'd prefer this quarrel to take place somewhere else.
The contest isn't on equal terms.

DIONYSOS. Why's that?

AISCHYLOS. In my case what I composed hasn't died with me,
But *his* has died with him, so he'll have it to hand.
Nonetheless, since it's what you want, we must do these things.

DIONYSOS. Very well. [*Calling*.] Please bring me incense and fire to burn.
Before the clever exchanges begin I'll pray
That I'm able to judge this contest with expert finesse.
[*To* CHORUS] While I do, I'd like you to sing a song to the Muses.

[*An* ATTENDANT *brings out a small altar, on which* DIONYSOS *burns some incense while he makes gestures of prayer*.]

CHORUS. Nine maiden daughters of Zeus, you sacred
Muses, who look down on the subtly reasoning, intelligent minds
Of these shapers of thought, when they come together in strife
Pitting speech against speech in wrestling bouts of cogitation,
Come here to behold the power
Of mouths so formidable at producing
Words an artist's tools have cut to size.
Now's the moment for wisdom's great contest

To move into action.

DIONYSOS. You two must pray as well before you speak.
AISCHYLOS [*adding incense*]. Demeter, goddess who nourished my mind and thought,
Please make me worthy of what your Mysteries teach.*

DIONYSOS [*to* EURIPIDES]. You too must burn some incense.
EURIPIDES. I'd rather not.
There are different gods to whom I make my prayers.
DIONYSOS. You have personal gods, a new coinage?*
EURIPIDES. I certainly do!
DIONYSOS. Go on then, make your prayers to your private gods.
EURIPIDES. O Aither, where I pasture, and Pivoting Tongue,
Astuteness, Nostrils keen to follow the scent,*
Help me refute my opponent in all that he says.

[AGON: 895–1098]

CHORUS. We feel the most intense desire *Strophe*
To hear from both these clever men
Their finely choreographed words.
Begin to launch your verbal assaults!
Your tongues are ready for violent combat,
You both possess courageous spirit,
Your minds are primed for agile moves.
Our expectation is of course
That one will speak in elegant style
And language polished to finest finish,
While the other will tear up words like trees
From their roots and falling upon his foe
Will fill the air with a horse's thick dust-clouds of verses.*

LEADER. It's time to deliver your speeches now. Be sure to adopt a manner
That's full of wit and straight to the point and avoids repeating clichés.
EURIPIDES. As regards myself and the kind of poet my work reveals me to be,

I'll come to that at the end of my speech, but begin by exposing *him*.
I want to show what a charlatan and a fraudster he was in the theatre.
He kept on duping those stupid spectators who'd grown up with Phrynichos' plays.*
At the start of each work he liked to produce a veiled figure to sit on the stage,
For example Achilles, or Niobe too: he wouldn't reveal their mask
But used them for purely showy effect, just stuck there brooding in silence.*

DIONYSOS. I swear that's true!

EURIPIDES. But instead the chorus would dump great chains of songs,
Four lyric sequences strung together, with the characters stuck there in silence.

DIONYSOS. But I rather liked that silence, you know. It gave me just as much pleasure
As the figures who jabber in modern plays.

EURIPIDES. But *that*'s because you were mindless,
No doubt about that.

DIONYSOS. Well I rather agree! But why did this so-and-so do it?

EURIPIDES. Pure charlatanry! He wanted spectators to sit there on tenterhooks,
Not sure when Niobe's voice would emerge. And meanwhile the play plodded on.

DIONYSOS. The wicked old crook! And there was I, taken in by his fraudulent tricks!
[*To* AISCHYLOS] But why all this twitchy and peevish movement?

EURIPIDES. Because I'm exposing his faults!
[*Resuming*] Then when he'd finished with all this nonsense and half the play had passed,
He'd give his character twelve huge words, each one as large as an ox,
And all of them shaggy with eyebrows and crests, like frightening bogey faces.

They were words that nobody understood.

AISCHYLOS [*roaring*]. I can't take any more!

DIONYSOS. Keep quiet!

EURIPIDES. His language was never remotely clear—

DIONYSOS [*to* AISCHYLOS]. Will you please stop grinding your teeth!

EURIPIDES. But perpetual talk of Skamander rivers and ditches and emblems on shields
Of griffin-eagles in beaten bronze.* His words were enormous crags
That were hard to interpret at all.

DIONYSOS. By the gods, I can certainly vouch for that!
I once lay awake the whole night long unable to sleep while I puzzled
Over what kind of bird he might have meant by his phrase the 'tawny horse-cock'.*

AISCHYLOS. It's a sign they painted on prows of ships—your ignorance knows no bounds!

DIONYSOS. Did they really? I thought that it must have meant Eryxis, Philoxenos' son.*

EURIPIDES. Well why was it right to mention cocks in dignified tragic verse?

AISCHYLOS. You god-forsaken wretch, what about the things that *you* composed?

EURIPIDES. But I never mentioned horse-cocks for sure, nor goat-stags either, like you—
The sorts of things you see depicted on fabrics imported from Persia.
When *I* took over the tragic art from you, I found her condition
Unhealthily bloated from constant bombast, all swollen with ponderous language.
So straight away I made her diet and removed that excess weight:
I slimmed her down with versicles and walks and lots of white beet.
I gave her the juice of babbling speech which I squeezed from the books I own.

Then I fed her up on monodic songs and mixed Kephisophon in.*
I didn't just talk any nonsense I liked nor heedlessly jumble my words.
Instead, the character first on stage would start with a direct statement
Of the ancestry of the plot.

AISCHYLOS. Which was bound at least to be better than *yours*!

EURIPIDES. From the opening lines I would never allow any character just to be idle.
It made no difference what sort they were: so wives and slaves as well,
And masters and maidens and old women too—they all spoke the same.

AISCHYLOS. Then surely
You deserved to die for such recklessness.

EURIPIDES. Not at all, in Apollo's name!
This way of writing was *democratic*.

DIONYSOS. Don't pursue this line, old chap.
It's not a direction of argument that promises well for you.*

EURIPIDES [*points at audience*]. Moreover I taught these people here to chatter away –

AISCHYLOS. Too true!
But before you'd managed to teach them that I wish you'd been split down the middle!

EURIPIDES. And how to apply to language itself fine measuring-rods and set-squares,
And to think, to observe, to comprehend, to wriggle and always be crafty,*
To cultivate a suspicious mind, to ponder all things—

AISCHYLOS. Yes, too true!

EURIPIDES. And I staged *domestic* affairs of the kinds we all habitually live with,
The sorts of things spectators know well. So *if* I'd got anything wrong,

They would have found fault with my artistry. But I didn't, like you, employ bluster
To distract their minds from serious thought, nor did I cause frissons of horror
With Kyknos-type figures or Memnons as well, whose horses have bells on their harness.*
You can tell us apart by the kinds of men who are products of *his* plays and mine.
Phormisios belongs to him, and Megainetos the Phrygian:
All trumpets and lances and long beards they are, the sort who rip trees with their teeth.
But *my* disciples are Kleitophon and nimble Theramenes too.*

DIONYSOS. Theramenes, hey? He's certainly clever and quick-witted too in all things.
If ever he finds himself in trouble or even comes anywhere near it,
He always escapes with a lucky throw—for him, nothing dicey goes wrong!*

EURIPIDES. Well, that's the sort of cogitation
I introduced in the lives of these people,
By making reasoning part of my art
And enquiry too, which means they now ponder
And thoroughly grasp all manner of things,
Especially how to improve the way
They organize their domestic affairs
And constantly ask 'Well how's this going?',
'Where's such and such?', and 'Who took that?'

DIONYSOS. I swear by the gods we've reached the point
Where every Athenian enters his house
And shouts at the top of his voice to the slaves
With urgent demands: 'Now where's that pot?
Who's eaten up the head of that fish,
The sprat I mean? That bowl of mine
I bought last year is finished for good.
And where's that garlic from yesterday?
Who's nibbled away at the olives as well?'
Yet in the past they were mindless dimwits
Who gaped as helpless as tiny babies
And sat there like nincompoops.

[*While singing and dancing the following, the* CHORUS *gestures in the direction of* AISCHYLOS.]

CHORUS. 'Beholdest thou this, noble Achilles?'* *Antistrophe*
Come then, what answer will you give?
Be sure of this one thing:
Don't let your anger seize hold of you
And sweep you outside the chariot-tracks.
Terrible charges he's brought against you.
But even so, magnanimous man,
Don't let your reply be driven by anger.
Instead reduce your vessel's canvas,
Make use of merely the tips of the sails,
Then gradually, gradually gather your speed
While watching out for the moment when
You catch a wind that's smooth and steady behind you.

LEADER. O first of all Greek poets who built a tower of mighty words
And adorned a realm of tragic nonsense, be bold and spout your speech.

AISCHYLOS. These circumstances fill me with rage, my guts are wrenched with anger.
To think that *I* must respond to *him*! But in case he should say I'm confounded—
[*To* EURIPIDES] Just answer me this: what kinds of things should prompt our praise for a poet?

EURIPIDES. Sophistication and moral advice. And because it's our task to improve
All the people who live in the cities of Greece.

AISCHYLOS. So if you have *failed* to achieve that
And you took good people of noble mind and turned them instead into rabble,
What penalty will you agree you deserve?

DIONYSOS. He should die! No need to ask *him*.

AISCHYLOS. Consider then whether the sorts of people I passed on to him at the start

Were of noble mind and stood tall and proud, not turn-and-run cowards in battle
Nor vulgar loafers nor dirty tricksters nor rogues like people today.
They breathed the spirit of lances and spears and headgear with flashing white plumes
And helmets and greaves and mighty mettle of seven full ox-hides in strength.*

EURIPIDES. Here we go, as I thought, with this awful stuff. He'll grind me down hammering helmets.
What actions of *yours*, could you please explain, taught the people to be quite so noble?

DIONYSOS. Answer him, Aischylos. Don't keep brooding in arrogant, wilful rage.

AISCHYLOS. I composed a play that was full of Ares.

DIONYSOS. Which one?

AISCHYLOS. The *Seven against Thebes*.*
Every man who saw that play performed would have longed for a warlike spirit.

DIONYSOS. Well that's a terrible thing that you did! You made the Thebans become
Far braver in war than they'd been before. And for that you deserve to be beaten.

AISCHYLOS. You Athenians too could have trained more for war; it's your fault, not mine, you chose not to.
Later on when I staged the *Persians* too I taught people always to want
To defeat their opponents, and at the same time I glorified what we'd achieved.*

DIONYSOS. Yes, it gave me a thrill when the dead Dareios delivered a speech in that play
And the chorus immediately clapped their hands and chanted 'iauoi', 'iauoi'.

AISCHYLOS. We expect our poets to do these things. Go back to the earliest times
And consider how all the noble poets have helped us to lead our lives.
We were taught by Orpheus mystic rites and how to abstain from killing.

Musaios taught us cures for disease, and oracles too, while Hesiod
Taught working the land, the seasons of crops, when to plough.
As for Homer divine,*
Why else did he win such honour and fame if not by teaching so well
About army formations and valour and armour?

DIONYSOS. But he failed to teach Pantakles that,*
The clumsiest man in the whole wide world. He was recently in a procession
And was trying to fasten his helmet on first before fixing the crest on the top!

AISCHYLOS. But he taught many other fine men nonetheless—brave Lamachos, just to name one.*
My mind in turn was moulded by Homer; I wrote about heroes like his,
The lion-heart types like Patroklos and Teukros. My aim was to rouse every man
To emulate great figures like them when the trumpet of war sounded out.
But I never created a whore like Phaidra, nor that other one too, Stheneboia,*
And no one can name a woman of mine who suffers from sexual passion.

EURIPIDES. But that's because your work lacks Aphrodite's allure.

AISCHYLOS. A good thing!
Whereas you and yours fell victim to her in a quite spectacular way:
She crushed you down with all her force.

DIONYSOS. By Zeus, she certainly did!
All the things you'd written about other women afflicted your very own life.*

EURIPIDES. What harm, you blackguard, was done to the city by women like my Stheneboias?

AISCHYLOS. You persuaded noble women, the wives of noble husbands as well,
To poison themselves with hemlock, ashamed by *your* Bellerophon story.*

EURIPIDES. But didn't the story I wrote about Phaidra exist already before me?
AISCHYLOS. It did, but still it's the poet's duty to draw a veil over evil
And not to stage or teach such matters. For just as smaller children
Have a teacher who tells them things, so poets are teachers to those who are adults.
We've a serious duty to say what's best.
EURIPIDES. So when *you* use mountain-sized words,
Lykabettos in size or as big as Parnassos, is *that* then teaching what's best?*
A poet should speak in a human voice.
AISCHYLOS. But we poets, you wretch, have to strive
To give birth to words that match the greatness of all our thoughts and ideas.
With characters too who are semi-divine you expect that they'll use bigger words,
In the very same way that the clothes they wear are far more majestic than ours.*
I set the standards in all these ways but *you* defiled them.
EURIPIDES. Just how?
AISCHYLOS. For one thing you dressed your kings in rags. You wanted to make them seem
More pitiful in the spectators' eyes.*
EURIPIDES. What harm did I do by that?
AISCHYLOS. It's because of these things that nobody rich is willing to pay for a warship.*
Each one of them wraps himself in rags and laments and claims to be poor.
DIONYSOS. By Demeter, they do, while wearing a thick woollen tunic beneath their rags!
When they've managed to take people in with their fraud, they're seen buying fish in the market.
AISCHYLOS. You've also taught people to cultivate bad habits of blather and chatter.
It's this which has emptied the wrestling-schools and worn away the buttocks

Of all the young men immersed in their chatter.* It's persuaded the Paraloi too
To dare to argue with those in command: when *I* was alive, by contrast,
They only knew how to call for bread and to shout 'yo-ho' from their benches.*

DIONYSOS. By Apollo, not half, though they also knew how to fart on the rowers below them
And to smear their messmates' faces with shit and to nip onto shore for some crime.
These days they argue and hardly row. The ships wander round on their sails.

AISCHYLOS. What evils *hasn't* he helped to cause?
He's shown us women as go-betweens
And women in childbirth in sacred places
And women who sleep with their very own brothers
And women who say that life is death.*
The consequence of all these things
Is our city's now teeming with minor officials
And buffoons who serve as public monkeys
Deceiving the people at every turn,
And nobody's able to carry a torch*
Since nobody trains in gymnasia now.

DIONYSOS. How true! I laughed myself dry of tears
At last year's Panathenaia. I saw
A runner all hunched and moving so slowly,
White-faced and fat and lagging behind
In a desperate state. At the Kerameikos*
The people standing there by the gate
Slapped his stomach and ribs and sides and buttocks,
And feeling the smacks from the palms of their hands
He started farting
And ran off while blowing his torch.

CHORUS. Momentous the issue, immense the strife, intense the approaching war. *Strophe*
A difficult task to decide between them

When one exerts its massive force
While the other can wheel around and resist with vigour.
The pair of you mustn't remain in your camps.
Many the openings still for further attacks of clever ideas.
So whatever resources you have for competing,
Speak now, advance now, anatomize
These subjects ancient and modern.
Both take the risk of speaking some subtle and clever thoughts.

In case you're both afraid stupidity may prevent the minds *Antistrophe*
Of these spectators watching here
From grasping subtleties that you speak,
Feel no anxiety on that score—the situation's changed.
These people are all old soldiers now,
Each of them has a book and understands sophistication.*
Their natures are strong in other respects
And now their wits are whetted.
So have no fear about that.
Launch an all-out attack in confidence that these are clever spectators.

EURIPIDES [*to* AISCHYLOS]. Very well, I'm going to turn to your prologues now.
[*To* DIONYSOS] I intend to take the opening part of a play
And put to the test his supposedly skilful work.
He was always obscure in explaining dramatic events.

DIONYSOS. Which prologue of his will you test?

EURIPIDES. A very large number.
[*To* AISCHYLOS] But start by reciting that one from the *Oresteia*.*

DIONYSOS. Let everyone else keep quiet. Speak, Aischylos.

AISCHYLOS. 'Hermes below, watching over the father's power,

Become my saviour, my ally in time of need.
I come back to this land, returning from exile I come.'

DIONYSOS. Do you find any fault with these lines?

EURIPIDES. Yes, more than a dozen!

DIONYSOS. But the lines themselves don't add up to more than three.

EURIPIDES. But each of the lines contains some twenty mistakes.

[AISCHYLOS *starts to make rumbling sounds of indignation.*]

DIONYSOS. Keep quiet, I warn you, Aischylos. If you don't,
I'll fine you more than these three iambic lines.

AISCHYLOS. I'm supposed to keep quiet for *him*?

DIONYSOS. If you take my advice.

EURIPIDES. He starts straightaway with an error as broad as daylight.

AISCHYLOS. You see what nonsense you speak.

EURIPIDES. I don't care what you think.

AISCHYLOS. What error d'you claim I made?

EURIPIDES. Recite it again.

AISCHYLOS. 'Hermes below, watching over the father's power—'

EURIPIDES. Well doesn't Orestes say this at the tomb
Of his father after he's died?

AISCHYLOS. I don't deny it.

EURIPIDES. Is the point he's making that when his father had died
A violent death at the hands of his very own wife
In a secret plot, Hermes was 'watching over'?

AISCHYLOS. That wasn't his point. He called Eriounian Hermes*
As protector of souls in the earth, and his words explained
That Hermes possesses this role as a gift from his father.

EURIPIDES. Then you made an even bigger mistake than I thought.
If Hermes possesses this underworld role from his father—

DIONYSOS. It would mean on his father's side he's a robber of tombs!

AISCHYLOS. Dionysos, the wine you drink has a nasty stench.*

DIONYSOS. Recite some more, [*to* EURIPIDES] while *you* watch out for the flaws.

AISCHYLOS. 'Become my saviour, my ally in time of need.
I come back to this land, returning from exile I come.'

EURIPIDES. He said the same thing twice, clever Aischylos!

DIONYSOS. How twice?

EURIPIDES. Consider the words, and I'll explain.
'I come back to this land', he says, and 'return from exile.'
But 'come back' and 'return' just mean the very same thing.

DIONYSOS. It's as if, by Zeus, someone should say to his neighbour
'Please lend me a kneading-trough—or a trough for kneading.'

AISCHYLOS. Not at all—you've been overwhelmed by his blather, you have!
The two things don't mean the same. It's poetic phrasing.

EURIPIDES [*sarcastically*]. How's that? Do please enlighten me what you mean.

AISCHYLOS. 'Come back' is something that any inhabitant does.
It applies when no special circumstances exist.
But a man who's been in exile 'comes back and returns'.

DIONYSOS. I like it! But what do you say then, Euripides?

EURIPIDES. I flatly deny that Orestes returned to his home.
He came back secretly and without permission.

DIONYSOS. I like that too! But I don't really know what you mean.

EURIPIDES [*to* AISCHYLOS]. Continue the next bit then.

DIONYSOS. Yes do, continue,
Keep going, Aischylos. [*To* EURIPIDES] *You* watch for faults.

AISCHYLOS. 'Upon the mound of this tomb I beseech my father
To hearken, to hear—'*

EURIPIDES. Another example again!
'To hearken, to hear', it's blatant they both mean the same.

DIONYSOS. It's because he was calling the dead, you stupid bonehead!
We can't even make them hear if we call *three* times.
But how did *you* compose your prologues?

EURIPIDES. You'll see.
If you catch me ever repeating myself or find padding
That doesn't belong to the plot, you can spit on my work.

DIONYSOS. Come on then, speak. I really need to listen

To the standards of diction your prologues exemplify.*

EURIPIDES. 'A time there was when Oedipus was happy.'*

AISCHYLOS. Completely false! He was damned when he came into being!
He must have been, since even before he was born
Apollo foretold he was going to murder his father.
So how could a man like this have ever been happy?

EURIPIDES. 'His fortunes changed: he became most wretched of mortals.'*

AISCHYLOS. Completely false! He was wretched right from the start.
It must have been the case, since when he was born
They put him inside a jar and exposed him in winter,
To make sure that he didn't grow up to murder his father.
He came to Polybos' court with his swollen feet.*
Later still, he married a woman much older than him—
And not just a woman, his very own mother in fact!
He eventually blinded himself.

DIONYSOS [*sarcastically*]. Ah, happy indeed—
Provided he served alongside Erasinides!*

EURIPIDES. What nonsense you're talking. My prologues are beautifully written.

AISCHYLOS. I can't bear to continue this word-by-word dissection
Of every verse. With the help of the gods on my side
I'll use a miniature oil-jar to rubbish your prologues.*

EURIPIDES. A miniature *oil-jar* to deal with my prologues?

AISCHYLOS. Just one.
Your style of writing means any old object will fit—
A fleecelet, a miniature oil-jar, a little old sack—
The iambic lines you compose. I'll show you at once.

EURIPIDES. Oh you will, will you?

AISCHYLOS. Yes.

EURIPIDES. All right then, listen to this.
'Aigyptos, so prevailing tradition relates,
With fifty sons traversed the sea by oar,
Put in to Argos and—'*

AISCHYLOS. lost his miniature oil-jar!

DIONYSOS. What's the point of the miniature oil-jar? It's damned annoying.

Recite him a further prologue—let's see what it means.

EURIPIDES. 'Dionysos, equipped with thyrsoi and wearing fawnskins,
Among the pine-trees down Parnassos's slopes
Went leaping in dance and—'*

AISCHYLOS. lost his miniature oil-jar!

DIONYSOS. Oh no, he's struck us again with this miniature oil-jar!

EURIPIDES. I'm not concerned by that. Now *here's* a prologue
To which he won't be able to tag on an oil-jar.
'No man exists who's happy in all respects.
Perhaps born noble he falls in penury's way.
Or low by birth—'*

AISCHYLOS. he loses his miniature oil-jar!

DIONYSOS [*confidentially*]. Euripides—

EURIPIDES. What's wrong?

DIONYSOS. Let's lower the sails.
This miniature oil-jar's about to blow a huge gale.

EURIPIDES. I swear by Demeter I'm not remotely troubled.
I'll show you now—I'll knock the thing from his hand.

DIONYSOS. Well recite another, but please avoid his oil-jar.

EURIPIDES. 'In ancient times, departing from Sidon his city,
Kadmos, Agenor's son—'*

AISCHYLOS. lost his miniature oil-jar!

DIONYSOS [*to* EURIPIDES]. I beg you, friend, please *purchase* the oil-jar from him,
To stop him from tearing your prologues to pieces.

EURIPIDES. You what?
You think I should buy this from *him*?

DIONYSOS. If you take my advice.

EURIPIDES. I certainly won't. There are numerous prologues of mine
To which he won't be able to tag on an oil-jar.
'When Pelops, the son of Tantalos, came to Pisa
With his dashing horses—'*

AISCHYLOS. he lost his miniature oil-jar!

DIONYSOS. You see? He's managed to tag on the oil-jar again.
Please pay him his price, my good man—it's not too late.

You'll be getting a very fine oil-jar for only an obol.*

EURIPIDES. I certainly won't, not yet. I've lots more prologues.
'Oineus once from the land—'

AISCHYLOS. lost his miniature oil-jar!

EURIPIDES. Allow me first to get to the end of the line!
'Oineus once from the land took abundant crops
And making first sacrifice—'*

AISCHYLOS. lost his miniature oil-jar!

DIONYSOS. What, in the act of sacrifice? Who filched it?

EURIPIDES. Ignore him, please. Let him try to respond to *this*.
'Zeus, as we're told by the truth of ancient reports—'*

DIONYSOS. You'll finish me off! He'll say 'lost his miniature oil-jar'.
This oil-jar's now a wart on the face of your prologues,
Just like the styes that grow on people's eyelids.
Turn instead, in the name of the gods, to his choral songs.

EURIPIDES. I *will*! What's more, I'll prove that he's no good as well
At composing songs: he always writes the same thing.

CHORUS. What's about to happen next?
Perplexed I am, I cannot imagine
What kind of faults he'll find
With a man who's composed so many songs,
The most beautiful ones of those we know
From all tragic poets who've lived.

Astounded I am and wonder how
He'll try to fault this man,
The bacchic master himself,
For whom I feel afraid.*

EURIPIDES [*sarcastically*]. Amazing songs indeed! We're about to find out.
I intend to condense all his different songs into one.

DIONYSOS. I'll take some pebbles and count the number you use.

[EURIPIDES *gestures to the aulos-player to accompany him, adopts a suitably parodic pose, and proceeds to sing a jumble of Aischylean lyrics in a ludicrously portentous manner.*]

EURIPIDES. Phthian Achilles, why, when you hear the man-slaying,

Alas, alas, toil of battle, comest thou not to our aid?
Hermes our ancestor we worship, we the people round the lake.
Alas, alas, toil of battle, comest thou not to our aid?

DIONYSOS. That's two toils, Aischylos, for you.

EURIPIDES. Most glorious of Achaians, wide-ruling son of Atreus, hear me.
Alas, alas, toil of battle, comest thou not to our aid?

DIONYSOS. A third toil, Aischylos, that was.

EURIPIDES. Sacred silence! Bee-keepers approach to unlock Artemis's temple.
Alas, alas, toil of battle, comest though not to our aid?
I speak with authority of the destined power of men as they start their journey.
Alas, alas, toil of battle, comest though not to our aid?*

DIONYSOS. Zeus king of the gods! I'm losing count of these toils.
The only thing I want is to go to the baths:
These toils have given me swellings around the kidneys.

EURIPIDES. Don't go till you've heard another collection of songs,
This one constructed from nomes meant for kithara music.*

DIONYSOS. Very well, continue, but please leave toil aside.

[EURIPIDES *continues in much the same manner, but this time introduces exaggerated vocal imitations of the strumming of a kithara-lyre.*]

EURIPIDES. When the twin-throned power of the Achaians, of Greece's youth,*
Thrum-splat, thrum-splat, thrum-splat,
Sends the Sphinx, the dog that presides over evil days,
Thrum-splat, thrum-splat, thrum-splat,
With spear and avenging hand a furious bird,
Thrum-splat, thrum-splat, thrum-splat,
Leaving prey for dauntless, air-traversing hounds,
Thrum-splat, thrum-splat, thrum-splat,
The throng converging on Ajax,
Thrum-splat, thrum-splat, thrum-splat.

DIONYSOS [*to* AISCHYLOS]. What on earth's this 'thrum-splat' sound and where did you hear it?
In Marathon's fields or the songs of a rope-hauling man?*

AISCHYLOS. Not at all. My finest plays used the finest sources.

My poetic flowers were not those that Phrynichos culled:*
I went to a different part of the Muses' meadows.
[*Gesturing*] But *he* takes stuff from high and low: whores' ballads,
Meletos' drinking songs, plus Karian pipe-tunes*
And dirges and dances as well. I'll show you right now.
Bring any old lyre—though come to think of it, why?
I'll dispense with that. But call that woman who plays
The potsherd castanets—Euripides' Muse!
She's just the right person to go with these songs that I'll sing.

[*Enter from the stage building* EURIPIDES' MUSE, *a down-market female performer with a pair of ceramic castanets in each hand. She writhes around in a louche manner during the parody of Euripidean lyrics delivered by* AISCHYLOS.]

DIONYSOS. Well here's a Muse who never found work on Lesbos!*

AISCHYLOS [*singing parodically*].
Halcyons, who by the sea's ever-flowing
Waves mouth all your blather,
Dipping your wings in the moist
Liquid, bedewing their skin,
And you who in angles beneath the rafters
Sp-i-i-i-i-i-in with your fingers, o spiders,
Your loom-taut spool-threads,
A singing shuttle's exercises,
Where the pipe-loving dolphin gambols
Near prows with dark-blue ramming rods
In oracular fashion and in competition.
Gleaming glory of the vine's wine-flower,
Grape-cluster's toil-ending tendril,
Throw your arms around, o child.
Do you see this dance-step?*

EURIPIDES. I do.

AISCHYLOS. Well then, and this one too?

EURIPIDES. I do.

AISCHYLOS. And though you compose such things
You dare to find fault with *my* songs,
When your lyrics use a dozen contortions

That would suit Kyrene the courtesan?*

Well that will do for your choral songs. But I want
To take to pieces the style of your monodies too.*

[AISCHYLOS *starts to sing again, producing another mishmash of pastiche and partial quotations.* EURIPIDES' MUSE *continues to cavort.*]

AISCHYLOS. O Night's black-gleaming darkness,
What is this anguished dream
You send me, emerging from invisible Hades
With a soul that is no soul,
Black Night's shuddering child,
Apparition horrendous,
Draped corpse-like in black,
Blood-filled, blood-filled look in its eyes,
Possessing huge talons.
Come, attendants, light me a lamp,
Scoop dewy liquid in pitchers from rivers
And heat the water,
So I may ablute this god-sent dream.
Hail deity of the sea!
Just what I expected. Occupants of the house,
Behold these portents! My cock's
Been snatched by Glyke, who's fled.
Mountain-born Nymphs!
O Mania, help me to catch her.*
Poor woman that I am
I happened to be concentrating
On my work, a spindle full of flax
I was sp-i-i-i-i-i-ining in my hands,
Producing thread, so that
At dawn I might go to the Agora
And take it with me to sell.
But my cock has flown, has flown up high
On the lightest extremities of his wings,
He's left woes, woes for me
And tears, tears from my eyes
I've shed, I've shed in my misery.

Come Cretans, children of Mount Ida,*
Take your bows and come to my defence,
Agitate your limbs
As you surround her house.
And with you may Diktynna, lovely child,*
Bring her pack of delicate bitches and come
Through the palace in every direction.
And you, daughter of Zeus, brandishing
Twin-flamed, blazing torches in your hands,
Hekate, light my way into Glauke's house
To guide my search for the stolen goods.

DIONYSOS. You must both now stop these lyrics.

AISCHYLOS. I've had enough too.
I want to make him come to the weighing-scale challenge.
This alone will fully assess our talents as poets.
It's the *weight* of our words that will prove the definitive test.

DIONYSOS. Come here then, both, if I really have to do this
And treat the art of poets like cheese for sale!*

[*During the following ode one of the* ATTENDANTS *brings out an enormous pair of scales and* DIONYSOS *starts to examine them before making the two tragedians take up position on either side of the equipment.*]

CHORUS. How meticulous clever people are!
Here's yet another prodigious thing,
Unprecedented, full of absurdity—
Who else could have thought of it?
Upon my word, if anyone else
Had told me this, there isn't a chance
I would have believed him. I'd simply suppose
He was talking pure balderdash.

DIONYSOS. Right then, both stand beside the scales.

AISCHYLOS AND EURIPIDES. Okay.

DIONYSOS. Both hold a pan and utter a verse in turn
And don't let go till I give you the cuckoo's call.

AISCHYLOS AND EURIPIDES. We're holding now.

DIONYSOS. Then say your words in the scales.

EURIPIDES. 'If only the Argo's hull hadn't winged its way—'*
AISCHYLOS. 'O river Spercheios and grazing lands of cattle—'*
DIONYSOS. Cuckoo!
AISCHYLOS AND EURIPIDES. We've let go.
DIONYSOS. Well well, the scales have dropped
On Aischylos' side.
EURIPIDES. But what's the reason for that?
DIONYSOS. It's because he put in a whole river: just like wool-sellers
He made his verse weigh more by making it moist,
While *you* put in a verse that was winged and light.
EURIPIDES. Well, let him quote something else and compete again.
DIONYSOS. Then hold the pans once more.
AISCHYLOS AND EURIPIDES. Okay.
DIONYSOS. Now speak.
EURIPIDES. 'Persuasion has no shrine but speech itself.'*
AISCHYLOS. 'Alone among the gods Death craves no gifts.'*
DIONYSOS. Let go.
AISCHYLOS AND EURIPIDES. We've done so.
DIONYSOS. It's tilting to *him* again.
He put death in the scale, the heaviest evil we know.
EURIPIDES. But *I* put in persuasion—my verse is perfect.
DIONYSOS. But persuasion is something light and lacking in thought.
Try one more time to find a ponderous weight
Whose size and mass will tilt the scales on *your* side.
EURIPIDES. Now where, oh where can I find such a thing?
DIONYSOS. I'll tell you.
[*Facetiously*] 'Achilles threw—three dice, two ones and a four!'*
[*To both*] Please speak again, since this is the final weighing.
EURIPIDES. 'Hefted with the iron the club he grasped in his hand—'*
AISCHYLOS. 'Chariot piled on chariot, corpse on corpse—'*
DIONYSOS [*to* EURIPIDES]. He's managed to fool you again.
EURIPIDES. But how's he done it?
DIONYSOS. By placing in two chariots and two corpses,
Too much for even a hundred Egyptians to lift!*

AISCHYLOS. Let him stop putting into the scales just lines of verse,
Let him, his children, his wife, Kephisophon too
All sit in the scales, let him take in his books as well.*
I'll still outweigh him with any two verses of mine.
DIONYSOS [*despairingly*]. These men are both my friends: I can't choose a winner!
I've no intention of being at odds with either.
I think that one of them's wise, the other I like.*
PLOUTON [*stepping forward*]. So it seems you won't achieve what you came here to do.
DIONYSOS. But suppose I decide?
PLOUTON. You'll leave with one of these men,
Whichever you choose—so your journey won't prove to be wasted.
DIONYSOS. Such kindness! I wish you well. [*To the poets*] Now listen to me.
I came down here to find a poet. And why?
To save the city and safeguard its festival plays.
So whichever of you is able to give the city
The best advice, it's *him* I've resolved to take back.
Tell me first the view that each of you holds about
Alkibiades.* The city's in pangs over him.
AISCHYLOS. Well what's the view of the city?
DIONYSOS. You want to know?
It pines for him yet loathes him but wants to *have* him.
But I need you both to tell me your thoughts about him.
EURIPIDES. I hate a man who'll always prove to be
Reluctant to help his homeland but quick to harm it—
A man who advances himself but hinders the city.
DIONYSOS. Hurrah for that, by Poseidon! [*To* AISCHYLOS] And what's your view?
AISCHYLOS. Don't rear the whelp of a lion inside the city. 1431a
Ideally don't rear a lion inside the city, 1431b
But if one's bred, be sure to tend to its needs.*
DIONYSOS. By Zeus the Saviour, I just can't choose between them!
The one spoke wisely, the other in lucid style.
[*Thinking*] Look, each of you give me a single further idea
Which you think would help to promote the city's survival.*

EURIPIDES. Suppose Kleokritos flew with Kinesias-wings*
And he soared on currents of air out over the sea—

DIONYSOS. What a ludicrous sight it would be! But what's the *point*?

EURIPIDES. If they took with them vinegar jars, during naval battles
They could spray the vinegar down in our enemies' eyes—

[DIONYSOS *seems about to interrupt, but* EURIPIDES *is determined to continue*.]

I know the solution. I'd like to explain it.

DIONYSOS. Go on then.

EURIPIDES. As soon as we start to trust what's now untrusted
And to lose our trust in what's trusted—

DIONYSOS. I'm baffled already!
Explain yourself in a clearer, less erudite way.

EURIPIDES. I mean the citizens whom we currently trust:
If we lost our trust in these but used instead
The ones we don't use now, we might be saved.
If our present leaders are bringing us close to ruin,
We'd surely be saved if we switched to the opposite ways?

DIONYSOS. You're a true Palamedes, a genius, what a fine thought!
Who's idea was this: your own or Kephisophon's then?*

EURIPIDES. It was mine—though Kephisophon thought of the vinegar jars.

DIONYSOS [*to* AISCHYLOS]. Well what about *you*?

AISCHYLOS. Tell me first what kind of leaders
The city has now. Are they really the best?

DIONYSOS. You're joking!
It simply loathes such people.

AISCHYLOS. And *likes* bad leaders?

DIONYSOS. Well, not exactly—she has no choice but to use them.

AISCHYLOS. Then how could anyone save a city like this
When it doesn't know whether a cloak or a goatskin will fit?*

DIONYSOS. That's the problem for *you* to solve, if you want to go back!

AISCHYLOS. I'll say what I think back there, but not down here.

DIONYSOS. No, no, you can't. You must send up your help from down here.
AISCHYLOS. As soon as they start to believe that the enemy's land
Belongs to themselves, while their own is their enemy's land,
And believe that the fleet is their wealth, all their other wealth void.*
DIONYSOS. I agree—though our juries consume all the wealth that we have.*
PLOUTON. It's time for you to judge.
DIONYSOS. Well here's my judgement.
[*Solemnly*] I'll choose the one my soul desires to have.
EURIPIDES. Remember the oath you swore by the gods before
That you'd take me home. Be sure to choose your friends.
DIONYSOS. 'It's my tongue that swore'—but Aischylos is my choice!*
EURIPIDES. What on earth have you done, you revolting person?
DIONYSOS. What, me?
I've judged that Aischylos wins—and what's to stop me?
EURIPIDES. Can you look me in the eye after being so shameless?
DIONYSOS. 'What's shameful if those watching don't think it's so?'*
EURIPIDES. You brute, you mean you'll leave me to die like this?
DIONYSOS. 'Who knows if life is really the same as death',*
If breathing is eating, if sleeping is merely a blanket?
PLOUTON. Go inside, Dionysos, with Aischylos too.
DIONYSOS. What for?
PLOUTON. I'd like to feast you before you sail back.
DIONYSOS. That's kind,
By Zeus, I don't object to an offer like that.

[DIONYSOS *leads* AISCHYLOS *back into the stage building, followed by* PLOUTON *and, skulking behind them,* EURIPIDES.]

CHORUS. Happy indeed the man who has *Strophe*
Sharp astuteness in his grasp.
Many the things that make this clear.
Now his intelligence can be seen,
Aischylos is the one who'll go home
Bringing good to the citizens,

Bringing good, what's more, to his own
Kith and kin and friends as well,
All because he's astute in mind.

Pleasing, then, not to sit around *Antistrophe*
Talking hot air with Sokrates,*
Treating the Muses' work with contempt,
Spurning the most important things
About the art of tragic drama.
As for pretentious arguments,
Quibbles of nit-picking drivel:
Devoting an idle life to *those*
Is the mark of someone crazy!

[PLOUTON, *carrying a sword, some nooses, and a mortar and pestle, reappears from the palace door, leading out* AISCHYLOS *and* DIONYSOS.]

PLOUTON. Depart then, Aischylos, farewell!
Your task is now to preserve our city
With good ideas. And educate
The stupid folk—no shortage of them!
Take this sword and give it to Kleophon,
And these nooses here for the revenue board,
For Myrmex and Nikomachos too,
And give this hemlock to Archenomos.*
Tell them all to rush down here to me
Without delay. If they don't come quickly,
I swear by Apollo I'll treat them like slaves:
I'll brand them and shackle them up together
With Adeimantos, son of Leukolophos,
And dispatch them to Hades at once.

AISCHYLOS. I'll do as you say. And you meanwhile
Please place my throne in Sophokles' care.*
He must keep it safe, in case I return
Back here. He's the poet I judge to be
Next best in artistry to me.
But be sure the *other*—that scoundrel I mean,
The peddler of lies who plays the fool—
Can't occupy that throne of mine
Not even by accident!

PLOUTON [*to* CHORUS]. Now light the way for him, you people,
With your sacred torches. Escort him onwards
With songs belonging to plays of his own
And resounding chants.

[ATTENDANTS *have brought torches for the* CHORUS, *which sings its final song as it prepares to depart.*]

CHORUS. Grant as our first prayer a prosperous journey for this departing poet
As he rises back up to the world of light, o deities beneath the earth,
And grant to the city good thoughts productive of great benefits.
In this way we hope for a final end to our great afflictions
And the grievous clashes of battle. Let Kleophon fight,
Together with anyone else who wants, in his *own* ancestral fields.*

[*Exit* CHORUS.]

APPENDIX

THE LOST PLAYS OF ARISTOPHANES

THE purpose of this appendix is to give general readers an impression of the scope of Aristophanes' oeuvre as a whole by providing a brief account of what we know about each of the lost plays, together with a small selection of some of the more notable fragments. The numbering of fragments follows the standard edition of Kassel and Austin, *Poetae Comici Graeci*; the same numbering is used in Henderson's bilingual Loeb, *Aristophanes: Fragments* (for both works see Select Bibliography, 'Fragments'). The plays are listed in alphabetic order of their Greek titles. Incompleteness in the original is indicated by . . . , omissions from the translation by [. . .]. Abbreviations for the surviving plays of Aristophanes are the same as in the notes to the translation.

Aiolosikon (Aiolos-Sikon)

There were two versions of the play, the later staged near the end of Aristophanes' life (*c.*388–385) in the name of his playwright son Araros; cf. on *Kokalos* below. It is possible that at least the second version, like the surviving *Assembly-Women* and *Wealth*, had a diminished choral element and no parabasis, though fr. 9 shows that there was a chorus of women in at least one of the versions, and fr. 8 too is choral. The title (as the protagonist's name) is a compound of Aiolos (guardian of the winds: cf. Homer, *Odyssey* 10.1 ff.) and Sikon, possibly here a cook's name: the protagonist presumably had something in common with both identities. There were certainly references to food: a bakery (fr. 1), shopping in the Agora (fr. 2), boiled pig's trotters (fr. 4), onions (fr. 5), cooking utensils (fr. 7). A gluttonous Herakles (see note on *F.* 62) was either mentioned or brought onto stage (fr. 11). It is likely that there was some relationship to Euripides' tragedy *Aiolos* (cf. n. on *C.* 1372), in which Makareus and Kanake committed brother–sister incest and later (after they failed to be paired in a lottery for incestuous marriages of all Aiolos' children) killed themselves. But nothing remotely like a plot can be reconstructed. There are several references to the world of women: in addition to frs. 8 and 9 there was a reference to a woman's 'perfume-case' (fr. 16).

fr. 8 (choral, probably referring to a woman, possibly to diaphanous attire: cf. *L.* 48):

> And we see gleaming through,
> Just as with a new lamp,
> Everything (beneath?) the off-the-shoulder dress.

fr. 9 (female chorus singing):

No wonder, women,
The men always lambast us
With every kind of abuse.
When we do our terrible deeds
We're caught by them.

Amphiaraos

Staged at Lenaia 414, directed by Philonides (who also produced *Frogs* and possibly *Wasps*: cf. on *Proagon* below). At least part of the play was set at the oracular shrine (near Oropos, to the north of Attika) of the healer-hero Amphiaraos: visitors slept in the shrine ('incubation') in the hope of finding a cure. Compare the similar procedures with the healer-god Asklepios at *We.* 653–748; fr. 21 represents/reports Amphiaraos addressing his own daughter Iaso (the same name as a daughter of Asklepios at *We.* 701). Fr. 29 may refer to a character's sexual impotence; but the plot cannot be reconstructed. The parabasis, as in several earlier Aristophanic plays, contained reflections on the playwright's own career (frs. 30–1).

fr. 21 (probably a husband addressing his wife; in preparation for incubation at the shrine?):

In the name of Zeus, go and fetch us out of the bedroom
A cushion and pillow, from the ones that are made of linen.

fr. 28 (recitative metre, speaker and addressee uncertain):

And the snakes you supply
Seal up in a basket,
And stop your selling of drugs.

fr. 29 (hexameters, indicating an oracular utterance delivered from Amphiaraos' shrine):

And make the old man's loins wiggle vigorously, like a wagtail's.
This way (the god?) will effect a healing spell.

fr. 30 (choral, from the parabasis, probably in the voice of the poet):

I know I'm doing something old-fashioned, I'm not unaware of that.

fr. 31 (choral, almost certainly, like fr. 30, from the parabasis; cf. *Geras*, fr. 130 below):

. . . since the time I recognized the comic bogey-mask.

Anagyros

Date uncertain, but probably *c.*417. Anagyros was the eponymous hero of an Athenian deme, Anagyrous (subject of a passing joke at *L.* 67–8). The main known myth about him involved a story pattern somewhat like that of Theseus, Phaidra, and Hippolytos: Anagyros took revenge on an old Athenian by making the man's concubine fall in love with his son then falsely accuse the latter of a sexual crime; when the father punished the son and discovered the truth, both he and the concubine committed suicide. Whether/how Aristophanes' play used this myth is entirely unclear. The fragments contain several references to horses, including (fr. 43) the same kind of thoroughbred racehorse mentioned at *C.* 23, 438. Other topics include the rich and poor using the same bath-houses (fr. 59). Given the 'Phaidra complex' theme (above, with Index of Names), it is striking that Euripides, *Hippolytos* 219–22 (where Phaidra deliriously imagines hunting with Hippolytos) is parodied in fr. 53. Fr. 58 is apparently a charge of plagiarism (or derivativeness) against another poet, possibly Eupolis (cf. *C.* 554).

fr. 53 (recitative, female speaker):

> In the name of the gods, I lust to eat cicadas
> And crickets, after hunting them myself
> With a delicate reed.

fr. 58 (choral recitative, from the parabasis, representing the poet's viewpoint):

> From the cloak belonging to me he made three simple tunics.

Babylonians

An early landmark in Aristophanes' career; cf. the general Introduction, 'Aristophanes' Career in Context'. Staged at Dionysia 426, with Kallistratos as producer, it may have won first prize; it certainly caused some political controversy. If we can trust the poet's own allusions to the affair at *A.* 377–82, 502–3, 630–1, the leading politician Kleon launched an official complaint to the Council (but not, so far as we can tell, a legal prosecution) that Aristophanes had 'slandered the city in the presence of visitors'. All we know for certain is that the chorus consisted of tattooed Babylonian mill-slaves (frs. 71, 90, 95, 99). The god Dionysos was a character (fr. 75); he presumably brought the chorus with him to Athens, where he was put on trial (for what, we do not know), but given a chance to bribe demagogues to win an acquittal (fr. 75, cf. fr. 68); one of those demagogues was probably Peisander (fr. 84; cf. later references to him at *B.* 1556, *L.* 490), another *may* have been Kleon himself (if *A.* 5 8, as some scholars suppose, refers to a scene in *Babylonians* and not to a historical event). The successful general Phormion (cf. *K.* 562, *P.* 348, *L.* 804) was also mentioned (fr. 88). If, again, we can safely glean something from Aristophanes' own words at *A.* 633–42, which it is hard not to understand as related to *Babylonians*, the play seems to have satirized the supposed ease with which Athenian assemblies could be impressed (and turned into 'gaping-mouthed citizens', *A.* 635, cf. fr. 67 below) by the rhetoric of allied ambassadors; it apparently also made comic material out of Athens' treatment of her allies (*A.* 642). But how exactly these themes fitted into a plot with Dionysos and the Babylonian chorus remains obscure.

fr. 67 (probably from a narrative account of an Assembly meeting):

> Every one of them had a gaping-wide mouth, just like
> Mussel-shells cracked open when roasting upon hot coals.

fr. 81 (recitative; someone anticipating the entry of the chorus):

> I expect they'll march in rows and screech in horrid barbarian tones.

Georgoi (Farmers)

Probably staged at some point during 424–421, the play exploited similar thematic contrasts (war vs. peace, city vs. countryside) to those of *Acharnians* and *Peace*: nostalgia for the supposedly easy life of rural Attika was clearly evoked. But details of the plot are unknown. The sons of Hippokrates (see *C.* 1001 with n.) were mocked for the abnormal shapes of their heads (fr. 116). One fragment (102) depicts the general Nikias as a figure keen to escape from front-line politics; it may, but need not, allude to his withdrawal from command of the Pylos campaign in summer 425 (Thucydides 4.28; cf. n. on *C.* 186).

fr. 102:

> (A) I want to farm the land. (B) Who's stopping you then?
> (A) You and your friends. If I pay a thousand drachmas,
> Will you let me escape from office. (B) We'll accept the money.
> With the payment Nikias made, that makes two thousand.

fr. 109 (choral recitative):

> Let's leave the city behind us now and return to the countryside.
> We should have gone long ago to soak in the bath and take it easy.

fr. 111 (choral song):

> Peace, bringer of deep wealth, and my little pair of oxen,
> How I wish I could give up this war and then
> Dig the soil, dress the vines, have a bath and quaff
> Some wine, with a gleaming loaf and a radish.

fr. 117 (referring to a tragic poet called Meletos: cf. on frs. 156, 453 below, with n. on *F.* 1302; for Kallias cf. *F.* 428, fr. 583):

> . . . he penetrates Kallias . . .

Geras (Old Age)

Date uncertain. The chorus appears to have consisted of rejuvenated old men (fr. 129). Various female characters appeared, including a mother and daughter (fr. 131), a woman abandoning a lover for a bridegroom (fr. 144), and a bread-seller (fr. 129, cf. *W*. 1388 ff.). Fr. 128 *may* be an elaborate culinary metaphor for the difference between Euripides and Aischylos (cf. *F*. 941–4). Incidental details include references to someone vomiting on statues in the Agora (fr. 135) and to allotment machines (cf. *AW* 681) used for allocation of jurors to courts and for the selection of Council members from deme nominees.

fr. 128:

> This vinegary, silphium-flavoured stuff, all bulbs and beet,
> Sour sauce, fig-leaves with animal brain, oregano—
> It's utter crap compared to a big piece of meat.

fr. 130 (cf. fr. 31 above):

> Who can tell me where I'll find Dionysos' shrine,
> The one where bogey-masks hang on the walls?

fr. 148 (speaker possibly a brothel-keeper, male or female):

> Old man, do you like your courtesans quite ripe
> Or very young, as firm as salted olives?

Gerytades

The title is the mock-name of a male character, roughly meaning 'Proclaimer'; we have no idea why. Our one piece of information about the plot is that it involved an embassy of poets who went down to Hades, presumably in some way to consult past masters of the art—so something a little akin to *Frogs* (though we cannot be sure of the relative chronology of the two works). We get a lively glimpse of this scenario from fr. 156. Other fragments include references to the operator of the theatrical 'crane' (fr. 160, cf. *Daidalos* fr. 192 below and *P*. 174), to someone praising the poetry of Aischylos (fr. 161), and to people eating the wax off their writing-tablets (fr. 163). It is possible that the embassy brought back personified Poetry: cf. fr. 591.84–5 (unattributed) below.

fr. 156 (beginning with a near-verbatim quotation of Euripides, *Hekabe* 1):

> (A) And who to this vault of corpses and gates of darkness
> Has dared descend? (B) For each poetic genre
> We elected one man at a meeting of all the poets:
> We chose the ones we knew were Hades-tourists
> And liked to come down here. (A) You mean to say

You have Hades-tourists up there? (B) We certainly do.
(A) You mean like tourists to Thrace? (B) Exactly right.
(A) And who are these men you mean? (B) Sannyrion first
From the comic poets, and then from tragedy's ranks
Meletos, with dithyramb's envoy Kinesias.[1]
(A) How thin and slender the hopes you're riding upon!
These men are so slight they'll be snatched and carried away
By the mighty force of the river of diarrhoea![2]

Daidalos

Daidalos was a mythical Cretan craftsman, designer for King Minos of the labyrinth at Knossos, and father of Ikaros, with whom he eventually fled after incurring Minos' anger (cf. on *Kokalos* below). So the play was presumably a mythological burlesque. Daidalos' ability to make 'moving statues' was referred to (fr. 202). Zeus was mentioned, or even depicted, as using metamorphosis to engage in mischievous behaviour (fr. 198). A character was suspended at one point on the theatrical crane and addressed the crane-operator (fr. 192, cf. *Gerytades*, fr. 160 above).

fr. 191 (for the motif cf. e.g. *WT* 392, 417, *L.* 107, 212–13):

All wives are the same in this respect at least:
They arrange to keep an adulterer as a side-dish.

Daitales (Banqueters)

Aristophanes' very first play, staged in 427 (probably Lenaia), with either Kallistratos or Philonides as producer. The parabasis of *Clouds* (528–33, with my nn.) refers back to it as a precedent for *Clouds* itself, in being aimed at clever, sophisticated spectators—i.e. for being itself an 'intellectualizing' comedy (see my Introduction to *Clouds*). The link involved comic treatment of clashing educational/cultural values in contemporary Athens, in the case of *Banqueters* through the relationship between a father and a contrasting pair of sons, 'one bashful, the other an arsehole' (*C.* 529). The thematic threads were complex; there were affinities, but not a complete correspondence, with (a) the Strepsiades–Pheidippides relationship and (b) the debate between Moral and Immoral in *Clouds*. The sons, one traditional and one 'modern' in conduct, diverged at an early stage in their

[1] Sannyrion: a minor comedian whose plays included one called *Laughter*. Meletos: possibly the tragedian who took part in the prosecution of Sokrates; see Plato, *Apology* 19b–c, 23e, etc. Cf. the same name in fr. 117 above, 453 below. Kinesias: see Index of Names. All three figures are supposed to have been notoriously gaunt and, by comic exaggeration, suitably corpse-like for a trip to Hades.

[2] Cf. the 'river of shit' at *F.* 146.

upbringing (fr. 206). The modern son was corrupted, according to the father, into a life of sybaritic hedonism (fr. 225); he refused to countenance traditional work on the land (fr. 232); and he abused his father with language which the latter associated with contemporary orators, showy aristocrats like Alkibiades (cf. fr. 244), and fashionable teachers of rhetoric (fr. 205, where Thrasymachos is the rhetorician memorably depicted at Plato, *Republic* 1.336b ff.). This same son, it seems (fr. 233), was reluctant to answer questions (of the kind a schoolteacher might ask) about the meaning of certain words in Homer; instead, he challenged his father and brother to explain archaic *legal* terms in Solon's law-code. Fr. 235 probably depicts the father inviting the decadent son to sing traditional sympotic poetry (and presumably being rebuffed with a more 'modern' choice of poets: cf. *C.* 1354–72). The chorus consisted of a kind of religious dining-club (a *thiasos*) which met in a shrine of Herakles, but their status vis-à-vis the characters is not clear.

fr. 205 (the sophisticated son abusing his father):

(A) You coffinette and funeral myrrh and pile of wreaths!
(B) Hah, 'coffinette'! Lysistratos gave you that word.
(A) It won't be long before you find you're wrong-footed.
(B) You've learnt 'wrong-footed' as well from the orators' lingo.
(A) Your words will have an upshot, of that I'm sure.
(B) That's Alkibiades' term, to have an 'upshot'.
(A) Why these conjectures and all this abuse of men
Who cultivate distinction? (B) Oh Thrasymachos!
Which legal advocate uses these flashy retorts?

fr. 206 (one brother—probably the 'modern' one—speaking to the other):

Do *you* have the clever ideas that *I* acquired?
Did you not play truant from school at the earliest stage?

fr. 225 (the father describing the decadent son; recitative metre, probably from an agon):

When I sent him to school it wasn't these things he learnt, but instead
To drink, then sing in a rotten way, and to eat rich food
From Syracuse, and to feast as the Sybarites do [. . .]

fr. 229 (same metre as fr. 225; probably a description of the decadent son):

His skin as smooth as that of an eel, his hair in golden ringlets.

fr. 232 (the 'modern' son speaking; recitative metre, probably from an agon):

When I've worn myself down with all that practice on music for pipes and lyres,
Do you really expect me to dig the soil?

fr. 235 (the father speaking? See above. For the poets named, cf. *WT* 161–2):

Pick up the lyre, sing a drinking-song from Alkaios or Anakreon.

fr. 247 (for the possible theme, cf. *C.* 1044–54):

We [or 'he'] washed in cold water.

Danaids

Evidently a play with an element of mythological burlesque: for the story of Danaos' fifty daughters and their flight from Egypt to Argos, see esp. Aischylos, *Suppliants*. There are only faint traces of the Danaid theme as such in frs. 267 (an Egyptian word for sourdough bread), 270 ('very Danaos-like'), 272 (Lynkeus, husband of one of the Danaids). Otherwise the fragments preserve miscellaneous details, including references to buying cheap octopus/fish in the market (fr. 258), a box for storing actors' equipment (fr. 259), and sellers of emetics/purgatives (fr. 269). We know that there was a parabasis from the following two fragments, which reflect on the history of comedy itself (cf. e.g. the parabases of *Knights* and *Peace*), though quite what fr. 264 envisages (primitive, rustic costumes? and food for the post-play party?) is uncertain.

fr. 264 (recitative metre):

The chorus used to dance while draped with rugs and sacks of bedding,
And ribs of beef tucked under their arms—yes, sausage and radishes too.

fr. 265 (same metre, and probably from the same passage, as fr. 264):

That's how little trouble it was for them to compose their verses back then.

Dionysos Shipwrecked

Virtually nothing is known about this play. It was included in lists of Aristophanes' works, but it was one of four plays whose authorship was disputed by some (and attributed alternatively to the late 5th-century playwright Archippos).

Dramas I (also *Centaur*) and II (also *Niobus*)

Aristophanes appears to have written two plays called *Dramas*, though some ancient scholars questioned the attribution of *Dramas* II to Aristophanes (and assigned it to the late 5th-century playwright Archippos instead; cf. the previous entry). Euripides was a character in one of the two. Little is known about the contents of either. *Dramas* I may have been connected to Herakles' visit to the centaur Pholos and his subsequent fight with other centaurs (cf. Index of Names). Incidental references in the fragments include urination (fr. 280), a brothel (fr. 283), and lewd dancing (fr. 287).

The alternative title of *Dramas* II may denote a male equivalent of Niobe (see n. on *F.* 912), who was mentioned in the play (fr. 294). There seems to have been a scene set in Hades (fr. 289, someone speaking for 'those of us here below'); fr. 290, in which someone's lamp goes out, might also belong there. There was mention of Chairephon, Sokrates' companion (see Index of Names), as a 'thief' (fr. 295).

One of the two plays included the ritual of weighing sacrificial animals for the Apatouria (nn. on *WT* 558, *F.* 798): a speaker asks another to press down the scales to make an animal seem heavier than it is (fr. 299).

Eirene (Peace) II

We cannot be sure whether this was a revised version of the surviving *Peace* or a separate work. But it must in any case have involved a thematic contrast between war and peace, including the association of the latter with the rural life of Attika (compare *Georgoi* above, *Nesoi* below): personified Farming was a character (fr. 305). There are only a handful of fragments; one contains a reference to triangular notice-boards on which military rosters were displayed in Athens (fr. 309).

fr. 305:

(Farming) Of Peace, so dear to all of human kind,
Her faithful nurse, her steward and helper and aide,
Her daughter, her sister—I was all these things to her.
(B) Then what's your name? (F) You want my name? I'm Farming.

fr. 306:

Well take the shield
And use it at once as a lid on top of the well.

Heroes

Named after its chorus ('heroes' in the sense of semi-divinized figures from the past). But we know nothing at all of the plot. Incidental details include references to a device like a neck-brace to prevent slaves from eating dough while kneading it (fr. 314), a bull-roarer for whirling round the head on a string (fr. 315), a hermaphroditic deity (fr. 325), and Dieitrephes (fr. 321), known to have been an Athenian military commander in the period 414–411 (cf. *B.* 800).

fr. 322 (sung by the chorus, probably as part of its parodos or entrance):

So for these reasons, men, take care
And worship us these heroes, since
We are the stewards of all things,
The sufferings and the good things too.
Our eyes are peeled for unjust people,
Like thieves and highway robbers:

These are the ones we cause diseases—
Enlargement of spleen and coughs and dropsy,
Catarrh and scabies and gout,
Insanity and ulcerous skin,
Swollen lymph nodes, shivers, fever
. . . —that's what we give to thieves.

Thesmophoriazousai (Women at the Thesmophoria) II

Probably later than the surviving play of the same name, this one was set on the third day (called Kalligeneia: cf. *WT* 300) of the women's Thesmophoria festival; Kalligeneia spoke the prologue (fr. 331). One fragment contains an extraordinarily detailed list (from, it seems, a disbelieving male speaker) of women's toiletries, clothes, cosmetics, and jewellery (fr. 332). There was at least one reference to Agathon (fr. 341), who actually appears at *WT* 101–265; but there is no reason to suppose the play had much to do with Euripides. The Thesmophoria as an interruption in marital relations is presumably the background to fr. 344. Frs. 347–8, in similar lyric metres, contain reflections on the earlier history of comedy which probably belong to the parabasis (for the reference to Krates in fr. 347, cf. *K.* 537–40). Also from the parabasis must have been fr. 346 (preserved only in an Arabic paraphrase of a work by Galen), where Aristophanes claimed, whether factually or fictionally, that he had been ill for four months (with a shivering cold and a fever).

fr. 334 (naming wine from various Greek islands; the last line is sexual):

I won't allow the drinking of Pramnian wine
Nor Chian nor Thasian nor wine from Peparethos,
Nor any other that will raise your battering-ram.

fr. 338 (cf. fr. 664, *WT* 139, 251, 638, though the Greek term here is different):

. . . she'd just undone the flap of her little dress
As well as the bands which held her tiny breasts.

fr. 341 (a reference to literary style that puns on effeminate lack of facial hair):

. . . and an antithesis that's shaved in Agathon's style

fr. 344:

I wish to mount my wife.

fr. 347 (where it is important that 'salt fish' was a cheap food in Athens):

Indeed the words and music of comedy's art provided a tasty dish
At the time when Krates regarded his salt fish 'ivory-textured'

And 'glistening bright' and 'effortlessly called to mind'
And had thousands of other such things to make his audience giggle.

fr. 348 (where the 'director' is probably also the playwright; cf. e.g. *A.* 628, *K.* 507):

. . . nor summon the Muses with their curling tresses
Nor call upon the Olympian Graces to join the dance:
They're with us already here, so says our director . . .

Kokalos

The play was staged near the end of Aristophanes' life (*c.*388–85) in the name of his playwright son Araros, possibly at the Dionysia of 387 (when we know that Araros won first prize); cf. on *Aiolosikon* above. Ancient critics claimed that the plot, with 'rape, recognition (sc. of identity) and other elements', anticipated typical features of New Comedy; but we have no idea how. Kokalos was king of Kamikos (later Akragas) in Sicily, where Daidalos (see above on the play named after him) took refuge from Minos, who was subsequently killed by Kokalos' daughters. Aristophanes' plot possibly had a parodic relationship to Sophokles' *Kamikioi* (Men of Kamikos), though the latter may itself have been a satyr-play. The few surviving fragments are entirely miscellaneous: e.g. references to chilblains (fr. 359), old women drinking unmixed wine (fr. 364), someone vomiting after drinking unmixed wine (fr. 365), and Korinthian prostitutes (fr. 370, cf. *We.* 149).

Lemniai (Lemnian Women)

A mythological burlesque, probably from the late fifth century and parodying parts of a set of myths used by several tragedians. The women of Lemnos, afflicted with a horrible odour by Aphrodite, were rejected by their husbands; in revenge, the women murdered all the men of the island—with the exception of Hypsipyle, who saved her father Thoas. The women subsequently became the lovers of the visiting Argonauts, Hypsipyle being Jason's mistress. Fr. 373 mentions Hypsipyle and the previous reign of Thoas, fr. 374 the women's killing of their husbands, and fr. 375 may refer to the arrival of the Argonauts. But we cannot reconstruct the plot as a whole.

fr. 375:

Every colonnade is swarming with foreign men.

fr. 382:

The women are fencing off their fannies.

fr. 383 (referring to a game like jacks and supposedly played especially by women):

<Playing> five-stones with broken bits of a pot.

Nephelai (Clouds) I

The surviving *Clouds*, as we are told by ancient scholars, is an extensively but incompletely revised version of the original play of 423: cf. my Introduction to the play. Three parts in particular were, we know, substantially changed by Aristophanes: the parabasis (which, in the surviving version, at 520–33, actually refers back to the 'failed' first performance), the agon between Moral and Immoral (where the contestants may have been presented as fighting-cocks in the first version), and the burning of Sokrates' school in the final scene. Among a handful of small fragments of the original text of 423 are the following.

fr. 392 (referring to Sokrates; cf. n. on *F.* 1492):

> The man who writes Euripides' plays for him,
> Those loquacious, clever plays—well, *this* is the person!

fr. 393 (referring to Chairephon and/or others like him; see Index of Names):

> They'll lie like a pair of moths that are fucking each other.

Nesoi (Islands)

The title refers to the play's chorus, which might have consisted of personified islands belonging to the Athenian empire (though other scenarios are possible). We know nothing at all about the plot: the idealized contrast between rural and urban life in fr. 402 does not point to a specific historical context (cf. on *Georgoi* and *Eirene* II above). This was one of four plays whose attribution to Aristophanes was questioned by some ancient scholars: see above on *Dionysos Shipwrecked*.

fr. 402 (compare *Georgoi*, fr. 111):

> You fool, you fool, all these things are enjoyed when there's peace.
> This man can live in the fields on his small plot of land,
> Quite free from all the troubles the Agora brings,
> And possessing his own trim pair of oxen as well.
> He can hear the calls of his flock of bleating sheep
> And the sound of new wine being filtered into a pot.
> For food he'll enjoy small finches and thrushes too—
> No need to spend time in the Agora looking for fish
> That's three days old, overpriced, and weighed for him
> By a seller who really cheats him by pressing the scales.

fr. 403 (with reference to the chorus's entry via an *eisodos*; compare *C.* 323–7):

> (A) But what do you mean? Where exactly are they?
> (B) They're here, coming through the entrance you see over there.

(?)*Odomantopresbeis* (Envoys to the Odomantians)

Highly dubious: both the title and the attribution to Aristophanes involve conjectural reconstructions of an entry in an inscription (*IG* II² 2321.87–8) recording comic performances at the Lenaia of uncertain date. The Odomantians were a Thracian tribe; cf. *A.* 156–64.

Holkades (Merchant-Ships)

Probably belongs to the late-420s; Lenaia 423 is one possibility. Ancient evidence indicates that the play's themes involved war and peace. The title suggests a chorus of personified ships (cf. *K.* 1300–15 for the trope), which are generally assumed to have represented Athens' extensive trading activity (impeded by war). There was an encounter between an Athenian and a Spartan (fr. 415), who appear to have compared notes on the war.

fr. 415:

> Well I never, Spartan! So both our sides, it's clear,
> Had lots of trouble of greasy and onerous kinds.

fr. 416 (describing a flatterer's exaggerated attentiveness—but to whom? Cf. *K.* 908):

> He scratches that person's dandruff and always plucks
> His grey hairs from his beard.

fr. 422 (for Straton, cf. *A.* 122, *K.* 1374):

> . . . beardless boys, Straton . . .

fr. 424 (for Euathlos, cf. *A.* 710, *W.* 592):

> We too have a wretched archer who's state prosecutor
> The way that Euathlos is for you younger men.

Pelargoi (Storks)

References to the politician Neokleides (fr. 454, cf. *AW* 254, 398, *We.* 665, etc.) and to the rich miser Patrokles (fr. 455, cf. *We.* 84) suggest a date in the early fourth century. A tragic poet called Meletos was described as 'the son of Laios' with reference to his trilogy of plays on the Oedipus myth; he was possibly the same person as in fr. 156, but probably not as in fr. 117: the relation of all these figures to the Meletos who was prosecutor of Sokrates remains uncertain (cf. n. on *F.* 1302). The scanty fragments give no clues either to the plot or to the point of the title.

fr. 444 (for sympotic singing, cf. *A.* 979, *C.* 1364, *W.* 1225, 1238):

> He held the myrtle branch to sing 'Admetos',
> But the other insisted on the 'Harmodios' song instead.

Ploutos (Wealth) I

This play was staged in 408, twenty years earlier than the surviving *Wealth*. We do not know whether the latter was a revision of the former or a completely new work: compare the cases of *Eirene* and *Nephelai* above.

fr. 459 (cf. *F.* 1093–8 for the scenario envisaged here):

> . . . for those who find themselves coming last in the torch-race
> It's the cause of flat-handed slaps.

Poiesis (Poetry)

One of four plays whose attribution to Aristophanes was questioned by some ancient scholars: see above on *Dionysos Shipwrecked*. The title probably indicates that the play contained a female personification of poetry: one of only two surviving fragments refers to a group of people seeking all over Greece for a particular woman (fr. 466.3–4); a scenario in which Poetry had (symbolically) hidden herself away is a possibility.

fr. 467 (from a context comparing old and new musical styles; cf. the contest in *Frogs*):

> . . . not the sort of early songs, monotonous seven-stringed pieces, they used to sing.

Polyidos

Polyidos was a Korinthian seer who, among other things, used magic to restore to life Glaukos, son of King Minos of Crete. We do not know what the play made of him, though fr. 469 shows a Cretan connection, since Phaidra was also daughter of Minos; whether coincidentally or not, the Athenian Theseum (temple of Theseus, later husband of Phaidra) was also mentioned (fr. 475, cf. fr. 577).

fr. 468 (the second line is identical to Sophokles, *Elektra* 1173):

> To be afraid of death is a load of nonsense:
> All human beings are bound to suffer this fate.

fr. 469 (speaker and addressee uncertain):

> So there, I give you this woman to be your wife,
> Phaidra here: I'm no doubt adding fuel to the fire.

Proagon (Preview)

Our best evidence is that *Proagon* was staged at Lenaia 422, the same festival as *Wasps*. This creates a puzzle about how one poet could have two plays staged in the same competition: the likeliest solution, but not certain, is that *Proagon* was produced in Philonides' name (and won first prize), with Aristophanes himself producing *Wasps* (which won second prize). The proagon was a ceremony at which (only tragic?) dramatists and actors gave a preview of forthcoming plays at Athenian dramatic festivals: see Plato, *Symposium* 194b. We have no idea how this shaped the plot of Aristophanes' comedy, but we are told Euripides was a character and we know the work contained parodic treatment of the story of Thyestes (who unwittingly ate his own children); Euripides had handled this story in at least two tragedies (cf. *A.* 433).

fr. 477 (probably Thyestes speaking, after having eaten his own children):

O wretched me, what's churning up my stomach?
Oh hell! Where on earth can I find a chamber-pot?

fr. 478 (Thyestes speaking: the second line is in lyric metre, for singing):

I tasted, o miserable me, a sausage of children.
How then behold a roasted pig-snout?

Skenas Katalambanousai (Women Pitching Tents)

The title refers to women claiming sites for temporary accommodation at a festival (cf. e.g. *WT* 624, 658); the women in question probably formed the chorus. There were individual female characters as well, one of whom called a wine-flask her 'fellow-festival-goer' (fr. 487). An ancient source claims that Aristophanes himself was a speaking character (fr. 488), though this has been doubted.

fr. 488 (Aristophanes himself describing his relationship to Euripides?):

I use the rounded style that belongs to his voice
But the thoughts I compose are far less vulgar than his.

fr. 490 (possibly referring to a comedy by Strattis about Kallippides, a leading tragic actor known for his hyper-realistic style):

Just as in *Kallippides*
I sit on the floor in the rubbish that's swept together.

fr. 494:

'The leopardess' is the name they give that strumpet.

Tagenistai (Frying-Pan Men)

The play may have involved the utopian fantasy of a 'life' of feasting in the underworld (see fr. 504). All we know for sure is that there was an abundance of references to food and drink: several fragments suggest feasting that takes place on stage.

fr. 504 (for Plouton, see the Index of Names):

How on earth would Plouton ever have got his name
If he hadn't acquired what's best? Here's one example

Of how the world below outdoes Zeus's realm.
Whenever you weigh with scales, the heavier side
Goes *downwards*, the empty side up to Zeus.
. . .
. . .   It would never have been the case
That our heads wear garlands . . .
When our corpses lie on the bier . . .
If there weren't a drinking-party awaiting us there.
That's the reason why the dead are called 'the blessed'.
For everyone says 'The blessed man has left us',
'He's fallen asleep', 'he's happy, he'll feel no pain'.
And we sacrifice sacred offerings to the dead
The way we do to the gods. We pour libations
And ask them to send all good things up to us here.

fr. 506 (for Prodikos, cf. *C.* 361; for books, see n. on *F.* 1114):

This man's been corrupted: the cause is either a book
Or Prodikos or some other blathering type.

fr. 513 (recitative; spoken perhaps by the chorus-leader?):

We've had a little too much to drink, my fellows, and eaten well.

fr. 514 (recitative):

This soup before us that's in the pots is hot and bubbling away.

fr. 515 (from a passage of recitative; for the names cf. e.g. *WT* 858, *F.* 293):

(A) And chthonic Hekate
Entwined with coiling snakes.
(B) . . . Why summon Empousa?

fr. 516 (in lyric metre; not necessarily literal: cf. *B.* 463–4):

Bring water for handwashing quickly, slave,
And pass the towel around.

fr. 520 (in lyric metre):

Enough whitebait for me!
I've been laid flat
Scoffing things cooked in oil.
Bring me instead some liver
Or a young boar's
Neck. Otherwise a rib or a tongue
Or a spleen or intestine or an autumn pig's
Womb—bring me this with bread-rolls
That are warm.

Telemesses (Telemessians)

The chorus were people from Tel(e)messus, a city in Lykia (SE Asia Minor) which possessed an oracle of Apollo and belonged to the Delian League (in effect, the Athenian empire), at least in the mid-fifth century. We are practically clueless about the scenario. Sokrates' companion Chairephon (see Index of Names) was satirized as a *sukophantes*, a kind of blackmailer or malicious prosecutor (fr. 552). Aristyllos (cf. *AW* 647, *We.* 314) was also mentioned. The play is likely to belong to the second half of Aristophanes' career.

fr. 543 (possibly from the play's prologue):

> We're not holding this contest in just the same old way
> That used to be done, but our business is novel . . .

fr. 545:

> (A) Bring us out a table
> That has three legs—it really mustn't have four.
> (B) But where on earth will I find a three-legged table?

Triphales (Tri-Phallus?)

The title may involve wordplay on the name Phales, personification of the phallus (see *A.* 263–76); there was at least one mention of large penises and/or a priapic god (fr. 567). We do not know to whom the title referred; but his mother was either shown or described giving birth to him (fr. 562). The sons of Hippokrates were mocked: see above on *Georgoi.* In fr. 563 someone is afraid of the political power of Theramenes (cf. n. on *F.* 541). Other references include Iberian mercenaries (cf. Thucydides 6.90.3) and the city walls of Athens (fr. 569). There is no secure basis for the conjecture that the play had something to do with Alkibiades.

Phoinissai (Phoenician Women)

The play probably stood in a parodic relationship to Euripides' *Phoinissai* (*c.*409), which deals with the fateful conflict between the two sons of Oedipus. Among the handful of fragments is a reference to a *theatropoles* (fr. 575), an entrepreneur who held a franchise from the city for selling theatre-tickets.

fr. 570 (possibly from the prologue; reminiscent of a tragic messenger-speech):

> On Oedipus' pair of sons, the twofold boys,
> Ares crashed down: for single-combat's contest
> They now stand ready.

Horai (Seasons)

The play apparently contained a 'trial' of foreign gods like Sabazios (fr. 578) and their expulsion from Athens. One long fragment (581) involves an argument from an agon between representatives of old and new gods, though the identity of the speakers has been widely disputed. The chorus presumably represented the seasons of the year. The play may partly have thematized major changes brought about by the cosmopolitanism of Athenian culture in the later fifth century (cf. e.g. Thucydides 2.38.2 on Athens' import of goods from 'the whole world'). The butts of individual jokes in the play included Kallias (fr. 583, cf. fr. 117 above) and Chairephon, called 'child of night' (fr. 584; see the Index of Names).

fr. 577 (spoken perhaps by a foreign god as though a slave seeking 'sanctuary'; cf. *K.* 1312):

It's best for me to run to Theseus' shrine
And stay there till we find a buyer for me.

fr. 578 (for Sabazios cf. *W.* 9–10, *B.* 873, *L.* 388):

. . . the Phrygian, the pipe-player, Sabazios . . .

fr. 581 (it is uncertain whether A is a traditional or new god, e.g. Athena or Sabazios):

(A) You'll see that even in winter's depths cucumbers, grapes and fruit grow.
There'll be garlands of violets too. (B) More likely, a blinding cloud of dust.
(A) The same man's stall sells thrushes and pears and honeycombs, olives as well,
Beestings, stuffed tripe, swallows, cicadas, and animal embryo flesh.
You'd see baskets of figs and myrtle-berries abounding everywhere.
(B) I assume that means they sow the seeds of pumpkins and turnips together,
So that nobody knows any longer precisely what time of year it is?
(A) Well doesn't it count as the greatest good if right the way through the year
A person can get anything he desires? (B) The greatest *evil*, you mean!
If it just couldn't happen, they'd lack the desires. And they'd save their money as well.
I'd personally let them try these things for a while then take them away.
(A) But that's what I do with *other* cities—these things are only for Athens.
And the reason they have this privileged state is because they worship the gods.
(B) You think, it seems, it's their reward for worshipping you. (A) Don't you?
(B) Their city's no longer Athens at all—you've turned it into Egypt!

Fragments Unattributed to Specific Plays

I translate a very small selection of some striking items in this category.

fr. 591.84–6, 89–91 (one of several quotations embedded in a fragmentary ancient commentary on a lost play by Aristophanes; the goddess *may* be personified Poetry: cf. on *Gerytades* and *Poiesis* above):

> Right, let me take this goddess I've brought back up
> To the Agora, and dedicate her with ox-sacrifice.
> Come, mistress, follow me here. It's noble for you
> To quickly heed my prayer.

fr. 592.15–30 (two female speakers; possibly from *Thesmophoriazousai* II. Cf. *L.* 108–10):

> (A) Well, what's to happen? (B) Look, answer me this question.
> What's the thing they say Milesian women employ
> To have some fun? I'm asking. The leather thing.
> (A) That's empty nonsense, outrageous to consider,
> And besides a cause of shame and a laughing-stock.
> To use this thing is the same as handling those eggs
> That are full of nothing but air, no chicks inside.
> It's exactly the same. Whenever your husband's away
> You resort to this, but it's just not worth the trouble.
> (B) And yet they say this thing resembles a willy,
> The real thing itself. (A) By Zeus, my dear, no more
> Than the moon resembles the sun. In colour perhaps
> There's some likeness to see—but the moon will never *heat* you!
> (B) You don't think it's worth it? (A) . . .
> (B) Look, suppose we share this business of ours with our slaves.
> What d'you think of that? In secret . . .

fr. 596 (for Kephisophon see n. on *F.* 943–4):

> Kephisophon, you finest, swarthiest man,
> You lived for most of the time with Euripides
> And helped him compose, they say, his lyric songs.

fr. 656 (someone speaking about Euripides):

> . . . (the tongue) with which he used to clean his . . . words.

fr. 664 (female speaker; cf. fr. 338 above):

> . . . but with my breast-band undone
> My nuts fell out.

fr. 682:

> . . . like a tangled fleece in his art, Euripides.

fr. 691 (lyric metre; describing an intellectual: cf. n. on *C.* 179):

> . . . who ponders things out of sight
> But eats what's on the ground.

fr. 694 (recitative; referring to Euripides. For the idea, cf. esp. *WT* 167):

. . . the sorts of things he makes his characters say
Are just what he's like himself.

fr. 696 (recitative metre; two separate passages: the first spoken by Aischylos, the second *to* him. The *Phrygians* was related to events in *Iliad*, book 24):

. . . I myself composed the dance-steps for my choruses.

I know this from watching your *Phrygians*,
When they came to accompany Priam in ransoming his dead son
And they made many moves like *this* and *this*, and *this* way, in their dances.

fr. 699:

You people mix our city like wine then sell it in cups to the poor.

fr. 706 (recitative metre):

. . . he has the city's middling style of speech,
Not the somewhat effeminate urban type
Nor the somewhat rustic and slavish kind.

fr. 719 (lyric metre; probably a parabasis song):

. . . a display of fancy language and witty jokes,
All fresh from the bellows and freshly sculpted.

fr. 720:

. . . darkness since the death of Aischylos

fr. 732 (describing a young man unable to speak; for weasels, cf. n. on *WT* 559):

He's swallowed a weasel.

fr. 821 (attesting a unique verb; for the brain's hemispheres, cf. *F.* 134):

. . . to be half-brained . . .

fr. 910:

. . . with make-up under her eyes . . .

EXPLANATORY NOTES

The Explanatory Notes are designed to provide concise guidance on historical and other details which might puzzle a modern reader. Fuller information about most points can be found in the Oxford commentaries cited in the Bibliography. The following abbreviations are occasionally used in the notes:

DK *Die Fragmente der Vorsokratiker*, ed. H. Diels and W. Kranz, 6th edn. (Zurich, 1962)

IEG *Iambi et Elegi Graeci*, ed. M. L. West, 2nd edn., 2 vols. (Oxford, 1989–92)

OCD^{4} *The Oxford Classical Dictionary*, ed. S. Hornblower and A. Spawforth, 4th edn. (Oxford, 2012)

PMG *Poetae Melici Graeci*, ed. D. L. Page (Oxford, 1962)

The fragments of comic and tragic poets are cited, respectively, from the following editions:

Poetae Comici Graeci, ed. R. Kassel and C. Austin (Berlin, 1984–)

Tragicorum Graecorum Fragmenta, ed. B. Snell *et al.* (Göttingen, 1971–2004)

Aristophanes' play titles are abbreviated as follows:

A. *Acharnians*
AW *Assembly-Women*
B. *Birds*
C. *Clouds*
F. *Frogs*
K. *Knights*
L. *Lysistrata*
P. *Peace*
W. *Wasps*
We. *Wealth*
WT *Women at the Thesmophoria*

CLOUDS

7 *punish my slaves*: there was a higher risk during wartime that (ill-treated) slaves would desert to the enemy; cf. e.g. Thucydides 2.57.1.

14 *grow long*: long hair was associated with, among others, the young cavalrymen (n. on 120) of Athens; see *K.* 580 and cf. n. on 349–50.

15 *chariot-racing*: the chariot mentioned here is a two-horse vehicle (*sunoris*); there were races for these in e.g. the Panathenaia festival (see Index of

Names). Cf. notes on 28, 69, 122 below for other kinds of chariots mentioned in connection with Pheidippides.

17 *twentieth*: Athenian months were 29/30 days long; Strepsiades is dreading the latest demands of his creditors at the end of the month.

21 *Twelve minas*: a fifth of a talent or 1,200 drachmas; the price of a very good horse (cf. 1224) but a huge amount for most Athenians (skilled workers around this time might be paid a drachma a day). For other prices cf. nn. on 118, *WT* 1195, *F.* 173.

23 *dashing*: the Greek specifies a horse branded with a special letter (*koppa*) to show its thoroughbred status; the same term is used in line 438.

28 *war-carts*: these were also two-horse chariots (cf. n. on 15) with their own races at the Panathenaia.

30 *'What burden . . . '?*: a phrase adapted from the lyrics of an unknown play by Euripides (fr. 1011). The names Pasias and Ameinias (cf. 686–92) need not denote real individuals here.

32 *rolled clean*: a horse would have its sweat removed after exercise by making it roll on the dusty ground of an enclosure; cf. the metaphor at *F.* 904.

35 *seize my goods*: the law sometimes allowed a creditor to seize property (which might have been pledged as security in advance) in lieu of unpaid interest; cf. 241.

37 *debt enforcer*: Strepsiades refers to a demarch, a local deme magistrate (cf. n. on 134), who seems to have been responsible, among other things, for enforcing the penalties on certain debt contracts. For the pun on bedbugs, cf. 'being bitten' at 12.

41b *matchmaker*: arranged marriages, common in Athenian society, were sometimes negotiated with the help of a female matchmaker.

46 *Megakles*: the name was associated with the Alkmaionids, an old but controversial Athenian aristocratic family (see *OCD*[4] 54) whose recent members included Perikles (see Index of Names) and Alkibiades (n. on *F.* 1423). For the nature of Strepsiades' marriage, see my Introduction to the play. It was standard for respectable Athenian women to be publicly identified by the names of male relatives; cf. e.g. *WT* 605, 619, 840–1.

48 *Koisyra*: this name too (cf. 800) was found among the Alkmaionidai; see also *A.* 614.

51–2 *she . . . cults*: Strepsiades associates his wife not only with an expensive lifestyle (saffron was used for dyeing dresses: see n. on *WT* 138–9) but also with sexual sensuality and involvement in cults of Aphrodite and other deities (cf. n. on *WT* 130).

65 *Pheidonides*: Strepsiades gives a lengthened form to the name Pheidon (see 134), whose etymology means 'sparing', by implication connoting stinginess in Strepsiades' mind. The mother's suggestions all contain the *-(h)ippo* element ('horse') which was a feature of traditionally aristocratic names.

69 *Akropolis*: if the imagined context is the cavalcade of the Panathenaia (see Index of Names), as illustrated on the N and S friezes of the Parthenon, then Pheidippides would be driving an *apobates* chariot, i.e. with a hoplite warrior alongside him. But it is uncertain whether such chariots actually ascended the Akropolis during the Panathenaia. Cf. *WT* 811–12.

83 *Hippios*: lit. '(god) of horses'; for this title of Poseidon's, cf. *K.* 551.

94 *Thinking Institute*: the image of an esoteric community of intellectuals may have been influenced by Pythagoreanism, the only philosophical movement of which this was a feature at this date.

97 *charcoal*: the analogy between cosmic phenomena and everyday objects (here a lid heated by being placed over charcoal) is of a kind used by early Greek thinkers; cf. e.g. Anaximenes A7.6 DK on heavenly bodies turning like a felt cap round the head, with Herakleitos A16.130 DK for another analogy with charcoal. See *B.* 1001 for the same baking-lid analogy, which had apparently been made by Hippon of Samos (mid-5th c.), earlier satirized for it in Kratinos fr. 167.

104 *Chairephon*: see Index of Names. Pheidippides invokes a stereotype of intellectuals as pale-faced (on account of their supposedly indoor life) and going barefoot (cf. nn. on 362–3, 1167).

109 *Leogoras*: a rich Athenian, father of the orator Andokides; his family had various connections with the Alkmaionids (see n. on line 46), but he is mentioned chiefly in comedy for his luxurious lifestyle (pheasants being bred by some aristocrats at this time as an exotic status-symbol). Cf. *W.* 1269.

113 *stronger . . . weaker*: Protagoras had boasted he could teach his students how 'to make the weaker argument into the stronger' (A21, B6b DK), which in the present play means above all making an *immoral* argument defeat a (conventional) moral position; see 882 ff. and cf. my Introduction to the play.

118 *obol*: a sixth of a drachma; for comparative prices cf. n. on 21 with 612, 864, 1235, *WT* 1195, *F.* 140, 173–7, 1236.

120 *cavalry men . . . complexion*: the 'cavalry men' are the knights (*hippeis*), a class of Athenian citizens who owned their own horses. On Pheidippides' concern about his complexion, cf. 103.

122 *fancy horses*: the reference includes those for four-horse chariots (*tethrippa*), which raced in the Panathenaia and Olympic games. Cf. nn. on lines 15, 28, 69.

132 *Hello there!*: for various door-knocking routines in Aristophanes see e.g. *F.* 37 ff., 460 ff., *A.* 395 ff., *B.* 57 ff.

134 *Kikynna*: the location of this rural deme (one of the *c.*140 administrative districts into which Attika was officially divided) is uncertain but probably lay SE of the city beyond Mount Hymettos. For Strepsiades' father's name, see 65 with note.

137 *aborted*: lit. 'made to miscarry'. Sokrates uses the same term in connection with his self-image as 'midwife' of ideas at Plato, *Theaetetus* 150e. Related

vocabulary is used of impeded/misguided thought at Empedokles B2.2, 110.7 DK.

145 *a flea can jump*: ironically, the mechanics of a flea's jump still interest modern scientists: see <http://jeb.biologists.org/content/214/5/836.full.pdf±html>.

150 *both its feet*: Aristophanes ignores (or is unaware of) the fact that a flea has six legs.

151 *Persian slippers*: a luxurious form of soft female footwear; cf. *WT* 734 (a baby's).

156 *Sphettos*: it is unclear why Chairephon's deme (see on line 134) is mentioned at this point; there may be a joke of some sort.

179 *stole a cloak*: the abrupt shift from a geometry lesson to an act of theft is an extreme example of a *para prosdokian* ('contrary to expectation') punchline. The joke-form erases any plausible psychology on the Student's part. But the gap between abstract ideas and material life is a telling motif: cf. Eupolis fr. 386 (Sokrates has intellectualized everything—except where to get enough to eat), fr. 395 (Sokrates steals a jug at a symposium), and Aristophanes fr. 691 (Appendix).

180 *Thales*: philosopher-scientist of the early 6th cent. (see *OCD*[4] 1448), a legendary polymath. Strepsiades means, of course, that he is even more impressed by what he has just heard about Sokrates. Cf. *B*. 1009.

184 *tableau* [stage direction]: there are various theories about how this scene was staged; one involves use of the wheeled platform, *ekkuklêma* (see the general Introduction, 'Stage Directions', n. 87).

186 *Pylos . . . Lakonian*: Spartan troops who had surrendered at Pylos in summer 425 and had been brought back to Athens (Thucydides 4.30–41). Strepsiades is referring to the dishevelled and emaciated appearance of the students.

188 *under ground*: this echoes a formula ('things up in the air and under the earth') used to mock the unworldly interests of some intellectuals; see Hippokrates, *Ancient Medicine* 1, Plato, *Apology* 18b, 23d.

192 *Erebos . . . Tartaros*: primordial parts of the cosmos (cf. *B*. 693, 698) which had become associated with the underworld's darkest recesses.

195 *master*: Sokrates.

203 *cleruchies*: a cleruchy was a colony in which parcels of land were allotted to Athenian citizens; see *OCD*[4] 333–4. Strepsiades' instinct that only practical 'geometry' (lit. 'earth-measuring') is useful matches the view ascribed to Sokrates himself at Xenophon, *Memorabilia* 4.7.2–3.

205 *the people at large*: Strepsiades thinks the cleruchy principle (see n. on 203) is being extended to claim the whole world as Athenian land and will accordingly benefit the entire *demos* or citizen body.

206 *map*: for the existence of 'world maps' at this time, see Herodotos 4.36, 5.49.

208 *jurors*: the Athenians came to think of their elaborate jury-court system, and the possibilities of litigiousness that went with it, as a salient feature of the democracy; in addition to *Wasps*, cf. 863–4, with the jokes at *B*. 40–1, 109, *F*. 1466.

210 *Kikynnian*: see 134.

211 *Euboia*: the largest island in the W Aegean, running roughly parallel to the mainland of Greece.

213 *laid them out*: the Athenians, with Perikles as general, had quashed a Euboian revolt more than twenty years previously, in 446 (Thucydides 1.114).

225 *Air-walking*: an invented verb in the Greek; cf. the famous reference to this passage in Plato, *Apology* 19 c.

228 *higher*: lit. 'up in the air'; cf. n. on 188.

233 *moisture of . . . thoughts*: Diogenes of Apollonia (roughly contemporary with Sokrates), who believed mind/soul was itself air (B4 DK; cf. Anaximenes B2 DK for the same view), suggested that moisture could impede thought (A19.44 DK).

241 *seizing my goods*: cf. n. on 35.

249 *iron coinage*: responding to Sokrates' metaphorical use of 'currency' (cf. *F*. 890), Strepsiades makes a (feeble?) joke about real currency; the Byzantines still used iron coins, where cities like Athens used (mostly) silver (see n. on *F*. 720–6). The whole passage may have a subtext: coins as bearers of images of the gods.

254 *holy couch*: but the reality is probably a cheap bed of some sort; cf. 633.

257 *Athamas*: a Boiotian king who found himself facing sacrifice as an expiatory victim but was rescued at the last minute; there is probably an allusion to a scene in a lost play by Sophokles where Athamas stood at an altar wearing a wreath. One of Athamas's wives was the goddess Nephele, 'Cloud', which may have added a tacit resonance to the humour!

260 *floury*: Sokrates uses a term meaning lit. 'fine flour' and metaphorically 'a subtle speaker'; the sprinkling of flour over Strepsiades is a sort of parodic ritual (sacrificial animals usually had grain thrown at them).

264 *earth up high*: Sokrates' words imply the view that the earth is held in its cosmic position by the surrounding air; for similar views see e.g. Anaximenes A20 DK. Diogenes of Apollonia (n. on 233) thought air was in some sense 'god' (B5 DK). Aither: see Index of Names. For 'measureless', cf. n. on 393.

270–4 *If now . . . heed our prayer*: Sokrates uses a traditional Greek prayer form, invoking the deity to come from its current abode and promising it continued worship; cf. n. on *WT* 319. In traditional Greek mythology, Ocean was a primordial river-god (Hesiod, *Theogony* 20, 133, etc.) often imagined as encircling the earth; the gardens are probably those of the Hesperides (Hesiod, ibid. 215–16). The Maiotian lake is the modern sea of Azov (NE of the Black Sea); Mount Mimas is on a headland in W Asia Minor.

275 *on the roof*: i.e. to be imagined as in the sky. Most scholars think the Chorus sang from entirely out of sight (until 323 ff.), but this poses acoustic problems for the audibility of their lyrics. Cf. the birds on the *skênê* roof at *B.* 267–93 and see the general Introduction, 'Formality and Performance'.

278 *father Ocean*: see 271.

300–1 *Pallas . . . Kekrops*: two periphrases for Athens/Attika. For Pallas see Index of Names; Kekrops was a mythical early king of Athens.

302–4 *awe . . . ritual acts*: a reference to the Eleusinian Mysteries (see Index of Names).

311–13 *spring . . . pipes*: a reference to the Great Dionysia festival, the most important of the Athenian dramatic festivals and the one at which the first version of *Clouds* itself was performed. See general Introduction, 'Aristophanes' Career in Context'.

323 *Parnes*: a large mountain range at the NW edge of Attika.

326 *entrance*: the Greek term *eisodos* denotes one of the side entrances to the *orchêstra*; see general Introduction, 'Stage Directions'. This is therefore a metatheatrical moment.

331–4 *clever . . . Muses*: Sokrates (in a voice which ironically undercuts his own supposed religion) lumps together all sorts of figures who might be cynically thought of as vapidly 'cloudy' in their pretentiousness (or, in their own terms, inspired by the Muses: see Index of Names).

335–9 *they wrote . . . wolfed down*: Strepsiades quotes snippets of 'airy' phraseology from dithyramb (a genre of choral song in honour of Dionysos) and pictures the poets being rewarded (by patrons) with lavish banquets. The giant Typhos (Typhoios) is the origin of winds at Hesiod, *Theogony* 869.

349–50 *Xenophantos . . . centaurs*: the target is Hieronymos, a dithyrambic poet (cf. n. on 335–9) and exceptionally hairy (cf. n. on 14), apparently the same person as at *A.* 388–9; there *may* be innuendo of pederastic behaviour in the present gibe. For centaurs, see Index of Names.

351 *Simon*: a contemporary politician and probably the same person as at 399.

353 *Kleonymos*: see Index of Names.

355 *Kleisthenes*: see Index of Names.

358 CHORUS: the context justifies chanting by the whole chorus at this point, though in dialogue scenes like this the chorus-leader alone normally speaks (as I assume from 412 onwards).

361 *Prodikos*: a contemporary polymathic intellectual or 'sophist' (see e.g. Plato, *Protagoras* 314–17); see n. on 659 and cf. fr. 506 (Appendix), *B.* 692.

362–3 *swaggering walk . . . face*: Alkibiades confirms this description at Plato, *Symposium* 221b. Sokrates' eyes were exceptionally protruding: see Xenophon, *Symposium* 5.5, Plato, *Theaetetus* 143e, 209c. His physiognomy and deportment were perceived by some as arrogant: see e.g.

Ameipsias fr. 9.3, Plato, *Symposium* 220c, Xenophon, *Symposium* 5.6. For his barefoot habit (cf. 103) see e.g. Plato, *Symposium* 220b, Xenophon, *Memorabilia* 1.6.2.

364 *Earth*: in early Greek mythology, the primordial wife of Ouranos (Sky); see Hesiod, *Theogony* 20, 45, etc.

373 *Zeus . . . sieve*: most Greeks did not take literally Zeus's traditional image as a rain-god (cf. *F.* 246); Strepsiades embodies ludicrous naivety.

380 *swirl*: several early Greek thinkers, including Empedokles (e.g. B35.4, 115.11 DK), posited a kind of cosmic vortex to explain processes of material change on the largest scale. The Greek word *dinos* used here can also mean a large wine mixing-bowl: a specimen of the latter stands outside the door of Sokrates' school (see n. on 1473).

385 *Panathenaia*: see Index of Names.

393 *endless*: Sokrates echoes the vocabulary of those Greek philosophers, starting with Anaximander in the 6th century, who took physical reality to be in some sense without limits, even 'infinite'; cf. 264.

394 *sounds themselves*: Sokrates actually says 'the words themselves', i.e. *brontê* (thunder) and *pordê* (fart), which have some phonological resemblance in Greek.

398 *Kronos*: see Index of Names.

399–400 *Simon . . . Theoros*: Simon (cf. 351), Kleonymos (see Index of Names), and Theoros (e.g. *A.* 134 ff., *W.* 42–51, 1220–42) were all minor politicians, the second and third associated with the leading demagogue Kleon (see 549, 586 ff.).

401 *Sounion*: the southernmost tip of Attika (cf. *B.* 868); Sokrates quotes a phrase from Homer, *Odyssey* 3.278. We do not know whether the first half of the line refers to a specific lightning strike on a temple of Zeus.

404–7 *dry wind . . . ignites*: the explanation is in the tradition of Ionian natural science; cf. esp. Anaximander A23 DK.

408 *Diasia*: a winter festival of Zeus Meilichios; see 864 and cf. Thucydides 1.126.6.

424 *Chaos*: originally the primeval void from which all reality came into being (cf. *B.* 693); but here as at 627 Sokrates associates it with the infinite air above (cf. 393). For Tongue as a pseudo-deity, cf. *F.* 892.

438 *thoroughbred*: see n. on 23.

451 *lip-smacking creep*: we do not know the exact meaning of this last term nor the precise slang sense of several other words in the preceding list.

475 *seek your advice*: the chorus picture Strepsiades as a legal consultant in great demand.

478–80 *disclose . . . defences*: this may evoke a distinctively Sokratic interest (seen in both Plato and Xenophon) in getting 'inside' individuals' ways of thinking; the theme is developed further at 695 ff.

494–6 *blows . . . charge*: for a scenario of this kind, with roles reversed, see lines 1297–1302, and cf. e.g. *W.* 1331–3.

499 *stolen goods*: in certain circumstances Athenian law permitted someone to enter another's house in search of stolen property, but the searcher was required to remove their clothing so as not to be able to 'plant' something.

503 *Chairephon*: see Index of Names.

507–8 *cake . . . cave*: visitors to the cave oracle of Trophonios in Boiotia took a honey-cake to placate the snakes believed to live in the cave.

518–19 *Spectators . . . Dionysos*: it soon becomes apparent that the chorus-leader is speaking (notionally) in the voice of the playwright, with Dionysos invoked as god of theatre/comedy. On the metre of this passage (eupolideans), cf. the general Introduction, 'Translating Aristophanes'.

524 *defeated*: the reference is to the first staging of *Clouds*, in 423; see my Introduction to the play.

528–32 *Ever since . . . so proudly*: a reference to Aristophanes' first play, *Banqueters* (427), which included a pair of brothers with sharply contrasting characters and values; see the Appendix, s.v. *Daitales*. The play was produced by Kallistratos or Philonides, hence the humorous trope of the unmarried girl who could not bring up her own baby: see the general Introduction, 'Aristophanes' Career in Context'.

534–6 *Elektra . . . hair*: the simile is loosely based on the story of Elektra living in hope of the return of her exiled brother Orestes, after the murder of Agamemnon by Klytaimnestra, and finding a lock of Orestes' hair on their father's tomb (cf. Aischylos, *Choephori*, esp. 166–211).

538–9 *leather . . . laugh*: i.e. the phallus often/standardly worn by comic actors but sometimes 'tied up' rather than left dangling. The ostensible disdain for blatant phallic humour is not a sincere Aristophanic attitude: see e.g. *WT* 236–48, 643–8.

543 *torches*: comically disingenuous in the light of 1490 ff.; see my Introduction to the play.

549–50 *struck him . . . flat*: the reference, cast in a metaphor from all-in-wrestling (*pankration*), is to the comic assault on Kleon (see Index of Names) in *Knights* (424). Cf. n. on 1047.

551–2 *Hyperbolos*: see Index of Names.

553–7 *Eupolis . . . Hermippos*: Eupolis, one of Aristophanes' main rivals, staged *Marikas* (a satirical sobriquet, of uncertain origin, for Hyperbolos) at Lenaia 421. Phrynichos, a somewhat older comic poet (cf. *F.* 13), had written a comedy in which Andromeda was threatened by a sea-monster (cf. n. on *WT* 1012). Hermippos's *Bread-Sellers* apparently contained a role for Hyperbolos's mother (cf. *WT* 840–5). There was also a *Hyperbolos* by Plato comicus.

559 *eel-fishing*: apparently a reference to *K.* 864–7, though we do not know which poet(s) had supposedly copied the image.

566 *trident's keeper*: Poseidon (see Index of Names).

571 *charioteer*: a traditional image of the sun (e.g. *Homeric Hymn to Demeter* 88–9).

580 *let you know*: adverse weather might be interpreted as an omen of divine displeasure; cf. n. on 581–3.

581–3 *tanner . . . thunder cracked*: the politician Kleon (allegorized as a Paphlagonian tanner in Aristophanes' *Knights*: cf. n. on 549) was elected general for 424–3, but the elections were initially postponed on account of meteorological omens (including a solar eclipse, 21 March 424). The quotation in 583 is from Sophokles' lost play *Teucer*, fr. 578.

591–2 *cormorant . . . stocks*: Kleon had already been called a cormorant at *K.* 956. Stocks or pillories, sometimes fastening just the neck (cf. *L.* 680–1, *We.* 476, 606) and sometimes the arms and legs as well (*K.* 1049; cf. n. on *WT* 931 for a particularly brutal form), were used to imprison/punish certain (low-grade) criminals.

596 *Kynthos*: the highest point on the island of Delos, birthplace of Apollo (Index of Names).

598 *deity*: Artemis (see Index of Names); her great 6th-century temple at Ephesos had benefited from Lydian contributions (Herodotos 1.92.1) and served the religious needs of both peoples.

602 *aigis*: traditionally a garment (often a snake-fringed cape) worn by Athena (see Index of Names), here treated, by an extravagant metaphor, as though it were a means of transport.

616 *confusion*: the Athenians used a calendar of twelve lunar months (cf. 1191) for their festival year, but had to make periodic intercalations to prevent major deviation from the solar year.

620 *trials*: Athenian courts (and other state institutions) were traditionally closed during religious festivals; cf. *WT* 78–80. On the torture of slaves for judicial purposes, see n. on *F.* 616.

622 *Memnon or Sarpedon*: non-Greek heroes with divine parents and both killed at Troy; the first (cf. *F.* 963) a Lykian, son of the goddess Dawn and killed by Achilles, the second an Aithiopian, son of Zeus and unforgettably mourned by his own father with tears of blood at Homer, *Iliad* 16.458–61.

623–6 *Hyperbolos . . . days of life*: Hyperbolos (see 551–8) had been elected Athens' sacred ambassador to the Delphic Amphictyony, but seems to have had an embarrassing experience on a ceremonial occasion; the passage may also imply he had been involved in official adjustments to the city's calendar (n. on 616).

627 *Chaos . . . Air*: see nn. on 264, 424. 'Respiration' is uniquely deified here, but in keeping with Sokrates' general emphasis on 'airy' gods.

638 *rhythms*: technical classification of metrical rhythms was an interest of several contemporary thinkers, including Damon (n. on 651) and Hippias (Plato, *Hippias Major* 285d).

642 *verses*: Sokrates' technical terms (trimeters and tetrameters: cf. the general Introduction, 'Translating Aristophanes') must have been familiar to anyone educated in or appreciative of poetry, especially drama (and therefore, practically by definition, the spectators of *Clouds* itself). Strepsiades thinks only of the measures in which grain was sold: his references are to a *medimnos* ('bushel') and the eight sub-units into which it was divided.

651 *'military beat' . . . 'bending finger'*: enoplian and dactyl (*daktulos*, lit. 'finger'). Both terms were recent metrical coinages by the musical theorist Damon (see Plato, *Republic* 3.400b), though we cannot be sure exactly which metres he designated by them.

653 *like this*: presumably an obscene gesture with the middle finger; related gestures are involved at *A*. 444, *K*. 1381, *P*. 549.

659 *rightly . . . gender*: an allusion to new ideas of systematic grammar, especially concepts of 'correct language' held by the likes of Protagoras (A24, A26–8 DK) and Prodikos (Plato, *Euthydemus* 277e). Cf. n. on *F*. 1181.

664 *for both*: the Greek *alektruôn* originally meant 'cock', but had become used also for the hen of the domestic fowl.

667 *Air*: cf. 627.

673 *Kleonymos*: see Index of Names.

676 *used himself*: lit. 'kneaded (himself) in a round mortar'. Evidently a sexual joke, though we do not know whether masturbation or anal sex is the point of the slang.

690 *Ameinia*: the vocative form of this name (cf. 31) lacks the final *-s*, producing an ending which coincides with that of some female names (e.g. Demetria, 684).

692 *military service*: a figure called Ameinias (or Amunias) was the butt of various jokes in this period (e.g. *W*. 74, 466, 1267); but we cannot be sure how precisely targeted this gibe is.

695 *think very deeply*: what follows parodies an exercise in intensive self-scrutiny and problem-solving which may well evoke the distinctive intellectual style of the historical Sokrates (roughly speaking, his preoccupation with 'the examined life': see Plato, *Apology* 38a); cf. n. on 478–80.

708 *ails you*: in the course of this exchange between chorus and character there are several parodic overtones of scenes of tragic suffering.

710 *Korinthian*: in Greek there is a phonetic pun (*koreis*, bedbugs, having the same first syllable as *Korinthioi*); the Korinthians were allies of Sparta and therefore on the enemy side in the Peloponnesian war at the time of the first production of *Clouds* in 423.

719 *shoes*: while inside Sokrates' school between 510 and 635, Strepsiades had been stripped of most of his clothes (cf. 497–500).

731 *Right then . . .*: the odd relationship of this line to 723 ff. may be the result of the incomplete revision of the play; an alternative is to take Sokrates off stage briefly between 726 and 731.

749 *sorceress*: the Greek world knew many women who practised assorted magic. 'Drawing down the moon' (cf. Plato, *Gorgias* 513a) seems to have been metaphorical for causing an eclipse, but Strepsiades has naively superstitious belief in the literal act.

758 *five talents*: an enormous sum of money; n. on 21.

763 *beetle*: in a children's game, a cockchafer's leg was tied to a piece of thread; the beetle was then released into the air.

768 *glass*: a rare commodity in classical Athens, here used as a burning-lens; cf. the glass vessels at *A*. 74.

772 *melt*: Strepsiades envisages a charge written on a wax tablet (cf. Strepsiades' own tablet at 19 ff.).

789 *crows*: more strictly, 'ravens'; for this colloquial curse (also in the Greek at 123, 133, 646, 871), see *WT* 1079, *F.* 187–9, and cf. *B*. 28 (with a situational pun).

800 *Koisyra-like*: see n. on 48.

804 *Antistrophe*: the antistrophe is longer than the strophe at 700–6, an irregularity which may reflect the incomplete revision of the play.

814 *Mist*: following his earlier experience in the School, Strepsiades is now inventing his *own* meteorological deities; but cf. 330.

815 *Megakles*: see 124 with n. on 46; 'colonnades' conjures up the image of a grand house.

827 *Swirl*: cf. 380–1.

830 *Melos*: island in the SW Aegean; Strepsiades confuses Sokrates with Diagoras the Melian (see *B*. 1073–4), a contemporary thinker with a scandalous reputation for challenging traditional religious beliefs.

831 *fleas' feet*: see 144–52.

837 *baths*: cf. 1044–54.

842 *know yourself*: an echo of the famous injunction on Apollo's temple at Delphi; see e.g. Plato, *Protagoras* 343b.

845 *court order*: Athenian legal procedure allowed a son to have control of family affairs transferred to him on the grounds of his father's dementia.

856 *lost your cloak*: see 497–505 with stage direction before 634.

859 *'special reasons'*: Plutarch, *Perikles* 23.1 records that Perikles used such a disingenuous phrase in his accounts as general in 445 to cover a large sum of money spent on a bribe to the Spartans.

864 *Diasia*: see n. on 408. Athenian jurors were paid on a daily basis: 3 obols (n. on 118) by this date (see esp. *W*. 684). Cf. n. on 208.

876 *Hyperbolos*: see Index of Names; Sokrates implies he had been a stupid pupil of forensic rhetoric and had needed hugely expensive teaching (for the value of a talent see nn. on 21, 758).

888/9 [*stage direction*]: the original version of *Clouds* would at this point have had a choral ode (during which the actor playing Sokrates would have changed into the costume of either Moral or Immoral). The evidence suggests it was cut but not replaced by Aristophanes in the unfinished revision of the play.

902 *Justice*: Dike is a deity, or at least a divine personification, in some Greek texts, the earliest being Hesiod, *Theogony* 902, *Works and Days* 256–62.

905 *father*: Kronos (see Index of Names). The argument is of a kind already used at Aischylos, *Eumenides* 640–2.

922–4 *Telephos . . . Pandeletos*: on Telephos, see the Index of Names. Pandeletos, mentioned also by Kratinos (fr. 260), is unknown: the name was probably proverbial.

964 *music lessons*: from a *kitharistês*, who taught boys poetry and music; cf. *K.* 992 and e.g. Plato, *Protagoras* 326a–b.

966 *fooling around*: the Greek refers to a boys' game of squeezing the thighs together, while seated, so as to make the penis protrude.

967 *'Pallas . . . lyre'*: openings/portions of two songs (i.e. lyric poems), both of uncertain authorship but implicitly representative of rather old-fashioned types; for Pallas see Index of Names.

971 [no line 970 in modern editions] *Phrynis*: a mid-5th-century professional performer who became known for use of a certain kind of modulation in his musical practices.

973 *wrestling*: a traditional element in athletic education, at least for those wealthy enough to afford it; cf. *F.* 729.

984–5 *Dipolieia . . . rites*: the Dipolieia was a summer festival of Zeus held on the Akropolis; a special ox-slaying ritual (Bouphonia) formed part of it. Cicada hair-brooches are mentioned as outmoded by Thucydides 1.6.3; cf. *K.* 1331. Kekeides was a dithyrambic poet (cf. n. on 335–9) of uncertain date.

986 *Marathon-fighters*: the generation of those who fought in the battle of Marathon (see Index of Names) became a byword for patriotic heroism.

988–9 *Panathenaia . . . Tritogeneia*: on the Panathenaia, see Index of Names; Tritogeneia is a very old title (e.g. Hesiod, *Theogony* 895) of Athena.

997 *apple*: throwing an apple is here a flirtatious gesture; the kind of dancing-girl envisaged is assumed to be also a prostitute (cf. *F.* 514–20, *A.* 1093).

1001 *Hippokrates*: probably the nephew of Perikles who served as general and died at the battle of Delion in 424 (Thucydides 4.101.2); his three sons were mocked by several comic poets for being simpletons (see fr. 116, Appendix). Cf. *WT* 273.

1005 *Academy*: a gymnasium/park to the NW of the city, later to become the location of Plato's philosophical school.

1019 *decree*: symbolizing engagement in the politics of the Assembly (see Index of Names).

1022–3 *Antimachos . . . arsehole*: we do not know whether Antimachos is the same man as at *A.* 1050. For the abusive sexual language, cf. 529, 909, 1083 ff.

1047 *in my grip*: as quite often in Aristophanes, the imagery is drawn from wrestling; similarly 126 and e.g. *F.* 878. Cf. n. on 549.

1051 *baths . . . Herakles*: hot springs, at least such as those at Thermopylai (Herodotos 7.176.3), were associated with Herakles (see Index of Names). 'Cold baths' could obviously be thought of as old-fashioned or primitive; the hot-water supply of public baths was a 'modern' urban amenity (cf. 837).

1055 *Agora*: see Index of Names.

1057 *agora-speaker*: Nestor is *agorêtês* (in Homeric Greek, 'assembly speaker') at *Iliad* 1.248, 4.293; the same term is used of e.g. Trojan elders, *Iliad* 3.150, and Peleus, 7.126.

1063 *knife*: Peleus (father of Achilles) virtuously resisted seduction by Hippolyte, who then falsely accused him. Hippolyte's husband, Akastos, left Peleus defenceless in the wild but the gods arranged for him to have a knife to protect himself.

1065 *Hyperbolos*: see Index of Names.

1067–9 *Thetis . . . bed*: Thetis, a sea-nymph, could never have lived in a normal ménage with a mortal; but Immoral represents her as abandoning Peleus, after they had produced their son Achilles, on grounds of sexual dissatisfaction.

1083 *radish and ashes*: an adulterer caught in the act could be physically abused by the wronged husband; having a radish forced up his anus and his pubic regions singed with hot ashes (cf. *WT* 537–8) are vivid examples of what might be done sadistically.

1085 *And suppose . . .*: the lines shorten here from iambic tetrameters to iambic trimeters, with a further shortening to dimeters at 1089 ff. (and some variations of length thereafter).

1131–4 *fifth . . . last*: the last ten days of the month were counted in reverse; the very last was known as 'old-and-new'. Cf. 1178–1200.

1149 *the one*: i.e. Immoral.

1150 *queen*: Strepsiades improvises a goddess of fraud (cf. 729), also using a term which echoes his address to the Clouds at 357.

1160 *tongue . . . sword*: cf. 1108–10.

1167 *emaciated*: the following scene suggests that Pheidippides appears in a different mask from previously, one which highlights his new ascetic look (cf. n. on 104).

1176 *Attic expression*: see Index of Names, s.v. Attika.

1179 *one day*: see n. on 1131–4.

1181 *deposit*: a plaintiff had to make a monetary deposit with a magistrate in order to institute proceedings leading to a court-case.

1187 *Solon*: Solon (*c.*640–560), the greatest statesman of archaic Athens, was popularly credited with being the city's first lawgiver (cf. *B.* 1660) and with having laid the foundations for 'democracy'.

1191 *moon*: the Athenian calendar was divided into twelve lunar months; cf. n. on 616.

1198 *tasters*: it seems that these were people who officially sampled food the day before certain festivals.

1209 *demesmen*: members of the same deme (cf. n. on 134).

1224–5 *minas . . . horse*: we are reminded of what Strepsiades said at 21–2.

1233 *gods*: an ironic echo of 246–7.

1235 *obols*: cf. n. on 118.

1237 *salt*: hides were rubbed with salt prior to tanning; 1238 shows what Strepsiades has in mind.

1251 *grammar*: Strepsiades is using the idea that Sokrates used with *him* at 669–80; 'one obol', cf. n. on 118.

1256 *deposit*: see n. on 1181.

1261 *Karkinos*: a tragic poet whose career had started more than two decades earlier; with his three sons, including Xenokles (see Index of Names), he is also the butt of jokes at *W.* 1499–1537, *P.* 781–95, 864, *WT* 440.

1264–6 *Harsh . . . Tlempolemos*: a parody of a tragic passage, possibly by Xenokles (n. on 1261). Tle(m)polemos was a son of Herakles (e.g. Homer, *Iliad* 2.653–70): it is possible that the tragedy alluded to here involved a chariot-crash (compare Sophokles, *Elektra* 698–756).

1300 *trace-horse*: one of the two outer horses of a four-horse chariot.

1327–30 *father-beater . . . roses*: compare 910–12; Pheidippides has learnt to model himself on Immoral's insouciant shamelessness.

1337 *stronger . . . weaker*: see n. on 113, with 882 ff. Strictly speaking, 1334 has already committed Pheidippides to taking the 'weaker', i.e. immoral, side of the argument.

1352 *chorus*: this kind of (extra-dramatic) self-reference by the chorus is more familiar in the parabasis; see 1115.

1354 *feasted . . . the way*: Strepsiades refers to a dinner of the kind that was followed traditionally by drinking and singing of songs.

1356 *Simonides*: a famous lyric poet (*c.*556–468). The song referred to (*PMG* 507) was a victory-song for a wrestler who had defeated an opponent called Krios, a name whose literal sense is 'ram'. Cf. *B.* 918–19.

1360 *cicadas*: these insects were proverbial 'singers'; cf. *B.* 39–40 and the famous story about them told by Sokrates at Plato, *Phaedrus* 258e–9d.

1364 *myrtle*: it was a sympotic custom sometimes to hold a myrtle-branch when singing; cf. fr. 444 (translated in the Appendix).

1367 *noisy ranting . . .*: very much the view of Aischylos taken by Euripides in the contest in *Frogs*; see my Introduction to that play.

1372 *brother . . . sister*: in Euripides' *Aiolos* Makareus committed incest with his sister Kanake; both characters ended up committing suicide. Cf. *F.* 1081, 1475, *P.* 114–19, with my Appendix on Aristophanes' *Aiolosikon*.

1378 *cleverest*: see my Introduction to *Frogs*.

1415 *the children . . .*: a perverted echo of Euripides, *Alcestis* 691, which is quoted in its proper form at *WT* 194 (see n. there).

1435 *you in turn*: Strepsiades is apparently preparing to make the point that any son of Pheidippides, according to the latter's new law, will *also* be entitled to hit his own father.

1450 *criminals' pit*: the pit, just outside the city walls and under the control of a public official, into which the corpses of executed criminals were thrown; cf. *F.* 574. There is a memorable image of the place in Plato, *Republic* 4.439e–40a.

1468 *'paternal Zeus'*: Strepsiades quotes a phrase that probably comes from tragedy; 'paternal' might alternatively be translated 'ancestral', but the point here is the implication that Zeus will support the demands of a father.

1471 *'It's Swirl . . .'*: Pheidippides quotes back line 828 at his father.

1473 *this pot*: a large wine mixing-bowl called a *dinos* has stood throughout outside the door of Sokrates' school; cf. n. on 380. The term *dinos* allows puns in Greek on Zeus's name (in oblique cases starting *Di*-).

1478 *Hermes*: a herm, i.e. a symbolic (and probably priapic) statue of Hermes, stands outside Strepsiades' house door. Cf. the reference at *L.* 1094 to the notorious scandal of the mutilation of many Athenian herms in 415 (Thucydides 6.27–9).

1485 *Xanthias*: a common slave-name (lit. 'blonde-haired') in Aristophanes; cf. Dionysos's slave in *F.*

1498 *cloak*: see 497–505 with stage direction before 634; cf. 856.

1503 *'Air-walking . . .'*: Strepsiades quotes back line 225 at Sokrates; see the n. there.

1507 *backside*: the noun can denote the position of a heavenly body but one of its other meanings is that of a person's bottom; cf. *WT* 133.

1507–8 *exit running*: some modern scholars talk about Sokrates and his pupils being 'burned to death' inside the school; but the text clearly indicates that they escape from the building and are chased off stage. See my Introduction to the play.

WOMEN AT THE THESMOPHORIA

1 *swallow*: herald of spring in Greek folklore; but the Kinsman means the question metaphorically, i.e. when will his misery end?

14–18 *Aither . . . hearing*: for Aither, see Index of Names. Euripides offers a mishmash of speculative cosmogony and science of the kind associated with presocratic Greek thinkers.

56 *model*: the Servant's elaborate mix of technical metaphors for poetic composition here alludes to the *cire perdue* method of creating a wax model (with a clay covering), which is then heated away to create a mould for bronze statue-making.

68 *verses*: the Greek term *strophê*, which refers to matching sections of choral lyric (cf. the general Introduction, 'Formality and Performance'), literally means a 'turning' and therefore allows a pun here on bending poetic timbers. The reference to winter suits the dramatic setting at the time of the Thesmophoria (Oct.–Nov.), soon to be mentioned (80).

78–80 *courts . . . underway*: cf. n. on *C.* 620.

83 *Thesmophorion*: lit. 'the shrine of the Thesmophoroi' (i.e. Demeter and Persephone); the location is not certain but was probably on the N slope of the Akropolis.

85 *bad reputation*: for the (exaggerated) idea that Euripides specialized in depicting scandalous female characters, cf. *F.* 1043–54, *C.* 1371–2, *L.* 368–9.

94 *crafty scheming*: Euripides boasts of such a (supposed) trait of his work at *F.* 957.

98 *Kyrene*: a well-known courtesan; cf. *F.* 1327–8.

100 *anthill tunnels*: a metaphor for musically/poetically intricate structures of the kind the Kinsman takes to belong to a pretentiously 'modern' style and which are in a sense exemplified by the song that follows.

101 *chthonic goddesses*: Demeter and Persephone; 'chthonic' means 'belonging to the earth/underworld'.

102 *free*: the implied scenario may be that of Troy during the period when the Greeks (deceptively) appear to have sailed away and abandoned the war.

110 *Simoeis*: one of the two main rivers of Troy (e.g. Homer, *Iliad* 4.475, 5.774); for Phoibos, see Index of Names.

118–22 *Leto . . . Phrygian Graces*: Leto was mother of both Apollo and Artemis; the Graces (see Index of Names) are assimilated to the 'Asiatic' associations of her cult.

130 *gods of the female domain:* Genetyllides, deities (literally of childbirth) linked with Aphrodite and associated in comedy with female sensuality; the singular Genetyllis occurs at both *C.* 52 and *L.* 2.

135 *Lykourgeia*: a tetralogy (three tragedies plus satyr play); in the first play, *Edonians*, the Thracian king Lykourgos resisted the introduction of Dionysiac rites. The following lines contain an uncertain mixture of quotation and parody of a scene where Lykourgos questioned Dionysos himself about his exotic dress and appurtenances, which the king regarded as mixing effeminate and masculine features.

138–9 *saffron dress . . . breast-band*: saffron-dyed dresses were fine women's wear (cf. 253 with e.g. *C.* 51, *L.* 44–51, *AW* 332, 879) but could also be Dionysiac (*F.* 46, Kratinos fr. 40); a breast-band supported a woman's breasts like a modern brassiere (cf. 251–5, 638, frs. 338, 664).

142 *Lakonian shoes*: a standard type of male footwear in Athens; 'Lakonian' (lit. from the territory of Sparta) designates the style, not the source of the shoes.

153 *kinky sex*: lit. 'you ride a horse' (sexually, of a woman sitting on a man; cf. e.g. *W.* 501). Phaidra: see Index of Names.

156 *role-playing*: Greek *mimêsis*, a term which was starting to be used for artistic 'representation' and 'expression' in general. Agathon offers a version of a theory of poetic composition that combines creative imagination with quasi-theatrical role-playing: cf. Aristotle, *Poetics*, ch. 17 for something similar.

157–8 *satyr-plays . . . erection*: satyrs (wild creatures with half-animal features) normally formed the chorus of satyr-plays written by tragedians; they were typically depicted in vase-painting as wildly oversexed.

161–3 *Ibykos . . . softness*: Agathon names three major 6th-century lyric poets; 'Ionian' refers here loosely to ideas of luxury and decadence (cf. *AW* 883, 918) which Greeks associated with Near Eastern influence.

164 *Phrynichos*: an early tragic poet (active *c.*510–470); cf. *B.* 749, *F.* 910, 1299.

167 *nature*: a different theory from the one Agathon put forward at 149–56.

168–70 *ugly . . . plays*: Kinsman names three late 5th-century tragic poets. Philokles (cf. *B.* 281, 1295) was a nephew of Aischylos; for Xenokles, see Index of Names; Theognis is a target of jokes also at *A.* 10–12, 138–40.

177–8 *'it's the mark . . . words'*: Euripides quotes from one of his own plays, *Aiolos* (fr. 28); cf. n. on *C.* 1372.

194 *'You're happy . . .'*: Euripides, *Alcestis* 691, where Pheres refuses to die on behalf of his son Admetos; cf. the parodic form of the line at *C.* 1415.

198–9 *'When disaster strikes . . .'*: Agathon quotes from one of his own plays (unknown), fr. 34.

222 *peg*: a reference to a technique used by butchers to force open a pig's mouth for inspection; cf. *K.* 375–81.

224 *Awesome Goddesses*: the Semnai, whose cave shrine was near the Areopagos hill and sometimes served as a refuge for those fleeing persecution (cf. *K.* 1312, Thucydides 1.126.11).

232 *manliness*: the Greek involves a pun, 'I shall serve in the army as *psilos*', the latter adjective meaning either 'smooth-shaven' or 'light-armed'.

235 *Kleisthenes*: see Index of Names. The joke will in a sense 'come true' at 574 ff.

237 *piglet*: slaughtered pigs had their bristles singed off before they were cooked; there may also be a sexual double entendre ('piglet' was slang for female genitalia: cf. 289, 537–40, with *A.* 764 ff.).

254 *By Aphrodite*: a type of oath especially used by women! Cf. *AW* 189–91.

272 *Aither*: see 14, 1068 and Index of Names. The line is based on Euripides fr. 487 (*Melanippe the Wise*); cf. *F.* 100.

273 *Hippokrates*: we do not know which individual is meant (cf. *C.* 1001 for one

such person), nor why his house (probably a kind of hostel with rented rooms) was good for a joke at this date.

275–6 *mind . . . tongue*: a partial, inverted quotation of the notorious line at Euripides, *Hippolytos* 612 ('My tongue has sworn but my mind is under no oath'); cf. *F.* 101–2, 1471, and for a later indication of the line's notoriety see Aristotle, *Rhetoric* 3.15, 1416a28–31.

278 *signal*: a signal of some sort was given for the start of the city's *ekklêsia* or political Assembly (see Index of Names). The implication of the present line is that the women's Thesmophoria assembly (cf. 84) will be a female equivalent to the *ekklêsia*; cf. nn. on 295–311, 335–8, 372–9.

279 *Thratta*: an ethnic name ('Thracian') used for some female slaves in Athens.

281 *hill*: the Akropolis; see n. on 83.

282 *Thesmophoroi*: Demeter and Persephone, patron deities of the festival; see my Introduction to the play.

287 *Pherrephatta*: the Attic form of 'Persephone' (Index of Names).

289 *Piglet*: see n. on 237.

291 *Willy*: a made-up name from the same slang term as used at 254 and 515; there may be parody of a mother's playful hypocorism for a small child.

295–311 *Let sacred silence . . . rejoice*: the Leader's proclamation, in prose, is partly reminiscent of the herald's announcement at the start of a meeting of the city's Assembly; cf. n. on 278. Ploutos ('wealth') was the son of Demeter. Kalligeneia (perhaps Demeter's nurse), lit. 'fair birth', gave her name to one of the days of the Thesmophoria; cf. fr. 331 from *WT* II (Appendix). Kourotrophos ('child-rearer') is a deity identified in later periods with Earth. 'Paion' is here an exclamatory prayer for good fortune. For Hermes and the Graces, see Index of Names.

319 *come here*: in Greek prayers, deities are standardly invited to come in person to their worshippers; cf. n. on *C.* 270–4. The gods mentioned after Zeus are Apollo and Athena (see Index of Names).

321 *Offspring*: Artemis (see Index of Names); for Leto, cf. 118–29.

327 *phorminx*: a large traditional lyre; cf. *F.* 231.

332–4 *Pythian . . . Delian*: see Index of Names under Delphi and Delos.

335–8 *plots . . . tyrant*: a (distorted) version of the curses delivered as part of the preliminaries of an Assembly meeting. 'Medes' was synonymous for Greeks with 'Persians', though the two peoples were originally distinct; on this passage and 365, see my Introduction to the play.

340–1 *surrogate baby . . . go-between*: the Leader's curses switch abruptly from political to sexual matters. The surrogate baby is envisaged either where a woman herself has not given birth (cf. 407–8) or where one child is swapped for another (see 564–5). For a slave go-between in an adulterous affair, see the legal case described in a speech of the Athenian orator Lysias (Lysias 1.19–20); cf. n. on *F.* 1079–82.

365 *Medes*: see n. on 335–8.

372–9 *decision . . . motion*: the formalities again follow those of the city's Assembly; cf. n. on 278. For the invitation to speak cf. *A.* 45, *AW* 130 (the latter in the women's *rehearsal* for the Assembly).

383 *swear . . . pretension*: the oath by Demeter and Persephone is distinctively female: cf. 594, 875, 916, *L.* 112, *AW* 155. But the woman's denial of self-interested motivation is a motif used by male orators in the city's politics.

387 *vegetable-seller*: a standing comic gibe at Euripides (possibly a satirical distortion of some kind of commercial activity on the part of his family); cf. 456, 910, *F.* 840, and e.g. *A.* 478.

390–1 *wherever . . . choruses*: i.e. every time a play by Euripides is performed; this could include stagings in local deme theatres as well as at the major city festivals (see n. 68 to the general Introduction).

392–3 *adultery . . . tongues*: ideas which chiefly belong to a *comic* stereotype of women; relevant to Euripides only in so far as he (but not alone among tragedians) sometimes depicted women with strongly erotic character and/or a capacity for boldly independent decision-making. Cf. my Introduction to the play.

395 *when they return*: the passage is often taken to indicate that most Athenian women did not normally attend the theatre in Athens; cf. *B.* 793–6 with n. 32 to the general Introduction. At this date, most seating in the Theatre of Dionysos consisted of wooden benches: see general Introduction, 'Stage Directions'.

401 *garland*: taken (on the husband's suspicion) to be some sort of dedicatory offering for a secret lover.

404 *Korinthian guest*: in Euripides' *Stheneboia* (cf. *F.* 1043–9) the heroine of that name was illicitly in love with the Korinthian guest Bellerophon (Index of Names); among other things, she even (superstitiously) 'dedicated' fallen/dropped objects to him.

407–9 *pregnant . . . birth*: see the idea of surrogate 'births' at 339–40; compare the scenario at Herodotos 5.41.

413 *'If . . . ruler'*: Euripides fr. 804.3 (*Phoinix*).

414 *women's quarters*: it was a standard practice for Athenian houses to be internally divided into male/female quarters, though exactly what this amounted to in practice would vary; cf. e.g. Lysias 1.9.3, Xenophon, *Oikonomikos* 9.5–6. The (clay) 'seals' in 415 are put on storeroom doors: see 424–8.

423 *Lakonian keys*: evidently an elaborate kind; cf. n. on 142.

430 *poison*: ironically this is itself an idea found in Euripidean tragedy; see esp. *Medea* 384–5. Cf. line 561.

432 *decree . . . scribe*: apart from the gender of the scribe (cf. 374), Mika talks like a male speaker proposing a decree in the city's Assembly.

433 *Strophe*: unusually, the matching antistrophe (see general Introduction, 'Formality and Performance') is not the next choral song (459 ff.) but the one after that (520 ff.).

440 *Xenokles*: see Index of Names; for Karkinos, cf. n. on *C*. 1261.

446 *Kypros*: we do not know of any Athenian actions on the island (under Persian control at this time) for several decades before this; there may or may not be a joke lurking here.

451 *gods*: the most extreme statement of atheism by a Euripidean character is Bellerophon's in fr. 286; passages such as *Hercules Furens* 1341–6 are somewhat less radical. Compare Sokrates at *C*. 247 ff.

456 *vegetable plots*: see n. on 387.

461–3 *verbiage . . . convincing*: a characteristic example of Aristophanic 'discontinuity' of characterization.

466 *Let me start*: various parts of the Kinsman's speech echo the defence speech of the disguised Telephos (see Index of Names and my Introduction to *WT*) in Euripides' play.

481 *scratched*: cf. *AW* 36 for scratching on a door as a prearranged signal.

486 *juniper*: juniper berries; the three ingredients are for a potion to settle an upset stomach.

489 *laurel*: sacred to Apollo; a pillar dedicated to the god stood outside some house doors (see n. on 748 and cf. *W*. 875).

495 *guarding the walls*: sentry duty on the city's walls was urgent at this date; see Thucydides 8.69.1.

499–501 *wife . . . house*: the scenario is taken from folktale, not ordinary reality—one of several symptoms of the Kinsman's absurd naivety.

504 *to help with the birth*: both drugs and amulets were sometimes used for this purpose.

518–19 *rage . . . we've done*: based on lines from Telephos's defence speech in Euripides' play (fr. 711).

520 *Antistrophe*: see n. on 433.

530 *orator*: this replaces 'scorpion' in the proverb referred to. Some scholars see here an allusion to current events in Athenian politics: see my Introduction to the play.

533 *Aglauros*: one of the daughters of the mythical Athenian king Kekrops (see *C*. 301); she committed suicide and had a shrine dedicated to her on the eastern slope of the Akropolis.

537 *ashes*: compare the violent genital depilation of an adulterer at *C*. 1083. Women sometimes used a lamp to singe off pubic hair (see *AW* 12–13, *L*. 828): Euripides' earlier treatment of his Kinsman at 215, 230 ff. was modelled on that practice. 'Pussy' in the next line is literally 'piglet'; cf. n. on 237.

547 *Melanippes . . . Phaidras*: Euripides wrote two plays about Melanippe, who

bore twins (after either rape or seduction) to the god Poseidon, and two about Phaidra (see Index of Names). The contrast with Odysseus's faithful wife is comically naive.

556 *scraper*: i.e. a 'strigil', a device with which athletes scraped olive oil (as a cleaning agent) off the body; the Kinsman probably envisages a type made of a hollow reed.

558–9 *meat . . . weasel*: the suggestion is that women bribe procuresses with meat left over from the Apatouria (a three-day festival which included a ritual, with animal sacrifice, for the admission of new members to the kinship group or phratry; cf. nn. on *F*. 417, 798) then tell their husbands it was taken by a weasel (kept as a vermin-killing house pet: cf. e.g. *W*. 363, *P*. 794).

561 *poison*: cf. n. on 430.

562–3 *Acharnian . . . bathtub*: Acharnai was one of the northernmost demes (n. on *C*. 134) of Attika; cf. *L*. 62 and the chorus of Aristophanes' *Acharnians*. The circumstantial details of these lines make one wonder whether there is reference to an actual sensational crime.

564–5 *boy . . . daughter*: economic reasons might lead to the preference for a boy over a girl; cf. n. on 340.

566 *two goddesses*: Demeter and Persephone; see nn. on 282, 383.

570 *gobbling*: the women were supposed to be fasting on this day of the Thesmophoria; cf. my Introduction to the play.

576 *spokesman*: Kleisthenes absurdly purports to be a *proxenos* (normally someone who semi-officially looked after another city's interests in his own city; cf. *B*. 1021) for the women.

586 *end . . . deed*: parts of the exchange between chorus-leader and Kleisthenes parody some of the stylized dialogue conventions of tragedy.

594 *goddesses two*: the Kinsman tries to use a typical female oath; cf. n. on 383.

602 *spokesman*: see n. on 576.

605 *Kleonymos*: see Index of Names. For the practice of publicly identifying women by the names of male relatives, see 619, 840–1, with n. on *C*. 46–7.

620 *Kothokidai*: a small, remote deme (n. on *C*. 134) in NW Attika.

624 *tent*: the women lived in a tented village on the Akropolis for the duration of the Thesmophoria.

638 *breast-band*: see n. on 138–9.

639 *she*: Mika incongruously continues to refer to the Kinsman as though he *were* a woman.

647–8 *isthmus . . . Korinth*: see Index of Names, s.v. Korinth.

654 *Prytaneis*: see Index of Names.

658 *Pnyx . . . tents*: the Pnyx was the hill west of the Akropolis where the Athenian Assembly met; the women are notionally on the Akropolis itself (83, 281) but in keeping with their Assembly-like procedures (nn. on 278,

295–311, 335–8, etc.) speak momentarily as though they were on the Pnyx. For tents, see n. on 624.

672 *the gods*: the chorus talk as though an infiltrator of their rituals would by definition be a non-believer in the traditional gods; cf. Kritylla's view of Euripides at 450–1.

690 *baby*: the Kinsman's seizure of the 'baby' (see 733) activates paratragedy based on Euripides' *Telephos*; cf. my Introduction to the play, with the Index of Names, s.v. Telephos.

697 *trophy*: normally erected on the battlefield by an already victorious army; here comically proleptic—or perhaps we are meant simply to infer that Mika is ignorant of military matters.

700 *Fates*: the Moirai, goddesses responsible for determining the length and other inescapable elements of each human life; see *B.* 1734, *F.* 453, with e.g. Hesiod, *Theogony* 217, 904.

727 *set him on fire*: for such comically extreme behaviour, cf. the male chorus's intentions at *L.* 269–70, as well as the form of Strepsiades' revenge at the end of *Clouds*.

734 *Persian bootees*: two of the tied ends of the wineskin have been fitted with miniature slippers (cf. *C.* 151), as seen in the illustration of the scene on an Apulian 4th-century vase cited in n. 91 to the general Introduction.

738 *No wonder*: i.e. because they are drunk.

741 *nine*: the Greek says 'ten', but that is a kind of inclusive counting.

746 *vintage*: the Greek refers to the Choes ('Wine-jugs') festival; cf. *A.* 1000–2. The Kinsman puns on counting a baby's years and the age of a wine.

747 *Dionysiac*: Athens had several Dionysia, festivals of Dionysos; all that matters is the allusion to Dionysos as god of wine.

748 *right here*: the Kinsman gestures towards a statue of Apollo outside the stage building; cf. n. on 489.

758 *perk*: a priest(-ess) would often be allowed to keep part of a sacrificial animal.

770–1 *Palamedes . . . oars*: a scene from Euripides' play *Palamedes* (see Index of Names), staged in 415; was there an ironic reference to Palamedes as himself the mythic inventor of writing?

773 *tablets*: wooden votive dedications lying on or near the altar.

781 *rho*: i.e. 'r'; one might imagine the Kinsman as having reached the third letter of Euripides' name.

785 *Step forward*: the Greek verb here is the one from which the term 'parabasis' derives; cf. *P.* 735 and see the general Introduction, 'Formality and Performance'. The present parabasis is in truncated form; it lacks songs and has only a single 'epirrhematic' section (contrast e.g. *C.* 510–626 for the full form).

790 *forbid . . . doors*: this presupposes a social protocol subscribed to (though

not necessarily upheld in all respects) by 'respectable' (and in practice wealthier) Athenian families, whereby women led much of their lives indoors and did not move freely in public; cf. e.g. *L.* 16, *AW* 335–41.

795 *visit . . . dancing*: women did socialize in this way, sometimes for festivals like the Adonia (*L.* 389–96); cf. *AW* 348–9, *L.* 700–1 (with a special twist).

797–9 *peek . . . peeking*: prostitutes might lurk alluringly in this way (cf. *AW* 924–5); but the passage interestingly hints at the sexual charge that might be generated even by such rare glimpses of 'respectable' women (cf. n. on 790). Compare *P.* 979–85.

804 *Nausimache . . . Charminos*: Nausimache means 'naval battle'; Charminos was a general who had suffered a recent naval defeat to the Spartans (Thucydides 8.41–3).

805 *Salabaccho*: a prostitute whose name occurs also at *K.* 765; Kleophon was a radical politician associated with an aggressive stance on the war (see n. on *F.* 678).

806–7 *Aristomache . . . Stratonike*: the first means 'best fighter', the second 'army victory'. Aristomache is called 'Marathonian' simply because the famous victory over the Persians at Marathon (Index of Names) was indeed remembered as the Athenians' 'best'. The logic, militarily speaking, is of course absurd.

808–9 *Euboule . . . somebody else*: Euboule means 'good council/counsel'; in 413–12 the Athenians had partly curbed the powers of the Council (see Index of Names) by the temporary appointment of a group of ten (later thirty) *Probouloi*, 'Commissioners' (see *L.* 387 with Thucydides 8.1.3).

811–13 *No woman . . . same day*: the Leader contrasts major misappropriation of public funds by a male politician (actual or generic is unclear), then pictured as hypocritically taking part in the Panathenaic procession (see n. on *C.* 69), with the petty domestic filching supposedly (i.e. comically) typical of Athenian wives.

823 *parasols*: in origin a Greek borrowing from the Near East; rarely used by Greek men, hence the piquancy of Prometheus's parasol at *B.* 1494–1551. For the idea of women as naturally conservative in habits, compare *AW* 221–8.

827–9 *thrown . . . parasol*: the women give an absurd twist to the idea of cowardly soldiers throwing away their shields in order to flee from battle.

834–5 *Stenia . . . our own*: the Stenia (just before the Thesmophoria) and Skira (cf. *AW* 18, 59) were examples of festivals exclusive to women.

838 *cropped close*: the reference is to a rounded hairstyle suitable only for a slave; cf. *A.* 849, *B.* 806.

845 *loans . . . loins*: the Greek puns on a noun (*tokos*) which can mean both interest on a loan and offspring; for Hyperbolos and Lamachos, see Index of Names.

850 *recent*: staged in the previous year (412).

855–7 *Lo . . . dwell*: these lines borrow Euripides, *Helen* 1–2, plus a line that starts from *Helen* 3 but then veers away from its model (and refers incongruously to an Egyptian fondness for purges: cf. *P.* 1253–4). The main correspondences to *Helen* in what follows (in some cases only parts of lines, and with some differences of detail) are: *WT* 859–60 ~ *Helen* 16–17, *WT* 862 ~ *Helen* 22, *WT* 864–5 ~ *Helen* 52–3, *WT* 866 ~ *Helen* 49, *WT* 868 ~ *Helen* 56, *WT* 871 ~ *Helen* 68, *WT* 874 ~ *Helen* 460, *WT* 878 ~ *Helen* 461, *WT* 881: cf. *Helen* 467, *WT* 886 ~ *Helen* 466, *WT* 905 ~ *Helen* 72 + 557, *WT* 906 ~ *Helen* 558, *WT* 907–12 ~ *Helen* 561–6.

858 *Hekate*: see Index of Names.

860 *Tyndareos*: King of Sparta, notional human 'father' of Helen, though Zeus himself had seduced her mother, Leda.

861 *Phrynondas*: a proverbial malefactor.

864 *Skamander*: one of the rivers of Troy; cf. *F.* 928.

868 *ravens aren't hungry*: lit. 'because of the poor quality of the ravens' (sc. in failing to eat you). Compare the curse 'To the crows/ravens' at line 1079, with n. on *C.* 789.

870 *deceive me not*: the first half of the line is actually based not on Euripides but on Sophokles fr. 493 (*Peleus*).

874–6 *Proteus . . . Proteas*: Proteus was an Egyptian king with whom, on the version followed in Euripides' *Helen* (line 4; cf. Herodotos 2.112–20), Helen resided for the duration of the Trojan War. Kritylla, using a female oath (cf. n. on 383), confuses him with a contemporary Athenian (the name is found as that of a general at Thucydides 1.45.2).

880 *Thesmophorion*: see n. on 83.

894 *to steal*: Kritylla makes a common-sense but mistaken assumption about why a man has infiltrated a women's festival.

897 *Theonoe*: in Euripides' *Helen* a priestess who gives Helen advice and assistance; 'crone' (896) rather suggests the abusive doorkeeper at *Helen* 437 ff. (whose words the Kinsman himself had adapted at 874, 886).

898 *Kritylla*: after her own name she identifies herself, as is the norm for respectable women in public (see n. on 605), by her husband and his deme (cf. e.g. *C.* 134).

902 *What did you say?*: what follows is based on the recognition scene between Helen and Menelaos at Euripides, *Helen* 526–96 (cf. n. on 855–7).

903 *cheeks*: the Kinsman alludes, with absurd incongruity, to his earlier shaving (221 ff.).

919 *Tyndareos*: cf. n. on 860.

931 *plank*: the reference is to a brutal form of imprisonment/torture (and sometimes execution) in which five metal clamps (1003) fastened a person's neck, arms, and legs to a wooden board. Cf. n. on *C.* 591–2.

935 *Egyptian sailor*: Kritylla says 'a sail-stitcher', probably an allusion to

Egyptian linen production and/or the rags in which Euripides is costumed.

949 *Pauson . . . fast*: Pauson is also mocked for poverty/hunger at *We*. 602 and as a parasite at *A*. 854; he may be the caricaturist painter of e.g. Aristotle, *Poetics* 2.1448a6. Here his hunger is satirically assimilated to the ritual fasting on this day of the Thesmophoria (Index of Names).

962 *slander*: a reference to the traditional expectation of satirical songs from a comic chorus. Is the passage an allusion to avoidance of political topicality at a time of dangerous political developments in Athens? See my Introduction to the play.

972 *victory*: the Chorus speaks momentarily in its theatrical rather than dramatic persona.

973–6 *Hera . . . marriage*: Hera, consort of Zeus, was traditionally a goddess of marriage.

988 *Bacchic god*: Dionysos (see Index of Names); the following part of the song celebrates him.

990–1 *Euios . . . Bromios*: two cult titles of Dionysos, the former derived from ritual exclamations ('euoi', 994); both are used frequently in e.g. Euripides' *Bacchae*.

996 *Kithaironian*: Mt Kithairon, near Thebes (birthplace of Dionysos).

1001 *'Ere den . . .*: for the Archer's 'pidgin' Greek, see the general Introduction, 'Translating Aristophanes'.

1012 *Andromeda*: daughter of Kepheus, king of the Ethiopians; she was tied to a rock by her father as propitiatory sacrifice to a sea-monster (sent by Poseidon to punish the family), but was rescued by the hero Perseus, returning from killing and decapitating the Gorgon Medusa (cf. 1102). Euripides' play on the theme was produced the previous year, 412 (at the same festival as *Helen*: n. on 855–7); see n. on 1015 with my Introduction to *WT*.

1015 *Dear maidens*: this opening is taken directly from the heroine's song to the chorus in Euripides' *Andromeda* (fr. 117). The precise extent of other borrowings from the play, obviously diluted by various comic incongruities, is uncertain; but the following quotations/adaptations are reasonably secure: *WT* 1018–19 ~ fr. 118, *WT* 1021–2 ~ fr. 120, *WT* 1029–39 ~ fr. 122, *WT* 1065–9 ~ fr. 114, *WT* 1070–2 ~ fr. 115, *WT* 1098–1100 ~ fr. 124.1–3, *WT* 1101–2 ~ fr. 123/124.5–6(?), *WT* 1105–6 ~ fr. 125.1–2.

1018 *you who sing*: i.e. Echo, who repeated parts of Andromeda's lament from a cave in Euripides' play.

1033 *Glauketes*: the name of a contemporary satirized at *P*. 1008 as a glutton.

1044 *saffron*: see n. on 138–9.

1061 *role*: a particularly ironic case of 'metatheatre'; see my Introduction to the play.

1069 *Olympos*: the name here connotes not just the mountain (Index of Names) but the whole sky.

1103 *Gorgos . . . scribe*: Gorgos was evidently secretary (n. on 372–9) to the Council at this time or in the recent past but is not otherwise known.

1130 *Bringing words . . .*: the line is a quotation from Euripides, *Medea* 298.

1142 *holder of the keys*: the reason for the term is not clear but the keys imagined may be those to the treasury in the Parthenon; for Pallas as a cult title of Athena, see Index of Names.

1149 *mistress deities*: Demeter and Persephone; see nn. on 83, 282.

1158 *Come now . . .*: cf. n. on 319.

1168–9 *denounce . . . secret*: Euripides alludes to the same male stereotype of women's behaviour used previously by the Kinsman in his speech at 466–519; for the assumption that most Athenian males are away on military campaigns, cf. *L.* 99–104.

1195 *drachma*: probably a high price for a prostitute's services; cf. nn. on *C.* 21, 118, *F.* 173.

1200 *Artemisia*: the best-known holder of this name was the queen of Halikarnassos who accompanied the Persian Xerxes on his invasion of Greece in 480; cf. *L.* 675, with Herodotos 7.99, etc. But it here serves as an amusingly pretentious name for a disreputable bawd of the kind Euripides impersonates.

1230 *Thesmophoroi*: see n. on 282.

FROGS

3 *hard-pressed*: i.e. by carrying a heavy load; Dionysos warns Xanthias off clichéd jokes about the physical labour of slaves. Cf. an ironic joke on the same Greek verb by the jester at Xenophon, *Symposium* 1.11.

13–14 *Phrynichos . . . Ameipsias*: three contemporary comic poets, the first and third both well established and successful; Phrynichos (cf. n. on *C.* 553–7) was actually competing against *Frogs* at this same festival with a play called *Muses*.

18 *a year*: a kind of temporal pun, since the major dramatic festivals were annual.

33 *sea-fight*: the battle of Arginousai in summer 406 (an Athenian victory but with heavy losses of men; cf. n. on 541), after which slaves who had fought for the city were given freedom and citizenship (cf. 190–1, 693–4).

38 *Centaur*: see Index of Names.

46 *saffron dress*: see n. on *WT* 138–9.

47 *boots*: high boots of a kind worn mostly by women (the same sort at *L.* 657, *AW* 346) but sometimes forming part of an 'effeminate' Dionysiac costume; cf. 557. The whole line resembles *WT* 136–40 and may echo the same Aischylean text as there (n. on *WT* 135).

48 *Kleisthenes*: see Index of Names.

49–50 *sea-fight . . . ships*: another reference to Arginousai (n. on 33).

52–3 *read to myself . . . Andromeda*: the context (on a ship) seems pointedly odd, but the line may still allude to the growing practice of reading plays in the late fifth century; cf. n. on 1114. For the *Andromeda*, see *WT* 1011 ff., with my Introduction to that play.

55 *Molon*: Dionysos probably refers ironically to someone (possibly a tragic actor) who was known for his considerable size.

62 *soup*: in comedy Herakles often had the persona of a glutton; cf. 107, 549 ff., with e.g. *W.* 60, *B.* 1583–90, and fr. 11 (Appendix).

73 *Iophon*: son of Sophokles and a tragic playwright himself for many years by this date. Sophokles had died a few months after Euripides in the second half of 406 (when Aristophanes was already writing *Frogs*). See my Introduction to the play.

82 *even-tempered*: our best evidence for Sophokles' personality is the vignette of him (going back to his contemporary Ion of Chios) at a dinner-party in Athenaios, *Dinner-Sophists* 13.603e–4f. Cf. n. on 788.

83–5 *Agathon . . . land of plenty*: for Agathon see Index of Names, with *WT* 29–265; the Greek puns on (i) the traditional idea of 'the islands of the blessed' (a privileged afterlife for a special few) and (ii) the luxury of the Makedonian court of King Archelaos, where Agathon was receiving patronage (as Euripides had done before him: n. on 953).

86–7 *Xenokles . . . Pythangelos*: for the former see Index of Names; Pythangelos was evidently also a minor tragedian, but is otherwise unknown.

100–2 *'Aither . . . mind'*: on Aither see Index of Names; Dionysos (mis-)quotes from Euripides fr. 487 (see n. on *WT* 272), *Bacchae* 889, and (*very* loosely) *Hippolytos* 612 (cf. nn. on 1471, *WT* 275–6).

111 *Kerberos*: guard-dog of Hades, usually depicted as three-headed; Herakles kidnapped him as one of his labours. Cf. 187, 467.

126 *freezing them*: hemlock is depicted as having this chilling effect on Sokrates in the famous passage at Plato, *Phaedo* 117e–18a.

129 *Kerameikos*: lit. 'Potters' district', in the NW part of the city, including Athens' largest burial-ground (part of the joke here?); cf. nn. on 422–7, 1093, with *K.* 772, *B.* 395. The tower in line 130 cannot be identified for certain.

131 *torch-race*: a type of event, found in several Athenian festivals, in which the runners carried torches; some evidently started in the Kerameikos. Cf. 1089–98.

134 *mincemeat . . . brain*: the Greek puns on a word which can mean (i) a fig-leaf stuffed with food (including animal brains: cf. fr. 128, Appendix), (ii) a hemisphere of the brain.

137–40 *lake . . . obols*: the Acherousian lake (or Acheron, cf. 471), over which souls of the dead are ferried in Charon's boat (180 ff.). 'Two obols', a third of a drachma (cf. nn. on 173, *C.* 118), combines (i) a reference to coins put in the mouth of the dead as a notional 'fare' for Charon's ferry, and (ii) an allusion to a daily dole paid to poorer citizens (on the proposal of Kleophon: see Index of Names) for certain periods during the later years of the war.

142 *Theseus*: mythological Athenian king/hero; he went down to Hades to help his friend Peirithoos and was eventually rescued by Herakles.

145 *mud*: this idea (cf. the Orphic beliefs at Plato, *Republic* 2.363d) may have been part of Eleusinian imagery; 'river of shit' is comic overkill (cf. fr. 156.13 in the Appendix).

151 *Morsimos*: minor tragic poet (and grand-nephew of Aischylos); cf. *K.* 400–1, *P.* 802.

153 *Kinesias*: see Index of Names; here apparently thought of as writing (bad) music to a type of dance in armour; cf. 366, 1437.

159 *proverbial donkey*: evidently denoting someone who does all the work without any reward; humorously harks back to the donkey in the play's opening scene.

165 *bedding*: part of the baggage consists of mats, pillows, etc., for sleeping on the journey; cf. slaves carrying bedding on a journey at Xenophon, *Memorabilia* 3.13.6.

173 *two drachmas*: cf. nn. on 137–40, *WT* 1195; no doubt a high price for a porter's service. Dionysos offers one-and-a-half drachmas (nine obols, 177).

185–7 *Plain of Forgetting . . . Tainaron*: the list of destinations jumbles traditional underworld geography, euphemisms for death, and a real place (Tainaron: the central S tip of the Peloponnese) where there was supposedly an entrance to Hades. 'Crows' end' links to the expression in 189 (for which see n. on *C.* 789).

191 *sea-fight*: see n. on 33.

204 *Salamis type*: the island of Salamis, off the W coast of Attika and location of the famous naval defeat of the Persians in 480, was a traditional source of good Athenian sailors/rowers; cf. *AW* 37–9.

215–19 *Nysa . . . precinct*: Nysa, a probably mythic mountain (outside Greece), was sacred to Dionysos. The frogs then refer to the third day ('Pots') of the Anthesteria festival, celebrated in the precinct of Dionysos 'in the marshes' (somewhere south of the Akropolis: Thucydides 2.15.4).

229–34 *Muses . . . marshes*: for the musical deities with whom the frogs identify themselves (as if they were in the 'high' tradition of Greek poetry) see the Index of Names. For Apollo's phorminx, cf. *WT* 327.

270 *two obols*: see n. on 137–40.

282 *There's nothing . . .*: an adaptation (with 'Herakles' for 'a man') of a line from Euripides, fr. 788.1 (*Philoktetes*).

293 *Empousa*: a bogey figure of Greek folklore with supposedly prodigious shape-shifting powers; cf. *AW* 1056 ('spook' in my translation), fr. 515 (apparently identifying Empousa with Hekate: cf. Index of Names).

297 *priest . . . later*: a priest of Dionysos (in whose shrine the theatre was located) was seated in the front row; Dionysos, as god of theatre, envisages a drinking-party (for the cast) after the performance. Cf. *A.* 1085–7.

304 *weasel*: the word is here a mispronunciation (a notorious slip by Hegelochos, a tragic actor) of a word meaning 'calm seas'; the line is taken from Euripides, *Orestes* 279. For weasels as house-pets, see n. on *WT* 558–9.

311 *Aither . . . time*: see line 100.

316 *Iakchos*: a divine name invoked during the procession of initiates from Athens to Eleusis and sometimes identified (outside *Frogs*) with Dionysos himself.

320 *Agora*: see the Index of Names; the procession to Eleusis probably started from the Agora.

338–9 *pig flesh . . . sausage*: piglets were (probably) sacrificed on one of the preliminary days of the Eleusinian Mysteries; some scholars also detect sexual doubles entendres here (for piglets as female genitalia cf. n. on *WT* 237).

354–71 *the following section* [stage direction]: this section has something in common with the 'anapaests' usually found in the parabasis (see general Introduction, 'Formality and Performance'). The parabasis proper in *Frogs* lacks such a section, as though it has been brought forward to this point, where it is a comic version of a proclamation (excluding the impure, etc.) made on the first day of the Eleusinian Mysteries.

357 *Kratinos*: the leading comic playwright of the period 450–420; cf. e.g. *A.* 849, *K.* 400, *P.* 700, with my general Introduction, 'Aristophanes' Career in Context'. 'Bull-eating' was a cult title of Dionysos: Kratinos is comically treated as the god of comedy (which is assimilated to a Dionysiac 'mystery' religion).

363 *Thorykion*: cf. 382 but otherwise unknown; presumably a real figure who had abused his position as collector of a 5 per cent tax on seaborne goods (see Thucydides 7.28.4) to sell contraband via the island of Aigina to Epidauros in the NE Peloponnese.

366 *who shits*: a reference to an embarrassing/impious episode (actual or maliciously invented) involving Kinesias (n. on 153); on Hekate, see Index of Names.

367 *fees*: we have no other evidence on how much money playwrights received for having their plays performed at dramatic festivals, but evidently some payment was involved.

378 *Saviouress*: probably Athena, but just possibly Persephone.

392 *playful humour*: cf. 374–5, 404, 416 ff.; there were in fact several opportunities for laughter and mirth in the course of the Eleusinian festivities; but the chorus's identity here is a sort of melding of Eleusinian and comic personae (cf. my Introduction to the play).

406 *rags*: some Eleusinian initiates deliberately wore old clothes which were

dedicated after the festival; cf. *We.* 845. The suggestion is that the producer of *Frogs* (Philonides) has saved costs by giving the comic chorus correspondingly cheap costumes.

417 *Archedemos*: a prominent politician at this date but here satirically accused of not being a legitimate Athenian citizen (hence not having been introduced as a young child into a traditional kinship group or 'phratry': see n. on 798); cf. 588. The Greek involves an untranslatable pun on growing teeth and belonging to a phratry.

422–7 *Kleisthenes' son . . . Anaphlystos*: we know nothing else about the son of Kleisthenes (see Index of Names), here obscenely depicted in behaviour which mixes gestures of bereavement with a desire to be sodomized (probably as a prostitute: 'tombstones' hints at one of the seedier associations of the Kerameikos area of the city; cf. n. on 129). Anaphlystos was an Athenian deme, but the context activates a pun on a slang term for 'masturbate'.

428–30 *Kallias . . . lion-skin*: Kallias was a member of one of the richest Athenian aristocratic families, a patron of intellectuals (Plato's *Protagoras* is set in his house) but ridiculed in comedy (cf. *B.* 283–4) for a profligate, sexually scandalous life-style; his father's name Hipponikos ('horse-victor') is changed to the obscene Hippobinos. Cf. frs. 117, 583 in the Appendix.

439 *same old story*: the Greek says lit. 'Korinthos son of Zeus', a proverb derived from the Korinthians' harping on their divine founder; cf. *AW* 828.

453 *Fates*: see n. on *WT* 700.

470–7 *Styx . . . Teithras*: the Doorkeeper, with quasi-tragic rhetorical vehemence, mentions three underworld rivers/lakes (cf. Homer, *Odyssey* 10.513–14), before bathetically linking the Gorgons (snake-haired monsters, including Medusa: see n. on *WT* 1012), as though they were merely feisty human women, to the real deme of Teithras in E Attika.

516 *trimmed*: i.e. their pubic hair; cf. e.g. *L.* 89, 151.

531 *Alkmene's son*: Herakles (Index of Names).

541 *Theramenes*: a politician with a reputation for side-switching adroitness; cf. 967–70. In 411 he helped both to set up and overthrow the oligarchy of the Four Hundred (cf. Introduction to *WT*): Thucydides 8.68, 89 ff. After the battle of Arginousai in 406 (n. on 33) he succeeded in pinning blame on the generals (six were executed: n. on 1196) for failing to pick up shipwrecked survivors, though he himself had failed to do so with his own ship. He was later part of the oligarchy of the Thirty imposed on Athens by Sparta at the end of the war; feuds within the group led to his execution.

542 *Milesian*: woollen fabrics from Miletos, a Greek city in Asia Minor, were prized for their fine quality (cf. *L.* 729).

545 *winkle*: the Greek here uses the term 'chickpea' in a slang sense.

546–8 *caught sight . . . mouth*: it is hard (one hopes) for a modern reader to get the humour of something which depends on imagining role-reversal in a scene in which a master violently punishes a slave for voyeurism.

557 *boots*: see n. on 47; the Innkeeper absurdly talks as though footwear could be the key to recognition of another person.

569–70 *Kleon . . . destroy*: see Index of Names for Kleon and Hyperbolos; they are imagined as (still) politically active on the side of ordinary people in Hades.

574 *pit*: see n. on *C.* 1450.

582–3 *'mortal slave' . . . 'Alkmene's son'*: Xanthias ironically echoes Dionysos's words at 531.

588 *Archedemos*: see n. on 417. The preceding line is, of course, an oath fit for an ordinary person, not a god.

590 *Strophe*: the metrical form of 590–604 corresponds to that of 534–48.

608 *Ditylas* . . .: all three names are probably parodic of non-Greek slave-names.

616 *torture*: Athenian law allowed the evidence of slaves to be adduced in court only if it had been extracted under torture; a defendant, as here, might offer his slaves as a supposed sign of his innocence. Cf. *C.* 620 and e.g. *We.* 875–6.

651 *Diomeia*: an Athenian deme just south of the city walls; the location of an important annual festival (at Kynosarges) in honour of Herakles.

661 *Hipponax*: late 6th-century author of vigorous satirical poems (*iamboi*) in which one can imagine a character exclaiming vehemently.

664–7 *Poseidon . . . depths*: Dionysos yelps with pain then tries to mask his reaction by quoting (loosely) from an invocation to Poseidon in Sophokles' *Laocoon* (fr. 371).

671 *Pherrephatta*: another name for Persephone (Index of Names).

674 PARABASIS: here in a shortened form; see n. on 354–71, with my general Introduction, 'Formality and Performance'.

678 *Kleophon*: see Index of Names; he is here depicted as of barbarian origin and in danger of being condemned in court even on a split vote (which in Athenian law usually produced an *acquittal*). Kleophon was in fact subsequently accused (and executed) by his political opponents on a dubious charge at the end of the war (Lysias 13.12, 30.13).

689 *Phrynichos*: a leading oligarchic conspirator in 411; see esp. Thucydides 8.48, 68, 92.

693–4 *those . . . masters*: another reference (see n. on 33) to the enfranchisement of slaves who fought at Arginousai, here compared with Plataians who had been made citizens of Athens after the destruction of Plataia (just to the NW of Attika) by Sparta in 427 (see Demosthenes 59.104).

704 *'Tossed on stormy waves'*: the phrase is taken from a poem by the 7th-century poet Archilochos (fr. 213 *IEG*).

706 *'If my eye . . .'*: a quotation from a tragedy by Ion of Chios (fr. 41).

709 *Kleigenes*: probably more than a bath-keeper; perhaps a political ally of Kleophon (678).

720–6 *old coins . . . stamped*: a reference to a change from Athens' traditional silver coinage (and some special gold coinage minted in 406) to inferior (probably silver-plated) bronze coinage; for later changes in coinage, cf. *AW* 815–22.

734 *idiots*: abuse of the audience is a stock element in Old Comedy (and affects the tone of the present passage); compare e.g. 276, 783, *C.* 1095–1102.

764 *dining rights*: in Athens such rights were bestowed on various people (certain politicians, officials, victorious athletes, and others); cf. e.g. *K.* 535, 766, *P.* 1084. Despite its name, the Prytaneion was not used by Prytaneis (see Index of Names).

788 *not like that*: this implies something similar to the idea of Sophokles' easy-going personality at 82.

791 *Kleidemides*: we have no idea who he was or in what sort of context he was supposed to have behaved in a manner analogous to Sophokles' attitude here.

798 *meat*: the reference is to a ritual at the Apatouria festival (cf. n. on *WT* 558–9), at which fathers weighed sacrificial meat before introducing their sons to the kinship group (phratry); cf. n. on 417, with fr. 299 (Appendix).

830 *the throne*: cf. 765–90. Some scholars think the chair was physically brought on stage (perhaps on the *ekkuklêma* or trolley: see the general Introduction, 'Stage Directions'), together with a throne for Plouton. But the text does little to encourage this view.

840 *'son of . . .'*: a distortion of Euripides fr. 885 (with 'fields' for 'sea') and a gibe at the supposed profession of the poet's mother (see n. on *WT* 387).

842 *beggars . . . rag-costume-stitcher*: Euripides had long had a (comic) reputation for creating tragic heroes (including Telephos: Index of Names) who appeared onstage as (disguised) beggars or in rags; cf. 1063, *A.* 412–34.

844 *'Don't let . . .'*: the line has all the hallmarks of an Aischylean quotation (fr. 468).

846 *cripples*: a running gibe against Euripides (see esp. *A.* 411, *P.* 146–8); one conspicuous case was that of Bellerophon (Index of Names), who in the play named after him fell from Pegasos and appeared onstage mortally wounded.

847 *black sheep*: sacrificed to avert a storm.

849–50 *monodies . . . incest*: monodies (solo songs) were characteristic of Euripides' later plays; see 944, 1330 (and the parody that follows it). Euripides wrote several plays with Cretan themes; cf. n. on 1356. For the motif of incest see 1081 with n. on *C.* 1372.

855 *Telephos*: Euripides' symbolic 'brains'; see Index of Names.

862 *sinews*: see n. 17 to my Introduction to the play.

863–4 *Peleus . . . Telephos: Peleus* probably dealt with the hero's life prior to his marriage to Thetis (cf. *C.* 1063–7) and his fathering of Achilles. For *Aiolos* see n. on *C.* 1372, for *Meleager* n. on 1240–1 below, for *Telephos* the Index of Names.

886–7 *Demeter . . . Mysteries*: Aischylos was born in the area of Eleusis; cf. Index of Names, s.v. Mysteries.

890 *coinage*: for gods as currency/coinage, cf. *C.* 247–9.

892–3 *Aither . . . Nostrils*: on Aither, which *characters* in Euripides sometimes treat as a god (e.g. fr. 941), see Index of Names. For Tongue as a quasi-sophistic deity, cf. *C.* 424. Astuteness: reclaimed for Aischylos at 1483, 1490. Nostrils: possibly implying contemptuous sneering.

904 *a horse's*: the reference is to a horse rolling on the ground after exercise to remove sweat; cf. n. on *C.* 32.

910 *Phrynichos*: an early tragic playwright (active *c.*510–470), thus different from those mentioned in lines 13 and 689. Cf. 1299, *WT* 164.

912–13 *Achilles . . . silence*: the reference is to protracted dramatic silences by the main characters in Aischylos' *Myrmidons* (= the Thessalian tribe of Achilles) and *Niobe* (where the heroine mourned the loss of her many children, killed by Apollo).

928–9 *Skamander . . . eagles*: for Skamander see *WT* 864; the compound (and unique) Greek noun for 'griffin-eagles' was probably found in Aischylos (fr. 422).

932 *'tawny horse-cock'*: a phrase from Aischylos' *Myrmidons* (cf. n. on 912–13), fr. 134; cf. *P.* 1177, *B.* 800. The hybrid figure in question was a kind of winged horse found in the visual symbolism of the late archaic period.

934 *Eryxis*: we know too little about this figure to guess why it was funny to identify him as a 'horse-cock'.

943–4 *books . . . Kephisophon*: Euripides was reputed to have a large private library; cf. 1409, with n. on 1114 for books more generally. For monodies, see n. on 849–50. About Kephisophon we know nothing for certain, but he is treated in comedy as a collaborator of some kind with Euripides and perhaps a member of his household (some later sources said a slave); cf. 1408, 1452–3, and fr. 596 in the Appendix.

953 *not a direction*: either because of some of Euripides' associates (see 968 with n.; and perhaps also Sokrates?, cf. 1492) or because he moved to the Makedonian court of Archelaos for the last part of his life (cf. n. on 83–5).

957 *crafty*: cf. *WT* 94. The ethos of Euripides' plays is characterized here as a sort of cross between philosophical questioning and neurotic suspiciousness.

963 *Kyknos . . . Memnon*: two victims of Achilles in the Trojan War; on Memnon cf. n. on *C.* 622. We do not know where Kyknos appeared in Aischylos, but Memnon was the subject of an entire trilogy of plays.

965–7 *Phormisios . . . Theramenes*: if Phormisios (probably a politician) is the same man as at *AW* 97, the joke here may depend simply on his shaggy appearance; Megainetos is unknown. Kleitophon and Theramenes (see n. on 541) were two figures towards the oligarchic end of the political spectrum who also moved in intellectual circles (Kleitophon is present at the conversation in Plato's *Republic*: 328b, 340a–b).

970 *dicey*: there is a pun in the Greek on dice-throws and place-names which no one has satisfactorily decoded; but Theramenes' ability to escape from tight corners is clearly the basis of the joke.

992 *'Beholdest . . . Achilles?'*: from the opening of Aischylos' *Myrmidons*, fr. 131, where the chorus beseech their silent leader, Achilles; cf. n. on 912–13.

1017 *seven full ox-hides*: an echo of the description of Ajax's shield at Homer, *Iliad* 7.220, etc.

1021 *Seven against Thebes*: produced in 467; it concerns the mutually fatal encounter between Oedipus's sons, Eteokles and Polyneikes (and is therefore hardly an encouragement to martial valour!).

1026–7 *Persians . . . glorified*: *Persians*, produced in 472, dramatizes Persian reactions to the news of Xerxes' defeat in the battle of Salamis; its 'glorification' of Athenian success is set against a partly tragic view of the enemy's sufferings. Dionysos's (approximate) recollection in 1028–9 of the scene involving the ghost of Dareios refers to *Persians* 681–851.

1032–4 *Orpheus . . . Homer*: various collections of poems passed apocryphally under the names of the mythical singers Orpheus and Musaios (the latter from Eleusis and occasionally treated as son of the former). Hesiod (*c.*700 BC) was author of, among other things, *Works and Days*, a didactic poem about farming. Homer's *Iliad* (*c.*700) could also be (naively) thought of as didactic in matters military.

1036 *Pantakles*: possibly a contemporary lyric poet of the same name.

1039 *Lamachos*: see Index of Names.

1043 *Phaidra . . . Stheneboia*: see Index of Names under Phaidra and (for Stheneboia) Bellerophon. Both women made false sexual allegations against men with whom they had fallen in love.

1048 *own life*: we do not have reliable biographical information to shed light on this apparently sexual allusion.

1051 *Bellerophon*: see Index of Names.

1057 *Lykabettos . . . Parnassos*: Lykabettos is a hill NE of the Akropolis in Athens; for Parnassos, see Index of Names.

1061 *clothes*: possibly a reference to theatrical tragic costume or to depictions in visual art.

1063–4 *rags . . . pitiful*: see n. on 842.

1065 *pay for a warship*: the costs of maintaining warships were charged to wealthy citizens as a form of taxation ('liturgy': see *OCD*[4] 850).

1070–1 *emptied . . . chatter*: the same charges brought against modern 'immoral' education at e.g. *C.* 1052–4.

1071–3 *Paraloi . . . benches*: the Paraloi were the rowing-crew of one of two Athenian triremes used for official state business; they had shown special loyalty to the democracy during the oligarch coup of 411 (Thucydides 8.86.9).

1079–82 *women . . . death*: the Nurse in *Hippolytos* acts as a go-between; the mother of Telephos (Index of Names) gave birth to him in a shrine in *Auge*; there was sibling incest in *Aiolos* (n. on *C.* 1372); for 'life is death', see n. on 1477.

1087 *carry a torch*: i.e. in a torch-race (cf. n. on 131) in the Panathenaia (see Index of Names).

1093 *Kerameikos*: cf. n. on 129, with n. on 131 for the torch-race in question.

1114 *a book*: this seems prima facie to refer to the availability of texts of (some) tragedies and the growing size of a 'reading public'; but there is much dispute about exactly what we can infer from the passage. Cf. nn. on 52, 943–4.

1124 *Oresteia*: the trilogy (produced in 458) comprising *Agamemnon, Choephoroi, Eumenides*. Aischylos proceeds to quote from the second play, *Choephoroi* 1–3 (spoken by Orestes).

1144 *Eriounian*: a traditional epithet of Hermes (see Index of Names), but of uncertain meaning.

1150 *wine . . . stench*: Aischylos uses the idea of malodorous breath (ironically of the god of wine) as a gibe conveying general disdain.

1172–3 *'Upon the mound . . .'*: Aischylos, *Choephoroi* 4–5.

1181 *standards of diction*: the terminology here is related to contemporary studies in proto-linguistics and stylistics by Protagoras and other intellectuals; cf. n. on *C.* 659.

1182 *'A time there was . . .'*: the first line of Euripides' *Antigone* (fr. 157).

1187 *'His fortunes changed . . .'*: Euripides fr. 158 (*Antigone*).

1192 *Polybos*: after being exposed at birth, Oedipus was brought up by Polybos, king of Korinth, and grew up mistakenly believing him to be his father; cf. Sophokles, *Oedipus Tyrannus* 774, 827.

1196 *Erasinides*: one of six generals executed the previous year for failing to pick up survivors after the battle of Arginousai (see nn. on 33, 541).

1220 *oil-jar*: a small container (for oil and perfume) used by athletes and others. The humour of the following passage has been variously explained; apart from a charge of formulaic writing, there may be sexual innuendo (an oil-jar resembling testicles?).

1206–8 *'Aigyptos . . . Argos'*: Euripides fr. 846 (play uncertain).

1211–13 *'Dionysos . . . dance'*: Euripides fr. 752 (*Hypsipyle*). For Parnassos, see Index of Names.

1217–19 *'No man . . . birth'*: Euripides fr. 661.1–3 (*Stheneboia*: cf. n. on 1043).

1225–6 *'In ancient times . . . Agenor's son'*: Euripides fr. 819 (*Phrixos*).

1232–3 *'When Pelops . . .'*: Euripides, *Iphigeneia in Tauris* 1–2.

1236 *an obol*: cf. n. on 137–40.

1240–1 *'Oineus . . . sacrifice'*: Euripides, fr. 516 (*Meleager*: cf. 864). Oineus was father of Meleager; his failure to sacrifice to Artemis made the goddess send the Kalydonian boar, which Meleager killed, but with a sequel that led to his own death (cf. Homer, *Iliad* 9.529–99).

1244 *'Zeus . . .'*: Euripides, fr. 481.1 (*Melanippe the Wise*).

1252–60 *Perplexed . . . afraid*: some scholars believe 1252–6 and 1257–60 are alternatives stemming from a partial authorial revision of *Frogs*; cf. my Introduction to the play, with nn. on 1431a–2, 1436 below. 'Bacchic master' associates Aischylos with Dionysos (see Index of Names).

1264–77 *Phthian Achilles . . . to our aid*: the farrago starts from Aischylos, fr. 132 (*Myrmidons*: cf. nn. on 912–13, 992) and repeats the second line (ungrammatically) as a refrain. Other phrases: 'Hermes . . .' = fr. 273 (*Psychagogoi*); 'Most glorious . . .' = fr. 238 (*Telephos*); 'Sacred silence!. . .' = fr. 87 (*Priestesses*); 'I speak with authority . . .' = *Agamemnon* 104.

1282 *nomes*: traditional songs for solo performance to the accompaniment of a large lyre (*kithara*).

1284 *When the twin-throned . . .*: the further farrago starts from *Agamemnon* 108–9, then continues: 'Sends the Sphinx . . .' = fr. 236 (*Sphinx*, a satyr-play), but with 'sends' transferred from *Agamemnon* 111; 'With spear . . .' = *Agamemnon* 111; 'Leaving prey . . .' = fr. 282 (play unknown); 'The throng . . .' = fr. 84 (*Thracian Women*).

1296 *Marathon . . . rope-hauling*: despite its great military associations, Marathon (see Index of Names) may have been thought of as a remote/rustic region of Attika; Dionysos also alludes to the simple songs of a workman operating a water-well.

1299 *Phrynichos*: see n. on 910.

1302 *Meletos*: identity uncertain; probably not the tragic poet(s) of frs. 117, 156, 453 (see the Appendix); 'Karian' here connotes the disreputably 'foreign' and vulgar (from a region of SW Asia Minor, a source of many Greek slaves).

1308 *work on Lesbos*: probably a double joke, implying (i) she could not find success in lyric poetry, (ii) she was not in demand for sexual services. The island of Lesbos had notable traditions of lyric (starting with Terpander, 7th century) but also a reputation for sexually expert prostitutes (cf. *W.* 1346, *AW* 920), though not usually 'Lesbians' in the modern sense.

1309–23 *Halcyons . . . dance-step*: a chaotic mélange of Euripidean and pseudo-Euripidean material, including fr. 856 ('Halycons . . . skin'), fr. 528a, *Meleager* ('exercises of a singing shuttle'), *Electra* 435–6 ('Where . . . rods'), fr. 765a, *Hypsipyle* ('Throw . . . child'). The protracted syllable 'Sp-i-i-i-i-i-in' (1314, cf. 1349) represents a musical mannerism.

1328 *Kyrene*: see n. on *WT* 98; there is some sort of comparison here between musical intricacy and sexual positions.

1330 *monodies*: see n. on 849–50. What follows is a continuation of the technique of 1309–23 but this one apparently involving more pastiche than quotation: a stream-of-consciousness monody, neurotic in manner yet about a banal incident (the theft of a cockerel), and correspondingly jumbling high and low linguistic registers.

1345 *Mania*: a female slave-name.

1356 *Come Cretans*...: from Euripides' *Cretans* (fr. 472 f), a play dealing with the consequences of the birth of the minotaur to Pasiphae after her mating with Minos' bull. 'Bows' in the next line reflects a specialist Cretan military tradition of archery (e.g. Thucydides 6.25.2).

1358 *Diktynna*: the name sometimes of a Cretan nymph but here probably an epithet of the goddess Artemis (see Index of Names).

1369 *like cheese*: compare Xanthias's similar sarcasm at 798.

1382 *'If only . . .'*: Euripides, *Medea* 1; the *Argo* was the ship that took the Argonauts to the Black Sea.

1383 *'O river Spercheios*...': Aischylos, fr. 249 (*Philoktetes*). The Spercheios, in central Greece, flows into the Malian Gulf.

1391 *'Persuasion has*...': Euripides, fr. 170.1 (*Antigone*).

1392 *'Alone among*...': Aischylos, fr. 161.1 (*Niobe*).

1400 *'Achilles threw* . . .': the start of the line is presumably from Euripides, but Dionysos creates the expectation of something weighty, only to make a joke out of throwing dice (which Achilles is shown doing in various Greek vase-paintings).

1402 *'Hefted... hand'*: Euripides, fr. 531 (*Meleager*).

1403 *'Chariot piled on chariot*...': Aischylos, fr. 38.1 (*Glaukos Potnieus*).

1406 *Egyptians*: reflecting Greek awareness of the scale of certain Egyptian monuments; cf. *B.* 1133–4.

1408–9 *Kephisophon... books*: see n. on 943–4.

1413 *one... the other*: this line (and likewise 1433) has been a source of unending disagreement; what matters most is that Dionysos is acknowledging poetic value in both playwrights (cf. my Introduction to the play).

1423 *Alkibiades*: one of the most controversial of Athenian politicians, who spent much of the period 415–407 working against Athens with the Spartans and/or Persians. Opinion in the city had long been divided over him (cf. esp. Xenophon, *Hellenika* 1.4.13–17, referring to 407). See *OCD*[4] 52–3.

1431a–2 *Don't rear . . . needs*: speculatively treated by some as a fragment of Aischylos (fr. 452), but more likely just a comic allusion to the famous Aischylean choral image at *Agamemnon* 717–36. Lines 1431a and 1431b appear to be alternative versions; cf. n. on 1252–60.

1436 *city's survival*: for this theme, cf. my Introduction to the play. From here to 1466 there are several vexed textual questions about the order of lines and the attribution of lines to speakers: compare nn. on 1252–60, 1431a–2. Most modern editors change the order of lines and/or posit more than one version of the play (see my Introduction); but since all remedies are debatable and there is no strong consensus, I retain the transmitted line-order.

1437 *Kleokritos . . . Kinesias*: probably fat and thin respectively (cf. *B*. 876, 1378); on the latter, see the Index of Names.

1451–2 *Palamedes . . . Kephisophon*: on the former see Index of Names with *WT* 769 ff., on the latter n. on 943–4.

1459 *a cloak or a goatskin*: probably proverbial for making a basic choice between alternatives.

1463–5 *enemy's land . . . the fleet*: i.e. a military policy, similar to that of Perikles at the start of the Peloponnesian War (Thucydides 1.142–3, 2.13.2), of using the Athenian fleet to raid enemy territory while allowing Sparta to make incursions into Attika.

1466 *our juries*: the expense of the Athenian jury system (with daily pay for serving jurors: cf. n. on *C*. 864) had long been politically contentious; cf. *W*. 656–63 (read by some as ironic).

1471 *'tongue that swore'*: the first half of Euripides, *Hippolytos* 612; cf. n. on 100–2.

1475 *'What's shameful . . .?'*: Euripides, fr. 19 (*Aiolos*), with 'those watching' (alluding to the theatre audience) substituted for 'those involved in it'.

1477 *'Who knows . . . death?'*: Euripides, fr. 638 (*Polyidos*); cf. line 1082.

1492 *with Sokrates*: Euripides had at least a comic reputation for being an intellectualizing acquaintance of Sokrates (see Index of Names), even for receiving poetic help from him (see fr. 392 in the Appendix). The motifs in the following lines, 'treating the Muses' work . . .' and 'nit-picking drivel', seem aimed more at Sokrates himself than at Euripides.

1504–7 *Kleophon . . . Archenomos*: on Kleophon see Index of Names; oddly, Nikomachos (a legal official) was later accused by some of having caused Kleophon's death (Lysias 30.13); Myrmex and Archenomos are otherwise unknown.

1516 *Sophokles*: cf. 787–94.

1532–3 *Kleophon . . . ancestral*: a reprise of the gibe at 678–82.

INDEX OF NAMES

Listed here are those proper names (excluding the purely fictional) of people, places, and institutions that are not glossed in the Explanatory Notes. References are selective; fragments of Aristophanes cited here are mentioned in the Appendix. Capitals within entries indicate cross-references. For abbreviations of play-titles see p. 255.

MORE ABOUT **OXFORD WORLD'S CLASSICS**

The Oxford World's Classics Website

www.worldsclassics.co.uk

- Browse the full range of Oxford World's Classics online
- Sign up for our monthly e-alert to receive information on new titles
- Read extracts from the Introductions
- Listen to our editors and translators talk about the world's greatest literature with our Oxford World's Classics audio guides
- Join the conversation, follow us on Twitter at OWC_Oxford
- Teachers and lecturers can order inspection copies quickly and simply via our website

www.worldsclassics.co.uk

MORE ABOUT **OXFORD WORLD'S CLASSICS**

American Literature
British and Irish Literature
Children's Literature
Classics and Ancient Literature
Colonial Literature
Eastern Literature
European Literature
Gothic Literature
History
Medieval Literature
Oxford English Drama
Philosophy
Poetry
Politics
Religion
The Oxford Shakespeare

A complete list of Oxford World's Classics, including Authors in Context, Oxford English Drama, and the Oxford Shakespeare, is available in the UK from the Marketing Services Department, Oxford University Press, Great Clarendon Street, Oxford OX2 6DP, or visit the website at www.oup.com/uk/worldsclassics.

In the USA, visit www.oup.com/us/owc for a complete title list.

Oxford World's Classics are available from all good bookshops. In case of difficulty, customers in the UK should contact Oxford University Press Bookshop, 116 High Street, Oxford OX1 4BR.

A SELECTION OF **OXFORD WORLD'S CLASSICS**

	Classical Literary Criticism
	The First Philosophers: The Presocratics and the Sophists
	Greek Lyric Poetry
	Myths from Mesopotamia
APOLLODORUS	The Library of Greek Mythology
APOLLONIUS OF RHODES	Jason and the Golden Fleece
APULEIUS	The Golden Ass
ARISTOPHANES	Birds and Other Plays
ARISTOTLE	The Nicomachean Ethics
	Politics
ARRIAN	Alexander the Great
BOETHIUS	The Consolation of Philosophy
CAESAR	The Civil War
	The Gallic War
CATULLUS	The Poems of Catullus
CICERO	Defence Speeches
	The Nature of the Gods
	On Obligations
	Political Speeches
	The Republic and The Laws
EURIPIDES	Bacchae and Other Plays
	Heracles and Other Plays
	Medea and Other Plays
	Orestes and Other Plays
	The Trojan Women and Other Plays
HERODOTUS	The Histories
HOMER	The Iliad
	The Odyssey

A SELECTION OF **OXFORD WORLD'S CLASSICS**

Horace	The Complete Odes and Epodes
Juvenal	The Satires
Livy	The Dawn of the Roman Empire Hannibal's War The Rise of Rome
Marcus Aurelius	The Meditations
Ovid	The Love Poems Metamorphoses
Petronius	The Satyricon
Plato	Defence of Socrates, Euthyphro, and Crito Gorgias Meno and Other Dialogues Phaedo Republic Symposium
Plautus	Four Comedies
Plutarch	Greek Lives Roman Lives Selected Essays and Dialogues
Propertius	The Poems
Sophocles	Antigone, Oedipus the King, and Electra
Suetonius	Lives of the Caesars
Tacitus	The Annals The Histories
Thucydides	The Peloponnesian War
Virgil	The Aeneid The Eclogues and Georgics
Xenophon	The Expedition of Cyrus

A SELECTION OF **OXFORD WORLD'S CLASSICS**

Thomas Aquinas	**Selected Philosophical Writings**
Francis Bacon	**The Major Works**
Walter Bagehot	**The English Constitution**
George Berkeley	**Principles of Human Knowledge and Three Dialogues**
Edmund Burke	**A Philosophical Enquiry into the Sublime and Beautiful** **Reflections on the Revolution in France**
Confucius	**The Analects**
René Descartes	**A Discourse on the Method** **Meditations on First Philosophy**
Émile Durkheim	**The Elementary Forms of Religious Life**
Friedrich Engels	**The Condition of the Working Class in England**
James George Frazer	**The Golden Bough**
Sigmund Freud	**The Interpretation of Dreams**
G. W. E. Hegel	**Outlines of the Philosophy of Right**
Thomas Hobbes	**Human Nature and De Corpore Politico** **Leviathan**
David Hume	**An Enquiry concerning Human Understanding** **Selected Essays**
Immanuel Kant	**Critique of Judgement**
Søren Kierkegaard	**Repetition and Philosophical Crumbs**
John Locke	**An Essay concerning Human Understanding**

A SELECTION OF **OXFORD WORLD'S CLASSICS**

Niccolò Machiavelli	**The Prince**
Thomas Malthus	**An Essay on the Principle of Population**
Karl Marx	**Capital** **The Communist Manifesto**
J. S. Mill	**On Liberty and Other Essays** **Principles of Political Economy and Chapters on Socialism**
Friedrich Nietzsche	**Beyond Good and Evil** **The Birth of Tragedy** **On the Genealogy of Morals** **Thus Spoke Zarathustra** **Twilight of the Idols**
Thomas Paine	**Rights of Man, Common Sense, and Other Political Writings**
Jean-Jacques Rousseau	**The Social Contract** **Discourse on the Origin of Inequality**
Arthur Schopenhauer	**The Two Fundamental Problems of Ethics**
Adam Smith	**An Inquiry into the Nature and Causes of the Wealth of Nations**
Mary Wollstonecraft	**A Vindication of the Rights of Woman**